CLINICAL NURSING TECHNIQUES

CLINICAL NURSING TECHNIQUES

NORMA DISON
R.N., B.A., M.A.

Clinical Instructor, Medical-Surgical Nursing,
Department of Nursing,
Rochester Community College, Rochester, Minnesota

THIRD EDITION

With 691 illustrations by Marita Bitans

THE C. V. MOSBY COMPANY

SAINT LOUIS 1975

Library of Congress Cataloging in Publication Data

Dison, Norma Greenler.
  Clinical nursing techniques.

  First-2d ed. published under title: An atlas of
nursing techniques.
  Includes bibliographies and index.
  1. Nurses and nursing. I. Title. [DNLM: 1.
Nursing care. WY150 D611a]
RT65.D5 1975   610.73   74-28411
ISBN 0-8016-1307-8

VH/VH/VH 9 8 7 6 5 4 3 2 1

To cure sometimes, to relieve often, to comfort always.

—attributed to
Edward L. Trudeau

Preface

The basic purpose of this book remains that of providing explanatory text and meaningful illustrations of techniques used in nursing.

The general format of the book is similar to that of the previous editions. Some content has been rearranged, and new content has been added. All material has been carefully evaluated and rewritten when necessary.

Content new to this edition includes the use of sterile disposable gloves, heel and elbow protectors, commercial restraints, blow bottles, Asmastik unit, MA-1 Respirator Unit, sterile aspiration of tracheal secretions, weaning from the respirator, destruction of used needles and syringes, intravenous site care, intravenous tubing incorporating an airway, permanent ostomy appliances, dilation of a stoma, and Aquamatic K-pad.

Again many persons shared their time and knowledge with me. Those who were especially helpful were Dr. H. Frederic Helholz, Jr., Consultant in Physiology, the Mayo Clinic; Bernard Gillis, Orvis Dahl, and Burdette Polk of the Mayo Clinic; Jane Daniels, Head Nurse, Rochester Methodist Hospital; Eva Bennett, Inservice, Saint Marys Hospital; and Jean Skar, Librarian, Rochester Methodist Hospital. Other members of the staffs at the Mayo Clinic, Rochester Methodist Hospital, Saint Marys Hospital, and Rochester Community College also contributed of their knowledge. Permission to illustrate commercial products is appreciated also. Again, the illustrations were done by Marita Bitans, medical illustrator, who deserves special appreciation. The comments of those who used the book were most helpful.

NORMA DISON

Contents

1

Infection and allergen control

Certain nursing techniques are designed to increase the patient's safety by lessening the risk of infection. A number of means are used to reduce the transmission of organisms. Others reduce contact with allergens.

Hand washing

The hands are washed to remove bacteria and other contaminants to which they have been exposed before and after caring for the patient, feeding him, handling food, preparing and administering medications, using bathroom facilities, and touching any part of the body or objects that may possibly be contaminated. This includes used linen and objects that have been in the patient's room or in contact with a contaminated area such as the floor.

An effective method of cleansing the hands is to wash them thoroughly with an approved cleansing agent. This may be soap or a germicidal compound in either liquid or solid form. The length of time required for effective hand washing depends on the amount and kind of contamination, the amount of friction used, and the cleansing agent. Removal of bacteria appears to be directly related to the amount of friction used. Grossly contaminated hands should be washed thoroughly at least twice.

Before washing the hands, the wristwatch should be moved well above the wrist or removed. Rings other than a plain wedding band are removed also. The temperature and flow of the water are adjusted to comfort. The hands are directed downward during the washing and rinsing processes; this permits the flowing water to wash away contaminants.

1

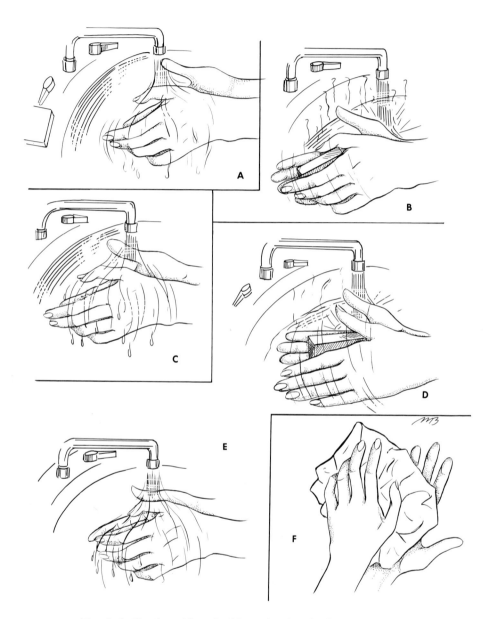

Fig. 1-1. Hand washing. **A,** After adjusting the flow and temperature of the water, moisten hands. **B,** Apply soap until a heavy lather covers the area to be cleansed, rubbing the hands against each other to produce friction. **C,** Rinse thoroughly. **D,** Apply more soap and repeat step **B. E,** Rinse well. **F,** Dry hands thoroughly. Using a paper towel to shut off flow of water avoids contamination from hand-operated faucets.

After wetting the hands and wrist areas, the cleansing agent is applied in the amount needed to make a lather. Liquid forms of cleansing agents are preferred. If a solid soap is used, the nails may be pressed into it to force soap beneath them. Bar soap should be held in the hands throughout the cleansing process. Efforts to clean the areas beneath the nails and the spaces around the cuticle are important because these areas are known to harbor bacteria. The hands are rubbed together, interlacing the fingers to cleanse the spaces between them, and then the back of each hand is rubbed with the palm of the other. Each surface should be rubbed a minimum of ten times to ensure cleansing. The hands, still directed downward, are rinsed thoroughly and dried with a disposable towel or a forced air blower. It is usual to consider the faucets contaminated. Therefore a paper towel is used to turn hand-operated faucets and to maintain the clean state of the hands (Fig. 1-1).

Skin preparation

Preparation of the skin precedes surgical incision. The procedure may be done in the patient's room, in a special area, or in the operating room. Little seems to be known of advantages to the patient of one method of preparation over another. Some procedure policies include surgical cleansing of the surface area prior to the patient's entrance into the operating suite. The method of hair removal may utilize depilatory agents or a razor. If a wet shave is given, a liquid soap solution or another wetting agent is used to soften the hair and reduce friction. Powder reduces friction if a dry shave is given with a safety razor. It is thought that fewer epithelial cells are removed with the dry method. Avoiding irritation and abrasion of the skin is important because irritation and abrasion cause discomfort, alarm the patient, and injure the skin, which acts as a natural barrier to infection. To determine that a clean shave has been obtained, the dry surface should be viewed against an adequate source of light.

The nature of the surgical procedure and the location and extent of the incision determine the area of the skin to be prepared. This area will be considerably larger than the predicted incision. Commonly designated areas of skin preparation should never be used contrary to the order of the physician, who may specify a somewhat different area (Fig. 1-2).

It is wise to obtain a specific order from the physician as well as the written permission of the patient if certain areas are to be freed of hair: the face or neck of the female patient, the eyebrows, or the head. If the head must be shaved, removed hair should be saved until the patient has recovered and indicates that it may be destroyed.

3

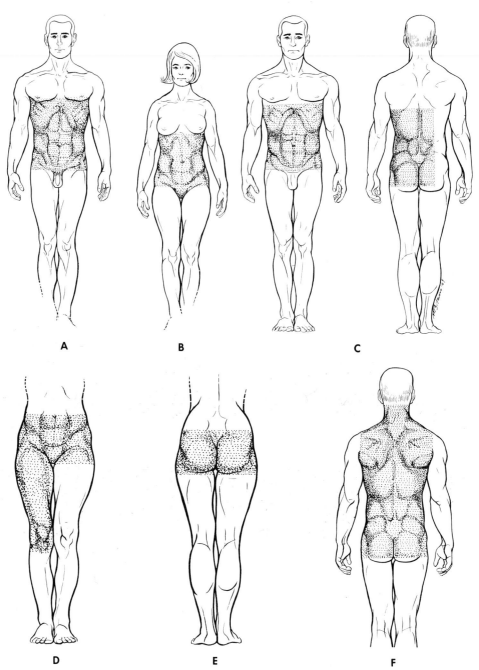

Fig. 1-2. Commonly designated areas of skin preparation. **A,** Abdominal surgery: the nipple line, symphysis pubis, and lateral aspects of the body serve as demarcation lines. **B,** Complete abdominal preparation (abdominoperineal preparation): abdomen and pelvic and perineal areas are prepared. **C,** Nephrectomy: abdominal area and three fourths of the back on the designated side are prepared. **D,** Inguinal hernia: lower abdomen plus anterior and lateral aspects of thigh are prepared. Preparation extends below the knee when fascial repair is planned. **E,** Rectal surgery: buttocks, anal area, and perineum are prepared. **F,** Neurosurgery and orthopedic surgery of the back: the entire back is prepared. Outermost borders of the area extend to top of scapula, lateral aspects of trunk, and distal portion of buttocks. If a bone graft is planned, the entire leg will be prepared to the ankle.

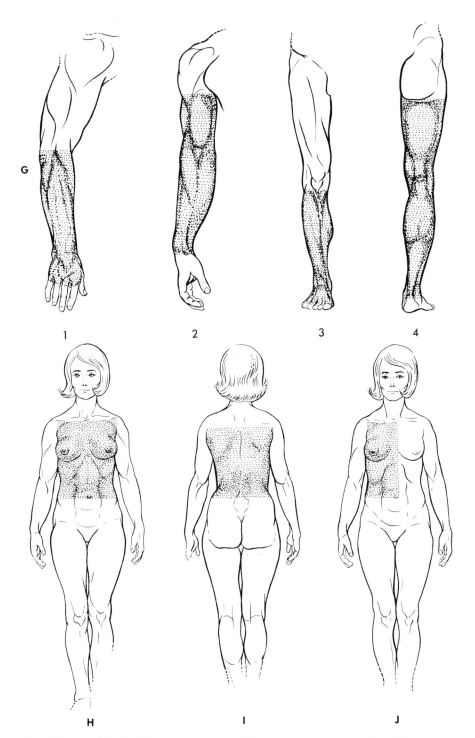

Fig. 1-2, cont'd. G, Other areas prepared for neurosurgery and orthopedic surgery include: **1,** lower arm and hand; **2,** arm; **3,** lower leg and foot; and **4,** entire leg. **H** and **I,** Chest surgery: the anterior area is demarcated by clavicle and umbilicus; the posterior area extends to upper border of scapula; the axilla is usually included. **J,** Unilateral mastectomy: clavicle, umbilicus, and opposite breast serve as demarcation lines; the axilla and the inner aspect of the upper arm are included.

Continued.

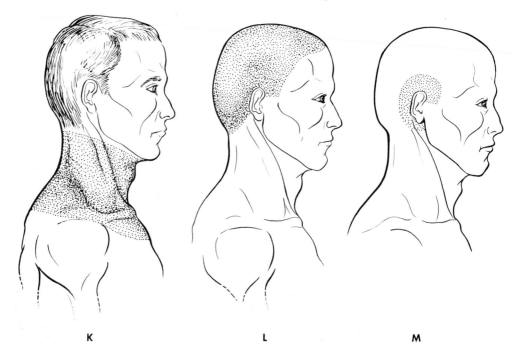

K   L   M

Fig. 1-2, cont'd. K, Neck: male patient may be permitted to shave the designated area; a female patient is not usually shaved. **L,** Head: written permission should be obtained from the patient prior to this preparation. **M,** Ear: the area extends 1 to $1\frac{1}{2}$ inches behind, above, and below the external ear; male patients are asked to shave the beard in front of the ear.

Sometimes, women wish to fashion this hair into a hairpiece. In the event of the patient's death, it may be possible for a mortician to simulate a natural appearance if he is furnished with the hair that has been removed.

The person who prepares the skin for surgery should provide privacy for the patient, explain the planned procedure and why such preparation is necessary, and reassure the patient.

Surgical scrub

The surgical scrub renders the hands and arms as free of contaminants as is possible with mechanical and chemical means (Fig. 1-3). The effectiveness of scrubbing depends on mechanical action, which helps remove organisms from the ducts of the sebaceous glands in which they grow. As yet no means of rendering the skin sterile is available. The effectiveness of scrubbing also depends on the chemical agent used. The system used should be chosen to fit the surgical procedure planned. An agent that acts slowly but over a long period of time is preferred when long procedures are planned. A rapid-acting agent is preferred for shorter procedures.

The scrub system used varies with institutional policy and individual preferences. Some prefer a scrub timed by the clock; others use a counted-stroke method. The time of the scrub or the number of strokes used varies also. This is affected by the cleansing agent used, the length of time between scrubs, the amount of contamination present, and the use of a preliminary wash or scrub or both. Differences of opinion exist concerning whether the scrub should extend to or above the elbow, whether a chemical rinse should follow the scrub, and what solution or solutions should be used for terminal rinsing. New systems of scrubbing are being investigated. If the system used is uniform, microbial studies can be obtained and used to determine when changes are indicated.

PREPARATION FOR SCRUBBING

The surgical scrub is begun after dressing appropriately for the operating room. This means wearing a clean surgical dress or suit, conductive footwear, a cap that covers the hair completely, and a mask that covers the mouth and nose. If, during the scrubbing technique, any part of the hands or forearms touches the sink, faucet, or an unsterile object or surface, the scrub must be restarted from the beginning. For all of the described scrubs, the hands and arms are directed upward so that these parts are above the level of the elbow. With the hands and arms held in this position, water used in scrubbing will drip from the elbow. Prior to beginning the scrub, the temperature and flow of water are adjusted to comfort because the water is left running throughout the scrub. Several methods of scrubbing are described. Variations from the described procedures may be used depending on institutional policy.

METHODS OF SCRUBBING

Routine surgical scrub (long scrub). When using the *timed method* of the routine scrub, the hands and arms are moistened thoroughly, and the cleansing agent is applied. To remove surface contamination, the hands and arms are washed directionally from the fingertips to the elbows for approximately a minute. Then the hands and arms are rinsed, more cleansing agent is applied, and these areas are scrubbed. A sterile brush or sponge adds gentle friction. Scrubbing proceeds in short or circular strokes until the entire area is covered. This should take about 4 minutes. If more lather is needed, additional water or soap may be applied. Next the brush is discarded and the hands are rinsed thoroughly. The nails are cleaned with a sterile nail file or orangewood stick. This is discarded after use. More cleansing agent is applied, and another sterile brush is used to scrub all surfaces of the hands and forearms for approximately 4 minutes. After rinsing the hands and arms thoroughly, a sterile towel is used to blot the hands and arms to dry them.

The *counted stroke method* of the routine scrub differs from the timed method in that the hands and arms are scrubbed by applying a specific number of strokes to each part. The scrub is begun with an initial washing and rinsing as described under the timed method. It is suggested that the first scrubbing be completed as follows: twenty strokes to the nails, ten strokes to all surfaces of the fingers and nails, and six strokes to all surfaces of the arms. After rinsing the hands and arms and cleansing the nails with a sterile nail file or orangewood stick, a second scrub is done. The number of counted strokes that are applied during the second scrubbing is as follows: ten strokes to the nails, six strokes to the surfaces of the fingers and hands, and three strokes to each surface of the arms.

Short surgical scrub. The short surgical scrub may be used between cases unless the hands or arms have been contaminated. The gown and gloves that were worn during the previous surgical case are not removed until one is ready to begin the short surgical scrub.

In the *timed method* of the short surgical scrub, after removing the gown and gloves, the hands and forearms are moistened thoroughly. The cleansing agent is then applied, and the areas are scrubbed with a sterile brush for 3 minutes. The brush is discarded, and the hands and arms are rinsed thoroughly and dried with a sterile towel.

When using the *counted stroke method* of the short surgical scrub, the hands and arms are wet thoroughly. The cleansing agent is applied, and a sterile brush is used to cleanse the parts as follows: twenty strokes to the nails, ten strokes to the surfaces of the fingers including the nails, and six strokes to the surfaces of the arms. After rinsing, the hands and arms are dried with a sterile towel. The primary difference between the *long counted stroke method* and the *short counted stroke method* is that for the latter, the scrub is considered to be complete after the initial scrubbing.

pHisoHex scrub, surgical wash, and surgical scrub.* The pHisoHex wash, surgical wash, and surgical scrub are used widely. pHisoHex is said to leave a minimal number of bacteria on the skin with a shorter scrub than when ordinary soap is used. In addition, it leaves a film on the skin that helps keep resident bacteria to a minimum. The surgical wash is useful for those whose skin is irritated by the trauma of scrubbing with a brush. When pHisoHex is used, small

---

*Use of pHisoHex must comply with the regulations established by the Federal Food and Drug Administration.

pHisoHex preliminary wash, surgical wash, and surgical scrub*

Preliminary wash (precedes surgical wash and surgical scrub)

1. Wet hands and forearms.
2. Apply about 2 ml. of pHisoHex.
3. Wash (without brush) for 30 seconds, adding small amounts of water. Avoid washing off lather.
4. Clean under nails (keep nails short and clean).
5. Rinse.

Surgical wash

1. Apply 2 to 4 ml. of pHisoHex.
2. Wash (without brush), as follows, while frequently adding small amounts of water.

Frequency of pHisoHex wash	Wash for	Benzalkonium (Zephiran) rinse
Routinely (twice daily or more often)	2 minutes	Unnecessary
Once daily	4 minutes	Optional
Infrequently	6 to 8 minutes	Recommended

3. Rinse.
4. Terminal rinse with benzalkonium solution 1:750. Do not rinse with alcohol alone.

Surgical scrub

1. Apply 2 to 4 ml. of pHisoHex.
2. Scrub (with brush), as follows, while frequently adding small amounts of water.

Frequency of pHisoHex scrub	Timed scrub	Counted stroke "anatomic" scrub (number of strokes of brush, lengthwise, for every area)		Benzalkonium (Zephiran) rinse
		Skin	Nails	
Routinely (twice daily or more often)	2 minutes	9	15	Unnecessary
Once daily	4 minutes	15	25	Optional
Infrequently	6 to 8 minutes	30	50	Recommended

3. Rinse.
4. Terminal rinse with benzalkonium solution 1:750.

---

*Courtesy Winthrop Laboratories, New York.
Use of pHisoHex must comply with the regulations established by the Food and Drug Administration.

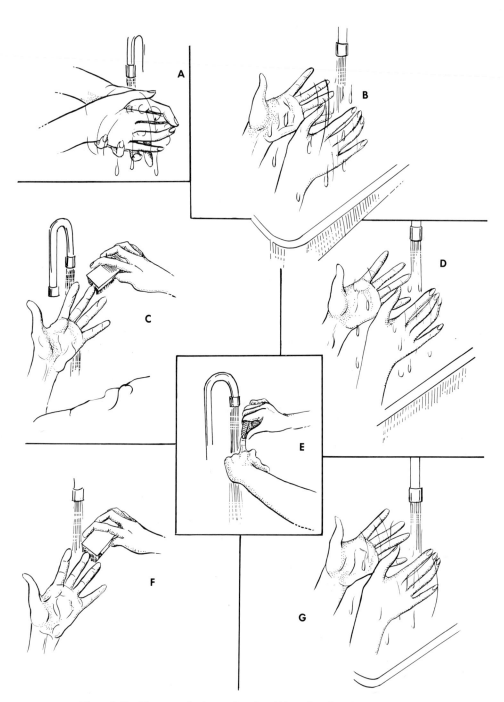

Fig. 1-3. The surgical scrub. **A,** Wet the hands and arms thoroughly, apply the cleansing agent, and wash the arms and hands. **B,** Rinse the hands and arms. **C,** Use a sterile brush or sponge to add gentle friction. **D,** Use additional water as needed to increase the lather. **E,** Clean the nails with a sterile file or orangewood stick. **F,** Apply more cleansing agent and use another sterile brush to scrub all surfaces of the hands and forearms. **G,** Rinse the hands and arms thoroughly.

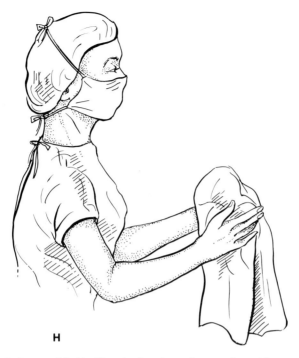

H

Fig. 1-3, cont'd. H, Blot the hands and arms dry with a sterile towel after the scrub is completed.

amounts of water are added as needed to produce more suds. Adding more pHisoHex is neither necessary nor desirable.

DRYING HANDS AND ARMS WITH A STERILE TOWEL

After the surgical scrub, the hands and forearms are dried with a sterile towel (Fig. 1-3, *H*). The towel is picked up by one corner and raised high enough above the table to prevent it from contacting anything that is unsterile as the towel unfolds. To prevent contamination of the towel, one should step into a space away from any objects and hold the towel well away from the body. The towel is held in one hand and used to blot the surfaces of the fingers, hand, and arm until they are dry. The dry hand is then moved to the opposite end of the towel to hold it while drying the other hand. During this process, the towel is manipulated as necessary to provide a dry surface. After drying the hands and arms, the sterile gown is put on.

Putting on a sterile gown

The method for putting on a sterile gown differs from the method illustrated for putting on an isolation gown. The sterile gown is folded in a manner that permits the hands to touch the inside of the

11

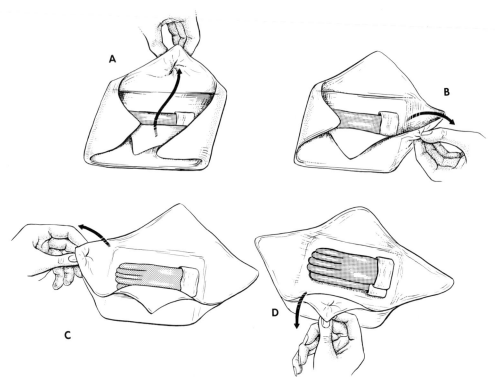

Fig. 1-4. Unwrapping sterile gloves. **A,** Unseal the package, fold the upper corner back, and open it away from the package. **B,** Reach the hand around the sterile field to unfold the next part of the wrapper by grasping the outside of the wrapper. **C,** Retract the next fold similarly. **D,** Expose the contents of the package.

gown only. The gown is grasped from the inside and held up and away from unsterile areas when it is unfolded. After the scrubbed nurse's hands have been slipped into the sleeves, the circulating nurse may touch the inside parts of the outer edges of the back of the gown to adjust it and to tie the ties.

Methods of gloving

Two methods of gloving may be used. The open method is also used when gloving is required for a technique not requiring the use of a gown, such as for catheterization.

OPEN METHOD, STERILE, REUSABLE GLOVES

After the package of sterile, reusable gloves is opened (Fig. 1-4), the turned-down cuff of the glove for the right hand is grasped with the left hand and picked up (Fig. 1-5, *A*). The right hand is slipped into the glove. Next, the gloved hand is placed beneath the cuff

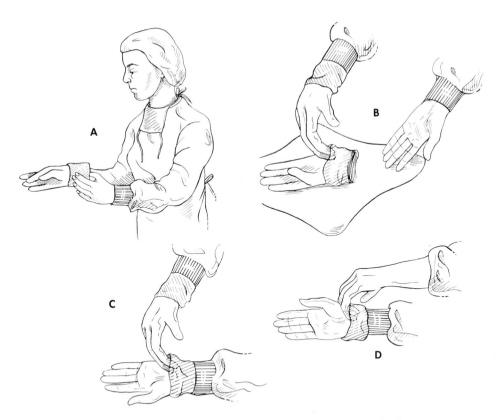

Fig. 1-5. Putting on sterile, reusable gloves, open method. **A,** After washing and drying the hands, the right hand is slipped inside the right glove. Care must be taken to prevent contamination of the exterior part of the glove. This is done by touching only the turned-down portion or cuff of the glove. **B,** The gloved hand is placed beneath the cuff of the left glove to hold it while the left hand is slipped inside it. **C,** The gloved right hand, still positioned beneath the cuff of the glove, is used to pull it over the cuff of the gown. When a gown is not worn, the cuff extends over the wrist area. **D,** As the cuff of the glove is pulled up, care must be exercised if contamination of the exterior portion of the glove is to be avoided. The position of the thumb of the hand that is manipulating the cuff is crucial to maintaining sterility.

of the left glove (Fig. 1-5, *B*) to hold the glove while the left hand is placed into it and to pull the cuff of the glove over the cuff of the gown when one is worn (Fig. 1-5, *C*). The cuff of the right glove is pulled over the cuff of the gown (Fig. 1-5, *D*). It is important to observe the position of the thumb when putting on gloves and when pulling the cuffs of the gloves over the gown. It may be helpful to tuck the thumb into the palm of the hand when placing the fingers beneath the cuff of the glove.

13

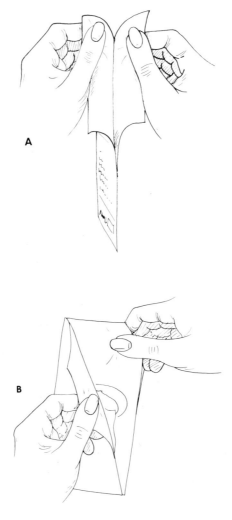

Fig. 1-6. Use of sterile disposable gloves (Dispos-A-Glove). **A,** After washing and drying the hands, open the individually packaged glove by grasping the exposed edges of the packet and pulling to expose the sheet inside, which contains the gloves. **B,** The sheet to which the disposable glove adheres lightly is opened by grasping the marked corners. **C,** The sterile glove is exposed by placing one thumb on the cuff extension and exerting moderate tension on the opposite end corner of the paper. **D,** The thumb continues to exert pressure on the extension of the cuff while the other hand is placed inside the glove. **E,** The inside, sterile portion of the paper to which the glove had adhered may be used to position the hand in the glove if necessary. (Courtesy Arbrook, Inc., Arlington, Texas.)

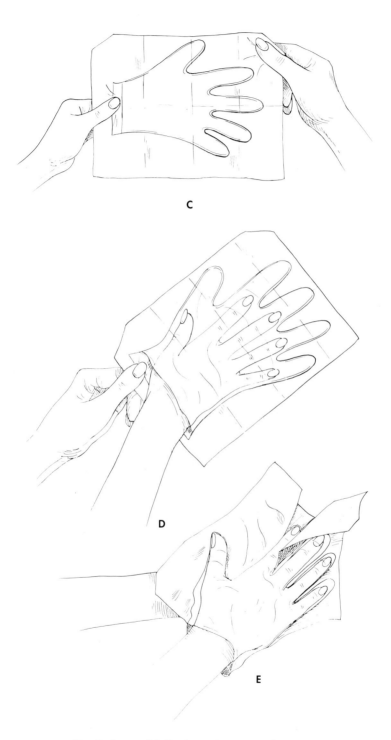

C

D

E

Fig. 1-6, cont'd. For legend see opposite page.

OPEN METHOD, STERILE, DISPOSABLE GLOVES

Sterile, disposable gloves may be used whenever sterile technique is indicated. Usually each glove is packaged individually. The glove may be sealed lightly to the wrapper, and one part of it may extend at the wrist level. This extension may be grasped and held like a cuff while gloving (Fig. 1-6). The same principles should be followed when opening the package containing the sterile, disposable gloves and when gloving as are used with reusable gloves. The manufacturer's packaging may necessitate some modification in the procedure. If the gloves are individually packaged and two gloves are to be worn, two packages will need to be opened before gloving.

CLOSED METHOD

The closed method of gloving may be used as an operating room technique. This method is described and illustrated by Brooks and Tyler.*

Isolation

If transmission of organisms to or from a patient constitutes a hazard to health, isolation is practiced. If this is done to prevent transmission of organisms from the patient to others, it is commonly said that isolation technique or isolation precautions are in effect. In the reverse situation, when transmission of organisms to the patient is to be avoided, a modified type of isolation referred to as reverse or protective isolation precautions may be used. It should not be confused with reverse isolation in its absolute form.†

The exact procedure followed will vary with the physical facilities, the materials used, and the nature of the infection. The patient must be in an area or room equipped with facilities for hand washing and disposal of contaminated materials and waste. The effective practice of isolation precautions depends on correct application of principles derived from a knowledge of medical asepsis.

The purpose of isolation precautions must be understood if principles drawn from microbiology are to be applied correctly. An understanding of what is to be considered clean or contaminated is essential. The source of contaminating organisms and mode of transfer will influence the techniques used.

---

*Brooks, H. L., and Rockwell, V. T.: Simple procedure for processing and donning surgical rubber gloves; closed glove method, Operating Rm. Nurs. 2:41-54, July-Aug., 1961.
†Seidler, F. M.: Adapting procedures for reverse isolation, Amer. J. Nurs. 65:108-111, 1965.

For the purpose of reducing transmission of pathogens, sterilization of equipment with steam under pressure, in a gas sterilizer, or with chemicals is useful. Because of damage that ensues if these methods are applied to certain materials, a less than perfect method of frictional cleansing or airing, preferably in sunlight, may be necessary. Choice of method and cleansing agents differ with the established policies of institutions.

The use of disposable equipment, when practical, is recommended to reduce the transmission of organisms and is particularly important when organisms causing certain diseases such as infectious hepatitis are present. It is possible to obtain disposable items such as gowns, gloves, syringes, and dishes at relatively low cost. Lining waste containers and linen hampers with bags made of plastic material increases the safety with which waste and linen can be removed from the room. The bag can be sealed by folding the top and securing it with a rubber band or a tie. When the contaminated bag is removed from the room, it is placed within a second clean bag held by an assistant who stands near the entrance to the isolation area. Isolation linen should be plainly marked to warn laundry personnel that special precautions are in order. Plastic laundry bags that disintegrate in hot water are available.

Certain aspects of medical asepsis used when isolation is in effect are routinely incorporated into daily nursing practice. Hand washing (Fig. 1-1), for instance, is essential after known or possible contact with contaminants.

USE OF GOWN

Clothing is protected by avoiding direct contact with contaminated areas or by wearing a gown. When isolation is used to prevent transfer of organisms from a well-dressed wound, it may be permissible to take an oral temperature without gowning if it is certain that physical contact with the patient, furniture, or linen will be avoided.

Gowns are available in various styles and materials, each with some advantages. They may be made of paper, plastic, or cloth. Design determines whether the gown has an open, semiclosed, or closed back. Fig. 1-7 illustrates the single use of a disposable gown. The gown shown features complete covering of the back, easy removal, and polyethylene construction. It is impervious to moisture and is considered disposable.

Cloth gowns continue to be used in isolation technique (Fig. 1-8). A supply of clean cloth gowns should be readily available. The contaminated gown should be discarded after use. This is referred to as single gown or discard technique (Table 1-1).

Text continued on p. 22.

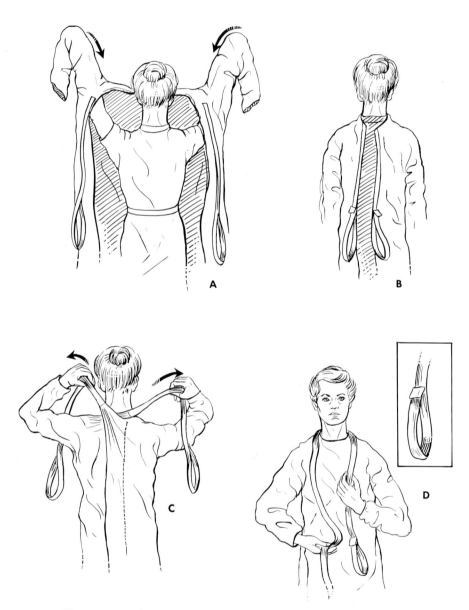

Fig. 1-7. Single use of a disposable protective gown. **A** to **F,** Gowning procedure. **A,** Open the gown and put it on with the opening in the back. **B,** View of gown before it is tied. **C,** Cross the ties and bring them forward over the shoulders. **D,** Each tie may be lengthened by gently pulling the tab near the end of the tie.

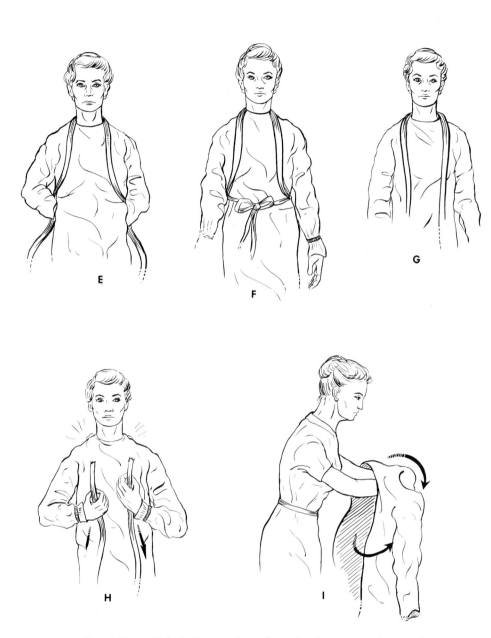

Fig. 1-7, cont'd. E, Ties are brought under the arms and crossed in the back. **F,** Ties are adjusted in front until comfortable and are tied. **G to I,** Removing the gown. **G,** To remove the gown, untie the ties and bring them to the front. **H,** Break ties from the shoulders by exerting a firm pull on them. **I,** Remove gown by folding the inside over the outside. This avoids self-contamination. (Courtesy E. C. Ricter Co., Rochester, Minn.)

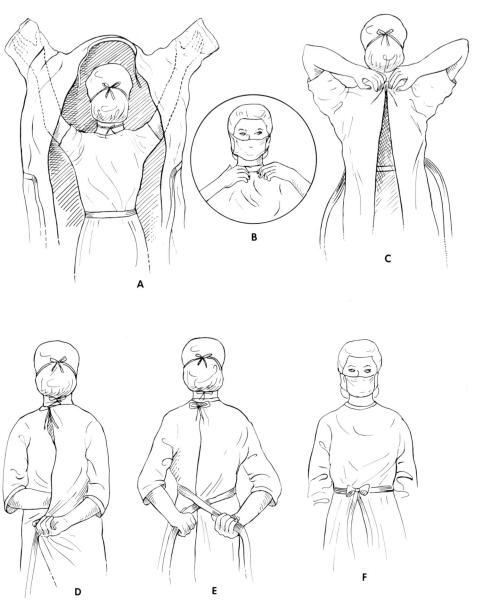

Fig. 1-8. Single use of cloth gown. **A** to **F,** Technique of putting on gown. **A,** After washing and drying the hands, grasp the gown inside the back of the neck opening and slip the hands into the sleeves. **B,** Adjust the neckband so that it fits comfortably and rather snugly. **C,** Secure the gown at the neck by tying it. **D,** Bring the left side of the gown across the back and then bring the right side of the gown over the left so that the back is completely enclosed by the gown. **E,** Bring the ties to the back and cross them. **F,** Tie the gown in front if possible. If ties are short, they may be tied in the back of the gown.

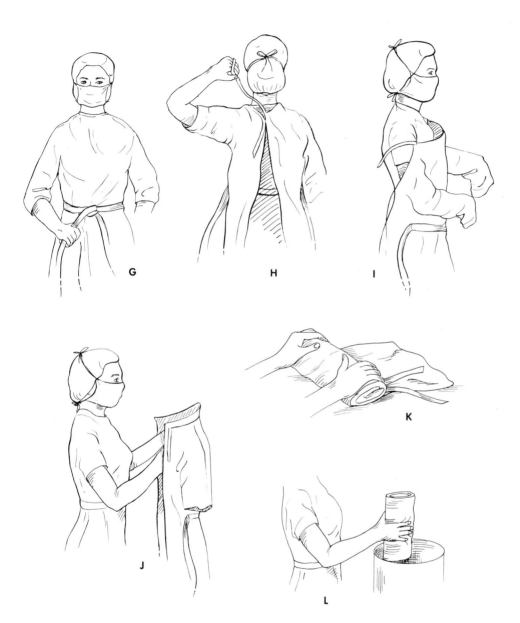

Fig. 1-8, cont'd. G to **L,** Technique of removing the gown and discarding it. **G,** Untie the gown at the waist. **H,** After washing and drying the hands, untie the gown at the neck. **I,** Slip hands out of the gown, using care to prevent unnecessary contamination through contact with the outside of the gown. **J,** Grasp the inside of the gown by its shoulder seams and turn the inside of the gown to the outside. **K,** Fold or roll the used gown prior to disposal. Note that the inside or clean side of the gown is exposed to the environment. **L,** The gown is placed into the receptacle for contaminated linen, and the hands are washed and dried thoroughly.

TABLE 1-1. Single use of gowns

Technique	Problem	Explanation or solution
Slip the hands into the sleeves and put on the gown; adjust the neckband so that it fits rather snugly but comfortably and fasten the neck ties.	The natural reaction to discomfort due to fit of the gown is to attempt to rearrange the gown.	It is difficult if not impossible to adjust the gown, once contaminated, without touching oneself or one's clothing.
Bring the left side of the gown across the back and the right side of the gown over the left; cross and tie the belt.	Any clothing that is exposed may become contaminated.	The gown provides a barrier between the clothing and the environment.
After use, untie the gown at the waist, wash hands, and unfasten the neck ties.	Contaminated hands transmit organisms.	The hands must be clean and dry when contact with the body may occur.
Slip the hands out of the gown, avoiding any contact with outside surfaces of the gown.	Contact with the outside surfaces of the gown results in contamination.	Organisms may be transmitted by handling contaminated materials.
Carefully roll or fold the gown so that the inside of the gown is exposed and the outside of the gown is enclosed; discard the gown.	The outside of the gown has been exposed to environmental contamination.	Folding the outside of the gown to the inside and discarding it prevents contamination of others through contact with contaminated materials.
Wash and dry the hands.	Unclean hands may transmit organisms.	Moisture and warmth of hands provide a favorable environment for organisms; the hands are contaminated from having touched the gown.

USE OF MASK AND HAIR COVERING

If transmission of organisms to or from the nasopharynx and hair is to be avoided, a mask and a hair covering are worn. Both are applied prior to gowning. The mask should cover the mouth and nose, and all hair should be tucked under the cap. The method of removal depends on their design.

Dust-free environment

Preparation and maintenance of a dust-free environment are essential to the control of certain allergenic responses. In addition, this environment serves to control transmission of organisms that dust transports.

Ideally, the room is emptied and scrubbed thoroughly to remove all traces of dust. All parts of the bed are scrubbed with soap and water, but the bed is not removed from the room.

The allergies of the patient will determine the exact precautions used. Permissibility of oiling or waxing the floor must be evaluated in light of known allergy history and the ingredients of the product used. Flaxseed is one ingredient found in these products to which allergic reaction may occur. The pillows, mattress, and box springs are enclosed in a dustproof cover, and the closures are sealed with adhesive tape. The need to do so when these items are said to be dustproof is determined by the allergist. His decision is based on experience and on knowledge of the porosity of such materials.

Linen for the bed must be freshly laundered and changed frequently. Choice of blankets necessarily eliminates those that have not been laundered, are fuzzy, or contain down. Wool blankets are preferred and are tolerated well.

Air conditioning and various types of filters that prevent entrance of dust or pollen are used appropriately. Hot air ducts are treated with a filter or are sealed. Filters should be constructed in such a way that they may be cleansed thoroughly. Certain reusable filters retain particles of dust even after thorough washing, and some disposable filters are inadequate. Windows and doors should be kept closed.

Control of allergens, including dust, is further reinforced by storing clothing, stuffed articles such as toys, and fur materials outside the dust-free area. If curtains and drapes are used, they must be washed frequently.

After the initial preparation, this environment is maintained with a thorough cleaning each week and daily dusting of the furniture and the floor with a damp cloth or mop. If possible, the patient should move to another area during the cleaning, and the room should be sealed for an hour after it has been cleaned. If the patient must remain in the room during the cleaning, he should be furnished with a mask. Cloth masks should be of double thickness and should be moistened to increase filtering power. Disposable surgical masks that filter efficiently when worn dry are available. Moistening these masks increases discomfort, for the material becomes flimsy and is drawn into the nostril or mouth with inhalation, obstructing respiration.

Questions for discussion and exploration

1. What are the differences between the ways the hands are held for hand washing and for surgical scrubbing? List situations in which hand washing is necessary.
2. What areas of the skin do the surgeons in your hospital commonly ask to be prepared for surgery?
3. If, during skin preparation, the patient tells you or indicates by his

nonverbal communication that he is frightened about his forthcoming surgery, what can you do to help him?

4. A woman who has consented to have brain surgery objects to having her head shaved. For what reasons may she be concerned? How can you relieve her immediate anxiety? What alternatives can you offer until her own hair has grown back?

5. What are the basic differences between the short and long surgical scrubs used in your hospital? How do they differ from those described in the text?

6. What are the basic principles that should be followed when sterile technique is used?

7. Are the inside, outermost edges of a sterile package considered clean, sterile, or contaminated? Why?

8. What are the basic principles and concepts used in isolation technique? How can the nursing staff help the patient feel less lonely? What teaching must you do for the patient and his visitors?

9. What are the basic principles for opening a package of sterile gloves and putting them on?

10. If a person is being admitted to the hospital with severe asthma related to dust allergies, what preparations should be made to control his environment? What special attention should be given to his environment during his hospitalization? What teaching does he and his family need prior to dismissal? Of what value might follow-up visits at his home be?

11. What are the advantages and disadvantages of reusing the same gown for isolation technique? Of using paper, cloth, or plastic gowns?

Selected references

Ballinger, W. F., Treybal, J. C., and Vose, A. B.: Alexander's care of the patient in surgery, ed. 5, St. Louis, 1972, The C. V. Mosby Co.

Berry, E. C., and Kohn, M. L.: Introduction to operating room technique, ed. 4, New York, 1972, McGraw-Hill Book Co.

Dumas, R. G.: Psychological preparation for surgery, Amer. J. Nurs. 63:52-55, 1963.

Feinberg, S. M.: Allergies and air conditioning, Amer. J. Nurs. 66:1333-1336, 1966.

Foster, M.: A positive approach to medical asepsis, Amer. J. Nurs. 62:76-77, 1962.

Fuerst, E. V., Wolff, L., and Weitzel, M. H.: Fundamentals of nursing, ed. 5, Philadelphia, 1974, J. B. Lippincott Co.

Gallivan, G. J., and Tovey, J. D.: Isolation for possible and proved Staph., Amer. J. Nurs. 67:1048-1049, 1967.

Ginsberg, F., Brunner, L. S., and Cantlin, V. L.: A manual of operating room technology, ed. 2, Philadelphia, 1970, J. B. Lippincott Co.

Hoeller, M. L.: Surgical technology: basis for clinical practice, ed. 3, St. Louis, 1974, The C. V. Mosby Co.

Kline, P.: Isolating patients with staphylococcal infections, Amer. J. Nurs. 65:102-104, 1965.

Kretzer, M. P., and Engley, F. B., Jr.: Effective use of antiseptics and disinfectants, R.N. 32:48-53, 1969.

Laduke, M. M., Hrynus, G. W., Johnston, M. A., Alpert, S., and Levenson, S. M.: Germfree isolators, Amer. J. Nurs. 67:72-79, 1967.

LeMaitre, G. D., and Finnegan, J. A.: The patient in surgery, ed. 2, Philadelphia, 1970, W. B. Saunders Co.

Matheney, R. V., Nolan, B. T., Hogan, A. E., and Griffin, G. J.: Fundamentals of patient-centered nursing, ed. 3, St. Louis, 1972, The C. V. Mosby Co.

Perkins, E. W., and Cibula, M. E.: Aseptic technique for operating room personnel, ed. 2, Philadelphia, 1964, W. B. Saunders Co.

Riley, R. L.: Air-borne infections, Amer. J. Nurs. 60:1246-1248, 1960.

Rockwell, V. T.: Surgical hand scrubbing, Amer. J. Nurs. 63:75-81, 1963.

Sather, M.: Environmental care of an asthmatic child, Amer. J. Nurs. 68:816-817, 1968.

Scheffler, G. L.: The nurse's role in hospital safety, Nurs. Outlook 10:680-682, 1962.

Schneewind, J. H.: Medical and surgical emergencies, ed. 3, Chicago, 1973, Year Book Medical Publishers, Inc.

Seidler, F. M.: Adapting nursing procedures for reverse isolation, Amer. J. Nurs. 65: 108-111, 1965.

Smith, A. L.: Microbiology and pathology, ed. 10, St. Louis, 1972, The C. V. Mosby Co.

Tyler, V. R.: Gas sterilization, Amer. J. Nurs. 60:1596-1599, 1960.

U. S. Department of Health, Education, and Welfare: Isolation techniques for use in hospitals, Public Health Service Publication No. 2054, U. S. Government Printing Office, Washington, D. C., 1970.

Werrin, M., and Kronick, D.: Salmonella control in hospitals, Amer. J. Nurs. 66:528-531, 1966.

Yeager, M. E.: Operating room manual, ed. 2, New York, 1965, G. P. Putnam's Sons.

2
Optimum activity and safety

Maintenance and promotion of optimum activity are important nursing responsibilities. The degree of mobilization must be individualized for each patient; for some patients, periods of immobility may be necessary, and this would represent optimum activity for them. The selection and carrying out of an individualized program of positioning and exercise should be consistent with the needs of the patient and with the activity or restrictions prescribed by the attending physician. Involvement of physical therapists does not relieve the nurse from responsibility for the patient's musculoskeletal function.

The selection of techniques that promote optimum activity is guided by the amount and kind of assistance needed by the patient. Factors influencing the selection and frequency of using techniques involving positioning and exercise include the patient's level of consciousness, state of health, age, surgical trauma, and degree of mobility or paralysis. Unconscious and paralyzed patients require more assistance than those who respond to stimuli or who voluntarily change position. The needs of patients for whom a period of immobilization is prescribed differ from those of ambulatory patients.

Pressure, friction, or moisture between the patient and linen, casts, braces, and other objects is damaging to the skin and underlying tissues. Knowledge of this should guide the modification of techniques used. For instance, pressure on bony prominences can be relieved by proper placement of pillows and other devices, friction from the rough edges of a cast can be reduced with petals of adhesive tape and positioning with pillows, and the perineal area of a body cast can be protected with waterproof material.

Use of the principles of body mechanics combined with adequate assistance of other personnel when lifting, turning, or helping the patient to ambulate can avoid strain or trauma to the patient and the nurse. Mechanical devices are helpful in moving the dependent patient.

Whenever a positioning or exercise program is to be followed after discharge from the hospital, the nurse should teach the patient and at least one responsible family member of the plan and techniques involved. Ideally, such teaching begins early, providing time for those involved to practice and gain confidence.

Positions

Proper positioning is a part of preventive nursing. Pillows, lumbar pads, trochanter rolls, and other accessory aids help to maintain good body alignment and prevent prolonged pressure that results in complications. In addition, frequent rotation of selected positions that alternate flexion, extension, abduction, and adduction promotes range of motion and prevents contractures, muscle spasms, and other symptoms of disuse.

Keeping the foundation linen of the bed tight and free of wrinkles helps prevent irritation to the skin. Sheepskin or a substitute properly positioned reduces friction. Sponge rubber pads, silicone gel–filled pads, alternating air mattresses, and other commercial equipment may be used to redistribute pressure. Doughnut-shaped devices are likely to restrict circulation further, interfering with adequate oxygenation of the affected cells.

Prolonged pressure on certain points, such as a bony prominence or edges of the ribs, cheeks, nose, and ears, contributes to excoriation and formation of blisters and decubiti. Similarly, circulatory problems and nerve damage may result from incorrect positioning. For example, "gatching" the foot of the bed may produce pressure in the popliteal area that, along with the dependent position of the lower leg, contributes to the development of thrombophlebitis.

Elevation of the head of the bed produces gravitation of abdominal contents away from the chest, permitting the lungs to expand more fully. Conversely, flexion of the neck interferes with an adequate airway, and clothing tightened over the chest restricts respiration. Pressure from an arm lying across an injured chest further restricts respiration.

Correct body alignment should be maintained with each position. The nurse may profit from assuming these positions and thus gain awareness of discomforts that result from improper positioning. For example, one can readily feel the tension on the muscles of the leg if the side-lying position is assumed without elevating the uppermost leg.

27

The patient's position must be changed frequently to avoid complications that result from immobilization. Such complications may occur in a relatively short period of time. Although position changes are often planned for 2- to 3-hour intervals, the frequency should be dictated by the needs of the patient and his pathophysiologic condition.

TABLE 2-1. Back-lying position

Technique	Problem	Solution or explanation
Move the patient toward the head of the bed if necessary. To do this, flex his knees, cradle his head and shoulders in your arm, and place your other arm under his thighs. Ask the patient to push with his feet on the count of three. Rock back and forth, facing the head of the bed, counting as you begin to rock towards the head.	The weight of the patient may be difficult to move.	Pushing efforts of the patient will add leverage; cradling the head and shoulders relieves friction; rocking increases momentum.
Check the alignment of the patient's body.	Movement may distort body alignment.	Incorrect alignment causes discomfort and muscular and nerve problems. The body should be as straight as possible.
Place one or two pillows beneath the head for comfort.	Tension on the neck and shoulder muscles may occur; flexion of the neck may also occur.	Pillows should extend between the sixth thoracic and first cervical vertebrae and should be of a thickness equal to the thickness of the shoulder.
A lumbar pad may be placed beneath the small of the back.	Tension on the small of the back causes muscular discomfort.	A pad may be formed by folding a bath blanket or towels to fit this area.
Place a trochanter roll along each thigh.	Outward rotation of the thigh may occur.	A trochanter roll is formed by folding a bath blanket lengthwise into thirds, then in half, and placing it beneath the thighs and rolling the ends firmly under to form a tight roll against the thigh.
Place a folded towel between the calf and the heel or apply heel protectors.	Pressure on the heels may predispose to decubiti formation.	Heel protectors serve to reduce friction.
Support the feet with a footboard.	Footdrop may develop; if the head of the bed is elevated, the patient will tend to gravitate toward the foot of the bed.	Alignment of the feet helps to prevent footdrop. Use of a footboard prevents gravitation.

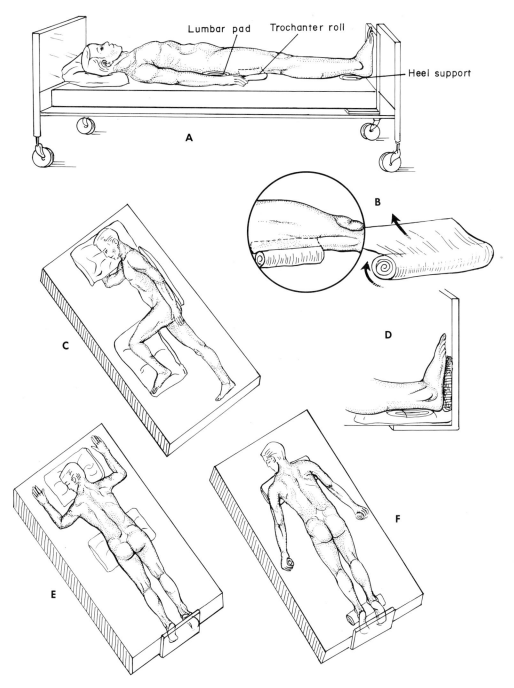

Fig. 2-1. Positions. **A,** Back-lying position showing the trochanter roll, heel support, and lumbar pad. **B,** The formation of a trochanter roll. **C,** Side-lying position. **D,** Support of the foot. **E** and **F,** Face-lying positions.

29

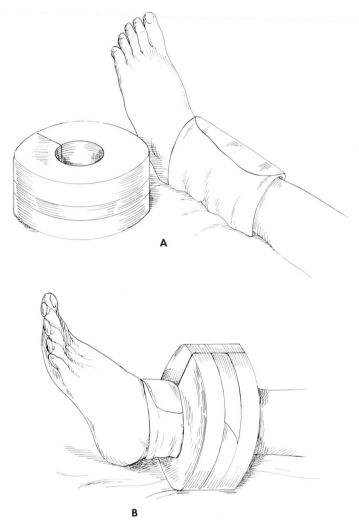

A

B

Fig. 2-2. Posey foot elevator. **A,** A flannel liner is wrapped around the ankle. **B,** The foam ring, which is encased in a plastic shell, is placed over the liner and fastened. (Courtesy J. T. Posey Co., Pasadena, Calif.)

BACK-LYING POSITION

When the patient is in the back-lying position (Table 2-1), one or more pillows may be used to align the head. The pillows should extend to a level between the sixth cervical and first thoracic vertebrae, thereby preventing tension on the neck and shoulder muscles and flexion of the neck (Fig. 2-1, *A*). If only one pillow is used, it should equal the thickness of the shoulders. A second pillow may be placed on top of the first pillow, with its lower edge near the base of the neck to provide alignment and comfort.

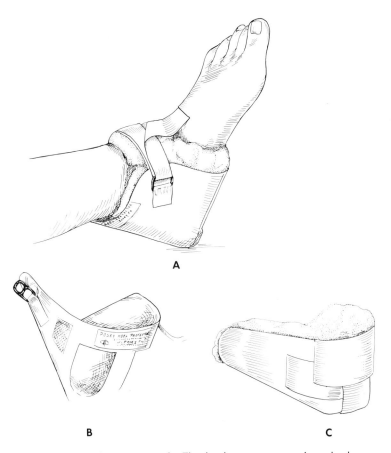

A

B   C

Fig. 2-3. Heel protectors. **A,** The heel protector as viewed when it is applied. The plastic shell is lined. The strap, which contains a Velcro fastener, has been placed through the buckle, then folded back onto itself to secure the protector. **B,** Rear view of the plastic shell showing the openings in it, which provide ventilation. **C,** Back view of the protector showing the synthetic wool liner in place. (Courtesy J. T. Posey Co., Pasadena, Calif.)

A lumbar pad, formed by folding a bath blanket or towels to an individualized size, may be placed under the small of the back for added comfort. A trochanter roll may be formed by folding a bath blanket into thirds lengthwise, then in half, tucking it under the thigh, and rolling it firmly under itself to correct outward rotation of the thigh (Fig. 2-1, *B*). A folded towel under the area between the calf and the heel will support this area and relieve pressure on the heel (Fig. 2-1, *D*). The foot may be completely elevated to prevent pressure on it (Fig. 2-2). Heel protectors and elbow protectors may be used to reduce friction and pressure on these joints (Figs. 2-3 and 2-4).

31

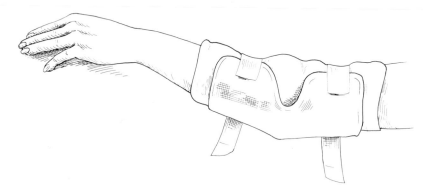

Fig. 2-4. Posey elbow protector (flannel-lined model). Protection of the elbow reduces irritation and pressure on the tissues; this prevents tissue damage due to friction and pressure. A liner is placed around the elbow, and then a foam-lined plastic shell is positioned over the liner and fastened. (Courtesy J. T. Posey Co., Pasadena, Calif.)

A substantial footboard supports the feet and holds the top linen off the toes. It should be nearly the width of the mattress and should be constructed sturdily because if the head of the bed is elevated at all, the patient tends to gravitate toward the footboard (Fig. 2-1, *A* and *D*).

SIDE-LYING POSITION

The back, in the side-lying position, should be as straight as if the patient were standing (Fig. 2-1, *C*). The lower arm is flexed to cradle the head in the hand and to maintain the position of the hand and extension of the fingers. A pillow placed between the head and the hand serves to align the head and reduce pressure on the hand.

Extension of the uppermost arm rests the hand on the hips, sustains extension of the fingers, and prevents pressure on the chest. Alternate positioning of this arm necessitates the use of pillows, hand rolls, and support of the wrist.

The uppermost leg is flexed and elevated with bolster pillows to prevent adduction and muscle tension. Padding or foot protectors may be needed to reduce pressure on the malleolus. Additional support of the foot maintains this position and prevents foot drop. The vertical bars of a side rail, previously attached to the bed, furnish a method of supporting the foot. A sandbag, folded towel, or other padding supports the instep area of the foot and prevents direct contact with the rail.

The stability and comfort of this position may be increased by placing pillows securely behind the back, tucking one edge under the patient while depressing the mattress, then pushing the free edge of the pillow under the anchored portion.

FACE-LYING POSITION

The face-lying position is used unless it is contraindicated by conditions such as abdominal incisions and advanced pregnancy, which would cause discomfort. The patient's feet project beyond the mattress to maintain their alignment and prevent pressure on the toes. When a footboard is in place, adequate toe space can be assured by placing 4-inch-square blocks at the outside edges of the footboard, between it and the mattress. A thin pillow under the abdomen aligns the spine and protects the breasts (Fig. 2-1, *E*). It is unnecessary to support the area between the lower ribs and pelvis of most children.

The head may be turned to either side. Prominences such as the ears, cheeks, and nose are positioned to prevent distortion and pressure. Abduction and external rotation of the arms promote full expansion of the chest. Shoulder rolls, made by rolling a towel, correct inward rotation of the shoulder when necessary. Two washcloths that have been formed into a roll limit flexion of the fingers if placement of the hands palms down with fingers extended is ineffective (Fig. 2-1, *F*).

Range of motion

Rotation of the previously described bed positions produces range of motion unless effort is used to prevent it. Often, additional exercises are needed to maintain or regain optional range of motion in the ill or injured. These are conducted slowly, smoothly, without force, and within the existing range of motion. If pain occurs, exercises are discontinued until further instructions are obtained from the physician, who also prescribes limitations to be observed, special devices such as skates, slings, and pulleys, and exercise programs designed to regain or increase range of motion.

Planning the bed bath, positioning, and other nursing care to include either active or passive range of motion may eliminate the need for designated exercise periods. Observation of alignment and correction of faulty movements, such as raising the shoulder during neck exercises, increase effectiveness of the exercises. Exercises for the normal range of motion are described as the patient might be instructed to do them.

Neck. To exercise his neck the patient bends his head forward until his chin rests on his chest. Then he bends the head back as far as possible, turning his head toward his left shoulder, then his right. Finally he tilts his head toward each shoulder in an attempt to touch his shoulder with his chin (Fig. 2-5, *A*).

Text continued on p. 38.

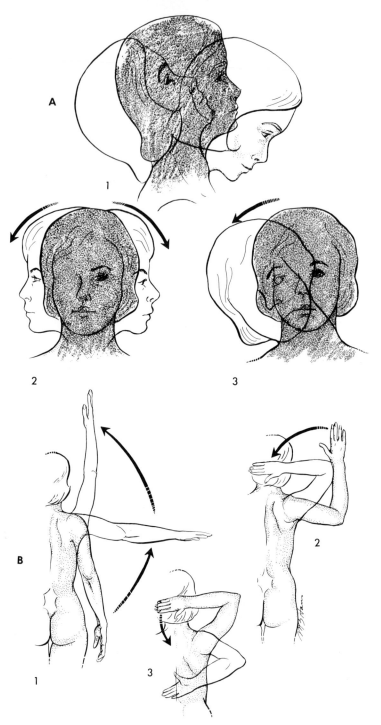

Fig. 2-5. Range of motion. **A,** Neck: **1,** the patient bends the head forward until the chin rests on the chest, then backward as far as possible; **2,** the patient turns the head toward the left shoulder, then toward the right shoulder; **3,** the head is tilted toward the right shoulder, then toward the left shoulder, attempting to touch the shoulder with the chin each time. **B,** Shoulder and elbow: **1,** the patient extends arm at the side with the palm of the hand turned toward the hip and raises the extended arm up and backward until it is held directly above the head; **2,** the elbow is then bent and the palm of the hand moved behind the head; **3,** the hand is then moved to the small of the back.

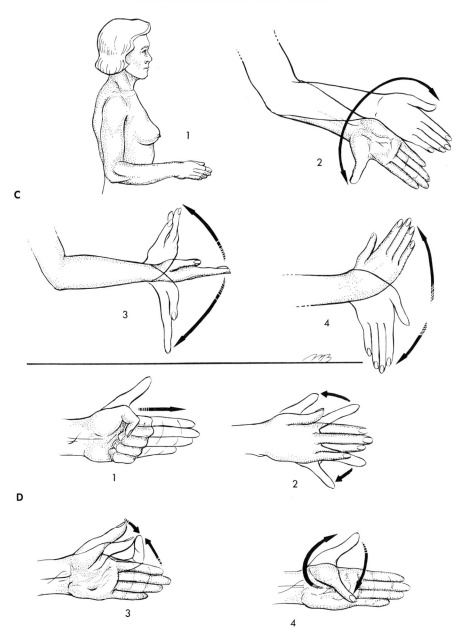

Fig. 2-5, cont'd. C, Wrist and lower arm: **1,** the patient holds the upper part of the arm in contact with the side of the body with the elbow at a right angle to it; **2,** the palm is turned up, then down; **3,** extending the fingers, the patient bends the hand down as far as possible, then up as far as possible; **4,** the patient aligns the hand with the lower arm, keeping the elbow bent, and moves the hand to either side as far as possible; then the hand is rotated over and back as far as possible. **D,** Fingers and thumb: **1,** the patient makes a fist and then straightens the fingers and thumb; **2,** the fingers and thumb are spread apart and then brought together; **3,** the patient touches each finger with the thumb; **4,** the patient rotates the thumb.

Continued.

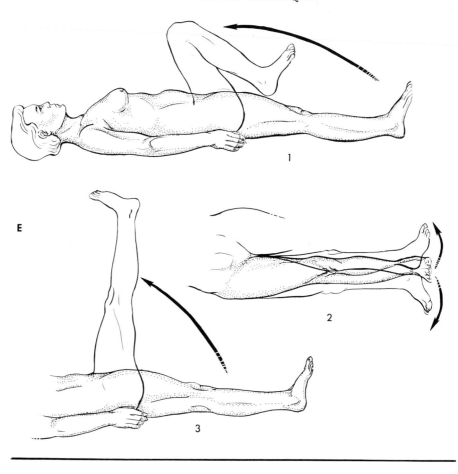

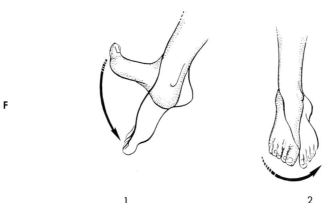

Fig. 2-5, cont'd. E, Hip and knee: 1, after assuming a back-lying position, the patient bends the knee toward the body as far as possible; 2, the patient straightens the leg, rolls it inward as far as possible, and then outward as far as possible; 3, the patient raises the leg straight up. F, Ankle and foot: 1, after assuming a sitting position with the feet dangling, the patient bends the foot and toes downward, then upward; 2, the patient rotates the entire foot inward, then outward and points the toes inward, finally circumducting the ankle.

Fig. 2-5, cont'd. G, Trunk: **1,** the patient bends the upper trunk to the left, then to the right, and then twists the upper trunk to the left, then to the right; **2,** with the knees straight, the patient touches the toes with the tips of the fingers and then bends the body backward.

Shoulder and elbow. To exercise the shoulder and elbow, the patient extends his arm at his side with the palm of his hand turned toward the hip. Keeping the arm extended, the patient raises it up and backward through an arc until he holds it directly above his head, then bends his elbow and moves the palm of his hand behind his head, and finally to the small of his back (Fig. 2-5, *B*).

Wrist and lower arm. In exercising his wrist and lower arm, the patient holds the upper part of his arm in contact with the side of his body, with his elbow at a right angle to it. He turns the palm up, then down. Extending his fingers, he bends his hand down as far as possible, then up as far as possible. He aligns his hand with his lower arm, keeping the elbow bent, and moves his hand as far as possible to either side. He finishes by rotating his hand over and back as far as possible (Fig. 2-5, *C*).

Fingers and thumb. To exercise his fingers and thumb, the patient makes a fist, straightens the fingers and thumb, spreads them apart, and brings them together. He touches each finger with the thumb, then rotates the thumb (Fig. 2-5, *D*).

Hip and knee. The hip and knee are exercised by having the patient, in a back-lying position, bend his knee as far toward the body as possible. Then, straightening the leg, he rolls it inward, then outward as far as possible. Finally he raises the leg straight up. He sits on the edge of the bed to dangle the lower leg and moves the foot inward, outward, forward, and back. He raises his knee toward his chest (Fig. 2-5, *E*).

Ankle and foot. To exercise the ankle and foot, the patient sits with his feet dangling. He bends the foot and toes downward, then upward; he rotates the entire foot inward, then outward; then he points the toes inward, finally circumducting the ankle (Fig. 2-5, *F*).

Trunk. Standing with the feet a few inches apart, the patient bends his upper trunk to the left, then to the right, and twists the upper trunk to the left, then to the right. With his knees straight, he touches his toes with the tips of his fingers and then bends backward (Fig. 2-5, *G*).

Transfers

The selection of transfer techniques is individualized. For example, horizontal transfer with a sheet moves patients with abdominal surgery from the stretcher to the bed, a three-man carry moves orthopedic patients through narrow doorways, mechanical devices such as lifts transfer patients with ease, and special frames or beds maintain body alignment during transfer. Precautions that prevent twisting or crepitation of the spine are employed in turning the patient with a spinal injury. If full range of motion is permitted, the patient may assist with the transfer or move himself independently.

Care to instruct the patient, to prevent trauma by positioning or supporting the extremities, to protect drainage tubes from tension, and to synchronize efforts of the persons involved contributes to safe, gentle transfer. The practice of transferring on the count of three helps to make the transfer gentle. Jolting or sudden movements are likely to cause physiologic adjustments that may result in complications such as shock. Some adjustment occurs with each position change, and the transfer may need to be completed over a period of time to accommodate resulting reactions. For example, it may be necessary to bring the orthopedic patient who has been lying in bed for a long period of time to a vertical position slowly with the use of a tilt table or CircOlectric bed.

PULL-SHEET TRANSFER

To prepare for transfer with a pull sheet, the bed and stretcher mattresses must be at the same height, with the bed linen folded to the side or foot of the bed.

Ideally, six persons combine their efforts for this transfer, although four persons can achieve a similar result. Two persons position themselves to support the chest and abdomen; two support the pelvis and hips; one, the lower legs and feet; and one, the head, neck, and shoulders. Better leverage and body mechanics are gained if a short person kneels on the edge of the bed. The pull sheet is tightened into a hammock by folding or rolling it toward the patient's sides. Efforts to pull and lift the patient from the stretcher to the bed should be synchronized (Fig. 2-6, A).

The patient is turned to his side to remove the pull sheet. The persons beside the bed reach across the patient, place the palms of their hands down on the posterior aspect of his shoulders, back, and hips, and roll him toward them. If immobility of the spine is desirable, his uppermost arm is held in extension on his hip, and his entire body is rolled like a log. This position of the uppermost arm prevents twisting of the torso. An alternate method of rolling the patient to his side uses the pull sheet rather than the hands. The patient is supported on his side until the pull sheet is folded or rolled tightly against his back, and its edge is tucked under him by depressing the mattress slightly. Then the patient is rolled to his opposite side, completely freeing the pull sheet. Forceful removal of the pull sheet disregards the comfort and alignment of the patient and produces skin damage that will become more apparent with time.

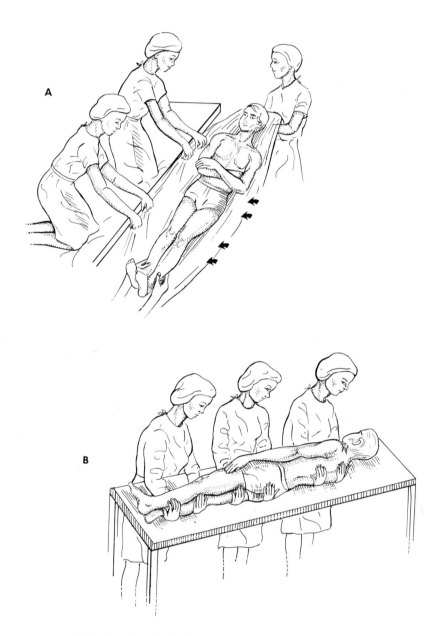

Fig. 2-6. Transfers. **A,** Pull-sheet method of transfer; arrows indicate placement of the hands of other assistants. **B,** Lifting the patient in preparation for transfer with a three-man carry.

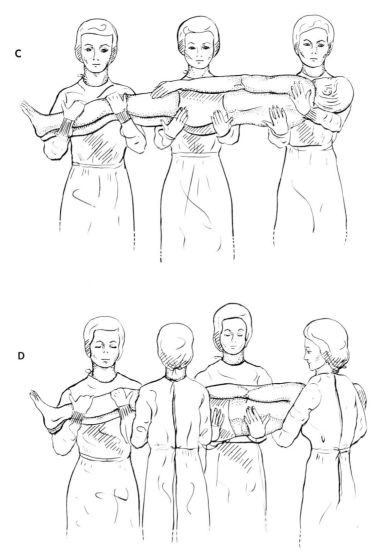

Fig. 2-6, cont'd. C, The patient is lifted and rolled onto the chests of the persons executing the three-man carry. **D,** Four-man carry.

THREE-MAN CARRY

For the three-man carry, three persons, all standing on the same side of the patient, slip their hands, palms facing up, beneath the patient (Fig. 2-6, *B*) and cradle him in their arms so that his weight rests against their chests and he faces them (Fig. 2-6, *C*).

FOUR-MAN OR SIX-MAN CARRY

To do the four-man carry, two persons stand on each side of the patient and place their hands beneath him to form a hammock (Fig. 2-6, *D*). Two persons are added to the basic four-man carry if the patient is tall or heavy.

Mechanical devices
HYDRAULIC LIFT

The hydraulic lift, also called a patient lifter or invalid lifter, enables one person to transfer a totally dependent patient with ease and safety to and from a bed, a wheelchair, a toilet, a tub, or a car. Depending on the needs of the patient, he is supported with a pair of slings, canvas seats with or without a head support, or a stretcher. The support is placed beneath the patient and attached to the swivel bar of the lift.

Most hydraulic lifts consist of a tripod type of base on casters, a mast, a boom, a hydraulic, mechanical, or electrical pump, and a sling, harness, or stretcher. Although design varies, their operation is similar to that of the Hoyer patient lifter illustrated in Fig. 2-7.

When canvas slings are used, the larger of the slings is placed beneath the patient's thighs, with its lower edge above his knees. The smaller sling is placed behind the small of his back by elevating the head of the bed and sliding the sling down to its position or by rolling the patient to his side, then onto the sling (Fig. 2-7, *A*). Both slings are attached to the swivel bar with **S** hooks that have been incorporated into the design (Fig. 2-7, *B*). The exact position of the slings must be individualized until the so-called point of adjustment is reached. This is the point at which the patient is given proper support. When the patient is lifted with proper support, he does not tip forward or backward, nor does he experience a feeling of slipping between the slings.

After the slings have been fastened, the jack handle is pumped to elevate the patient. When he is sufficiently high to swing free (Fig. 2-7, *C*), he is assisted to face the mast by grasping the outer edges of the swivel bar to turn him. Then the release knob is turned to lower him to a sitting position. Some manual assistance may be necessary during the lowering process to guide him to the desired position.

The steering handle is used to guide the lift to the desired loca-

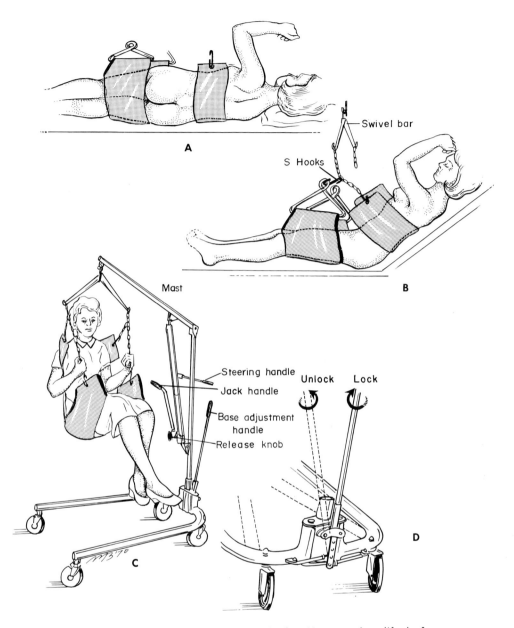

Fig. 2-7. Hydraulic lift (illustrated after Hoyer patient lifter). **A,** Placement of slings. **B,** Attachment of slings to swivel bar. **C,** A patient in the slings is swung free of the bed. The point of adjustment has been reached. The patient will turn to face the mast before the lift is moved. **D,** View of the base. To narrow the base, the handle is unlocked by rotating it counterclockwise and moving it to the left. The base is locked by turning the handle clockwise. The base is widened by unlocking the handle and moving it to the right, where it is locked in position. (Courtesy Ted Hoyer & Co., Inc., Oshkosh, Wis.)

tion. It is sometimes necessary to change the width of the base. Passage through a doorway requires a narrow base, whereas positioning the patient over a toilet requires a widened base. The narrow position should not be used unless it is necessary because a slightly widened base offers more stability. To change the width of the base, the base adjustment handle is unlocked by rotating it to the left (counterclockwise), then the handle is moved to the left to narrow the base or to the right to widen the base. The base is locked in this position by rotating the handle to the right (clockwise) (Fig. 2-7, D).

TURNING DEVICES

The Stryker turning frame, the Foster reversible orthopedic bed, and the CircOlectric bed provide means of changing the patient to and from the face-lying and back-lying positions with a minimum of personnel, maximum ease, and undisturbed body alignment.

Stryker frame and Foster bed. Basic padding of the frames is similar, although the materials and fasteners may vary. Each company supplies canvas covers, mattresses, sheets, and fasteners designed to fit its product. Additional accessories are a footboard, arm supports, a utility table for diversional materials and the serving tray, and provisions for attaching traction. All frames provide openings used for normal routes of elimination. The center section of the posterior frame is removed, and the receptacle is placed within the device attached to the frame for this purpose.

Although each has distinctive features, common principles apply in the use of all these devices. The position of the patient is stabilized similarly on all. Frequent changes of position prevent complications and facilitate nursing care. In addition, complete passivity of joints during transfer adds to patient comfort.

In the initial transfer to the posterior frame, previously described transfer techniques (pages 38 to 42) may be used, or a litter bearing the patient may be placed on the frame. To remove the litter without disturbing body alignment, the anterior frame is secured in position, and the patient is turned so that the posterior frame and the litter may be removed.

Mental preparation prior to use of a turning frame helps the patient to adjust to its use. Before each maneuver, the nurse tells him which direction he will be turned and informs him of sensations likely to occur because of changes in circulation. For example, vertical change of position may produce sensations of numbness, tingling, or light-headedness. Knowledge that he is securely and comfortably sandwiched between the posterior and anterior frames helps the patient develop trust. It may be helpful for nurses who are involved in caring for patients on these devices to experience the posi-

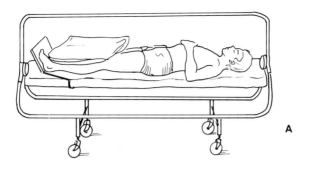

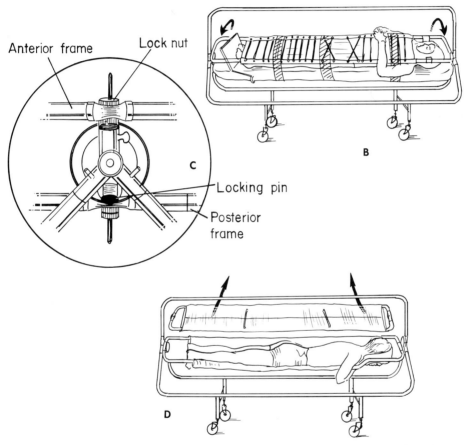

Anterior frame

Lock nut

Locking pin

Posterior frame

Fig. 2-8. Stryker turning frame. **A,** The top linen is removed, the pillow from the head is placed lengthwise over the legs, and the footboard is adjusted. **B,** The anterior frame is positioned with its narrow end and the face support over the face. This frame is locked securely with a knurled nut. The patient is secured with safety straps and permitted to grasp the frame. The locking pin is disengaged, and the patient is transferred laterally. **C,** End view of the turning assembly. Locknuts on each end of the frame must be tightened before the patient is turned. The locking pin at the end of the frame is pulled out, the patient is turned slightly, the locking pin is released, and the transfer is completed. **D,** After lateral transfer is completed, the posterior frame is unbolted and removed. (Courtesy Stryker Corp., Kalamazoo, Mich.)

tion transfers personally, thus increasing their sympathetic and instructional capacities.

Preparatory to lateral transfer with a Stryker turning frame or the Foster bed, a pillow is placed lengthwise over the patient's legs to protect the knees and stabilize the legs during transfer (Figs. 2-8, A, and 2-9, A). Depending on the size of the patient, an additional pillow may be needed. The pillow beneath the patient's head is removed and the face is protected with a face mask. Safety straps are

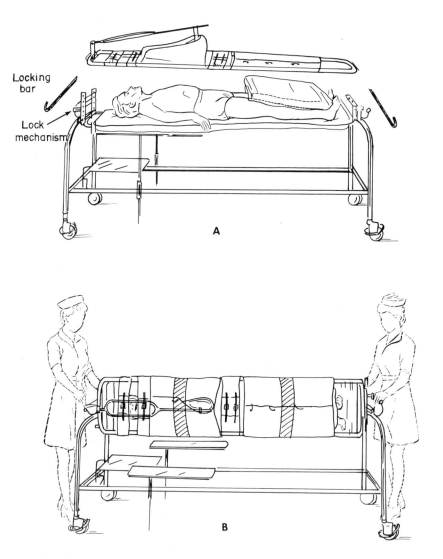

Fig. 2-9. Foster orthopedic frame. **A,** The anterior frame is installed and secured with locking bars. **B,** The lock mechanism is disengaged, and the patient is turned. Safety straps add security. Position of the nurses' hands should be planned for smooth transfer. (Courtesy Gilbert Hyde Chick Co., Oakland, Calif.)

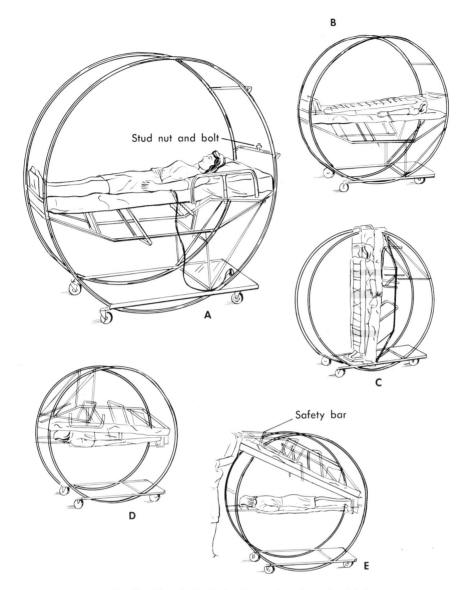

Stud nut and bolt

Safety bar

Fig. 2-10. CircOlectric bed. **A,** The patient is in back-lying position, with the hips centered at the gatch. The footboard is adjusted to prevent the patient from sliding downward during transfer. The pillow is used to pad the patient's legs and knees. A sponge rubber face mask is applied to protect the face. **B,** The anterior frame is installed and locked in place with a stud nut and bolt. **C,** After telling the patient the direction that he will be turned, the nurse rotates the bed electrically. Safety straps are necessary if the patient is unable to control his arms. **D,** The posterior stud nut is removed from the head of the frame, and the safety bar is pulled forward to disengage the posterior section. **E,** The posterior section is raised high overhead and locked into the circle frame with the safety bar. (Courtesy Stryker Corp., Kalamazoo, Mich.)

used to stabilize the head and prevent flexion or extension of the neck. The arm boards are removed and the patient, if he is able, is permitted to hug the frame during transfer (Fig. 2-8, *B*). If the patient is unable to do this, his arms are extended beside his body and maintained in this position with safety straps (Fig. 2-9). This prevents the arms from dangling and also prevents trauma when the patient is turned. After removing the footboard of the Foster bed, two nurses place the anterior frame over the patient and secure it (Fig. 2-9, *B*). It is imperative to have two persons handle the anterior frame of the Foster bed (Fig. 2-9, *B*). The safety straps should be fastened and checked by the nurse.

A nurse stands at each end of the frame, disengaging the pins that lock the frame to the base (Figs. 2-8, *C*, and 2-9, *A*). Each nurse grasps the frame preparatory to rotation, one tells the patient which direction he will be turned, and together they transfer him with a synchronized turn. Preplanned placement of the nurses' hands will make this maneuver smooth.

CircOlectric bed. The CircOlectric bed has features useful in progressive rehabilitation. Because it turns the patient vertically (Fig. 2-10, *C*) and can be stopped at any point, it serves as a tilt table. "Gatching" the posterior frame provides the same position attainable in the ordinary hospital bed; when combined with rotation in the circle frame, it brings the patient to a sitting position from which he can be easily transferred to a chair by means of slings, much as a patient is transferred with a hydraulic lift.

Preparatory to vertical transfer of the patient in a CircOlectric bed, the patient is protected from unnecessary movement by positioning the footboard, placing pillows over his legs, and applying the sponge rubber face mask (Fig. 2-10, *A*). The overhead frame is disengaged from its resting place on the circle frame with a downward pull and secured by tightening the nut on the prepositioned bolt (Fig. 2-10, *B*). Safety straps are then applied. After telling the patient in which direction he will turn, the nurse moves the switch button to "face" or "back" accordingly (Fig. 2-10, *C*). After the desired level of transfer is achieved, the posterior section is disengaged, raised high overhead, and locked into the circle frame with the safety bar (Fig. 2-10, *D* and *E*).

Ambulation

Whenever it is feasible, early ambulation is prescribed to promote independent activity. This avoids the complications and the discouragement that are likely to accompany inactivity.

The amount and kind of assistance needed vary. Factors such as fluid and electrolyte imbalance, inadequate nutrition, age, insecurity, limited joint motion, and paralysis increase the amount of assistance needed. If necessary, the patient is helped to progress through stages to independent activity. The patient may first be assisted to sit on the edge of the bed, then to stand briefly while being assisted to a chair, next to ambulate with necessary degrees of support, and finally to ambulate independently. Supports such as arm slings should be applied prior to ambulation. Moving the strongest part of the body first gives the maximum support, and this, combined with effort, increases independence. The hemiplegic would therefore transfer his uninvolved side first.

SITTING UP

To assist the totally dependent patient to sit up, the nurse elevates the head of the bed and places the left arm under his legs and the right arm under his shoulder. Then the patient's shoulders are lifted slightly and simultaneously his legs are pulled toward the nurse's body, pivoting him to a sitting position (Fig. 2-11, *A* and *B*). The nurse permits as much self-assistance as possible. The patient can be helped to maintain this position if the nurse stands facing him, with his hands on the nurse's shoulders and the nurse's hands at his waist.

An independent method of assuming the sitting position, preferred by many patients and especially useful if an abdominal incision is present, consists of instructing the patient to turn to his side before sitting up. The head of the bed is elevated to an angle of approximately 30 degrees; the patient is instructed to grasp the side rail with his uppermost arm for leverage and to push up with his lower arm, simultaneously moving his feet toward the edge of the bed until they hang free (Fig. 2-11, *D*). If some assistance is needed, the patient places his upper arm on the nurse's shoulder, and the nurse uses one arm to support his head and neck, moving his legs with the other arm (Fig. 2-11, *C*).

TRANSFER FROM BED TO CHAIR

To transfer a patient from the bed to a chair, an electric bed is placed in low position to permit the patient's feet to rest on the floor, and the patient is helped to a standing position. Depending on the placement of the chair, he may need only to pivot or take one step to place his back to the chair, then seat himself with assistance as necessary. Placing the chair against a wall or bracing one's foot behind the front leg of the chair will prevent the chair from slipping when the patient is being seated.

If the bed cannot be lowered, the patient, supported at waist level, places his arms on the nurse's shoulders, and is helped to slip to a

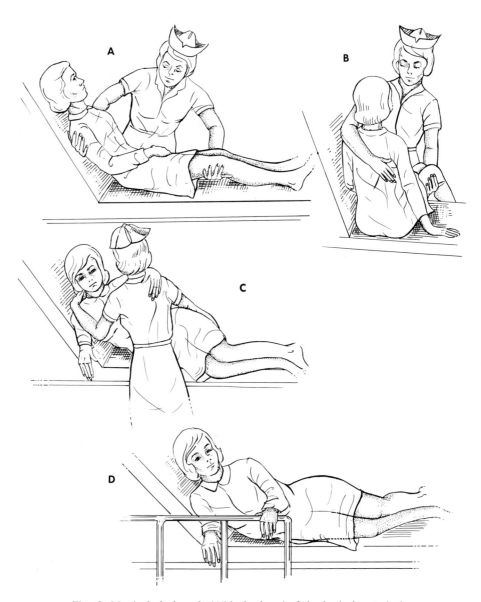

Fig. 2-11. Ambulation. **A,** With the head of the bed elevated, the nurse is preparing to pivot the patient to a sitting position. **B,** The pivot to sitting position is nearly complete. **C,** A patient receiving some assistance. **D,** Self-assisted method of sitting up.

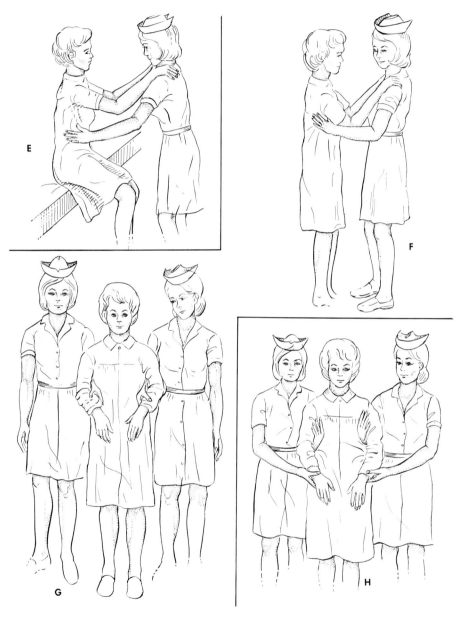

Fig. 2-11, cont'd. E, Assisting patient from edge of bed to standing position. **F,** Assisting patient to stand. Feet and knees may be braced with nurse's feet and knees for additional support. **G,** Supported ambulation. **H,** Convenient method of supported ambulation.

standing position (Fig. 2-11, *E*). Bracing his feet and knees helps stabilize the upright position (Fig. 2-11, *F*).

DEPENDENT AMBULATION: AIDS IN WALKING

To help a patient walk, the nurse, standing at the patient's left side, places the right arm around his waist and grasps his right forearm with the right hand and his left forearm with the left hand. If two nurses assist the patient, each may place the arm that is beside the patient so that it interlocks with the patient's arm and may grasp the patient's forearm for support (Fig. 2-11, *G*). Bilateral support without clumsiness during ambulation is obtained if two nurses, standing on either side of the patient, grasp the upper arm near the axilla with the arm nearest the patient. The other hand is used to grasp the patient's wrist (Fig. 2-11, *H*). Although the patient may tend to grasp the nurse's hand, it is important that the nurse control the points of support to utilize necessary leverage if the need arises.

Cane walking. To walk properly with a cane, the patient stands in normal walking position with the cane positioned about 4 to 6 inches away from the toe of the uninvolved extremity (Fig. 2-12, *A*). This prevents leaning toward the cane or having it accidentally kicked away. The patient moves the cane forward about the length of his foot (Fig. 2-12, *B*). Then he moves the involved leg forward until its toe is parallel to the cane (Fig. 2-12, *C*). He moves the uninvolved leg forward until its heel is parallel to the cane (Fig. 2-12, *D*). Alternative methods of cane walking may be used if this method is not satisfactory.

Crutch walking. As with any activity, good body alignment is essential for correct crutch walking and future rehabilitation. Holding the involved extremity in extension to prevent contracture and rotation and standing erect with the head held erect and the eyes looking ahead prevent errors commonly associated with crutch walking. Supporting the body weight on the hands necessitates keeping the elbows straight. Placing the crutches 4 to 6 inches to the side, but in front of the feet, adds stability.

Length of crutches. Numerous methods of measuring a patient for crutches are used. If the patient is able, he should stand against a wall, in a position of good posture. He must be wearing his walking shoes. Three points are used to determine the length of crutch needed: (1) a measurement from the outside of the toe of the shoe sole to a point 2 inches to the patient's side, (2) a measurement from this first point, straight forward for a distance of 6 inches, and (3) a measurement from the second point to 2 inches below the axilla. The third measurement indicates the length of crutches needed. If the patient is unable to stand, he lies on his back, arms extended at

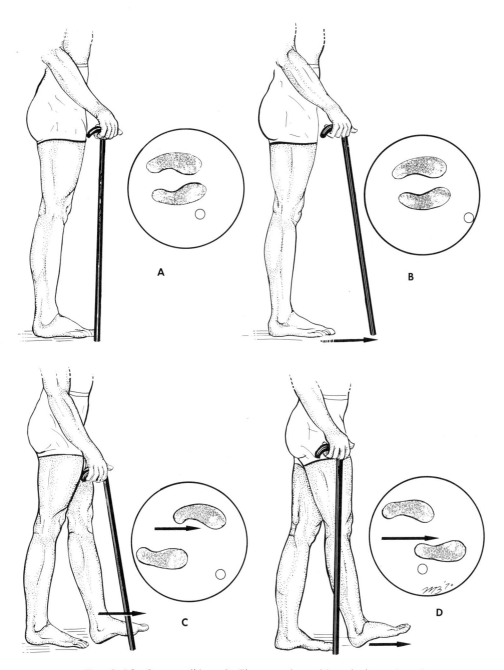

Fig. 2-12. Cane walking. **A,** The cane is positioned about 4 to 6 inches away from the toe of the uninvolved extremity. **B,** The cane is moved forward about the length of the patient's foot. **C,** The involved leg is moved forward until the toe is parallel to the cane. **D,** The uninvolved leg is moved forward until its heel is parallel to the cane.

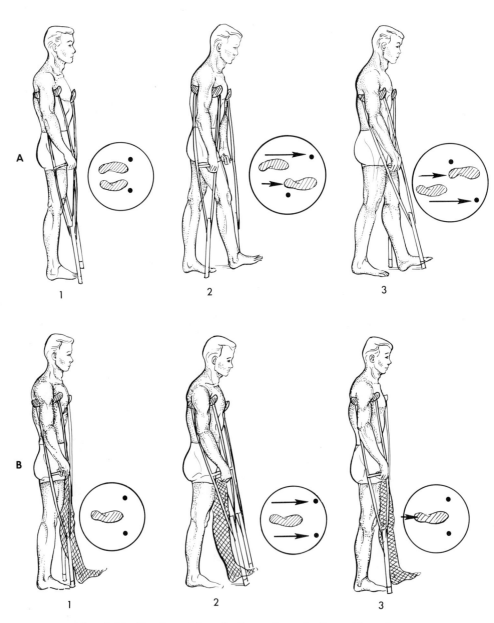

Fig. 2-13. Crutch walking. **A,** Two-point gait: **1,** position of rest; **2,** the left crutch and the right foot are advanced simultaneously; **3,** the right crutch and the left foot are advanced simultaneously. **B,** Three-point gait: **1,** weight is on the uninvolved extremity; **2,** with the weight on the uninvolved extremity, the crutches and the involved extremity are advanced; **3,** the uninvolved extremity is advanced.

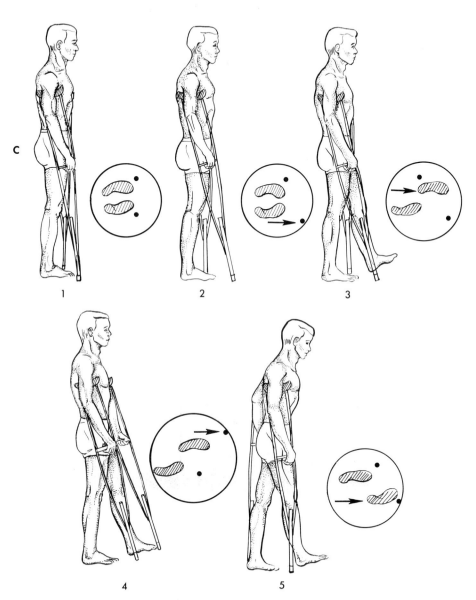

Fig. 2-13, cont'd. C, Four-point gait: **1,** position of rest; **2,** right crutch is advanced; **3,** left foot is advanced; **4,** left crutch is advanced; **5,** right foot is advanced.

his sides, legs aligned, feet slightly apart, with his walking shoes on. A measurement taken from the axilla to a point 6 inches out from the heel represents crutch length. Evaluation of the height of the hand bar and its adjustment to individual needs are basic for preventing pressure in the axillary region.

Crutch gait is prescribed according to the kind and amount of support required. Teaching crutch walking varies with the gait and the individual.

Two-point gait. When partial weight bearing is allowed, the two-point gait increases speed. The left crutch and the right foot are advanced simultaneously. Then the right crutch and the left foot are advanced simultaneously (Fig. 2-13, *A*).

Three-point gait. When bearing the weight on one extremity is permitted, the patient may use the three-point gait. The weight is shifted to the uninvolved extremity while the crutches are advanced. Then the uninvolved extremity is advanced (Fig. 2-13, *B*). The crutches and the involved leg are moved forward at the same time. Next the uninvolved leg is moved forward. These steps are repeated.

Four-point gait. The four-point gait is slower than the two-point gait but similar to it. The right crutch is advanced, then the left foot, the left crutch, and then the right foot (Fig. 2-13, *C*).

Additional aids

Not uncommonly, prescribed levels of activity necessitate additional aids, some of which serve to prevent complications related to body position.

FINISHING THE EDGES OF A CAST

When a cast is thoroughly dry, unfinished edges are covered with strips of waterproof adhesive tape that have been shaped for this purpose. This procedure is called petaling the cast (Fig. 2-14). Excessive sheet wadding is trimmed from the edges of the cast, and its stockinette lining is stretched over the edges of the cast prior to petaling.

The size of the petal used varies with the size of the cast. The shape of the petal may be influenced by its size; rounded edges seem to have less tendency to curl away from the cast. The tape may be folded so that the nonadhesive sides of the tape are together, or it may be placed on waxed paper or a similar material from which it is readily separated for cutting the petals to the desired size and shape. Tape 2 inches wide is used for large areas such as those on a body cast, whereas small areas are treated with 1-inch tape.

Each petal is applied by placing one end of the petal on the inside

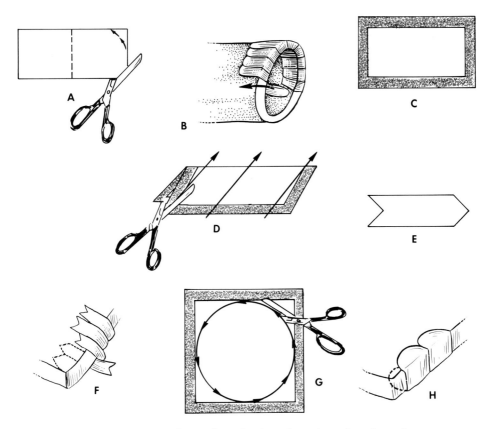

Fig. 2-14. Preparation and application of petals to the edges of a cast. **A,** The end of a piece of tape 2 inches wide and 4 inches long in rounded. **B,** The uncut end of tape is placed beneath the edge of the cast, and the petal is brought forward over the edge of the cast. Each petal overlaps the one previously applied. **C,** Tape 2 inches wide is placed on waxed paper. **D,** Tape and paper are folded lengthwise and cut diagonally to prepare the petal. **E,** The prepared petal. **F,** The petal is applied to the edge of the cast. **G,** A 2-inch square of tape is rounded. **H,** Application of round petals to the edge of the cast.

surface of the cast, bringing the petal over the edge of the cast, and smoothing its finished edges to the exterior part. Each succeeding petal overlaps the previous one by about ½ inch.

ARM SLING

A sling is used to support either the weight of a cast that has been applied to the arm or a completely dependent arm. It will, if applied correctly, elevate the hand slightly and support it, preventing edema caused by allowing the wrist and hand to hang down. It should not contribute to discomfort or poor body alignment. Fig. 2-15, *A* to *E*,

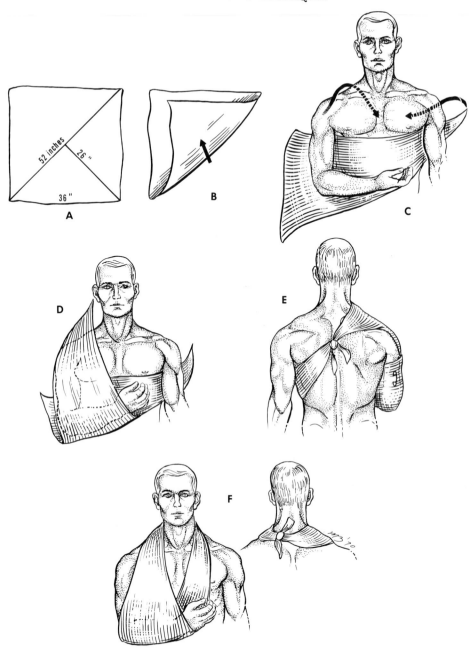

Fig. 2-15. Triangular arm sling. **A,** A square yard of material, showing the measurements of the sling. **B,** The material folded diagonally; the resulting triangle may be cut and hemmed. **C,** The apex of the triangle is placed at the elbow, with the end of the base of the triangle enclosing the arm; the arm is positioned to prevent dependent edema. **D,** Anterior view of the completed sling. **E,** Posterior view of the completed sling. The sling is pinned or knotted at the elbow to maintain position of the arm. **F,** Alternate method of applying sling.

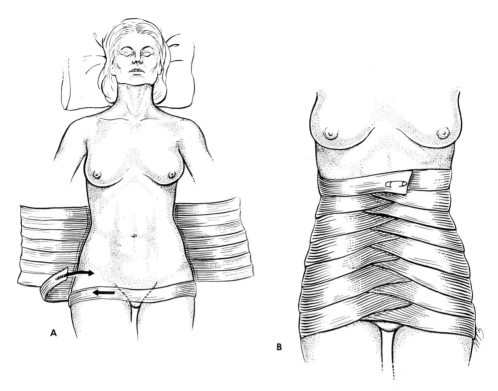

Fig. 2-16. Abdominal binder. **A,** A scultetus binder is placed beneath the patient, who is in a back-lying position. Distal tails of the binder are tightened across abdomen and tucked beneath the patient. **B,** The completed binder is fastened with a safety pin.

illustrates one method used to make and apply a triangular arm sling measuring approximately 26 by 36 by 52 inches. Another method of applying a sling is shown in Fig. 2-15, *F*.

ABDOMINAL BINDER

After surgery, an abdominal binder may be prescribed for support. Various types of binders are available, but all should be applied when the patient is in a back-lying position. They should be tightened from the most distal point upward across the abdomen and should be tucked beneath the patient for maximum support (Fig. 2-16). Care to provide even pressure and to avoid undue pressure on drainage tubes or respiratory structures is essential.

ELASTIC BANDAGES

Application of elastic bandages to the legs prior to ambulation is not unlike the application of wet dressings illustrated in Chapter 5. The stretchable bandage should be sufficiently taut to provide sup-

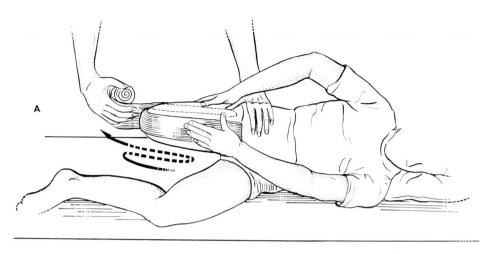

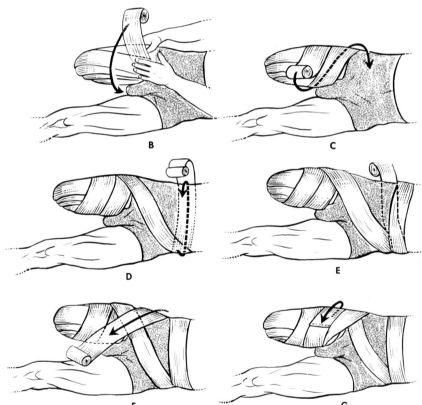

Fig. 2-17. Elastic bandage for stump shrinkage. **A,** The first turn of the bandage begins high on the front of the stump and extends across its center and to the top of the back of the stump. **B,** After making 2 to 3 turns over the end of the stump, the nurse turns the bandage for a circular spiral. **C,** Circular turns or spirals continue toward the top of the stump, then are brought across the back of the stump toward the waist. **D,** The bandage is brought across the abdomen to encircle the waist. **E,** Bandages circle the waist twice. **F,** The bandage is brought from the back of the waist to the front of the stump. **G,** The remainder of the bandage encircles the stump and is anchored in front with safety pins or tape.

port and increase venous return but not tight enough to produce stasis. A method of testing the tightness is to place one finger between the circular turns. If the bandage has been applied correctly, one finger will easily slip beneath the bandage as far as the first knuckle. The use of elastic stockings instead of elastic bandages requires less skill.

Preparatory to fitting an amputee with a prosthesis, the nurse may wrap the stump with an elastic bandage or apply a reducing sock. Either of these shapes the stump and supports the soft tissue, giving firmness to the stump and reducing edema.

To bandage the healed stump with compression, the nurse uses an elastic bandage. Its width is determined by the size of the stump. Frequently, a 4- to 6-inch width is used for the adult. The length of bandage needed also varies with the size of the individual. If more than one length of bandage is needed, sewing the two lengths of bandage together is likely to be more satisfactory than other methods of fastening. The nurse forms the bandage into a firm, even roll to facilitate its application. It must be applied with an even pressure that does not produce creasing of the skin. Pressure over the area of the healed incision is greater than that exerted at the upper portion of the stump. Frequently, each turn of bandage overlaps the previous one by about a third of the width of the bandage. Thus, if a 4-inch bandage is used, each turn overlaps the previous turn by about 1⅓ inches. Fig. 2-17 illustrates an elastic bandage being applied to a stump. The method used may be modified by using circular turns after the end of the stump has been enclosed.

REDUCING SOCK

The physician may recommend a reducing sock of a size that will fit the stump snugly without interfering with circulation. Periodically, it is replaced with a smaller size.

Restraints

In special circumstances a decreased level of consciousness, mental confusion, or physical disability may predispose a patient to self-inflicted injury. The method of choice for preventing such misfortune should be evaluated for each such situation. The nurse should not restrain a patient forcibly without a physician's order or unless it is absolutely necessary.

The purpose of any restraining device should be explained to the patient and his family. Adequate help during application must be available if injury to a highly active patient is to be avoided. The device itself must be applied correctly, for a carelessly applied restraint can be more dangerous than no restraint. For example, the nurse should not restrain one side of the patient's body only or fasten his hands to the head of the bed. It is safer to restrain opposite extremities, thus preventing potentially tragic activity. If inflexible materials are incorporated into the restraining device, the underlying tissues should be protected with sufficient padding. Padding must be used beneath a leather cuff to prevent skin damage. Methods of securing the selected device vary. Commonly, ties, buckles, or locks are self-contained in the device.

Periodic removal of these devices is essential to prevent tissue injury. The skin should be cleansed, powdered, and observed for signs of irritation, and extremities should be exercised. Normal range of motion exercises are discussed on pages 33 to 38.

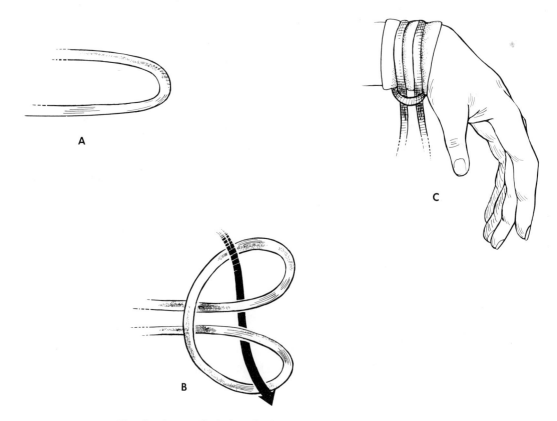

Fig. 2-18. Modified clove-hitch restraint. **A,** Form a loop. **B,** Fold the loop backward over itself. Enlarge the loop as necessary to place the patient's arm through the hitch as shown by arrow. **C,** Tighten the hitch over protective padding to restrain the extremity.

IMPROVISED RESTRAINTS

Modified clove-hitch restraint. Often the patient simply needs to be helped or reminded to restrain himself. A convenient method of reminding the patient that he is not to touch a particular wound is to apply a modified clove-hitch type of restraint. Its use in preventing self-inflicted injury after eye surgery may be combined with local application of a metal or other type of protective eye shield. A roller bandage 2 inches wide may be used to form the modified clove hitch (Fig. 2-18).

Clove-hitch restraint. A triangular bandage folded diagonally may be applied as a clove-hitch restraint. The free ends are tied to the bed frame in a manner that allots a range of permissible movement. A distance of 12 inches or less is often desirable (Fig. 2-19).

If the patient is restless or confused, the restraint should be knotted securely. This prevents the restraint from tightening and impairing circulation. In this instance, adequate padding should be applied between the restraining device and the patient's skin.

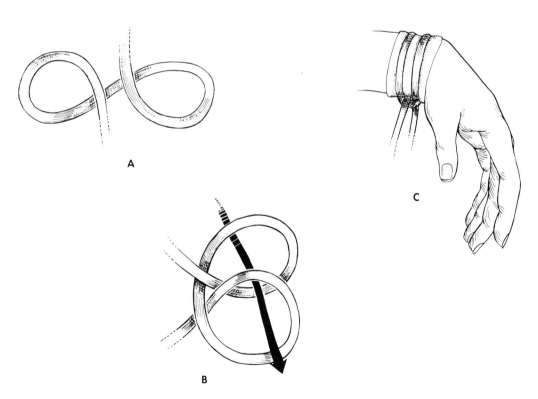

Fig. 2-19. Clove-hitch restraint. **A,** Make a double loop. **B,** Turn one loop in preparation for placing the extremity within the loops as shown by the arrow. **C,** Completed clove hitch showing placement of padding for protection of the tissues.

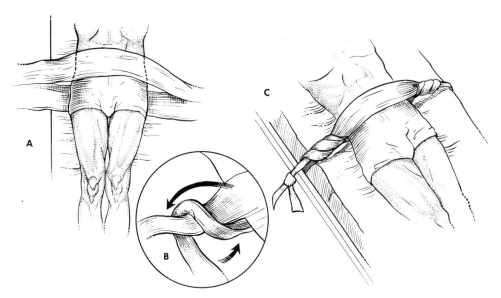

Fig. 2-20. Modified restraint with sheets. **A,** Fold two sheets diagonally. Place one under, the other over the abdominal area. **B,** Twist the ends of the sheets until they are snug. **C,** Tie the ends of the sheets to the bed frame.

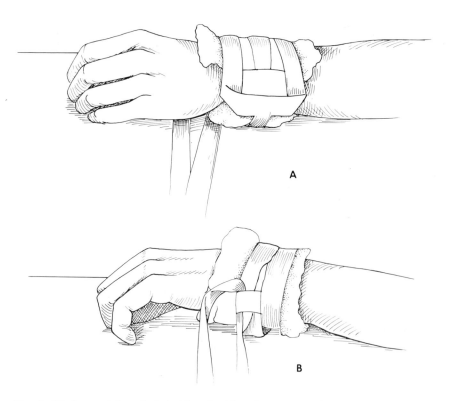

Fig. 2-21. Posey deluxe limb holder. **A,** After the strap on the narrow end of the holder is placed through the slit provided in the wider end of the holder, the hand is slipped into the restraint, which is adjusted for security and comfort and fastened with the Velcro fasteners. **B,** Both straps are threaded through the loop in back of the limb holder and tied securely to the bed frame. Note that the holder is lined with artificial fur. (Courtesy J. T. Posey Co., Pasadena, Calif.)

Sheets. Two sheets folded diagonally and applied around lower trunk may be used in an emergency to remind the patient stay in bed. One sheet is placed beneath the abdomen, and the oth on top of it. These must not extend over the rib cage, restricting respiration. The protruding ends of the sheets are twisted to form a snug cage around the body, drawn to the edge of the bed, and tied securely to its frame (Fig. 2-20).

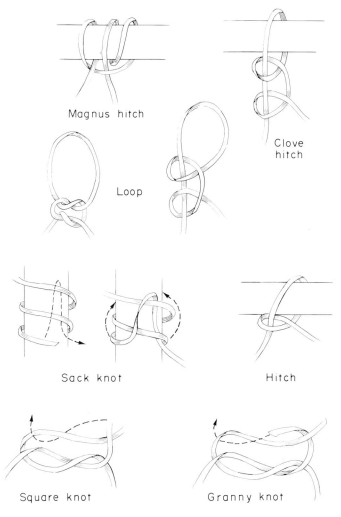

Magnus hitch

Loop

Clove hitch

Sack knot

Hitch

Square knot

Granny knot

Fig. 2-22. Kinds of knots used to secure restraining devices. Various kinds of knots may be used to secure restraining devices. Wetting the material allows one to tie the knot more securely. (Courtesy J. T. Posey Co., Pasadena, Calif.)

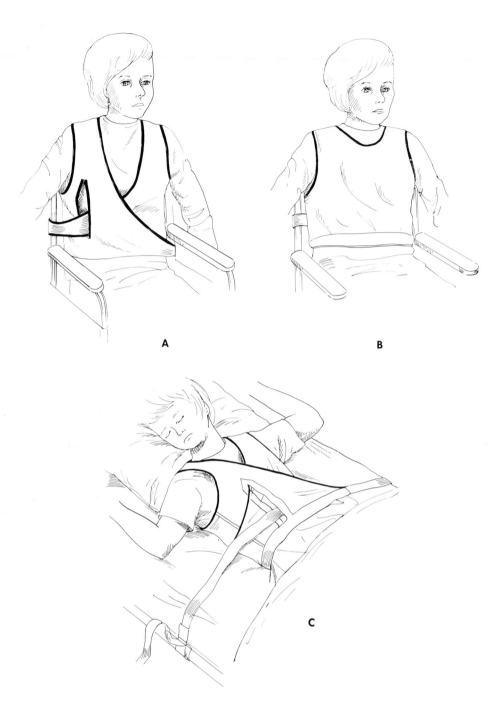

Fig. 2-23. Posey safety vest. **A,** The safety vest is positioned with the slot in front for maximum restraint of the wheelchair patient. **B,** For minimum restraint of the chair patient, the vest is placed with the slot behind the patient. **C,** The vest is applied to a bed patient with the slot in front for maximum restraint. **D,** Back view of the vest applied for minimum restraint when patient is sitting in a chair. The ties must be fastened securely. **E,** Back view of the vest applied to the bed patient for minimum restraint. (Courtesy J. T. Posey Co., Pasadena, Calif.)

COMMERCIAL RESTRAINTS

Many kinds of commercial restraints are available. Fig. 2-21 illustrates a type of restraint that is suitable for application to either the ankle or the wrist. Similar restraints containing built-in padding and locking devices are available. In the absence of padding and locking devices, padding is placed under the restraint as it is being positioned, and the ties of the restraint are knotted proximal to the extremity to prevent the restraint from tightening. Fig. 2-22 illustrates kinds of knots that may be used. Precautions discussed on pages 41 and 42 should be followed when using these restraints.

A safety vest is widely used to protect selected patients (Fig. 2-23). As a guide, the slot in the vest through which the strap is passed should be placed in front of the patient when maximum restraint is desired or behind the patient when minimal restraint is needed. The nurse's observations of the patient are helpful in determining the most effective direction of application of the vest. The straps are secured to the bedframe when the patient is in bed, or, if he is sitting, the straps may be secured to his chair.

A roll belt may be used to allow maximum freedom to turn from side to side and sit up in bed but to prevent the patient from falling out of bed (Fig. 2-24).

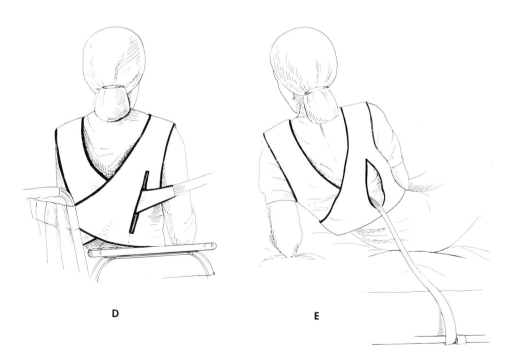

D   E

Fig. 2-23, cont'd. For legend see opposite page.

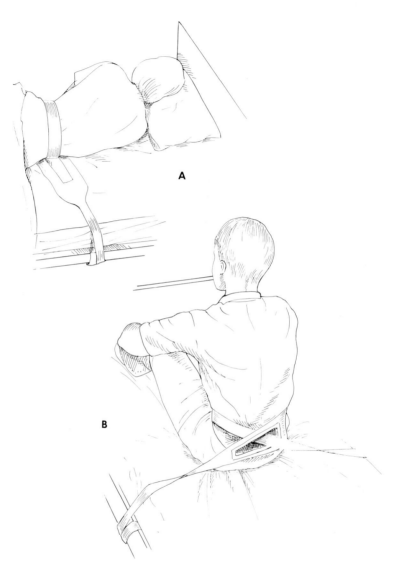

Fig. 2-24. Safety roll belt. **A,** The wide part of the pad is placed beneath the center of the patient's back. The short strap is anchored to the bed frame, and the long strap is placed around the patient's waist and through the slot in the back of the pad; then it is anchored to the other side of the bed. The belt should be snug but should allow a nurse to place the hand between the belt and the patient. **B,** In addition to rolling with the patient, as shown in **A,** the roll belt will also allow the patient to sit up in bed. (Courtesy J. T. Posey Co., Pasadena, Calif.)

Questions for discussion and exploration

1. What are some of the principles of teaching and learning that are useful in helping to prepare and carry out a plan of teaching?
2. If a patient complains of phantom pain in an extremity that has been amputated, how can you explain this phenomenon to him and at the same time provide emotional support?
3. After amputation of his lower leg, Mr. C. insists that elevating it on a pillow would be more comfortable than his present position. How should you deal with this request?
4. When relatives of Mrs. A., 90 years of age and bedridden, confide that they feel unable to care for her at home but cannot afford the cost of care in a nursing home or in the hospital, what additional information do you need to understand their reaction? How can you help them make use of the abilities they do have to care for Mrs. A.? What community agencies can become sources of help to them?
5. Mrs. D., who is recovering after fracturing her hip, wishes to return to her walk-up apartment where she lives alone. What teaching related to ambulation does she need prior to returning home?
6. You are asked to measure Mrs. D. for crutches. What methods might be used?
7. Mrs. D. is later fitted with a cane. How would you explain, demonstrate, and teach her to walk with the cane?
8. Although Mrs. D. will be able to ambulate with a cane when she returns home, she worries that she will be unable to shop for food or clean her apartment. What community resources are available to her?
9. Due to the nature of Mr. R.'s pathophysiologic condition, the physician agrees that he can be cared for at home if the family is able to obtain a CircOlectric bed and learn to operate it and to learn to care for Mr. R. Where can the family obtain this equipment? What adjustments might need to be made in their living arrangements? Develop a plan of teaching the patient and his family about the use of the CircOlectric bed.
10. Johnny B., 8 years of age, had a fracture of his arm reduced under anesthesia. Develop a plan for teaching Johnny and his mother about the use and application of a sling and positioning of the affected arm. For what reasons should they be instructed to consult the orthopedist prior to their next appointment?
11. It is likely that Johnny will be an active lad after his dismissal from the hospital. What play activities are permissable while he is wearing a cast? Is there a plan for his taking a shower or a tub bath?
12. When Mrs. Z. is brought to her room, partially awake, after abdominal surgery, what are your responsibilties concerning transfer of Mrs. Z. from the surgical cart to her bed? What are your responsibilities to her, the relatives, and the nursing staff during the immediate postoperative period?
13. If you are alone and a patient becomes very disturbed, how can you restrain him temporarily? What are your hospital policies regarding

the application of restraints? Where are various types of restraints and materials for improvised restraints kept in your hospital? What care specific to the use of restraints must be given to the patient? What are some possible reasons that a patient may become confused?

Selected references

American Rehabilitation Foundation: Rehabilitative techniques: 1, Bed positioning and transfer procedures for hemiplegia, 1962; 2, Selected equipment useful in the hospital, home, or nursing home, 1962; 3, A procedure for passive range of motion and self-assistive exercises, Minneapolis, 1964, American Rehabilitation Foundation.

Carini, E., and Owens, G.: Neurological and neurosurgical nursing, ed. 6, St. Louis, 1974, The C. V. Mosby Co.

Grabstetter, J.: Synthetic fat helps prevent pressure sores, Amer. J. Nurs. 68:1521-1522, 1968.

Harvin, J. S., and Hargest, T. S.: The air-fluidized bed: a new concept in the treatment of decubitus ulcers, Nurs. Clin. N. Amer. 5:181, 1970.

Hirschberg, G. G., Levis, L., and Thomas, D.: Rehabilitation: manual for the care of the disabled and elderly, Philadelphia, 1964, J. B. Lippincott Co.

Hrobsky, A.: The patient on a CircOlectric bed, Amer. J. Nurs. 71:2352-2353.

Kelly, M. M.: Exercises for bedfast patients, Amer. J. Nurs. 66:2209-2213, 1966.

Kerr, A.: Orthopedic nursing procedure, ed. 2, New York, 1969, Springer Publishing Co., Inc.

Knocke, L.: Crutch walking, Amer. J. Nurs. 61:70-73, 1961.

Kraus, Sister R. A.: Polyurethane foam pads, Amer. J. Nurs. 65:98, 1965.

Larson, C. B., and Gould, M.: Orthopedic nursing, ed. 8, St. Louis, 1974, The C. V. Mosby Co.

Lawton, E. B.: Activities of daily living for physical rehabilitation, New York, 1963, McGraw-Hill Book Co.

Noonan, J., and Noonan, L.: Two burned patients on flotation therapy, Amer. J. Nurs. 68:316-319, 1968.

Olson, E. W.: Hazards of immobility. With: Thompson, L. F.: Effects on cardiovascular function; McCarthy, J. A.: Effects on respiratory function; Johnson, B. J.: Effects on gastrointestinal function; Edmonds, R. E.: Effects on motor function; Schroeder, L. M.: Effects on urinary function; Wade, M.: Effects on metabolic equilibrium; Wade, M.: Effects on psychosocial equilibrium, Amer. J. Nurs. 67:779-797, 1967.

Pesczynski, M.: Why old people fall, Amer. J. Nurs. 65:86-88, 1965.

Rusk, H. A.: Rehabilitation medicine, ed. 3, St. Louis, 1971, The C. V. Mosby Co.

Senf, H. R.: Caring for the patient in the CircOlectric bed, Amer. J. Nurs. 60:227-230, 1960.

Skinner, G.: Nursing care of a patient on a Stryker frame, Amer. J. Nurs. 46:288-293, 1946.

Sorenson, L., and Ulrich, P. G.: Ambulation: a manual for nurses, Minneapolis, 1966, American Rehabilitation Foundation.

Stryker, R. P.: Rehabilitative aspects of acute and chronic nursing care, Philadelphia, 1972, W. B. Saunders Co.

Toohey, P., and Larson, C. W.: Range of motion exercise: key to joint mobility, Minneapolis, 1967, American Rehabilitation Foundation.

Walike, B. C., Marmor, L., and Upshaw, M. J.: Rheumatoid arthritis, Amer. J. Nurs. 67:1420-1426, 1967.

Works, R. F.: Hints on lifting and pulling, Amer. J. Nurs. 72:260-261, 1972.

3
Ventilation

Maintenance of the blood's access to oxygen is vital. If that access is inadequate, techniques that maintain ventilation may be ordered. Ventilation is the mass transport of air to and from the alveolar exchange surfaces so that carbon dioxide can be removed from the blood and be replaced by oxygen.

As air is transported from the atmosphere to the exchange surfaces, it is filtered and conditioned with heat and moisture. The level of its entry into the respiratory system affects conditioning. Gases inhaled through the nose are filtered, warmed, and moistened before reaching the exchange surfaces, but gases entering through the mouth pass less warm, moist surfaces. Gases that enter the trachea directly must be warmed and moistened by the tracheal and bronchial mucosa, which is not normally required to do this. During this process, removal of water from the mucous membranes subjects them to damage; the resulting inflammation causes increased production of secretions. These secretions tend to become viscous and may even crust, thereby impairing the sweeping action of the cilia. This may finally decrease the diameter of the bronchioles; obstruction inevitably results.

In health, certain spontaneous activities help to prevent or reverse changes that result in pulmonary complications. The use of simple nursing techniques for the same purpose must not be underrated or neglected. After operative procedures or concurrent with reduced activity, a regimen involving periodic turning from side to side, deep breathing, and coughing may be ordered and is indeed useful. Other measures that produce alveolar expansion, change gas concentrations, and loosen and expel secretions are also used. These are forms of inhalation therapy now available in most hospitals.

Breathing exercises

Adequate explanation, early instruction, guided practice, judicious use of drugs, and incisional splinting tend to increase coop-

71

TABLE 3-1. Deep breathing and coughing exercises

Technique	Problem	Explanation or solution
Assist the patient to a comfortable back-lying or sitting position. If pain is present, administer an analgesic prior to the deep breathing and coughing exercises.	Discomfort and position may interfere with the patient's ability to cooperate and breathe effectively.	Pain during breathing causes splinting of the thoracic wall. Positioning provides for effective expansion of the lungs and coughing; a sitting position allows abdominal contents to gravitate away from the thoracic region and relieves pressure on the diaphragm.
Encourage the patient to breathe deeply several times by inhaling through the nose and exhaling through the mouth.	Shallow breathing does not fully inflate the lungs or produce sufficient pressure for an effective cough.	Expansion of the lungs helps to dislodge mucus and foreign materials. Inhaling through the nose warms and humidifies air, which is less irritating than cold, dry air.
Support incisional areas during coughing by exerting gentle pressure on the abdominal wall just below the costal margin.	Pain and anxiety interfere with effective coughing; some patients are afraid that coughing will damage the incision.	Support can be given manually, by holding a pillow or book against the abdomen, or by tightening a towel or drawsheet around the abdomen.
Command the patient to cough.	Mucus remaining in the lungs or tracheobronchial tree interferes with gaseous exchanges.	Coughing, a forceful expulsion of air, is a normal method for cleansing the tracheobronchial tree of secretions.
Help the patient who is unable to cough effectively to sniff repeatedly until his lungs feel full; then encourage him to expel the air with several short, deep staccato coughs.	Reluctance or inability to breathe or cough deeply may be observed.	Sniffing is useful in expanding the lungs; short staccato coughs expel secretions. Both may be more comfortable for the patient.

eration when breathing exercises are used. Ideally, teaching occurs some time before the actual need is present; for example, the surgical patient should be taught these exercises during the preoperative period.

For the exercises in Table 3-1, it is desirable to assist the patient to a sitting position. If sitting up is contraindicated, the back-lying position will permit effective expansion of the lungs and effective coughing. Other positions are less effective.

The patient is encouraged to breathe deeply. If the nurse holds the hands just below the costal margin, exerting firm, gentle pressure on the abdominal wall, the abdomen will be felt to expand as the patient inhales. Pressing the hands firmly against this same area

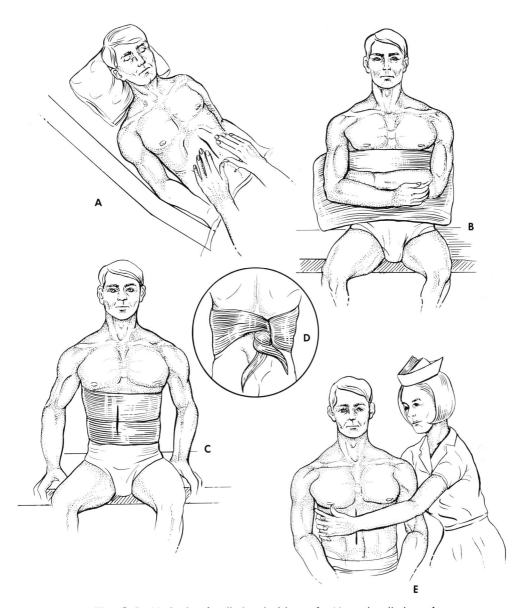

Fig. 3-1. Methods of splinting incisions. **A,** Manual splinting of incision. The nurse's hands exert firm, gentle pressure on the abdominal wall. The pressure is directed slightly toward the incision. **B,** A pillow pressed against the incisional area offers moderate support during coughing. **C,** Anterior view of the drawsheet folded into thirds and tightened smoothly over the incisional area. **D,** Posterior view of the drawsheet, showing the method of tightening it. The twisted ends are directly opposite the incision. **E,** Hugging the patient in this manner permits support of the incision as well as pressure that assists exhalation.

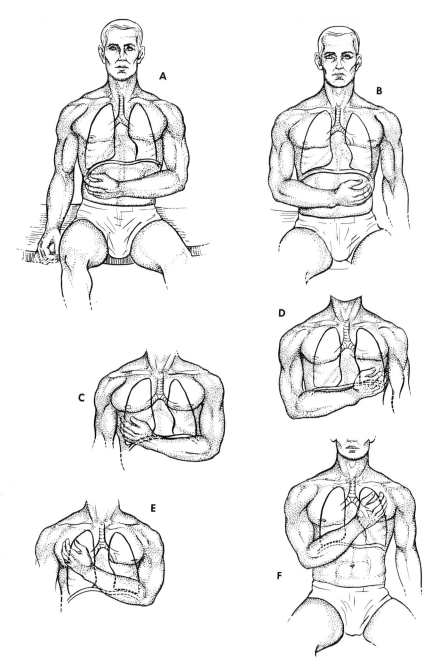

Fig. 3-2. Breathing exercises to encourage lung expansion. The patient is directed to concentrate on moving the prepositioned hand with each series of deep breaths. **A,** The left hand is placed over the right side of the diaphragm. **B,** The right hand is placed over the left side of the diaphragm. **C,** The left hand is placed above the base of the right lung. **D,** The right hand is placed on the area above the base of the left lung. **E,** The left hand is placed over the apex of the right lung, with the fingers lying in the depression above the clavicle. **F,** The right hand is positioned over the apex of the left lung.

during exhalation may help the patient exhale more completely. This will also provide support during coughing. If the patient finds it more comfortable, he may hold a pillow or book against his abdomen (Fig. 3-1, B). Fig. 3-1, C and D, shows the use of a drawsheet to permit support of the incision and to provide pressure that assists exhalation. Fig. 3-1, E, illustrates a method of hugging the patient to support the incision and to apply pressure that assists exhalation.

A simple breathing exercise consists of having the patient take three deep breaths by inhaling through the nose and exhaling through the mouth, slowly and gently. The patient expels a fourth breath forcefully with a cough. If an incision is involved, some method of supporting it by splinting should be used during coughing, as shown in Fig. 3-1, A.

A more extensive regimen consists of six series of five deep breaths, taken as described initially. Each series is followed by a short rest period. The thorax is divided into six areas. The nurse places her hand or the patient places his hand over a different area for each series of breaths, and the nurse directs the patient to concentrate on breathing against the hand, causing it to move (Fig. 3-2). At the conclusion of each series, the nurse encourages the patient to expel secretions from the lower respiratory tract with a forceful cough.

If the patient is unable to breathe deeply and cough effectively, comparable results may be achieved by commanding him to "sniff" with his nose until he feels his lungs are as full of air as possible. The patient may use several short, deep, staccato coughs instead of one forceful cough to expel secretions.

Blow bottles

Blow bottles are prescribed to prevent or treat atelectasis and to strengthen the abdominal muscles used in expiration. The purpose of the latter is to increase the force of coughing.

After the blow bottle unit is assembled, one of the chambers is filled with water to the 900 ml. mark. A dye tablet is added to the water. The tubing is placed into the chambers, and the caps are tightened.

The patient should be in a sitting or semisitting position when using the blow bottles. He is asked to seal the mouthpiece of the tubing leading to the filled chamber between his lips and with each breath to blow part of the solution into the other chamber. It may be helpful to specify an amount such as 100 ml. When all of the solution has been transferred, the patient is instructed to take a deep breath and to blow as much water as possible into the empty cham-

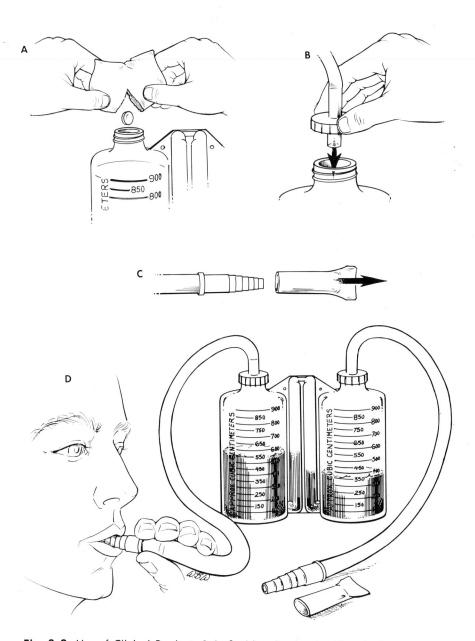

Fig. 3-3. Use of Clinical Products Spiroflo blow bottle. **A,** After the blow bottle unit is removed from the package, one chamber is filled with water to the 900 ml. level, and the tablet that is provided for coloring the water is dropped into the filled chamber and allowed to dissolve. **B,** A cap to which tubing is attached is screwed onto each chamber of the unit. **C,** Covers are removed from *both* mouthpieces and retained for later use. **D,** After taking a deep breath, the patient seals his lips around the mouthpiece on the tubing connected to the filled chamber and blows to transfer the water to the other chamber. The amount of water transferred with each breath and the number of times the solution is transferred is done in accordance with the physician's wishes. When the treatment is completed, the covers are replaced on the mouthpieces to protect them from environmental contamination. (Courtesy Chesebrough-Pond's, Inc., Hospital Products Division, Greenwich, Conn.)

ber. This may be repeated, if necessary, until all of the solution has been transferred. These two exercises are repeated as prescribed by the physician, commonly every 2 hours (Fig. 3-3).

After each treatment, a record should be made of the following: time of the treatment, total amount of solution displaced with 100 ml. per breath, total amount of solution displaced with maximum expiratory effort, the number of breaths needed to transfer the solution using maximal efforts, and comments related to the patient's tolerance of the treatment. Because expiratory efforts against resistance may cause a decrease in blood pressure, complaints of light-headedness or dizziness should be evaluated carefully.

Postural drainage

Postural drainage is the use of positioning to drain secretions from segments of the lungs and bronchi. Coughing will expel secretions that reach the trachea. Effectiveness of postural drainage depends on positioning that allows gravity to drain the secretions, liquefaction of secretions, ciliary action, and effective breathing. Secretions are liquefied by adequate hydration, humidification of gases, and the use of certain drugs. Drugs may be prescribed to dilate the bronchi also. These adjuncts must precede postural drainage if the effectiveness of this technique is to be increased.

During drainage, cupping and vibration may be used to dislodge and mobilize secretions. Percussion or cupping involves rhythmic percussion of the area with the hands held in a cupped position and the fingers and thumb held together in a manner that traps air between the nurse's hands and the patient's chest. It is begun gently and increased in forcefulness as the patient tolerates increased percussion. Cupping should never be done over breast tissue because this causes discomfort and serves no useful purpose. Vibration is done by placing the nurse's hands over the affected area and shaking from the shoulders, thus shaking the area and mobilizing secretions. This shaking is comparable to the type of shaking one does when one chills. After postural drainage, percussion, and vibration, the patient, if he has been in a head-down position, is helped to a position favorable for effective coughing. Percussion and vibration should always be followed by breathing deeply at least three times and coughing deeply at least twice.

Head injuries and certain cardiac conditions contraindicate the use of head-down positioning. Severe dyspnea does not necessarily contraindicate the use of a head-down position, but the patient must not be left unattended during such positioning. His tolerance to a head-down position will need to be developed gradually, start-

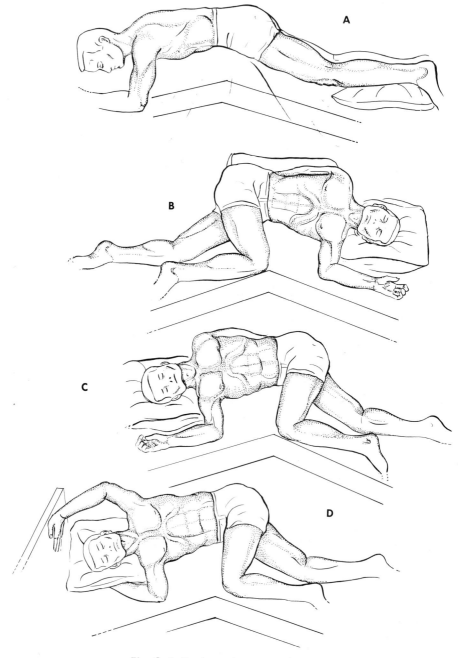

Fig. 3-4. For legend see opposite page.

ing with a minute or less and increasing the length of time as tolerated. The physician must be consulted to be certain that he wants the patient to have chest physical therapy if the patient has active hemoptysis, possible cerebral hemorrhage, cancerous lesions, or lung abscesses.

Postural drainage is begun at the patient's level of cooperation. Positioning may begin on a level surface with the degree of tipping the head down increased each time until the patient can tolerate full Trendelenburg positioning. The patient who is unconscious, severely dyspneic, producing more than a normal amount of secretions, or who has a decreased cough reflex must never be left alone during postural drainage. Equipment for removing secretions with

---

Fig. 3-4. Postural drainage. Selected positions used to promote drainage from various parts of the lungs. Pillows are used to promote maximum comfort and relaxation. A pillow should be placed between the legs with the knee of the uppermost leg resting on the pillow, and pillows should be used to support the back when the patient is placed in a side-lying position. Additional pillows are used to position the arms and to achieve the desired angle of head-down inclination if the bed cannot be adjusted for this purpose. After the patient has been in a position for the desired length of time and before he is changed from that position, he is encouraged to breathe deeply and to cough effectively. **A,** Posterior segments of both lower lobes. The patient's knees are flexed slightly and supported with a pillow to achieve a relaxed position. The head-down angle of inclination is altered according to the patient's tolerance. **B,** Right middle lobe. The patient is positioned on his left side with the thorax tilted slightly backward, the buttocks elevated, the lower extremities flexed, the left arm abducted and flexed, the right arm resting on the bed or on pillows, and the head supported with a pillow. The head-down angle of inclination is altered according to the patient's tolerance. **C,** Lingular segment of the left upper lobe. The patient is positioned on his right side with the thorax tilted somewhat backward, the buttocks elevated at the apex of the bed, the lower extremities flexed, the right arm abducted and flexed, and the left arm resting on the bed or on pillows. The head-down angle of inclination is altered according to the patient's tolerance. **D,** Left lateral segment of the left lower lobe. The patient is positioned on his right side, buttocks elevated, lower extremities flexed, right arm flexed, and the hand placed under the pillow to support the head. The left arm is abducted and flexed so that its palm and fingers rest on the head of the bed. The inclination of the head-down angle varies with the tolerance of the patient.

Continued.

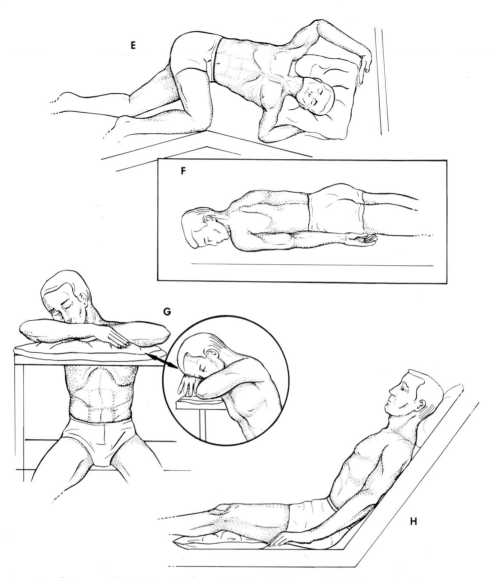

Fig. 3-4, cont'd. E, Lateral segment of the right lower lobe. The patient is positioned on his left side with his hips elevated, the lower extremities flexed, the left arm flexed, and the hand placed under the pillow. The right hand rests on the head of the bed, and the head is supported with a pillow. The angle of head-down inclination varies with the patient's tolerance. **F,** Superior segment of the right lower lobe. The patient is placed in a prone position on a bed that is absolutely flat. This position places the bronchus from the superior segment of the right lower lobe at a nearly 90-degree angle to the floor. **G,** Posterior portion of both upper lobes. The patient is seated, his feet are supported, the shoulders are rotated anteriorly, and the arms are flexed. The arms may be rested on a pillow placed on the table as shown, or the elbows may be rested on the thighs. **H,** Anterior portions of both upper lobes. The patient is positioned with his back leaning backward at about a 45-degree angle, and the upper extremities are relaxed. This position can also be achieved by having the patient lean backward while sitting on the edge of the bed if someone is available to support him in this position.

suction must be available if there is any evidence that the patient may be unable to expel secretions.

The physician identifies the areas to be drained with the aid of radiographic and bronchographic examination. The nurse individualizes positioning for each patient in a manner planned to promote relaxation. Properly placed pillows will enhance relaxation, promote drainage, help the patient maintain the desired position, and protect him from injury. Regardless of the positions used, the patient's spine should be as straight as possible to allow maximum expansion of the lungs. Because the patient's tolerance to a given position and the number of areas being drained vary, the time used for a given position will vary also. As a guide, one position may be used for a few minutes or for as long as a half hour.

After postural drainage or chest physical therapy, the patient should breathe deeply at least three times and then cough effectively at least two times. Because secretions leave an unpleasant taste and feeling in the mouth, oral hygiene is important. Such therapy should be planned to precede meals and sleep. This seems to reduce nausea and vomiting that could cause aspiration of stomach contents into the lungs.

Fig. 3-4 illustrates some basic positions used for postural drainage. The bed is placed in Trendelenburg position if the patient can tolerate a head-down position. The means by which this is accomplished depend on the design of the bed.

It is important that the patient understand what is expected of him during chest physiotherapy. This is taught to the patient verbally and by repeated demonstration. The areas that the nurse must consider include the following:

1. Relaxation is of utmost importance.
2. One must breathe in through the nose to humidify and moisten the inhaled air.
3. Exhalation takes place through pursed lips as though one is whistling or saying, "Oh."
4. One must concentrate on the area on which the hands are placed.
5. The surgical incision must be supported during coughing.

Adequate time must be spent in teaching the patient and his family as well as in motivating them if chest therapy is to be continued at home. The exact regimen planned will vary with the patient's condition. For example, the patient with bronchitis might be taught to cough after awaking in the morning if his chest feels rattly, then to breathe deeply three times, in through the nose and out through pursed lips, and, finally, to take another deep breath and cough deeply. He would be instructed to carry out this same regimen prior to meals and at bedtime.

Inhalation therapy

The physician evaluates the individual's need for and response to inhalation therapy. He prescribes what the gas concentration should be, how it is to be administered, and whether the treatment is to be continuous or intermittent. Table 3-2 shows oxygen concentrations possible with various equipment. Each general type of equipment has qualities that make it more desirable for some cases than for others.

OXYGEN

Regardless of the technique of oxygen administration used, the nurse must give the patient and his family some explanation, stressing the fact that the purpose of such therapy is to prevent damage due to hypoxia. This will combat the mistaken belief that oxygen is given only to the dying.

Precautionary measures to ensure the patient's safety must accompany the administration of oxygen. Materials that produce static electricity, sparks, or flame are dangerous. Therefore, alcohol rubs are prohibited when an oxygen tent is in use, wool blankets are not permitted within the tent, and either a mechanical extension is attached to the electric call signal or a hand bell is substituted. Matches, ashtrays, cigarettes, and candles should not be permitted in the room. If oil or related materials are used, personnel must be trained to cleanse their hands thoroughly before operating gas therapy equipment.

TABLE 3-2. Oxygen concentrations possible with various equipment

Equipment	Approximate percentage concentration of oxygen delivered
Mask	
Rebreathing	90 to 100*
Nonrebreathing	90 to 100
Close-fitting, disposable, without reservoir bag	30 to 45
Nasal cannula	30 to 45
Face tent	30 to 40
Oxygen tent	30 to 40
Bennett respirator	40 to 100
Bird respirator	40 or 100

*A percentage concentration of 100 indicates that the patient receives the gas delivered without outside air dilution; this gas is usually 99.7% oxygen.

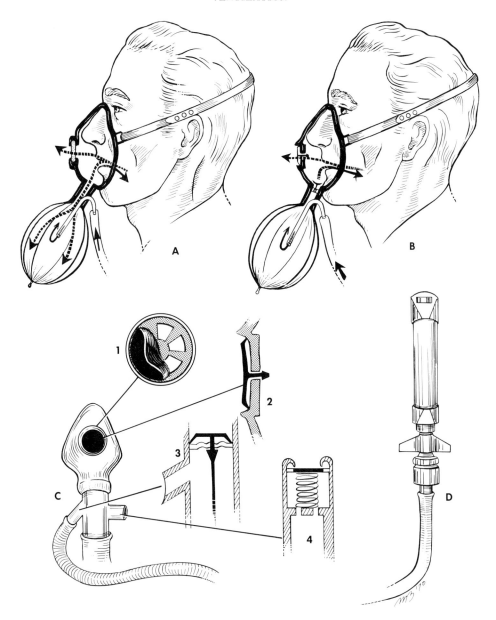

Fig. 3-5. Basic types of oxygen masks. **A,** Partial rebreathing mask. At end of inhalation, oxygen is flowing into the reservoir bag, and exhaled gases also flow into reservoir bag until it is filled. If oxygen flow is sufficient to fill the reservoir bag immediately, no exhaled gas will flow into the bag. **B,** Nonrebreathing mask. Construction of the mask prevents exhalation into the reservoir bag. **C,** Front view of a nonrebreathing mask, showing construction of the valves: **1,** front view of exhalation valve; **2,** side view of exhalation valve; **3,** one-way inhalation valve construction permits oxygen to flow into the reservoir bag but prevents exhalation into the bag; **4,** safety valve permitting inhalation of air, if malfunction occurs. **D,** A preset valve attached to the oxygen inlet determines the concentration of oxygen.

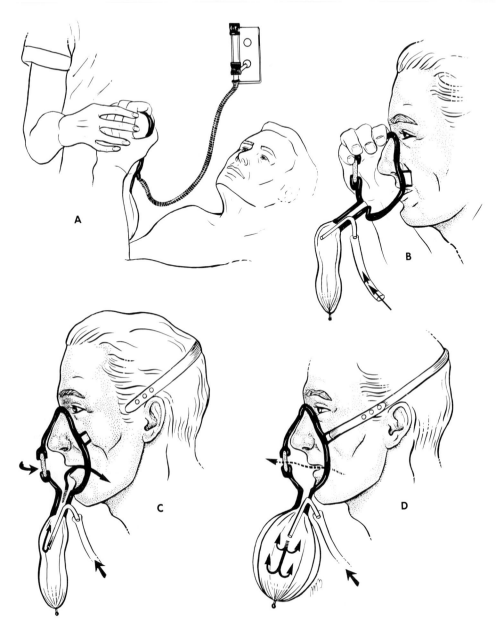

Fig. 3-6. Administration of oxygen by mask. **A,** The nurse should place the mask in the patient's hand and then place her hand over his. This permits the patient to control the mask until he becomes accustomed to it. Oxygen flow is set at 10 to 12 L. per minute during initial fitting. **B,** The narrow part of the mask is placed over the bridge of the nose. The mask is then brought over the mouth. **C,** Retaining straps are fastened after the patient has become accustomed to the feel of the mask. The reservoir bag collapses with inspiration; however, complete collapse indicates a need to increase oxygen flow. **D,** During exhalation the reservoir bag expands. When the patient is accustomed to breathing through the mask, oxygen flow is reduced as prescribed, often to 6 to 8 L. per minute.

Signs cautioning visitors and personnel that oxygen is in use and that smoking or other flames are prohibited must be displayed conspicuously. Direct communication that further emphasizes these precautions is recommended.

Oxygen masks. High concentrations of oxygen can be administered by mask. Essentially, the mask used will be either a partial rebreathing mask (Fig. 3-5, *A*) or a nonrebreathing mask (Fig. 3-5, *B* to *D*). The clinical technique involved is similar for both. If humidification of the oxygen is prescribed, the humidifier is prepared by filling it to the designated level with distilled water. The mask is attached to an oxygen supply and the flow is adjusted as prescribed, often at 6 to 8 L. per minute. It is unusual for the flow to be greater than 12 L. per minute. During the short period after the mask is first applied, the patient may breathe more rapidly than usual. It is advisable to increase the flow to 10 to 12 L. per minute during this time, and then readjust the flow to the prescribed level when a normal breathing rate is resumed.

The oxygen must be flowing before the mask is fitted to the face. For the fitting, it is helpful if the nurse places the mask in the patient's hand and then places her hand over his (Fig. 3-6, *A*). Doing so permits the patient to control the mask until he becomes accustomed to it. The mask is placed over the bridge of his nose first, then over his mouth (Fig. 3-6, *B*). When the patient is accustomed to the feel of the mask, the retaining straps are placed around the patient's head (Fig. 3-6, *C*) and adjusted until the mask fits snugly, but not tightly, against the face (Fig. 3-6, *D*).

Observation to ensure that the mask is fitted correctly and that the patient is breathing properly is essential. The reservoir bag will expand and collapse with normal breathing (Fig. 3-6, *C* and *D*). If the bag collapses completely, the oxygen flow needs to be increased. Leakage around the mask is corrected by repositioning.

If the mask is used for prolonged therapy, it should be removed periodically, washed and powdered lightly, or a new disposable mask should be used if one is available. Care of the facial skin must be meticulous if its healthy condition is to be preserved. Commonly, the mask and skin should be cared for every hour or two.

Nasal cannula. The nasal cannula may be used if the patient breathes through his nose. He must be discouraged from mouth breathing, for this dilutes the gas concentration with room air. The setting of the flowmeter determines the concentration of oxygen delivered.

The cannula is connected to a source of oxygen, the flow of the gas is set as prescribed (often at 4 to 5 L. per minute), the cannula is placed, and the retaining straps are fastened (Fig. 3-7). Higher flows of oxygen are uncomfortable and are rarely used. The gas

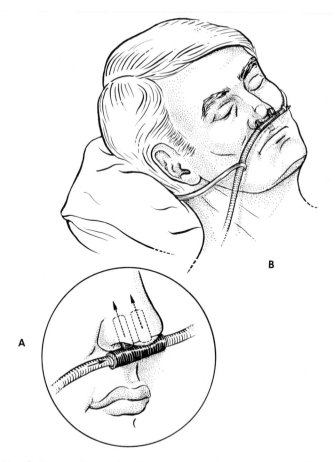

Fig. 3-7. Nasal cannula. **A,** A cross section showing insertion of cannula. Oxygen flow is set at a rate of 4 to 5 L. per minute. **B,** The cannula is held in place with retaining straps.

must be humidified to ensure patient comfort. The nasal cannula may be cleansed as necessary. If areas of irritation are present, a water-soluble lubricant or an anesthetic agent may be used for the patient's comfort.

Nasal catheter. The nasal catheter is used to administer oxygen nasopharyngeally. No additional benefit is gained from oropharyngeal placement; in fact, it stimulates the gag reflex. Initially, the catheter is placed oropharyngeally as a method of determining actual placement; however, it should be withdrawn 1 to 2 cm. ($\frac{1}{2}$ to 1 inch).

To approximate the depth to which the catheter should be inserted, the distance between the tragus of the ear and the external nares is measured (Fig. 3-8, *A*). This point on the catheter is marked and used as a guide when rotating the catheter between

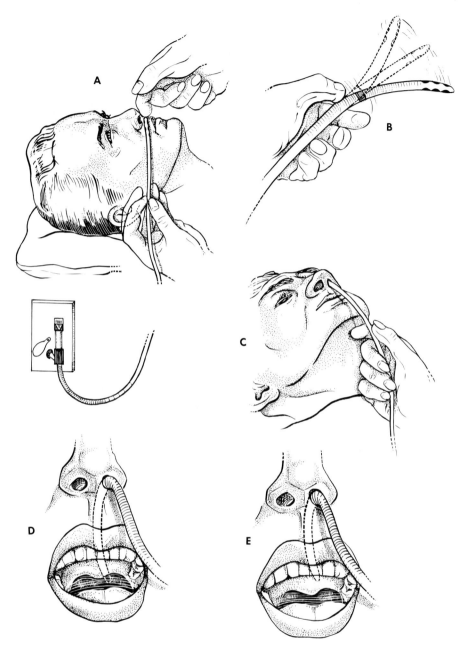

Fig. 3-8. Nasal catheter. **A,** Approximating the distance the catheter will be inserted by measuring the distance between the tragus of the ear and the external nares. **B,** Tape may be used to mark the predetermined distance of insertion. The catheter is rotated between the thumb and forefinger to find its natural droop. **C,** The catheter, lubricated with silicone grease, is inserted so that its curvature follows that of the nasopharyngeal passage. **D,** The tip of the catheter is seen behind the uvula. **E,** The catheter is withdrawn about 1 cm. (½ inch) to obtain correct placement.

the thumb and forefinger to determine its natural droop (Fig. 3-8, *B*). The catheter is inserted in such a way that its curvature follows that of the nasopharyngeal passage (Fig. 3-8, *C*).

Prior to insertion, the catheter should be tested for patency and lubricated. It is suggested that petroleum jelly or a nonflammable lubricant such as silicone grease be applied sparingly to avoid trauma to the mucosa during removal of the catheter. Water-soluble lubricants will not serve this purpose. Excess lubricant should be removed by wiping the catheter. There is no evidence that this method of lubrication, properly done, will cause respiratory problems. **However, any oily material must be completely removed from the hands before the oxygen regulator is touched.** This includes such substances as mineral oil, petroleum jelly, and glycerin. To test the patency of the catheter, the flow of oxygen is turned on and the end of the catheter is placed in a container of sterile water and observed. A bubbling action indicates that the catheter is patent.

After the catheter is inserted, its exact placement is checked visually. When the tip of the catheter is seen behind the uvula (Fig. 3-8, *D*), it is withdrawn about 1 cm., or approximately ½ inch (Fig. 3-8, *E*). The flow of oxygen is then regulated as prescribed. This may range up to 6 L. per minute. Flow rates above this are uncomfortable. As has been emphasized, humidification of gas for nasal catheters is essential. Frequent observations are necessary to determine that the catheter is patent. If the patient seems comfortable and the catheter is working well, cleansing is not indicated. Crust formation around the catheter or occlusion of its lumen indicates that the catheter should be changed.

Face tent. The face tent can be used to supply oxygen or mist. If it is used to increase concentrations of oxygen only, it is connected to the oxygen supply with small-bore tubing. If it is used to supply mist, a large-bore tubing must be used (Fig. 3-9). The humidifier must be filled with distilled water, and the volume of mist produced is checked visually.

Prior to application, the flow of oxygen is regulated as prescribed. This usually is 7 L. per minute or more.

The principles of applying the face tent are similar to those of applying masks. However, fitting presents no problem. The patient may prefer to hold the appliance in place. This permits its easy removal. Once the patient is accustomed to it, the retaining straps may be adjusted as desired.

Oxygen tent. The use of oxygen tents has decreased markedly in hospitals that have modern air conditioning. Occasionally, oxygen tents are used for patients who are too restless or are unable to cooperate in the use of other methods of administering oxygen or humidification. As stated previously, the patient needs reassurance and

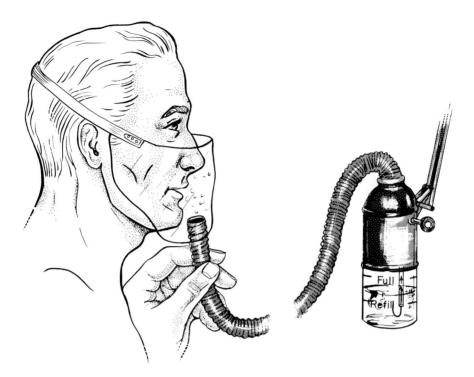

Fig. 3-9. Face tent. When the purpose of the tent is to supply mist, large-bore tubing and a humidifier are used. When its purpose is only to supply oxygen, small-bore tubing replaces large-bore tubing. (Courtesy MistOgen, Oakland, Calif.)

must be told its purpose before he is placed in an oxygen tent. The part of the mattress that will be within the tent is covered with rubber, plastic, or other material that oxygen cannot penetrate readily.

The tent is placed near the head of the bed (Fig. 3-10, *A*). If piped oxygen is not available, the placement of the cylinder of oxygen should be planned so that it does not interfere with nursing care.

The patient should be assisted to a comfortable position. Often a semisitting position is desirable. The top linen is folded to waist level unless the tent has a full, bed size canopy, the air conditioner of the machine is turned on, and the temperature control is set, usually at 70° F. The temperature is altered for comfort, but it is not usually changed more than 10°. There is no need to cover the patient's ears or to enclose his shoulders with a blanket. If he complains of being too cool, the temperature control should be reset. The flow of oxygen is usually set at 10 to 12 L. per minute.

After the canopy is lifted carefully over the patient and its skirt is tucked under the top and sides of the mattress, its lower edge is arranged around the thighs to minimize escape of oxygen (Fig. 3-10, *B* to *D*). Placing a folded bath blanket over the lower edge of the

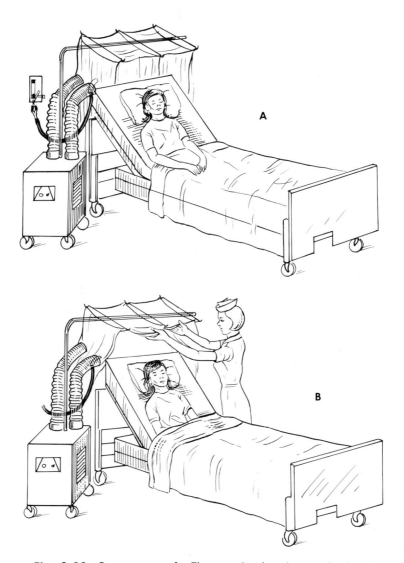

A

B

Fig. 3-10. Oxygen tent. **A,** The tent is placed near the head of the bed with its canopy draped behind the mattress. Oxygen flow is set at 10 to 12 L. per minute, the machine's air conditioner is turned on, and temperature is set at 70° F. (21.1° C.). **B,** The canopy is lifted over the patient, and the back of the canopy is tucked under the head of the mattress.

tent skirt and tucking it under the mattress will further secure the canopy. The top linen will serve the same purpose.

Initially, the tent is flushed with oxygen for a specified period of time (Fig. 3-10, *D*). Because the flushing process varies with equipment, it is suggested that the flowmeter be opened fully. If this causes the tent to billow, that is, bulge outward, full flow should be continued for at least a full minute. If the tent does not billow, it should be checked for leakage by determining that the zippered openings

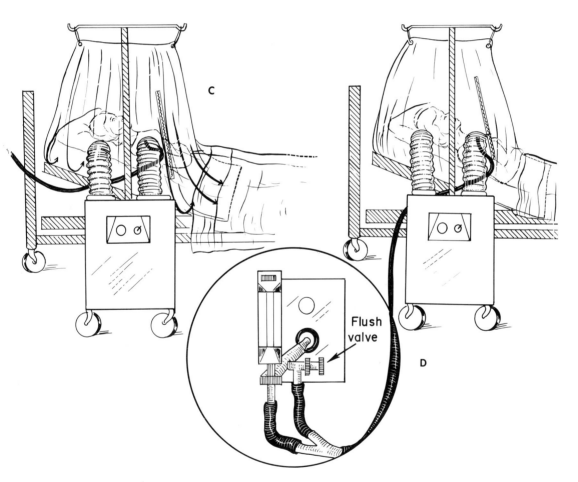

Fig. 3-10, cont'd. C, The sides of the canopy are tucked beneath the mattress, and the lower edge is arranged to conform to the patient's body. **D,** Linen that secures the lower edge of the canopy conforms to the body. The tent should billow when it is flushed with oxygen. The highest possible flow of oxygen should be continued for at least 1 minute.

are closed and that the canopy has been properly secured by tucking it smoothly beneath the mattress.

Each time care is given through the zippered openings, the tent should be flushed with oxygen for at least a full minute. For extensive care, the skirt of the canopy is moved to the upper chest of the patient. After this, or after the tent has been removed for a time, it is flushed with oxygen as specified initially.

Determining oxygen concentrations. When the patient is receiving oxygen-enriched gases, the oxygen content of the gases delivered is measured to ensure correct concentration initially and at frequent intervals until the desired concentration is reached—then at prescribed intervals, commonly three times a day.

An oxygen analyzer is used to determine oxygen concentrations. Several designs are available, operating on any of three principles: (1) that the magnetic susceptibility of oxygen produces changes in a magnetic field, (2) that the thermal conductivity of the atmosphere varies with the amount of oxygen present, or (3) that when oxygen is consumed by an electrochemical fuel cell, an electric current is generated in proportion to the amount of oxygen consumed.

Analyzers operated by magnetic susceptibility or thermal conductivity. The accuracy of analyzers operated by magnetic susceptibility or thermal conductivity may be influenced by the relative humidity, the temperature, the gas mixture sampled, the technique of obtaining the sample, and the position in which the analyzer is held. Usually a horizontal position is necessary. Silica gel crystals used to alter the relative humidity of the sample must be checked for color changes prior to the operation of the analyzer. Because the color change indicating excess moisture in the crystals varies with the particular analyzer, the manufacturer's directions should be consulted for details of use and proper care of this equipment. Analyzers operated by thermal conductivity should be used to measure oxygen-nitrogen mixtures only.

To determine oxygen concentrations within a tent, the sampling tube of the analyzer is inserted through an opening in the tent. Some tents contain a special opening for this purpose; the zipper opening may be used and may be preferable if mist production is used within the tent. The end of the sampling tube is placed well within the tent and distal to the source of mist because moisture tends to increase the need for maintenance of the analyzer. The sample is withdrawn with an aspirator, which consists of a rubber bulb attached to tubing. Compressing and releasing the bulb alternately a prescribed number of times allows its full expansion (Fig. 3-11, *A*). After aspiration, it is necessary to depress the switch button until the reading on the scale stabilizes (Fig. 3-11, *B*). A second reading is then taken for verification.

Fig. 3-11. Determining oxygen concentrations. **A,** With the oxygen analyzer held horizontally and the sampling tube inserted well within the tent, the bulb is squeezed a prescribed number of times to aspirate a sample. **B,** The switch button on the analyzer is depressed until the reading stabilizes.

Analyzers operated by generation of an electric current. The oxygen analyzer that operates on the principle of an electric current being generated by a fuel cell in proportion to the amount of oxygen available can be used to determine oxygen content in an oxygen-enriched atmosphere, or it can be fitted with adaptors to sample oxygen content of gases delivered by a ventilator. It differs from the analyzers described previously in that it is unaffected by relative humidity, ordinary temperature ranges, and the position in which it is held (Fig. 3-12). Maintenance involves changing the fuel cell. For details of this, consult the manufacturer's directions.

Determining accuracy of readings obtained by oxygen analyzers. Testing samples of room air and pure oxygen indicates whether the equipment is functioning properly, for atmospheric air contains 20.9% oxygen. The scales of all analyzers are calibrated from 0% to 100% oxygen. When determining oxygen content of gases being de-

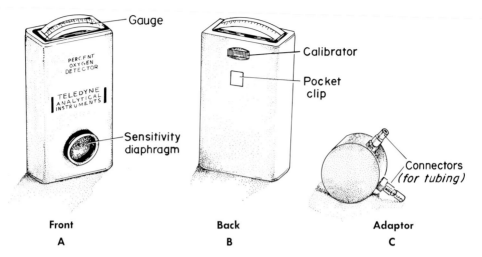

Fig. 3-12. Teledyne percent oxygen detector. A, Anterior view of the Teledyne percent oxygen detector showing the gauge and sensitivity diaphragm. The analyzer can be placed within any oxygen-enriched atmosphere to determine oxygen content. A reading can be taken within 30 seconds. B, Back view of the analyzer. The calibration button is used to calibrate the analyzer by turning the button until the pointer on the gauge matches the red line on the gauge. Calibration is done in room air. C, An adaptor can be placed over the sensitivity diaphragm and connected to tubes to sample the oxygen content of gases being delivered by ventilators. (Courtesy The Harris Calorific Co., Cleveland, Ohio.)

livered to the patient, a second reading should be taken. Duplicate readings are of value in determining the stability of gas concentrations. The reading obtained is compared to the prescribed oxygen concentration, and the oxygen flow is regulated accordingly. Erratic readings may indicate malfunction of the equipment, the presence of environmental factors that alter its accuracy, or improper technique.

OTHER GASES

Carbon dioxide. A mixture of 5% carbon dioxide in oxygen may be prescribed for its pharmacologic effects on blood vessels, to eliminate volatile substances from the body, or to stimulate respiration. The nurse administers it intermittently and for relatively short periods of time, often 5 to 15 minutes. When carbon dioxide is used to dilate the cerebral blood vessels, it is necessary to use drugs to control response of the respiratory center. This gas mixture should be administered by mask, using a technique similar to that described for oxygen masks.

Helium. A mixture of 80% helium and 20% oxygen reduces the work of breathing. When this mixture is used in some cases such as asthma, the physician may prescribe its further dilution with additional oxygen. The gaseous mixture should always be administered by mask.

HUMIDITY

Humidity of inspired gases can be improved as follows:
1. It can be increased approximately 10% with room vaporizers that disperse water vapor into the atmosphere or with a bubbler placed in the oxygen flowline.
2. It can be increased 90% with cool mist generators.
3. It can be increased 100% with heated mist generators when mists are delivered with a face tent or mask.

Room vaporizers. Adequate humidification can be obtained without boiling water. However, vaporizers that boil water to produce humidification are still in use. They are dangerous, and precautionary measures to prevent thermal injury must be observed. The vaporizer must be placed so that the vapor is projected from a safe distance—the distance required varies with the design of the equipment. In addition, placement of the vaporizer should be planned to prevent accidental contact with the vaporizer itself. This becomes extremely important when the nurse is dealing with children.

If the humidity of the air is to be increased appreciably by this means, the nurse should close the doors and windows of the room during therapy. Occasionally a croup tent is used to confine the vapor.

When the hot water vaporizer is used, loss of body heat may be interfered with and the patient may develop a fever.

Inline humidifiers. Incorporating a mist generator or humidifier into the flowline of equipment for administration of compressed air or oxygen provides increased humidity. Heating the gas increases its capacity for transporting moisture. This is accomplished best by heating the water through which the gas passes. Therefore, in clinical practice, a heating element may be used in conjunction with an inline humidifier. If cool mist is desired, either the unit is not connected to electricity or a unit without a heating element is used.

The reservoir is filled with sterile distilled water. The manufacturer's directions should be consulted to learn the method of filling a particular design of humidifier. This reservoir must be kept in an upright position so that it will function properly. If it is tipped, water may enter the delivery tube and block the flow of mist. Similarly, water may collect in the delivery tube as the result of condensation. If this occurs, the position of the humidifier must be corrected and the water must be removed from the delivery tube by draining it.

95

Opening the flowmeter fully will give adequate flow. The in-line compensated flowmeter will indicate oxygen flow. Total flow from the mist generator will depend on the air dilution accomplished. Flow of oxygen bears little or no relation to the percentage of oxygen delivered by this type of equipment. If mist is not produced, the equipment may need cleaning. The manufacturer's directions should be consulted, because the exact method of cleaning varies with the equipment used.

NEBULIZATION OF DRUGS

Certain drugs may be administered by inhalation. For this process, a nebulizer may be placed in the oxygen flowline. A nebulizer is inadequate for humidification purposes; therefore, if humidification is necessary, a large humidifier must also be incorporated into the flowline with the nebulizer.

The nebulizer is prepared by detaching it from its connection

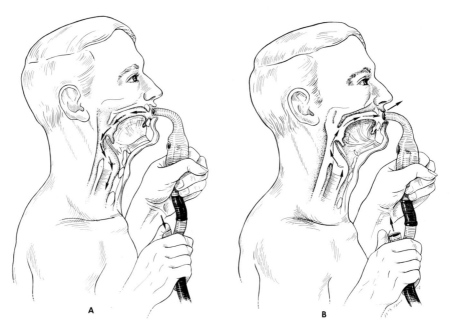

A   B

Fig. 3-13. Use of a hand nebulizer. **A,** After the drug is placed in the nebulizer, oxygen flow is set at 4 L. per minute, and the end of the nebulizer is placed in the patient's mouth. His lips must not close tightly around the nebulizer, and the small opening in the nebulizer should not be occluded. During inspiration, he occludes the free end of the **Y** tube to nebulize the drug. **B,** During exhalation, he removes his thumb from the end of the **Y** tube. Unless he does so, some drug will be wasted. If he desires, he may remove the nebulizer from his mouth during exhalation.

and placing the prescribed amount and kind of drug and diluent into it. The nebulizer is replaced in the line and nebulization is checked. Production of aerosol is related to the flow of oxygen.

Hand nebulizer. The hand nebulizer is connected to one extension of a Y tube supplied with oxygen. If the nebulizer is fitted with stoppers, these should be removed. Then the drug is placed in the nebulizer and a diluent added, if it has been prescribed. The flow of oxygen is turned on, usually to 4 L. per minute.

The patient is asked to place the free end of the nebulizer in his mouth. He must not close his lips tightly over the end of the nebulizer; rather he should be encouraged to keep his mouth open. Next, the patient is told to occlude the free end of the Y tube with his thumb during inspiration. This routes the oxygen through the nebulizer and converts the drug to an aerosol. The patient must be encouraged to inhale when he occludes the free end of the Y tube (Fig. 3-13, *A*) and to remove his thumb from the Y tube when he exhales (Fig. 3-13, *B*). The patient should not swallow the drug, for doing so may cause systemic effects. If a supply of oxygen is not available, an air compressor can be used. Some nebulizers can be fitted with a bulb that the patient compresses manually to force air past the drug to produce an aerosol.

Positive pressure breathing units (assisted ventilation)

In response to inspiration, positive pressure breathing units deliver compressed gas into the airway under positive pressure until a preset pressure is reached. This is followed by passive exhalation through a valve that can be moved close to the patient. The resulting respiration is called *intermittent positive pressure breathing, inspiratory,* commonly abbreviated as IPPB. Because the flow of gas is triggered by inspiration, the process is also termed assisted ventilation.

USE OF IPPB UNITS

Use of the IPPB units involves the combined efforts of the physician, inhalation therapy technician, and nurse. The adjustment of the control settings is determined by the physician in accordance with the needs of the patient. Indiscriminate manipulation of the controls is dangerous and should be prevented. After the controls are adjusted, these should be checked visually and the pressure indicator observed to make certain that the unit is functioning properly.

Before using the unit, the technician attaches a test lung to it to check the controls and to make certain that the unit is functioning properly. The test lung can also be used to demonstrate how the machine will help the patient breathe with less effort.

During the final preparation of the equipment, additional explanation is given, and the respiratory rate and rhythm of the patient are assessed. This information is used as a basis for determining whether the pressure selected is helpful to the patient. When the unit is applied to the patient, a decrease in respiratory rate means that the tidal volume is increased and that the patient is receiving assistance. If the respiratory rate increases, the pressure should be increased. The physician's approval is needed for this.

Observation of the pressure gauges during therapy is useful in determining that the unit is functioning properly and that the patient is breathing with the machine. Prior to inspiration, the needle on the breathing gauge rests on zero. With inspiratory effort, the needle will show negative pressure of one unit or less; then it should move into the positive pressure zone as the unit switches on and gas flows into the airway. At this point, the patient can and should relax and let the machine fill his lungs. The needle on the breathing gauge will continue to rise steadily until the control set is reached. Then the unit switches off and permits passive exhalation. Deviation from this pattern suggests that the patient is not breathing with the machine or that the settings need to be changed.

If, on inspiration, the needle on the breathing gauge moves farther than one unit into into the negative pressure zone, the patient is exerting excessive inspiratory effort. To correct this, the following measures should be carried out in this order:

1. Increase the pressure, which increases the tidal volume, thus improving the patient's ventilation.
2. Increase the flow in an attempt to meet the patient's demand for oxygen.
3. Urge the patient to cease inspiratory effort as soon as he feels gas beginning to flow into his airway.

If the unit does not switch on with inspiratory effort, its sensitivity is probably insufficient. If the unit has a special sensitivity control, readjust it to give the desired result. It must be emphasized that air should not be allowed to escape through the mouth or nose, or the unit will not switch off at the end of inspiration. If the patient finds it difficult to occlude his nose voluntarily when he is using a mouthpiece, apply a noseclip to prevent the escape of air through his nose. The patient must mold his lips around the mouthpiece. However, he should not clench the mouthpiece tightly between his teeth as though biting it, for this may permit air to flow around the mouthpiece or may even obstruct the flow.

If the unit switches off prematurely, the patient may be blowing into the mouthpiece before his lungs are filled with gas. He must be encouraged to let the machine fill his lungs completely and must be reassured that the unit will switch off automatically.

Pressure settings. Most units give little or no assistance if the pressure is less than 10 cm. of water. Pressure above this may be prescribed. The physician's prescription is, of course, limited by the capability of the machine.

Gas concentrations. IPPB units can be operated with compressed air or oxygen. When the latter is used, either 40% or 100% concentration is available with the Bird medical respirator, and a 40% to 100% concentration is available with the Bennett therapy unit. If the concentration of oxygen is critical, gas must be analyzed because ventilators vary considerably in concentration delivered.

Humidity. When the mouthpiece is used, humidification is desirable; when a tracheostomy is present, humidification is essential. When a mask is used, the inhaled gas may or may not be humidified, depending on the condition being treated. Humidification is recommended whenever oxygen is used as a driving force.

Use of the nebulizer. Preparation of the solution to be nebulized must be in accordance with the physician's prescription. Usually the prescribed drug is diluted with a suitable agent. If the drug is inhaled more rapidly than prescribed or if it is not completely used within a specified period of time, the physician should be consulted. Adjusting the nebulizer control will correct this on the Bennett valve. The nurse must assess the physiologic response to the drug and initiate nursing action that is appropriate. Permitting unused medications to remain in the nebulizer between treatments is dangerous. Not only does this predispose to inaccurate dosage, but also some drugs act as culture media for microorganisms; others may deteriorate and even produce toxic materials.

SPECIFIC UNITS USED FOR IPPB

Of the available positive pressure units, the Retec Model N-30, the Hand-E-Vent II, the Bird Asmastik, one model of the Bennett IPPB therapy unit, one model of the Bird medical respirator, and the Bennett Model MA-1 respirator unit are illustrated. The manufacturer's directions should be consulted for detailed information concerning the assembly, operation, and use of these and other models.

Retec Model N-30 (Fig. 3-14). The Retec Model N-30 has no moving parts; operation depends on the flow of gases through confined passages. It can be attached to piped or tank oxygen or to a compressed air source, and it will cycle automatically unless excessive leakage occurs. When aerosol production is desired, a nebulizer can be attached to the inlet. Pressure under which gas is delivered to the patient depends on the flow rate of the gas. Usually the flow rate is set between 6 and 10 L. per minute when the nebulizer is not incorporated into the system. It is set between 10 and 15 L. per minute when the nebulizer is incorporated into the system. These settings deliver gas under an inspiratory pressure between 10 and 20 cm. of water.

If the patient is breathing with this unit, he is seated comfortably, seals his lips around the mouthpiece, inhales until his lungs feel

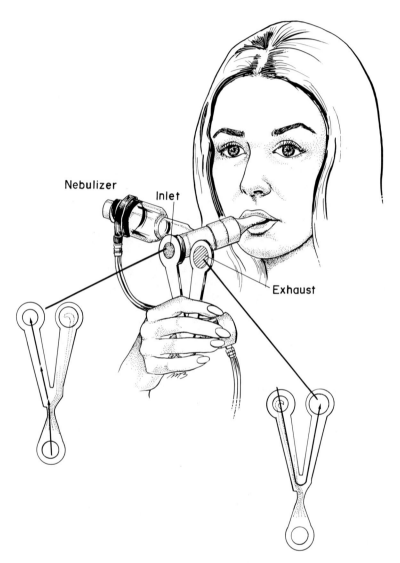

Fig. 3-14. Retec Model N-30. The prescribed medication and diluent are placed in the nebulizer. The flow of gas is set between 10 and 15 L. per minute. Arrows show the direction of gas flow during inhalation and exhalation. Intermittent manual occlusion of the exhaust port is used to control the rate of respiration as desired. (Courtesy Retec Development Laboratory, Portland, Ore.)

comfortably full, then exhales. The machine will cycle off when the preset pressure is reached and will cause exhalation on its own, also. Removal of the mouthpiece is neither desirable nor necessary for exhalation. The device is designed so that the desired gas and nebulized material can flow only into the lungs, and exhaled gases flow only away from the lungs through the exhaust part of the machine.

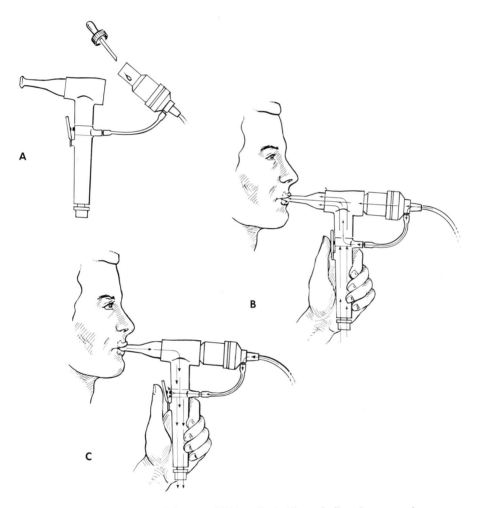

Fig. 3-15. Use of the Hand-E-Vent II. **A,** The nebulizer is removed from the Hand-E-Vent II and medication or distilled water is added as prescribed. **B,** The thumb is placed over the porthole in the handle of the Hand-E-Vent II during inhalation. **C,** The thumb is removed from the porthole during exhalation. (Courtesy Ohio Medical Products, Division of Air Reduction Co., Inc., Madison, Wis.)

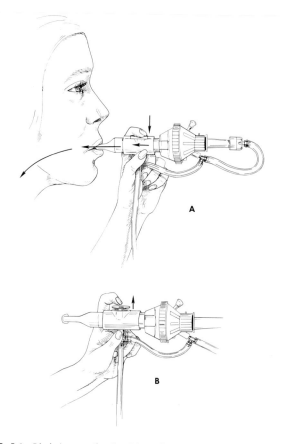

Fig. 3-16. Bird Asmastik. **A,** After the nebulizer is prepared, the unit is connected to oxygen, the pressure is set, and nebulization is tested. The patient seals the lips around the mouthpiece and depresses the valve during inspiration. **B,** For expiration, the patient removes the finger from the valve and allows passive exhalation to occur. It is not necessary to remove the mouthpiece during exhalation. (Courtesy Bird Corp., Palm Springs, Calif.)

If the machine is cycling automatically, the patient can voluntarily override its cycle.

Hand-E-Vent II. The Hand-E-Vent II can be connected to compressed air, an air pump, piped oxygen, or tank oxygen. If a relief valve is used with a compressor, the maximum amount of pressure delivered at the mouthpiece is fixed at 20 cm. of water. When a compressor with a needle valve and gauge or compressed air or oxygen fitted with a regulator valve is used, the maximum amount of pressure delivered to the mouthpiece can be preset. The pressure to be delivered to the patient is set by occluding the porthole and opening the needle valve by rotating the control knob until the prescribed pressure registers on the gauge. The gauge is calibrated in centimeters of water. The pressure prescribed is often between 10 and 15 cm. of water. The manufacturer's directions should be consulted for details regarding the use of pressure gauges and valves and for adjusting the pressure.

During use, the Hand-E-Vent II should be held in a horizontal position to ensure maximum nebulization and to avoid spillage. If the patient is too ill to cooperate in the use of the Hand-E-Vent II, another IPPB device may be indicated. Patients who are sufficiently strong to sit up and who are able to cooperate can usually learn to use this device and may continue its use at home, as prescribed by the physician.

Teaching the patient to use the Hand-E-Vent II involves teaching him to prepare the nebulizer (Fig. 3-15, A) as prescribed by the physician, having him learn to seal his lips around the mouthpiece and to inhale with the nasal passages occluded by the palate or a nose-clip. Once the patient has learned that he can inhale and exhale through the handle of the machine without removing the mouthpiece from his mouth, he is ready to begin inhalation with positive pressure on inspiration. To do this, he occludes the hole in the handle of the Hand-E-Vent II and breathes in slowly until his lungs feel comfortably full (Fig. 3-15, B). To exhale, he removes his thumb from the porthole and exhales through the mouthpiece and, therefore, through the handle of the machine (Fig. 3-15, C). He repeats this procedure for the prescribed length of time, usually about 15 to 20 minutes.

Bird Asmastik. After the pressure line from the Bird Asmastik is connected to a source of oxygen or compressed air, the nebulizer is prepared (Fig. 3-16). Then the pressure is set, usually at 10 to 15 cm. of water, and the function is checked. To do this, the nebulizer is disconnected from the handpiece, the valve is depressed, and vaporization is observed. After this, the nebulizer is connected to the handpiece, and the patient is instructed to mold his lips around the mouthpiece. He is told to depress the center valve when he begins inhalation and to continue to press on the valve until he feels that his lungs are full (Fig. 3-16, A). Then he releases the valve (Fig. 3-16, B) and exhales through the mouthpiece. These steps are repeated during the treatment period, which usually lasts about 15 minutes. The approximate number of deep inspirations per minute will be six to ten.

Bennett therapy unit (Model TV-2P). The Bennett therapy unit is connected to compressed oxygen with a regulator, to piped oxygen, or to compressed air. Prescribed medication or distilled water is placed into the bowl of the nebulizer (Fig. 3-17, A). After the prepared nebulizer has been replaced in the circuit, the oxygen to the nebulizer is turned on until a fine spray is produced (Fig. 3-17, B). If the humidifier has a heater (Fig. 3-17, C) and if heat is prescribed,

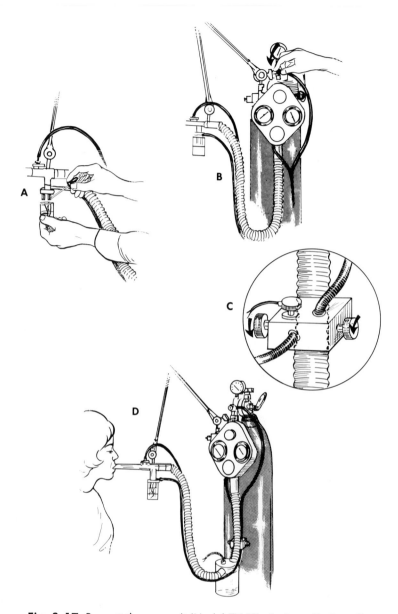

Fig. 3-17. Bennett therapy unit (Model TV-2P). **A,** Prescribed medication is placed into the bowl of the nebulizer. **B,** After the prepared nebulizer has been replaced in the circuit, the oxygen to the nebulizer is turned on (arrow) until a fine spray is produced. **C,** Valves when the heated mist unit is used. To regulate production of mist with the flow of oxygen to the nebulizer, the valve on the left side is closed, and the valve on the right side is opened, as shown by arrows. **D,** After the unit has been connected to oxygen, the nebulizer has been prepared, and controls have been set, it is used by the patient. (Courtesy Bennett Respiration Products, Inc., Santa Monica, Calif.)

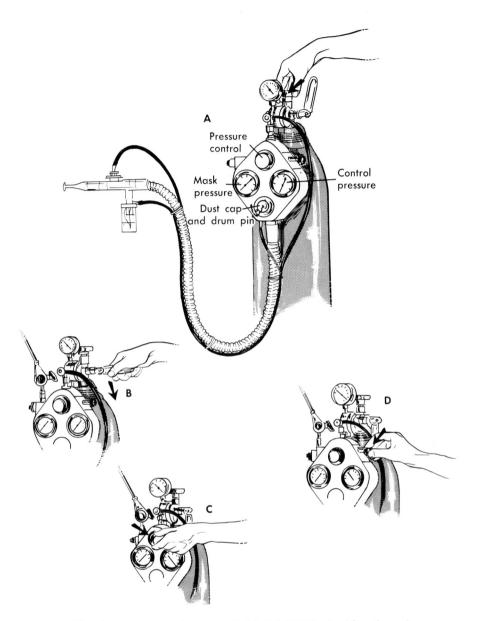

Fig. 3-18. Bennett therapy unit (Model TV-2P). **A,** After the unit has been connected to oxygen, the cylinder valve (arrow) is opened fully. If piped oxygen is used, the unit is connected directly to the outlet. A flowmeter is not used. **B,** The shutoff lever is pulled down completely to turn on the flow of oxygen. **C,** The control pressure is turned until the prescribed pressure is reached on the pressure control gauge. **D,** The oxygen concentration is selected. Pushing the lever in gives 40% oxygen; pulling the lever out as far as possible gives 100% oxygen. (Courtesy Bennett Respiration Products, Inc., Santa Monica, Calif.)

it must be connected to a source of electricity. Fig. 3-17, *C*, describes regulation of production of mist with the flow of oxygen to the nebulizer. Set controls as prescribed by the physician (Fig. 3-18).

The therapist first adjusts the oxygen flow to the nebulizer to produce a steady flow of mist. If the tube leading to the nebulizer pops off the connection, the oxygen flow to this point is too great and should be reduced. Failure of the nebulizer to function properly may also be related to loose connections. Tapping the side of the nebulizer will cause medication clinging to its walls to fall to the bottom so that it can be nebulized.

After assisting the patient to a comfortable position, preferably a sitting or semisitting position, the oxygen flow is turned on and the mouthpiece or mask is applied. The nurse should observe to determine that the patient is breathing with the unit and that it is functioning properly. (See also pages 97 and 98.) If the oxygen concentration is critical, gas must be analyzed.

Bird medical respirator (Mark 7). For the Bird medical respirator, the controls are set in the following order, beginning at the right side of the unit. The pressure control (Fig. 3-19, *A*) is set. Next, the oxygen (40% or pure O_2) concentration is selected. If 40% oxygen is desired, the airmix control (Fig. 3-19, *B*) is pulled out. If the oxygen concentration is critical, gas must be analyzed. The expiratory timer (Fig. 3-19, *C*) is then turned off, the sensitivity control (Fig. 3-19, *D*) is set, and the flow rate (Fig. 3-19, *E*) is adjusted. These settings serve as reference points only. The physician must assess the individual's ventilatory needs and must alter the settings accordingly. A starting point of 15 is suggested by the manufacturer for the pressure, sensitivity, and inspiratory flow rate settings. After this unit is connected to compressed oxygen, the controls are set, the humidifier and nebulizer (Fig. 3-20), are prepared, and the unit is applied to the patient (Fig. 3-19, *F*). (For further elaboration, see the discussion on use of IPPB units, page 97.)

Bennett model MA-1 respirator unit. The Bennett MA-1 unit operates with room air or oxygen. If the unit is used with tank oxygen, a regulator must be used; with piped oxygen a regulator is not necessary. Preparation of the unit and the adjustment of its settings is done by the physician or an inhalation therapist, as prescribed by the physician. First, with the power switch in the "off" position, the unit is connected to oxygen and to electricity. The humidifier is filled with distilled water to the full mark, and the temperature control is set at 6. If tubing of a different bore than that supplied with the unit is used, the control setting will differ. The sensitivity control is set so that 1 cm. of negative pressure or less will trigger the machine. Then the peak flow is set at the prescribed liters per minute and the normal pressure

106

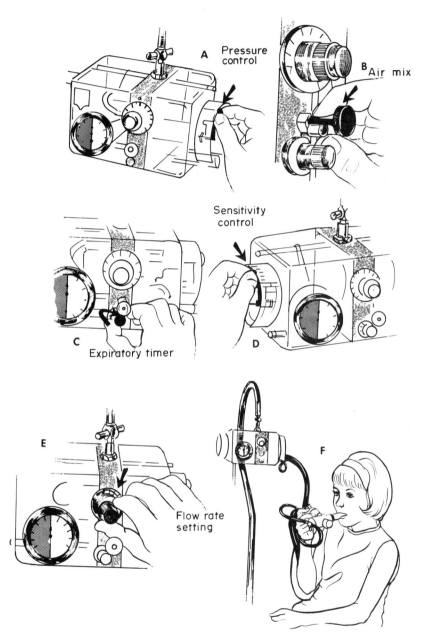

Fig. 3-19. Bird medical respirator (Mark 7). **A,** The pressure control is set as prescribed. **B,** The air mix control is pulled out if 40% oxygen is prescribed. If pure oxygen is needed, this control is pushed all the way in. **C,** The expiratory timer is turned off. **D,** The sensitivity control is set. **E,** The flow rate setting is adjusted. **F,** The unit is applied to the patient. (Courtesy Bird Corp., Palm Springs, Calif.)

limit is set as necessary to deliver the desired volume. Next the normal volume is set at the prescribed tidal volume. Commonly, this is slightly above 3 ml. per pound of body weight for adults. The desired cycles per minute are set on the rate dial. The sigh pressure limit is set at one and one-half times the tidal volume, and the sigh multiple is set at 1, 2, or 3, as prescribed. The oxygen percentage dial is set at the prescribed concentration. Then the expiratory resistance is set at "off" by turning the dial counterclockwise. The spirometer alarm is tested by turning the "on" switch and pressing the test button. This method is used to check the 20-second delay and to test the strength of the batteries. If the alarm is not heard clearly, the batteries should be replaced.

If optional attachments are used, these should be regulated. The negative expiratory pressure is set at its maximum setting by turning the dial fully counterclockwise. The positive end expiratory pressure is set at zero by turning the dial clockwise. After this, the machine is turned on, applied to the patient, and the filled nebulizer, if prescribed, is turned on.

After the machine is applied to the patient, the breathing pattern of the patient, the spirometer, the system pressure gauge, and the thermometer should be observed. If indicated, settings are readjusted as prescribed.

If the set tidal volume is not exhaled in approximately a 20-second

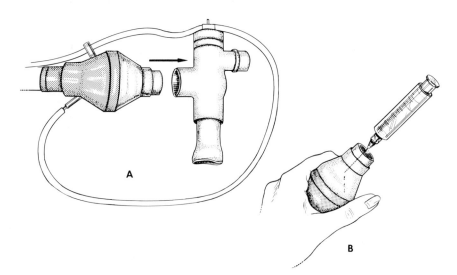

Fig. 3-20. Preparation of the nebulizer on the Bird medical respirator. **A,** The nebulizer is disconnected from the mouthpiece and exhalation valve. **B,** Medication is placed in the nebulizer, which is then replaced within the breathing circuit. (Courtesy Bird Corp., Palm Springs, Calif.)

interval, the alarm of the spirometer will sound. This is an additional alarm that is not supplied on all spirometers.

The indicators above the panel must also be observed. The system pressure gauge indicates pressure in the system ranging from −10 to +80 cm. of water. It is on this gauge that positive end expiratory pressure (PEEP), zero end expiratory pressure (ZEEP), and negative end pressure are read. The light of the assist indicator goes on when the patient triggers inspiration. It also lights when the unit self-

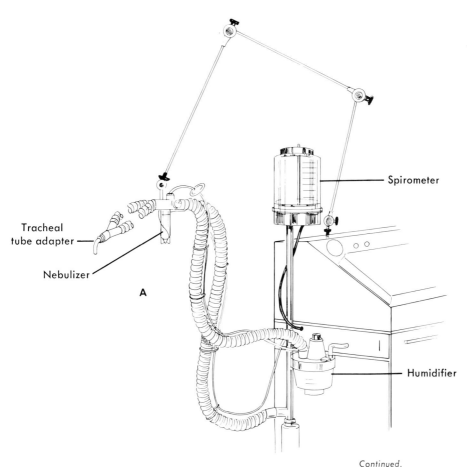

Continued.

Fig. 3-21. Bennett Model MA-1 respirator unit. **A,** View of the unit showing the spirometer, humidifier, nebulizer, tracheal tube adapter, and covered control panel. **B,** The control panel of the unit. During use, all but the top row of dials may be covered. For details regarding the dials and their setting, see pages 106 and 108 to 111. **C,** Negative expiratory pressure can be adjusted with an optional attachment for the unit. **D,** Control for positive end expiratory pressure (PEEP). (Courtesy Bennett Respiration Products, Inc., Santa Monica, Calif.)

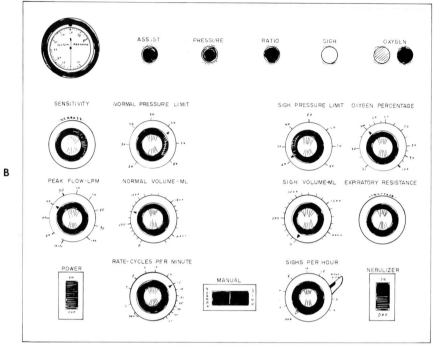

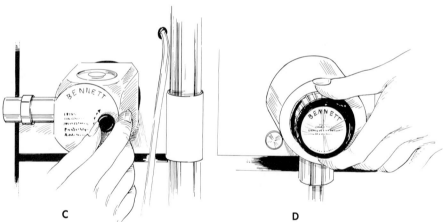

Fig. 3-21, cont'd. For legend see page 109.

cycles. To correct self-cycling of the unit, decrease the sensitivity control. The ratio warning light indicates that inspiration is longer than will be the length of the following expiration. The length of inspiration can be decreased by increasing the peak flow setting in liters per minute. The sigh indicator light goes on during the sigh part of the breathing cycle. The green oxygen light indicates that the oxygen percentage is set for enrichment. The red oxygen light, accompanied by an audible alarm, indicates that this is lower than the required pressure in the oxygen line. This alarm does not respond to improper oxygen concentrations. The manual and sigh inspiration start controls, located at the center of the lower panel, are used to start a single normal inspiration or a single sigh respiration (Fig. 3-21).

RESUSCITATION WITH IPPB UNITS

If inspiratory efforts are not present, IPPB units can be used as resuscitators. The patient is positioned as described for mouth-to-mouth resuscitation (pages 343 to 348), either an airway is inserted (Fig. 12-4, *A* and *B*) or the jaw is supported to relieve obstruction by the tongue (Figs. 12-2 to 12-4), and the mask is fitted snugly over the mouth and nose. Pressure should be set at 25 cm. of water or above.

The inspiratory phase is actuated by triggering the unit manually. On Bennett therapy units, the drum pin is flicked upward to initiate inspiratory flow (Fig. 3-22). With the Bird medical respirator, the control rod in the center of the sensitivity ring is pushed quickly toward the center of the machine. This rod must be released immediately if the unit is to function as desired (Fig. 3-23). On the Bennett model MA-1, the manual normal inspiration start button is depressed (Fig. 3-21).

If the mask is used for any extended length of time, air will flow into the stomach and must be removed. The air may be removed by gastric intubation or by external pressure on the epigastric region. Dangers that accompany the latter method are discussed on page 349. This problem is avoided when the units are used with a tracheostomy or tracheal tube.

Whenever resuscitation is necessary, the physician should be notified immediately.

Controlled respiration. When the patient is unable to initiate inspiration, IPPB units equipped with automatic cycling devices can be used as respirators. The decision to cycle the machine automatically, thus controlling respiration completely, involves a medical diagnosis. Therefore only the physician decides whether controlled respiration is indicated.

Constant vigilance is indicated when automatic cycling is used. The nurse should know that the characteristic sound of the unit cycling indicates only that the machine is operating, and she should realize the importance of observation to determine whether the machine is helping the patient's respiration. Methods of measuring expired volume are available. Also, various alarm systems may be incorporated into special units. When these are used, the nurse must find out how they work and must be familiar with the alarm system. If for any reason the mask or adaptor is displaced or the airway is

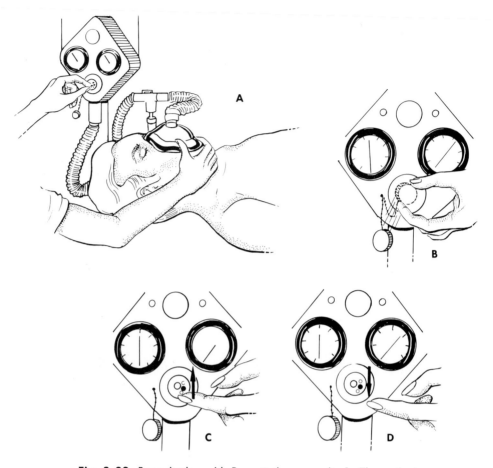

Fig. 3-22. Resuscitation with Bennett therapy unit. **A,** The patient is positioned to maintain patency of the airway, the mask is applied, and resuscitation is begun. **B,** Removal of the dust cap to expose the drum pin. **C,** The drum pin is flicked upward to initiate inspiratory flow. **D,** The finger is removed from the drum pin immediately. (Courtesy Bennett Respiration Products, Inc., Santa Monica, Calif.)

occluded, the purpose of the therapy is thwarted and life is jeopardized.

If the unit is capable of exerting negative pressure during expiration, close supervision is mandatory. Misguided application of negative pressure can be dangerous.

Periodic deep inspirations (sighing). With controlled ventilation, periodic deep inspirations or sighs tend to prevent atelectasis. When these are prescribed, they can be accomplished with the described IPPB units as follows:

1. With the Bennett therapy unit, at prescribed intervals for a

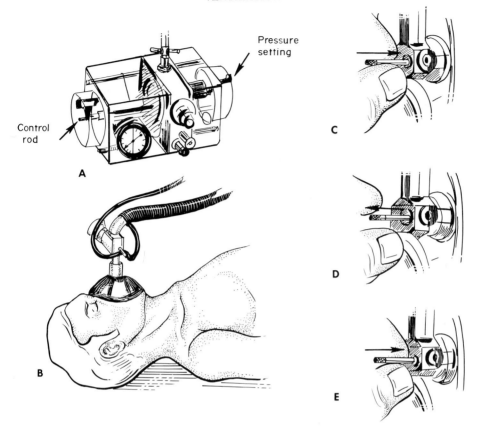

Fig. 3-23. Resuscitation with the Bird medical respirator. **A,** The control rod used to initiate inspiration is located within the sensitivity ring. Pressure is set at 25 cm. of water. **B,** Patency of airway is maintained with positioning and an artificial airway. The mask is applied. **C,** The control rod is pushed quickly toward the center of the ring. **D,** The control rod must be released immediately. **E,** After passive exhalation, the control rod is again pushed toward the center of the machine to start another inspiration. (Courtesy Bird Corp., Palm Springs, Calif.)

prescribed number of breaths, turn the pressure control (Fig. 3-18, *C*) fully clockwise, giving high pressure.

2. With the Bird medical respirator, push the control rod in and hold it until the prescribed pressure is reached (Fig. 3-23, *C*). At this point the control rod must be released immediately (Fig. 3-23, *D*). This action is repeated for the prescribed number of breaths.

3. The Bennett Model MA-1 respirator is set at sigh intervals per hour, or sighing can be accomplished by depressing the manual sigh inspiration start control (Fig. 3-21, *B*).

TABLE 3-3. Weaning from the respirator

Technique	Problem	Explanation or solution
The patient is told of the plan and is assured that the nurse will stay with him during weaning. An explanation is given that he is able to breathe without the respirator.	The person who requires controlled ventilation develops dependence on the respirator.	Explanation relieves apprehension. The nurse's presence reassures the patient that the respirator can be reapplied if it is needed. The physician orders weaning when there are indications that the patient is able to breathe spontaneously.
Suction the airway and ventilate the patient before weaning.	Secretions will interfere with gaseous exchange.	Suctioning removes secretions and foreign materials from the airway.
Remove the patient from the respirator for prescribed periods of time (often 3 to 5 minutes every 2 to 3 hours). During the weaning periods, supply increased concentrations of humidified oxygen and encourage the patient to take deep breaths. Observe chest excursions.	Synchronization of the respiratory muscles may be absent. Hypoventilation and maldistribution may cause arterial hypoxemia.	The patient must be helped to relearn how to breathe; synchronization of the muscles will occur as they gradually become stronger. Increased concentrations of oxygen help to prevent these conditions; inspired oxygen is humidified to reduce dryness and trauma to the mucosal lining.
Observe the vital signs, skin color and moistness, emotional state, chest excursions, and central venous pressure; discontinue weaning if any of these change markedly.	Marked changes in vital signs may occur; the patient may become cyanotic or agitated, or he may perspire profusely.	Recurrence of respiratory failure must be treated without delay.

Weaning from the respirator. The patient who requires controlled ventilation develops dependence on the respirator. The physician will order weaning from the respirator when there are indications that the patient no longer needs controlled ventilation (Table 3-3).

Before weaning, the patient should be told what is planned and reassured that the nurse will stay with him during the weaning periods. Patients are apprehensive during the weaning periods and fearful of being unable to breathe on their own.

The weaning is done as prescribed. The patient is usually removed from the respirator for 3 to 5 minutes every hour or two. He should be watched for synchronization of muscles used for respiration. He may need some help in learning to breathe all over again. The period of time spent breathing on his own is increased as rapidly as is tolerated by the patient. The length of time required to complete the weaning process varies with each individual. Even though the patient is able to breathe effectively without the respirator when he is awake, he may continue to need the respirator when he is asleep. Observations of cyanosis, increased rate and decreased depth of respirations, increased or decreased blood pressure, or increased pulse rate may indicate that the patient is not tolerating the weaning process.

Care of the temporary tracheostomy

A temporary tracheostomy may be necessary to preserve life. When the patient has a tracheostomy, humidification of inspired gas is essential, infection must be prevented, and secretions must be removed by a catheter introduced into the airway for aspiration. In addition, the inner cannula of the double tracheostomy tube is removed periodically for cleaning. If either the catheter or the inner cannula is handled carelessly, large numbers of microorganisms will be introduced, and this introduction of pathogens can result in overwhelming infections. The described technique is aimed toward preventing such an outcome.

For suctioning the tracheostomy, a suction apparatus fitted with a Y catheter is necessary unless the catheter is designed with a release valve. Sterile supplies include a catheter, a basin of sterile water, a tracheal tube brush, disposable gloves, and an external dressing. The diameter of the catheter used should be considerably smaller than that of the tracheostomy tube. For example, a No. 16 French catheter is used with a No. 6 or 36 French tracheostomy tube.

After washing the hands, the nurse opens the tray and connects the appropriate portion of the catheter to the Y connection. The hand that is used to introduce the sterile catheter must be gloved (Fig. 3-24, A). Although some references state that the catheter should not be introduced more than 4 to 5 inches, or the length of the cannula, when secretions are a problem it should be advanced farther. This method of removing secretions from the tracheobronchial tree is also referred to as deep suction. The need for deep suctioning may be lessened by the use of chest physiotherapy.

Tracheobronchial suction. To direct the catheter into the right main bronchus for tracheobronchial suction, the patient's chest is turned slightly to the right and his head is turned to his far left (Fig. 3-24, A). To suction the left bronchus, this position is reversed (Fig. 3-24, D). The catheter is observed to be certain that it curves toward and passes into the left bronchus. Suction is not applied until the catheter has been passed as far as possible without force. As it is withdrawn, suction is applied and the catheter may be gently rotated. When a collection of mucus is contacted, the catheter is moved back and forth until the mucus is removed. This process is repeated until the catheter is completely withdrawn. Then sterile water is aspirated through the catheter, giving attention to the rela-

115

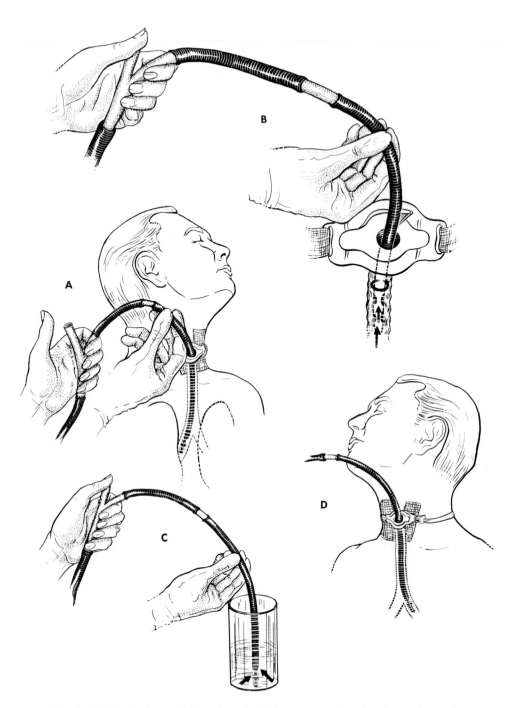

Fig. 3-24. Tracheobronchial suction. **A,** If the catheter is to be directed into the right main bronchus, the patient's chest is turned slightly to the right, and his head is turned to the far left. **B,** A sterile glove is worn on the hand used to introduce the sterile catheter. Suction is not applied until the catheter has been introduced. As the catheter is withdrawn, suction is applied and the catheter may be rotated gently. **C,** Sterile water is aspirated through the catheter, with attention given to the amount of mucus removed. **D,** The catheter is directed into the left main bronchus, and aspiration is repeated.

Fig. 3-25. Schematic drawing of a sterile aspirator. The specimen container is fitted with a rubber stopper through which hollow metal rods extend. These are connected to the catheter and the tubing that leads to the suction apparatus with plastic connectors. The small hole in the connector nearest to the suction apparatus serves as a release valve and permits insertion of the catheter without application of suction.

tive amount of mucus removed (Fig. 3-24, C). This process is repeated until the water appears clear after aspiration. However, the catheter must not remain in the airway for more than 10 seconds during any single aspiration. This same catheter is used throughout a single series of tracheobronchial aspirations unless it is contaminated. However, the next time secretions need to be removed, another sterile catheter is used.

Sterile aspiration of tracheal secretions. Sterile aspiration of tracheal secretions is done with a sterile aspirator. This consists of a sterile container fitted with a cap to which is attached a sterile catheter and tubing that will be connected to suction (Fig. 3-25). Aspiration is done as described on pages 115 to 117. During the collection of the specimen, the sterile container must be held somewhat perpendicular; if it is tipped too much to either side, the specimen will be suctioned through the vial and into the collecting bottle of the suction apparatus. After aspiration of the specimen, the cap to which the catheter is attached is removed, and the vial is covered with a sterile cap. The sterile cap may be packaged as a part of the collecting vial, often placed on the bottom of this vial, or it may be separate. The specimen is labeled and sent to the laboratory.

Care of the cannula. When the secretions have been aspirated from the airway, the inner cannula of a double-cannula tube is removed (Fig. 3-26, A and B) and placed in a basin of solution for cleaning. The solution used varies. Hydrogen peroxide is helpful in loosening secretions; however, soap and water or other mild agents may be used. The inner cannula is brushed until it is completely clean when it is subjected to visual inspection (Fig. 3-26, C). After

117

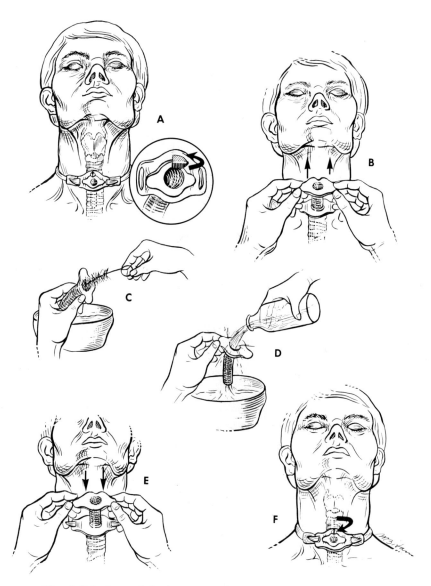

Fig. 3-26. Care of the inner cannula. **A,** The turnkey is unlocked in preparation for removal of the inner cannula. The inset shows turning the key to unlocked position. **B,** The inner cannula is removed. **C,** Cannula is cleansed with brush and cleansing agent. **D,** Cannula is rinsed thoroughly with sterile water. **E,** Cannula is replaced. **F,** Turnkey is moved to locking position.

this inspection, the cannula is rinsed thoroughly with sterile water (Fig. 3-26, *D*). It is then replaced in the outer cannula and locked in place (Fig. 3-26, *E* and *F*).

Inflation of cuffed tracheostomy tubes. When a tracheostomy tube is used for controlled ventilation, the inner cannula is removed, and the outer cannula is fitted with an adaptor that connects to the ventilator. The outer cannula and some single plastic tracheostomy tubes are surrounded by a single or double inflatable cuff. The cuff can be inflated to seal the space between the tube and the trachea.

Minimal inflation of these cuffs prevents leakage around the tube. The technique of inflation varies with the type of cuff or cuffed tube. Depending on the type of single cuffed tube used, it may be necessary to deflate the single cuff from time to time. If the tube has only one cuff, it may be deflated for 5 minutes of every hour to avoid damage to the trachea; if the tube has a double cuff, inflation of the two cuffs is alternated. *However, true low-pressure cuffs are not deflated.* No sure rules can be given for the prevention of damage to the trachea.

During initial inflation of the cuff, the tracheostomy tube is connected to the IPPB machine. Leakage between the trachea and the tube produces a gurgling sound. The person inflating the cuff must listen to this sound carefully. The cuff is inflated with air until the gurgling sound just barely disappears. The amount of air needed to inflate the cuff varies; it is often less than 5 ml. but may be as high as 20 ml. with some tubes. The method of inflating the cuff varies with the design of the tubing used for inflation. In some the end of the syringe, filled with air, is inserted directly into the tubing; in others a syringe fitted with a needle must be used. After the cuff has been inflated, the inflation tubing must be sealed or clamped unless it has incorporated into its design a one-way valve.

Before or at the time of deflation, secretions that have collected above the cuff must be removed by suctioning. This can be accomplished by placing the patient in the Trendelenburg position for a few minutes to drain the secretions by gravity and then removing them with a catheter attached to suction. If a second or double cuff is present, it is inflated when the other cuff is deflated.

To facilitate the removal of secretions, deflation of the cuff should coincide with exhalation when the patient is breathing with a ventilator. Conversely, the cuff is deflated during inhalation when the patient is breathing on his own.

The danger of aspirating secretions is reduced when the cuff of the tracheostomy tube is inflated. The cuff should remain inflated whenever the respirator must be removed from the tracheostomized patient. This commonly occurs during suctioning and during weaning from the respirator. The cuff should also be inflated when the patient is taking nourishment by mouth. As stated previously, deflation of low-pressure cuffs is unnecessary except when secretions need to be removed from the upper airway.

Ventilation during tracheobronchial aspirations. When tracheobronchial aspirations are done, replenishing the oxygen in the tracheobronchial tree increases the comfort of the patient and reduces the possibility of cardiac arrhythmias. This may require the assistance of a second person. For delivery of maximum concentrations of oxygen, a 3 L. anesthesia bag with a pop-off valve may be used. Alternatively, a respirator or a self-inflating resuscitator may be used. The resuscitator or anesthesia bag is connected to oxygen and fitted with an adaptor for tracheostomy tubes and applied to the tracheostomy tube. The bag is alternately compressed and released as described on pages 347 to 349. Compression of the bag should coincide with any spontaneous effort of the patient to inhale. It is common to ventilate the patient at least five times between aspirations of tracheobronchial secretions. This method is correctly referred to as hyperinflation; it is erroneously called "bagging" the patient.

When a ventilator or respirator is used, the patient is given pure oxygen for ten to fifteen breaths before disconnecting the machine and suctioning. The ventilator is used between aspirations to supply oxygen to the patient also.

Tracheostomy dressings. A bib dressing, fashioned by folding a 4- by 8-inch piece of gauze lengthwise and then into a V shape, or by splitting a 4- by 4-inch or 4- by 8-inch gauze dressing to approximately 1½ inches, is placed beneath the tie tapes and beneath the flange of the tube (Fig. 3-27, *A* and *B*). This protects the wound and the surrounding skin.

Changing tie tapes. The physician or the nursing coordinator usually assumes the responsibility for changing soiled tie tapes. During this procedure an assistant should hold the outer cannula securely but gently (Fig. 3-27, *C*), since manipulation or pressure will stimulate coughing, the force of which may dislodge the tube.

To change tapes, two strips of twill tape, ⅜ by 15 inches, are needed. The end that will be fastened to the flange of the tube is slit horizontally about an inch from the end of the tube. After the tapes are fastened to the tube (Fig. 3-27, *D*), they must be knotted securely. Placing the knot to one side of the neck is desirable. If venous congestion is observed, the tapes are too tight and must be loosened immediately.

Dislodgment of tube. If the outer cannula becomes dislodged, an infrequent but serious occurrence, the airway can be maintained by inserting a tracheal dilator or a sterile curved clamp into the stoma and spreading the incision apart. The physician will insert a sterile tracheostomy tube, which should be readily available. To do this, he

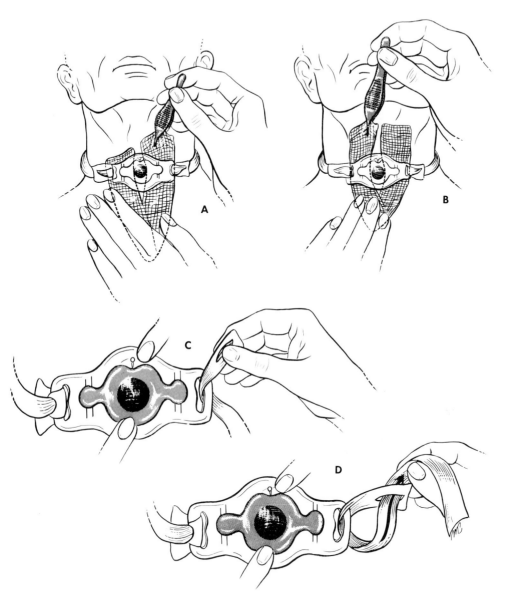

Fig. 3-27. Tracheostomy dressings and tie tapes. **A,** A prepared bib dressing is placed beneath the tie tapes and beneath the flange of the tube. **B,** Forceps are useful in positioning the dressing. **C,** An assistant holds the outer cannula to prevent its dislodgment when tie tapes are changed. Prepared tape is slipped through the opening in the flange of the outer cannula. **D,** The method of securing tape through the opening in the flange. After this, the tapes are securely tied together with a knot at one side of the neck.

lays aside the inner cannula and places the obturator within the outer cannula. After lubricating the tip of the obturator he slips the unit quickly into place. He immediately removes the obturator and attaches tie tapes to hold the outer cannula in place.

Questions for discussion and exploration

1. What natural methods do we normally use for humidifying inspired air?
2. Discuss the artificial methods for humidifying inspired gases, the advantages and disadvantages of each, and the relative importance of humidification depending on the anatomic point at which gases are delivered to the patient.
3. Mr. J. is scheduled to have abdominal surgery tomorrow. What will you teach him about deep breathing, turning, and coughing? What methods will you use to teach him?
4. If, during the postoperative period, Mr. J. is to receive oxygen by mask, what information must you know? What approach will enable him and his family to accept this therapy?
5. If a patient receives oxygen by nasal cannula, what factors will influence its effectiveness in delivering the percentage of oxygen prescribed? Why must he be encouraged to breathe through his nose?
6. If Mr. S. needs humidified gases, the physician might order mist with oxygen to be delivered to Mr. S. via a face tent. How can you troubleshoot the equipment used when it does not seem to be working well?
7. For what reason might a nasal catheter be used? How often does it need to be changed? What effects will the catheter have on the mucous membrane lining the nose if it is lubricated with a water-soluble lubricant and remains in place for several days?
8. Compare the flow rates used for a cannula, catheter, face tent, and face mask. How can you know if the prescribed flow rate is adequate?
9. What are the inherent dangers in using pure oxygen, pure helium, or a high pecentage of carbon dioxide for inhalation therapy?
10. Mrs. R. asks your opinion about a room vaporizer that she plans to purchase for use with her preschool children. What factors can you help her consider in making a selection?
11. Discuss the qualities of drugs used in your hospital for inhalation therapy. Would drugs with an oil base be prescribed? Why should the nebulizer be cleansed following use? Why must the nurse administering drugs by inhalation therapy know the side effects, toxic effects, and expected effects of drugs that are inhaled? Can you determine a common denominator for dosage of drugs given by this method?
12. If you are to assist a patient in learning to use an IPPB device effectively, what must you be able to explain to him as reasons for this therapy? How will you know if he is using the device correctly? If he uses it improperly, how can you help him learn to breathe properly with the device? What sort of emotional support should you be able to give him?

13. As you turn on the Bennett IPPB therapy unit and the patient begins to use it, a tube pops off and nebulization of the drug ceases. How can you correct this problem?

14. If one continues to aspirate tracheal secretions for an extended period of time, what is likely to happen to the patient that may necessitate emergency action? Why?

15. What are the differences in resuscitating someone with various IPPB devices?

16. Why should a mask being used with an IPPB machine for resuscitation be replaced with a tracheostomy or endotracheal tube as soon as possible?

17. Patients and the families of patients who have tracheostomies need a great deal of emotional support. How can you provide this? Compare the different reactions that can be anticipated if the tracheostomy is done as an emergency procedure to those expected if the patient and his family are told beforehand that a tracheostomy is necessary.

18. Why do you suppose that the use of sterile rather than clean technique for tracheostomy care is gaining increasing favor by many authorities in respiratory care?

19. If you note an unpleasant odor that seems related to soiled tie tapes on a tracheostomy tube, what action can you take? What precautions must be used in changing the tie tapes?

20. If a patient is to leave the hospital with a tracheostomy tube in place, what teaching would be needed? What supplies should be available to the patient at home?

21. If a patient has a permanent tracheostomy, how can he or she protect the fenestration so that foreign materials will not be inhaled and the opening will not be apparent? Consider the possibilities for men, women, and children.

22. If you learn that relatives are crying for unknown reasons and you are able to elicit from them that they are afraid that their relative is dying because he is receiving oxygen, how can you help them? How might this situation have been prevented if oxygen therapy were simply a part of the therapeutic plan?

Selected references

Adler, R. H., and Brodie, S. L.: Postoperative rebreathing aid, Amer. J. Nurs. 68:1287-1289, 1968.

Ballinger, W. F., Treybal, J. C., and Vosie, A. B.: Alexander's care of the patient in surgery, ed. 5, St. Louis, 1972, The C. V. Mosby Co.

Bendixen, H. H., Egbert, L. D., Hedley-Whyte, J., Laver, M. B., and Pontoppidan, H.: Respiratory care, St. Louis, 1965, The C. V. Mosby Co.

Betson, C.: Blood gases, Amer. J. Nurs. 68:1010-1012, 1968.

Burgess, A. M.: A comparison of common methods of oxygen therapy for bed patients, Amer. J. Nurs. 65:96-99, 1965.

Burn, H. L.: A pure fluid cycling valve for use in breathing equipment, Inhalation Ther. 69:11-19, 1969.

Bushnell, S.: Respiratory intensive care nursing, Boston, 1973, Little, Brown and Co.

Cherniak, R. M.: Care of tracheostomy, Canad. Anaesth. Soc. J. 12:386-397, 1965.

Conner, G. H., Hughes, D., Mills, M. J., Rittamanic, B., Sigg, L. V., and White, H. A.:

Tracheostomy: when it is needed, how it is done, postoperative care, care with a cuffed tube, Amer. J. Nurs. **72:**75-77, 1972.

Dyer, E. D., and Peterson, E.: Safe care of IPPB machines, Amer. J. Nurs. **71:**2163-2191, 1971.

Egan, D. F.: Fundamentals of respiratory therapy, ed. 2, St. Louis, 1973, The C. V. Mosby Co.

Flatter, P. A.: Hazards of oxygen therapy, Amer. J. Nurs. **68:**80-84, 1968.

Foley, M. F.: Pulmonary function testing, Amer. J. Nurs. **71:**1134-1139, 1971.

Foss, G.: Postural drainage, Amer. J. Nurs. **73:**666-669, 1973.

Gaskell, D. V., and Weber, B. A.: The Brompton hospital guide to chest physiotherapy, ed. 2, Oxford, England, 1973, Blackwell Scientific Publications, Ltd.

Grillo, H. C., Cooper, J. D., Giffin, B., and Pontoppidan, H.: A low-pressure cuff for tracheostomy tubes to minimize tracheal injury, J. Thorac. Cardiovas. Surg. **62:**898-906, 1971.

Hadly, F., and Bordicks, K. J.: Respiratory difficulty: causes and care, Amer. J. Nurs. **62:**64-67, 1962.

Hanamey, R.: Teaching patients breathing and coughing techniques, Nurs. Outlook **13:**58-59, 1965.

Helming, M., editor: Nursing in respiratory disease, Nurs. Clin. N. Amer. **68:**381-487, 1968.

Jacquette, G.: To reduce hazards of tracheal suctioning, Amer. J. Nurs. **71:**2362-2364, 1971.

Kurihara, M.: Assessment and maintenance of adequate respiration, Nurs. Clin. N. Amer. **68:**65-76, 1968.

Kurihara, M.: Postural drainage, clapping, and vibrating, Amer. J. Nurs. **65:**76-79, 1965.

Nett, L. M., and Petty, T. L.: Oxygen toxicity, Amer. J. Nurs. **73:**1556-1558, 1973.

Pitoral, E. F.: Laryngectomy, Amer. J. Nurs. **68:**780-786, 1968.

Robinson, F. N.: Nursing care of the patient with pulmonary emphysema, Amer. J. Nurs. **63:**92-96, 1963.

Seedor, M.: Therapy with oxygen and other gases: a programmed unit in fundamentals of nursing, Philadelphia, 1966, J. B. Lippincott Co.

Shafer, K. N., Sawyer, J. R., McCluskey, A. M., Beck, E. L., and Phipps, W. J.: Medical-surgical nursing, ed. 5, St. Louis, 1971, The C. V. Mosby Co.

Sovie, M., and Israel, J.: Use of the cuffed tracheostomy tube, Amer. J. Nurs. **67:**1854-1856, 1967.

Totman, L. E., and Lehman, R. H.: Tracheostomy care, Amer. J. Nurs. **64:**96-99, 1964.

Traver, G. A.: Assessment of the thorax and lungs, Amer. J. Nurs. **73:**466-471, 1971.

Wade, J. F.: Respiratory nursing care, physiology and technique, St. Louis, 1973, The C. V. Mosby Co.

4

Administration
of drugs

Interpretation and implementation of orders for drug therapy require considerable knowledge of the patient, the drug, and the plan of therapy. Knowledge of the nature of the drug, the usual range of dosage, dosage forms, methods and techniques of administration, expected effects, and symptoms of overdosage is needed. Reliable sources of information should be consulted whenever necessary. The reason the patient is receiving the drug, any history of previous drug reactions—including allergy and idiosyncrasy—and information transmitted by the physician is necessary to promote the patient's acceptance of drug therapy. Frequently the physician discusses the plan of therapy with the patient and his family. It is always wise to know what the patient has been told and his interpretation of this information. Special circumstances may restrict the information given to the patient. Such restriction precludes discussion of the therapy in these instances.

Clinical response to the therapy is used to alter drug therapy. For this reason, drugs are withheld prior to certain laboratory tests and in the presence of significant physiologic reactions. For example, morphine is withheld if the respirations are 12 or less per minute, and oral drugs are withheld if the swallowing reflex is absent or if the patient is persistently vomiting. Knowledge of these circumstances is used to guide the decision to consult the physician for further orders.

Thoughtful consideration of the patient's comfort will influence his acceptance of the therapy. The patient should be helped to a position that is comfortable and compatible with his condition and the method of planned administration. Unless it is contraindicated, a brief explanation should be offered of what is to be done, what is expected of the patient, the purpose of the medication, and any of its effects that might otherwise prove frightening. For example, the surgical patient who has epilepsy may be relieved to know that the injection he is receiving contains medication to control this condition, and a patient is less likely to be worried by discoloration of the sputum, stool, or urine if he has been forewarned. If the drug depresses the central nervous system appreciably, necessary limitations of activity should be explained and emphasized.

The patient's record should include notations concerning the drug and dose given, the method of administration, and the reaction to therapy. Additional records will be required if the drug is being investigated. Compliance with state and federal drug legislation necessitates additional records for narcotics and other habit-forming drugs.

Legally, the physician's order should state the preparation, dose, and method and frequency of administration. It may also contain additional directions. In all cases, the order is to be used intelligently, and the physician is to be consulted if a change in the order appears to be indicated.

The nurse may transcribe the order to a medication card, also called an identification card. Although these vary in form, they usually contain the full name of the patient, hospital room number, name of the drug, dose, times and method of administration, date the order was written, date the order expires when this is known, and initials of the person transcribing the order. This information should be rechecked prior to the preparation of each subsequent dose and should be used to identify the dose while it is being transported to the patient.

Frequently the exact times of administration become a nursing responsibility. Establishment of these times should be planned to provide for consistency and to promote the purpose of the therapy. Table 4-1 is planned to avoid meals served at 7:30 A.M., 11:30 A.M., and 5:30 P.M. A few drugs should be administered at mealtime, and sleep may need to be interrupted to maintain the blood level of certain drugs. No time is stated in the table for medications given at the hour of sleep, since this time is individualized, although it is frequently between 10 and 10:30 P.M.

A stock supply or an individual supply of medication is dispensed by the pharmacist and stored in a medication locker unless the patient is permitted to take the medication as the need arises. In this case, the physician may permit the medication to be left at the bedside.

Preparation of the single dose may involve mathematical computation, which becomes the nurse's responsibility. The use of prepackaged single doses of drugs tends to conserve nursing time and provides identification of the drug and the dose during transport.

TABLE 4-1. Suggested times for drug therapy*

Abbreviation	Interpretation	Time of administration
a.c.	Before meals	7, 11, 5
b.i.d.	Twice a day	9, 7
p.c.	After meals	9, 1, 7
p.r.n.	Whenever necessary	Dose may be repeated according to stated time interval
q.d.	Every day	9 a.m.
q.h.	Every hour	7, 8, 9, 10, etc.
q. 2 h.	Every 2 hours	7, 9, 11, etc.
q. 3 h.	Every 3 hours	6, 9, 12, 3, etc.
q. 4 h.	Every 4 hours	8, 12, 4, 8
q. 6 h.	Every 6 hours	6, 12, 6, 12
q.i.d.	Four times a day	9, 1, 4, 7
s.o.s.	If necessary	
stat.	Immediately	

*These are the suggested hours for drug administration if meals are served at 7:30, 11:30, and 5:30.

The name of the drug and the dose are printed on the wrapper of strip-packaged drugs; therefore the wrapper is left intact until the drug has been taken to the bedside and is about to be administered. Before preparing or administering a drug, the hands should be washed as clean as possible (Chapter 1).

After preparing the individual dose, the nurse is ready to administer the drug. Precautions must be taken to identify the drug and the patient by comparing the information on the medication card with the information found at the door, the bedside, and the identification bracelet. In addition, the nurse should ask the patient to state his name. The latter is useful when it is uncertain that the patient understands the nurse. If the patient is to continue taking the drug at home, it is important to teach him when and how to take it and to tell him what adverse effects should cause him to contact his physician. Teaching should begin early. It is helpful if written instructions to which the patient may refer are given to him.

Oral, sublingual, and buccal administration

The preparation of doses for oral, sublingual, and buccal administration is similar. Checking the label when the drug is removed from the shelf, before it is placed into the medication cup, and again when the stock medication is being returned to the shelf, is useful in making certain that the correct drug and dose are prepared. If the

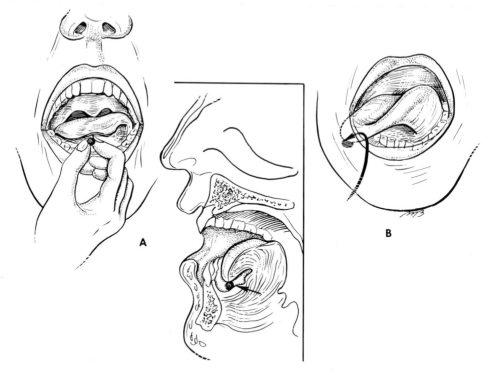

Fig. 4-1. Oral medications. **A,** Sublingual administration. **B,** Buccal administration.

medication is individually packaged, the wrapper enclosing it is imprinted with identifying information and should remain intact during transport to the bedside. Medications should be removed from a bottle without contact with the medication itself. Liquid preparations are measured into a calibrated medicine glass or with calibrated medicine droppers. For the former, the bottom of the meniscus rests on the calibration line. Manipulating the cover of the container enables the nurse to remove solid dosage forms without touching them.

Unless it is contraindicated, the patient should swallow oral medications with sufficient water to lubricate solid forms as well as to dissolve and dilute the drugs. Drugs that are harmful to the teeth are given through a straw. Preparations with disagreeable tastes should be disguised. The use of foods for this purpose should be avoided, if possible. If the patient is unable to swallow a solid medication, permission to use a more suitable form should be obtained.

Sublingual administration of drugs consists of placing the tablet beneath the patient's tongue and instructing him to retain it in this location until it has dissolved (Fig. 4-1, *A*). Buccal administration of drugs involves placing the tablet between the cheek and the teeth until it dissolves (Fig. 4-1, *B*).

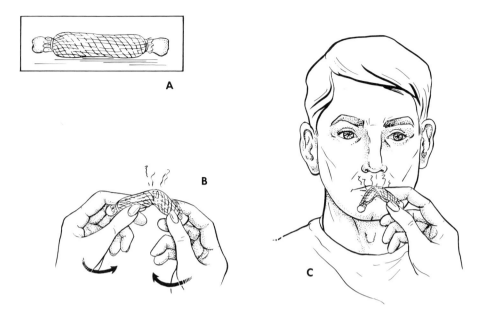

Fig. 4-2. Inhalation of vapors. **A,** A fragile ampule sheathed in loosely woven cloth. **B,** Crushing the ampule releases vapor. **C,** The saturated cloth is held near the patient's face for inhalation of vapor.

Inhalation

A few drugs are available in single, fragile ampules, also called pearls, which are sheathed in a loosely woven cloth covering (Fig. 4-2, *A*). These are crushed at the bedside (Fig. 4-2, *B*), and the saturated cloth is held near the patient's face so that he inhales the released vapor as it is passed back and forth (Fig. 4-2, *C*). Drugs such as amyl nitrite and spirits of ammonia act quickly, and overdosage is prevented by permitting only 2 to 3 inhalations per dose. Inhalation of nebulized drugs is discussed in Chapter 3.

Eyedrops and ointments

Care to instill the correct strength, amount, and drug into the correct eye is essential. The following abbreviations are commonly used to designate the eye to be treated: O.D., right eye; O.S., left eye; and O.U., both eyes. Prescribed strengths are necessarily dilute. Frequently a strength of less than 1% is used, although a few drugs may be used in a strength as high as 10%. Prior to instillation, the drug should be at room temperature and should be examined for signs of deterioration. Ointment dispensed in small tubes can be warmed

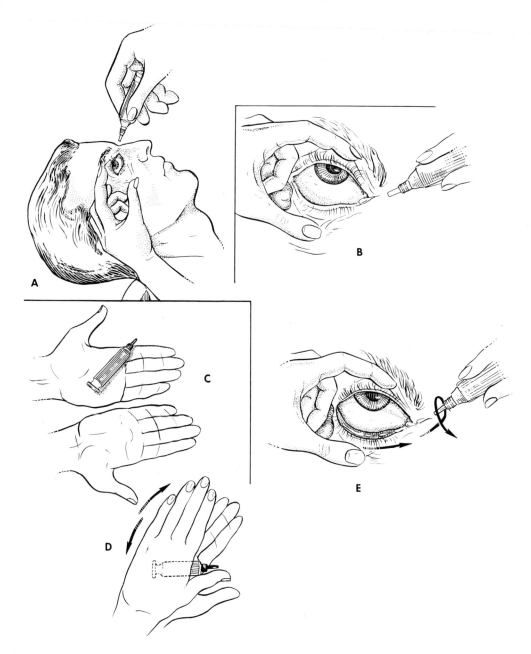

Fig. 4-3. Eyedrops and ointments. **A,** The cul-de-sac is exposed. **B,** Drops are placed in the lower cul-de-sac. The approach to the eye assists the patient in rotating his eye away from the point of instillation. **C,** Warming the ointment by holding the tube in the hand. **D,** The tube may be rolled gently between the hands to hasten the warming process. **E,** Ointment is squeezed from the tube into the cul-de-sac. The tube is rotated rapidly to detach the ointment from it. A cotton pledget held in the hand that retracts the lower lid is used to absorb excess drug.

by holding the tube in the hand for a few minutes (Fig. 4-3, C and D).

With the exception of suspensions, cloudiness or precipitation usually indicates deterioration of the drug. If cloudiness or sediment is seen in a solution that should be clear, a new supply of the medication should be obtained.

The patient should be positioned comfortably, either in a back-lying position with his face directed upward or in a sitting position with his head supported to maintain it in a chin-up positon. The cul-de-sac is exposed by gently retracting the tissue proximal to the lower eyelid (Fig. 4-3, A). This forms a pouch or sac into which the drops are instilled. The patient is instructed to look upward to move the sensitive cornea away from the point of instillation. Approaching the eye slowly from its inner angle across the bridge of the nose helps the patient to rotate his eye upward. The dispenser should not touch the eye, nor should the medication be placed directly on the cornea, since this causes a reflex squeezing together of the eyelids that can damage recent surgical repairs. The eyelid should be released slowly, and, unless contraindicated, the patient may be instructed to roll his eye a few times to ensure even distribution of the medication. A cotton pledget held in the hand that retracts the lower lid is used

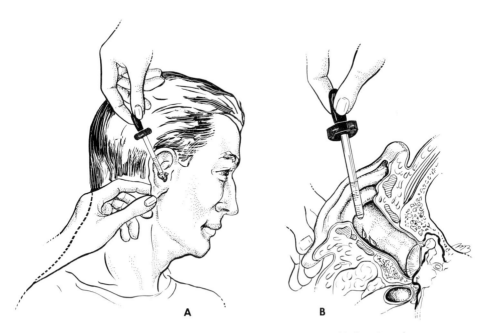

A   B

Fig. 4-4. Eardrops. **A,** The patient is asked to turn his head to the side so that the ear being treated faces upward. The external ear is manipulated gently to expose the external canal. **B,** The medication is directed toward the internal wall of the canal.

to absorb excess drug (Fig. 4-3, *A, B,* and *E*), or, if indicated, to remove excess drug. For this, the eye may be wiped gently from the inner to the outer canthus, that is, from the nose to the outside of the eye. When both eyes are medicated, clean pledgets should be used for each eye. This reduces the possibility of transferring organisms from one eye to the other.

Eardrops

Occasionally, instillation of eardrops is prescribed. To instill drops, the patient is asked to turn his head to the side so that the ear being treated faces upward. The external ear is then manipulated gently to expose the orifice of the external canal and drops the medicine against the internal wall of the canal (Fig. 4-4). Gentle retraction of the pinna of the external ear is directionally upward and posteriorly in a person over 3 years of age and downward and posteriorly in a child younger than 2 or 3 years.

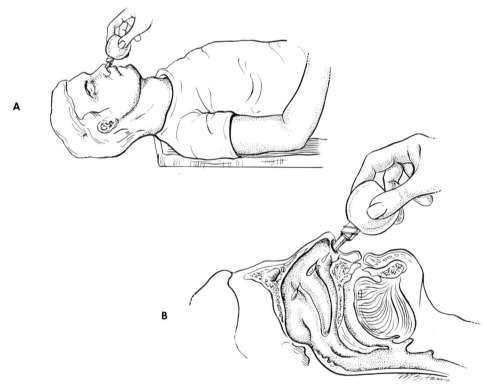

Fig. 4-5. Nose drops. **A,** The patient's head is tilted backward by elevating his shoulders. **B,** Cross section showing instillation of drops.

Nose drops

Infrequently, nasal instillations are prescribed. When drops are to be instilled, the patient's head is tilted backward by elevating his shoulders with pillows (Fig. 4-5, *A*). Unless doing so is contraindicated, the patient may lower his head over the edge of the bed, or, if he is in a sitting position, he may hyperextend his neck. The patient is instructed to breathe through his mouth while the drops are being instilled (Fig. 4-5, *B*). He should retain the position used for instillation for about 5 minutes to permit the medication to spread throughout the nasal cavities. If a nasal spray is prescribed, the patient is placed in a sitting position. Expectoration of medicine that enters the pharynx after instillation is desirable.

Genitourinary tract instillations

Prior to instilling medications into the genitourinary tract, the patient is assisted to a back-lying position with her legs flexed and partially adducted (Fig. 4-6, *A*). A lithotomy position or a modified

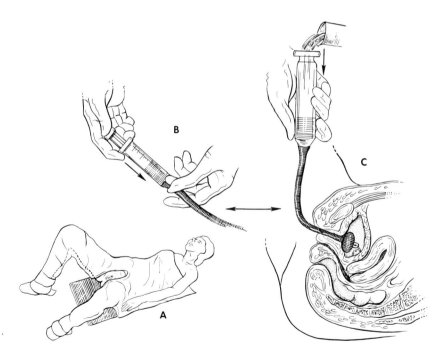

Fig. 4-6. Bladder instillation. **A,** Position of the patient. **B,** Medication may be instilled through the catheter with a syringe, or, **C,** it may be poured into a funnel attached to the catheter.

133

Sims' position may be used, if preferred. A drape is arranged so that the area is exposed. After washing her hands, putting on sterile gloves, and cleansing the area, the nurse locates the orifice and administers the drug. Every effort must be made to prevent introduction of organisms into the urethra and bladder.

Knowledge that a prescribed drug is likely to discolor clothing is useful in guiding the patient's choice of clothing after this treatment; sanitary pads may be provided to protect clothing from permanent staining.

Only mild medications are used because the mucous membranes of the genitourinary tract are sensitive. Medications can be absorbed systemically from the urethra and vagina; the amount of absorption increases when the mucous membranes have been traumatized.

BLADDER

Catheterization precedes instillation of medications into the bladder. Catheterization is described in Chapter 9 and illustrated in Fig. 9-2. After the bladder has been drained, the catheter is kept in place, and a sterile funnel through which the medication can be poured is connected to it (Fig. 4-6, C). Although the drug can be injected with a syringe, this must be done slowly and gently. The rate at which the injection is done should approximate the time required for the medication to flow into the bladder by gravity. This is controlled by rotating the plunger of the syringe rather than by pushing the plunger forward (Fig. 4-6, B). The catheter is withdrawn, and pressure is applied to the meatus with a soft sterile sponge. The patient should be instructed to retain the medicine for the designated period of time, which is frequently 20 to 30 minutes.

URETHRA

Often a urethral suppository is prescribed for administration immediately after bladder instillation. If the suppository only is ordered, the patient is prepared as described for bladder instillation immediately after she has emptied her bladder. After cleansing the meatus and adjacent areas, the tip of the suppository is lubricated with water or a water-soluble lubricant and inserted into the urethra (Fig. 4-7, A and B). Immediately after inserting the suppository, firm pressure may be applied to the meatus with a sterile sponge until the suppository melts or the spasms subside (Fig. 4-7, C); this is often about 10 minutes. The patient should be instructed to refrain from voiding for 15 to 30 minutes, if possible, because voiding will remove the medication. Fig. 4-7, D, shows the insertion of a suppository supplied in an applicator.

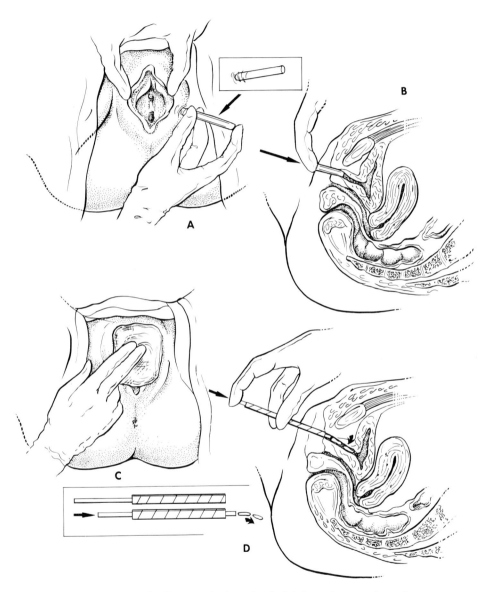

Fig. 4-7. Urethral suppositories. **A,** A lubricated suppository is inserted into the urethra, observing sterile precautions. **B,** Cross section showing insertion of the suppository. **C,** A sterile sponge is held against the meatus until spasms subside. **D,** A suppository supplied in an applicator is inserted by pushing it through the applicator with the plunger. Inset shows suppository supplied in an applicator.

135

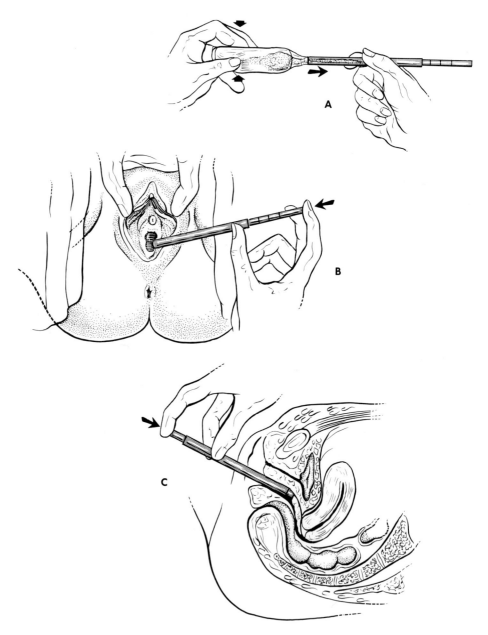

Fig. 4-8. Vaginal instillation. **A,** A vaginal applicator is filled directly from the tube of medication. **B,** The applicator is inserted into the vagina. **C,** As the plunger is pushed forward, medication is deposited, and the applicator is withdrawn.

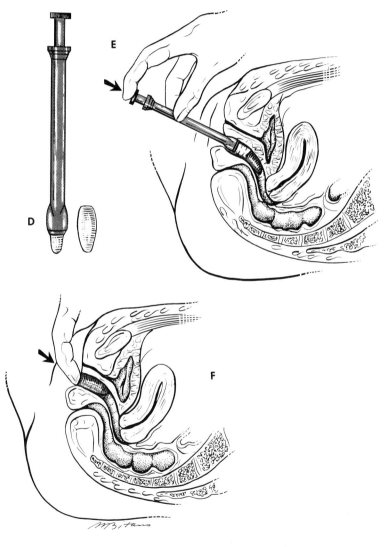

Fig. 4-8, cont'd. D, A device for inserting vaginal tablets. **E,** After insertion of the device, the tablet is deposited by pushing the plunger forward. **F,** A suppository may be inserted manually, using the index finger to position it.

137

VAGINA

The patient should void prior to vaginal instillation and should maintain a recumbent position after instillation. This must be explained to the ambulatory patient. Ideally, she should be told some time prior to instillation so that she can plan her activities accordingly. A glove is worn on the hand that is used to expose the orifice. If the medication is inserted manually, gloves are worn on both hands. Unless otherwise specified, clean technique is permissible.

Vaginal applicators are filled with medicated creams or jellies directly from a tube (Fig. 4-8, *A*). The filled applicator is inserted into the vagina to a depth of $1\frac{1}{2}$ to 2 inches (Fig. 4-8, *B*). As the plunger is pushed forward, depositing the medication, the applicator is withdrawn (Fig. 4-8, *C*). Immediately after use, the reusable applicator is disassembled and washed. Initial rinsing with cold water removes protein without causing coagulation. Disposable applicators are available.

Special devices for the insertion of vaginal tablets are available (Fig. 4-8, *D* and *E*). A suppository may be inserted by grasping it between the thumb and forefinger and then pushing it into the vagina until it is deposited near the posterior aspect of the cervix (Fig. 4-8, *F*).

Rectal instillations

After assisting the patient to a comfortable side-lying position with the lower leg extended and the upper leg flexed, the upper buttock is retracted to expose the anal area (Fig. 4-9, *A*). After unwrapping the suppository (Fig. 4-9, *B*), it may be lubricated with a water-soluble lubricant. Some suppositories are self-lubricating. When inserting the suppository, the nurse should either protect her thumb and forefinger with finger cots or wear a glove (Fig. 4-9, *C* and *D*). The suppository is pushed forward until it passes the anal sphincter. The administration of medicated enemas is prescribed occasionally. Fig. 8-1 shows the administration of a disposable enema. The purpose of the rectal instillation and the length of time it is to be retained should be explained to the patient.

Injections

The prevention of infection must accompany administration of drugs by injection. Both the equipment and the drug must be sterile. After the site for injection has been selected, the nurse cleanses an area about 2 inches square, usually with 70% alcohol, benzalkonium

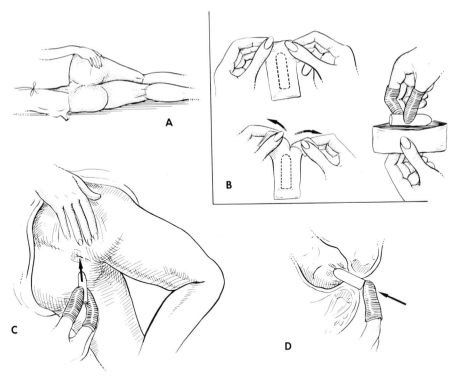

Fig. 4-9. Rectal suppositories. **A,** Position of the patient. **B,** The wrapper containing the suppository is opened and the suppository removed. **C,** The suppository is inserted. **D,** Cross section showing insertion of the suppository. The suppository will be advanced beyond the anal sphincter.

chloride, or benzine. Cleansing with a circular motion proceeds from the center of the site outward.

Disposable equipment reduces transmission of pathogens. This is essential if causative organisms of certain diseases such as viral hepatitis are present.

The preparation of the syringe and needle varies with the method of packaging. Individually packaged needles and syringes can be attached to each other without removing the needle from its container. Prefilled syringes may be supplied in a completely assembled state, or various amounts of assembling may be necessary. Some drugs are supplied in cartridges (Fig. 4-10). Labeling on these provides additional identification of the drug and the dose. The manufacturer usually supplies directions concerning the assembly of equipment.

SELECTION OF NEEDLE

Needle size is selected according to the desired depth of insertion and the viscosity of the drug that must pass through the needle. The

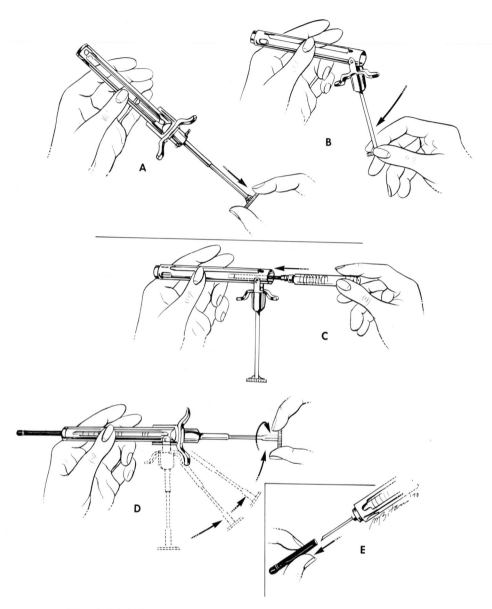

Fig. 4-10. Tubex sterile cartridge-needle unit. Prefilled or empty sterile cartridges may be used. Following assembly, the prefilled cartridge is ready to be injected; the prescribed dose must be drawn into an empty cartridge from a vial or an ampule. **A,** The barrel of the syringe is held in one hand and the plunger pulled back with the other hand. **B,** The plunger is pulled downward until it locks at a right angle to the barrel. **C,** A sterile cartridge is inserted into the barrel, needle end first. The cartridge is secured by turning it clockwise. **D,** The plunger is swung into place and the end of the plunger turned until it is fitted tightly onto the threaded end of the cartridge. **E,** The sheath covering the needle is removed prior to injection. (Courtesy Wyeth Laboratories, Philadelphia.)

length of the needle is relative to the depth of tissue that must be penetrated. A longer needle is used for deep intramuscular injections than for subcutaneous injections; a longer needle is needed for obese patients than for those who are thin. A viscous drug requires a needle with a large bore; a drug of waterlike consistency passes easily through a small needle without clogging. The bore, or inside diameter of the needle, increases in size as the gauge number becomes smaller. Thus a 13-gauge needle has a large bore and a 27-gauge needle has a small bore. As a guide, the size commonly used for subcutaneous injection is 2 cm. (¾ inch) long and 24- or 25-gauge; for intramuscular injection a needle 1 to 2 inches long and 19- to 22-gauge is selected.

SELECTION OF SYRINGE

The volume of drug to be injected influences the choice of syringe according to its size and calibration. Measurement of a small dose is most accurate if the syringe is of small diameter. For many injections, a 2 or 3 ml. syringe calibrated in minims as well as milliliters (cubic centimeters) is used; a 1 ml. tuberculin syringe calibrated in minims is used for small doses; and syringes calibrated in units are used for administration of insulin. In the latter case, the syringe should be calibrated with the same number of units per milliliter as the insulin preparation. The trend is to use 100-unit insulin syringes and 100-unit insulin preparations.

PREPARATION OF DOSE

Unless prefilled syringes are used, the dose is withdrawn from a sealed container. Throughout preparation, contamination of the drug is prevented by keeping sterile the needle, the inside of the syringe, and the part of the plunger that will be enclosed by the barrel of the syringe. In addition, the dose must be measured accurately.

Vial. If the drug is dispensed in a vial, the rubber stopper is cleansed with an antiseptic sponge before introducing the needle (Fig. 4-11, *A*). The antiseptic usually used is 70% alcohol. The plunger of the syringe is withdrawn until the tip of the plunger rests on the calibration that indicates the amount of solution needed (Fig. 4-11, *B*). The needle, which has been attached to the syringe, is inserted through the center of the rubber stopper, and the plunger is pushed forward, injecting into the vial a volume of air equal to the volume of solution that is to be withdrawn (Fig. 4-11, *C* and *D*). This increases the pressure within the vial, facilitating withdrawal of the dose. The vial and syringe are inverted, and the designated dose is withdrawn (Fig. 4-11, *E*). After preparing the dose, the needle is sheathed in a sterile protector during transport to the pa-

141

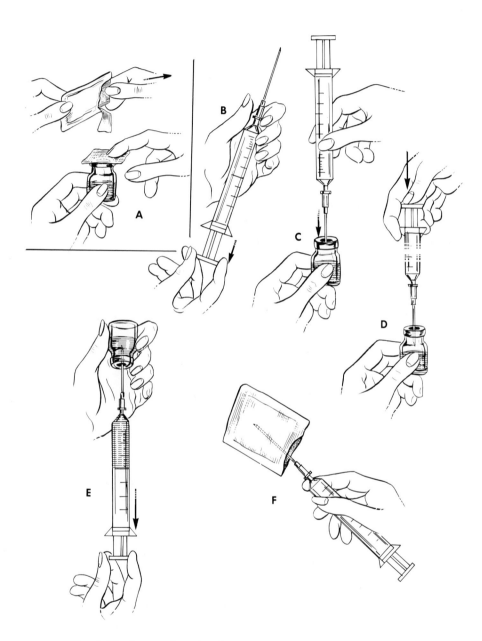

Fig. 4-11. Preparation of a dose from a vial. **A,** The rubber stopper is cleansed with an alcohol sponge. **B,** Air equal to the prescribed dose is drawn into the syringe. **C,** The needle is inserted into the vial. **D,** The air is injected into the vial. **E,** The vial is inverted to withdraw solution. **F,** The needle is sheathed in a sterile wrapper for transport.

tient care center. A sterile package containing an alcohol sponge will serve this purpose if the needle is not supplied in an individual sterile container (Fig. 4-11, *F*).

If two drugs are to be mixed in one syringe, every precaution must be taken to prevent contamination of one drug with the other. For example, when a mixture of insulin preparations is desired, a volume of air equal to the dose is injected into the vial of modified insulin and the needle is withdrawn; this procedure is repeated with the unmodified preparation, that is, regular insulin. The desired amount of unmodified insulin and then the modified insulin is drawn into the syringe. Next, air is drawn into the syringe, and it is tipped or rotated vertically so that the air bubble moves back and forth, mixing the solution. This should be done slowly and gently.

The pharmacist dispenses in crystalline form drugs that deteriorate rapidly after being placed in solution. Immediately before their use dry, soluble drugs are mixed with the amount and kind of diluent recommended by the manufacturer. Occasionally some agitation is necessary to dissolve the solid particles. Rolling the vial back and forth between the palms of the hands mixes the solution without producing air bubbles that interfere with accurate measurement. Repeatedly withdrawing the solution and reinjecting it forcefully against particles adhering to the wall of the vial tends to hasten solution, although repeated withdrawal and reinjection produces froth.

Ampule. Before breaking a hermetically sealed ampule, the apex of the ampule is tapped, causing solution trapped by the constriction in the neck to flow into the body of the ampule (Fig. 4-12, *A*). If the ampule is not designed with a break line, one is formed by drawing a file across the constriction several times. The same method may be used to remove the filed top of the ampule as is used to break an ampule with a ready-break line (Fig. 4-12, *B*). It is advisable to protect the hands during the breaking of the ampule by enclosing the area of the break line in alcohol sponges, pledgets, or gauze. Wiping the neck of the ampule with an antiseptic before breaking it will help in removing any external contamination.

If the needle used to withdraw the drug is sufficiently long, the ampule need not be inverted; however, the needle must not be permitted to touch contaminated parts of the ampule (Fig. 4-12, *C*). If the ampule is inverted to withdraw the solution (Fig. 4-12, *D*), care must be used to prevent contamination of the needle by the hands. Injecting air into the ampule is avoided because it would displace the drug, causing it to drip from the ampule and resulting in its loss. Unused solution should be discarded. The needle is sheathed in a sterile container during transport (Fig. 4-12, *E*).

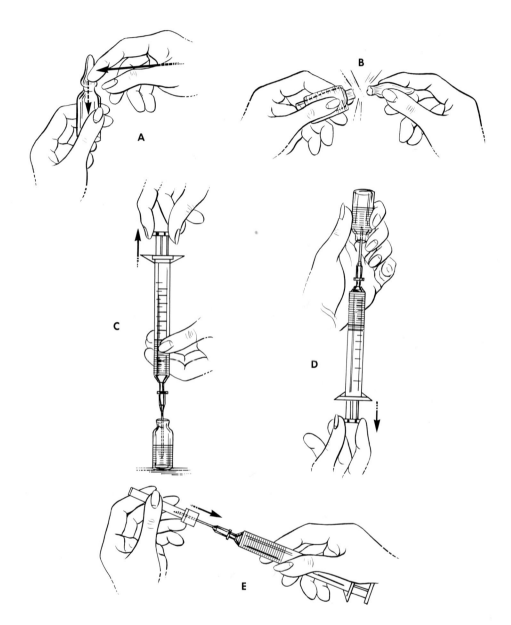

Fig. 4-12. Preparation of a dose from an ampule. **A,** Tapping the top of the ampule causes solution to collect in the body of the ampule. **B,** The ampule is opened by exerting pressure with the thumb and forefinger placed on each side of the constriction. **C,** If the needle is sufficiently long, the drug may be withdrawn without inverting the ampule. **D,** When a short needle is used, the nurse inverts the ampule. **E,** The needle is sheathed in a sterile container during transport.

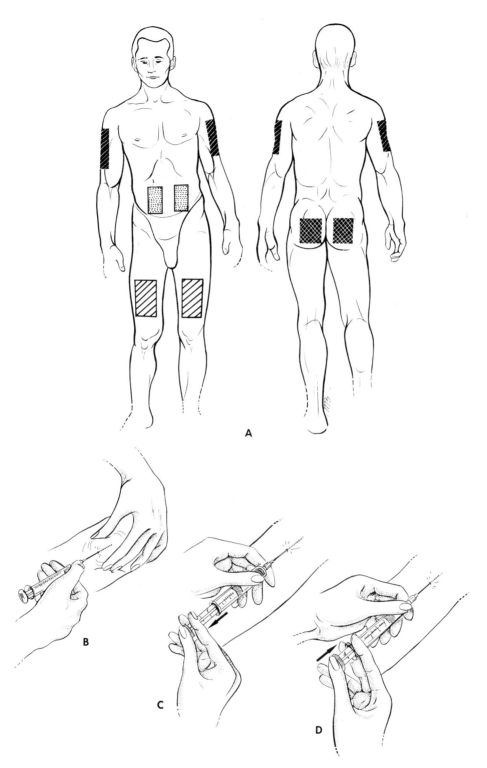

Fig. 4-13. Subcutaneous injection. **A,** Possible sites for injection. **B,** A method of tensing tissue during insertion of the needle; the area is cleansed just before the tissue is tensed. **C,** After insertion of the needle, the plunger is withdrawn slightly to determine that the needle is not located within a vessel. **D,** The drug is injected by pushing the plunger forward.

Continued.

SUBCUTANEOUS INJECTION

The sites most frequently used for subcutaneous injection are the upper arms and thighs, although other areas such as the abdomen may also be used (Fig. 4-13, *A*). If repeated injections are given, the site of injection should be rotated so that each succeeding injection is about 2 inches away from the previous site. A definite plan for rotating sites of injection and a record of the site injected is necessary if fibrosis is to be prevented.

After preparing the drug, the site is cleansed and grasped between the thumb and forefinger to tense it (Fig. 4-13, *B*). This also lessens the sensitivity of the site. The needle is inserted at an angle of about 45 to 60 degrees, piercing the skin quickly and advancing steadily to minimize pain. After aspirating to determine that the needle has not inadvertently entered a blood vessel (Fig. 4-13, *C*), the drug is injected slowly (Fig. 4-13, *D*). To do this may require changing the position of the hands. Taking care to minimize the

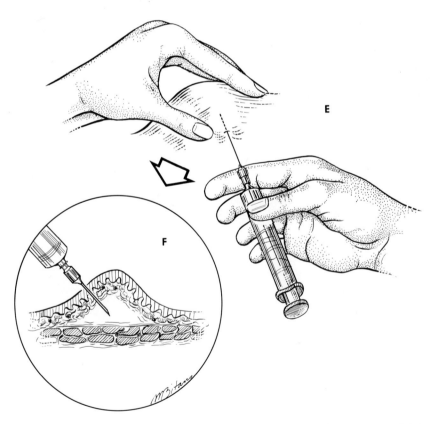

Fig. 4-13, cont'd. E, This method of tensing tissues is used for injection of irritating drugs such as insulin and heparin. **F,** Cross section showing relationship of the needle to the tissues.

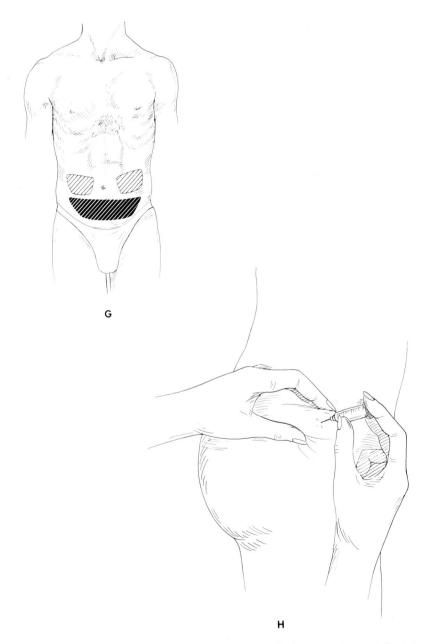

G

H

Fig. 4-13, cont'd. G, Areas on the abdominal wall that may be used for injection of heparin. The lower, darkly shaded area is preferred; the smaller, lightly shaded areas may be used if necessary. **H,** Technique of injecting heparin near the iliac crest. Note that the tissue has been grasped so that it forms a roll; this helps to ensure deposition of the drug into the deep subcutaneous tissues.

147

patient's discomfort by holding the needle steady is essential. When the drug has been injected, the needle is withdrawn and the area is massagèd with a sterile alcohol sponge.

If the drug to be injected is known to irritate the tissues, a modified technique is used to ensure deposition of the drug in the deep subcutaneous tissues. The tissue overlying the injection site is grasped with the thumb and forefinger to form an elevated roll (Fig. 4-13, *E*). After the site is cleansed, the needle is inserted before the hold on the tissue is relaxed. Opinions vary as to the angle at which the needle should be inserted. Often it is inserted at a right angle to the thumb (Fig. 4-13, *F*), but it may be inserted perpendicular to the tissue mass when drugs such as insulin, emetine hydrochloride, or sodium heparin injection are being administered. The most commonly used sites for injecting heparin are located on the abdomen (Fig. 4-13, *G*). A small area located above the iliac crest may also be used (Fig. 4-13, *H*).

INTRAMUSCULAR INJECTION

Selection of sites. Selection of sites for intramuscular injection frequently includes gluteal tissues, and, less often, the thighs and the upper arm. Various methods of selecting the site of injection have been described and may be used.

Posterior gluteal area. When the injection is to be given into the posterior gluteal area, maximum relaxation of the muscles can be achieved by positioning the patient correctly. Ideally, the patient lies on his abdomen with his toes pointed inward (Fig. 4-14, *A*). A pillow placed beneath the lower legs adds to the comfort of this position and increases relaxation. The arms may dangle over the edge of the table, or the patient may extend them at his side. When this position is uncomfortable or impossible, the patient may lie on his side with the lower leg extended and the upper leg flexed. The injection is given in the upper, outer gluteal area. It is inadvisable for the patient to stand during injection because this tends to increase tenseness of the muscles and permits a tensing reaction when the needle is inserted or when the drug is injected. Increased discomfort plus the possibility of needle breakage in a muscular person results from the increased muscular tension. Both the face-lying and the side-lying positions prevent the patient from seeing the approach of the needle. This is said to be of psychologic benefit.

The gluteal area is exposed and divided into quadrants. This area must not be equated with the buttocks. Instead, the anatomic area is determined by careful palpation of the landmarks. The gluteal area is bounded by the iliac crest, the anterior iliac spine, the inferior gluteal fold, and the division between the buttocks (Fig. 4-14, *B*). If, on palpation, gross deformity of the skeletal structures

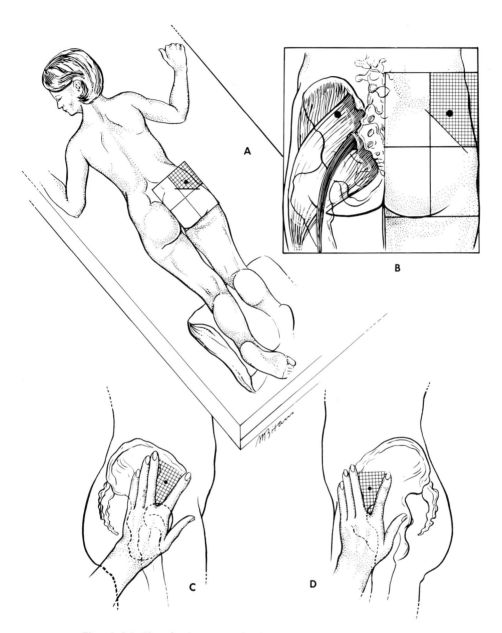

Fig. 4-14. Sites for intramuscular injection. **A,** Position of the patient when the posterior gluteal area is used. **B,** Diagram showing the anatomy of the posterior gluteal area and the method of finding the injection site. The large dot indicates the site of injection. **C,** Location of the site for injection into the right ventrogluteal area. **D,** Location of the site for injection into the left ventrogluteal area.

Continued.

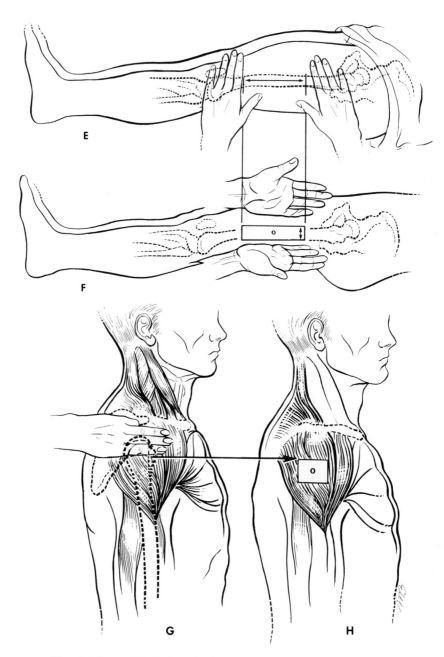

Fig. 4-14, cont'd. E, Location of length of the boundary for injection into the vastus lateralis. **F,** Location of breadth of the boundary for injection into the vastus lateralis. **G,** Location of the site for injection into the deltoid is two to three fingerbreadths below the acromion process. **H,** Injection should be made above the groove inferior to the deltoid.

appears to exist, the clinical specialist's or the physician's assistance in locating a safe site for injection should be sought. After the gluteal area has been outlined, it is divided into four quadrants with intersecting vertical and horizontal lines.

The injection is given in the upper outer quadrant. To be certain that this area has been identified correctly so that the sciatic nerve is well removed from the point of injection, a line is drawn from the posterior superior iliac crest to the head of the femur (Fig. 4-14, *B*). Injection lateral and superior to this line will be within the gluteal mass and will not traumatize the sciatic nerve.

Ventrogluteal site. Another site for intramuscular injection is the ventrogluteal site. This location is preferred for intramuscular injection in children and is recommended by some physicians for injection in adults. Major vessels and nerves are not found in this area if it is outlined properly.

The patient assumes either a back-lying or face-lying position for use of this site. The area is located by any of three methods. If the right ventrogluteal site is to be used, the nurse places the tip of the index finger of the left hand on the anterior superior iliac spine and rests the left hand on the hip, with the tips of the other fingers pointing toward the patient's head. The index and middle fingers are spread as far apart as possible, thus forming a V (Fig. 4-14, *C*). Injection is made between these two fingers and below the iliac crest. If the left ventrogluteal area is used, the nurse places the middle finger on the anterior superior iliac crest and moves the index finger away from it to form the V (Fig. 4-14, *D*). Another method of locating this site involves drawing imaginary lines from the anterior and posterior edges of the iliac crest to the greater trochanter. These lines also form a triangle within which the injection is given.

Vastus lateralis. The patient may assume a back-lying, face-lying, or sitting position when the vastus lateralis area is used. The area for injection approximates the distance of a hand breadth below the head of the greater trochanter and a handbreath above the knee (Fig. 4-14, *E*), the midanterior thigh, and the midlateral thigh (Fig. 4-14, *F*). The needle is inserted to a depth of 1 inch.

Deltoid area. Injection into the deltoid area is likely to produce more pain than at other sites of intramuscular injection. The area cannot be exposed satisfactorily by rolling up a sleeve; the gown or shirt should be removed. Injection should be 2 to 3 fingerbreadths below the acromion process (Fig. 4-14, *G*) and above the groove inferior to the deltoid (Fig. 4-14, *H*). Injection into the middle or lower third of the upper arm is avoided because it might injure the radial nerve.

Technique of intramuscular injection. After the site has been selected and cleansed, the tissue is stretched, reducing the amount
Text continued on p. 156.

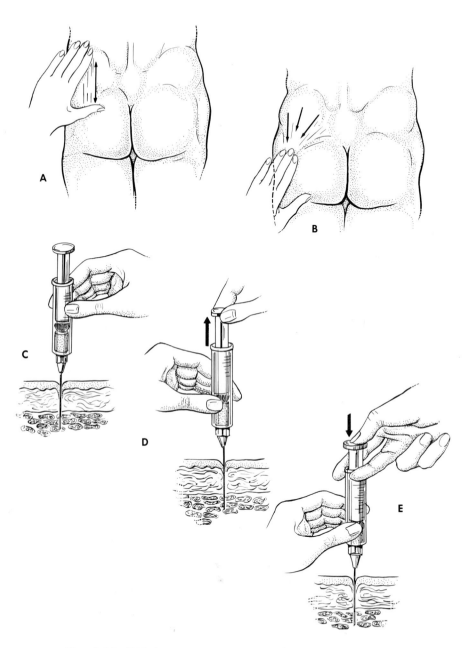

Fig. 4-15. Technique of intramuscular injection. **A,** One method of stretching the tissues. **B,** An alternate method of stretching the tissues. **C,** The needle is inserted at a right angle to the tissues. **D,** The plunger is withdrawn slightly to make certain that the needle is not located within a blood vessel. **E,** The solution is injected. Note the air bubble at the top of the solution, which clears the shaft of the needle of residual drug.

TABLE 4-2. Intramuscular administration of drugs

Technique	Problem	Solution or explanation
Establish rapport with the patient and explain the nature of the treatment.	Patient may dread injections; fear causes muscular tension to increase.	The patient's tension may be relieved by the nurse's manner and explanation of the care.
Select the equipment needed (a 19- to 22-gauge, 1- to 2-inch long needle, alcohol wipes, and identification card).	Nonsterile equipment contributes to infection.	Sterile, disposable equipment reduces transmission of organisms and is preferred.
Arrange to be free of interruptions and check the information on the identification card against the physician's orders.	Errors in medication carry legal responsibility.	Interruptions are distracting; verification of information minimizes errors; if the physician's order differs from the information on the identification card or is not understood, clarification must be sought.
Select and prepare the drug, comparing the label on the drug with the information on the identification card three times (when selecting the drug, before removing the drug from its container, and when replacing or discarding the container).	Error may occur in selection of the correct drug or dose for the patient.	Repeated checking helps to prevent errors and ensures accuracy.
Transport the prepared medication, alcohol wipe, and identification card to the nursing care center, keeping the card with the medication at all times.	Interruptions may disrupt one's thinking and prevent accurate recall of the contents of the syringe and the identification of the patient for whom the medication is intended.	Identification of the medication, dose, the person for whom it is intended, and his location in the hospital ensures administration of the drug to the correct person.
Check the hospital room number with the number on the identification card, check the chart to be sure the drug has not already been given, check the patient's name against his identification band, and ask him to state his name.	Patients sometimes respond to names other than their own or are unable to identify themselves appropriately.	Accuracy of administration of medication is a nursing responsibility.
Position the patient correctly and comfortably and expose the site for injection.	Difficulty inserting the needle may occur; pain may occur when the injection is given.	Relaxation of the muscles through correct positioning prevents pain.
Select the area and palpate it to locate areas of pain or nodules.	Penetration of sore muscles may cause severe pain. Injection into a nodule interferes with absorption of the drug.	Avoid sites that are tender or that have been injected repeatedly; select a site free of nodules, large vessels, or nerves.

Continued.

TABLE 4-2. Intramuscular administration of drugs—cont'd

Technique	Problem	Solution or explanation
Cleanse an area about 2 inches in diameter with alcohol sponge and friction.	Infections and abscesses have been known to occur after an injection.	Cleansing with a circular motion from the center outward may diminish the possibility of introducing infectious agents.
Stretch the tissue or pull it away from the site of injection.	Medication may leak into the subcutaneous tissue through the needle track; this may cause discoloration of the tissue, pain, and a change in the rate of absorption.	Displacing the tissue to one side during injection will allow the subcutaneous layer to seal the medication into the muscle. Stretching the skin or pulling it taut allows the needle to penetrate the skin more easily.
Unsheath the needle and leave a small air bubble in the syringe.	Some drugs continue to produce irritation in the tissues after injection.	An air bubble will clear the needle of drug and will help to keep medication from being dragged through tissue.
Divert the patient's attention and insert the needle deep into the tissue with a quick thrust, holding the needle perpendicular to the tissue.	Patients who concentrate on the injection appear to experience more pain than those who are concerned with other thoughts.	Having the patient take a deep breath, converse, wiggle his toes, etc., distracts his attention from the injection.
Release the grasp on the tissue and pull back on the plunger of the syringe to be certain that the needle is not in a blood vessel; if blood is aspirated, withdraw the needle and reinsert it.	It is possible, although unlikely, that the needle will enter a blood vessel.	Drugs intended for intramuscular injection may be harmful if given intravenously; intravenous administration of drugs gives immediate absorption and action.
Inject the contents of the syringe slowly.	Rapid injection may cause discomfort.	Slow injection allows the solution to disperse into the tissues.
Hold an alcohol sponge near the needle, exerting enough pressure on it to prevent pulling of the tissue as the needle is withdrawn.	Some pain is felt as the needle passes through the tissues.	Pulling on the skin as the needle is withdrawn increases the amount of pain because of the disruption of nerve endings.
Apply pressure over the injection site with an alcohol sponge if bleeding occurs.	Bleeding may occur if the needle passes through a capillary, and this is alarming to patients.	Direct pressure will stop the bleeding; an explanation of the reason for applying pressure allays the patient's worries.
Massage the area for 30 to 60 seconds unless massage is contra-indicated.	Physical discomfort may occur at the site of the injection.	Massage reduces pain, discoloration, and induration, and alters absorption rate. It is contra-indicated after injection of drugs containing heavy metals.

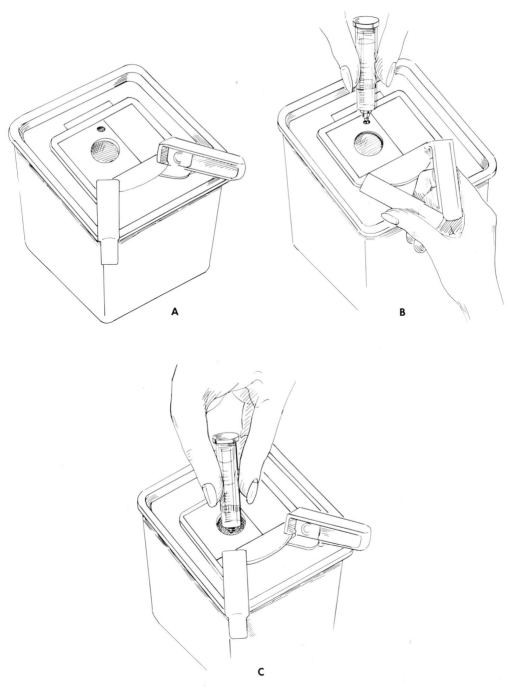

Fig. 4-16. Destruction of needles and syringes. **A,** View of a commercial device for destruction of syringes and needles. The top lifts off the box for emptying and cleaning purposes. **B,** The needle, still attached to the syringe, is inserted as far as possible into the small opening. Holding the syringe steady with one hand while squeezing the handles together rapidly shears the shaft of the needle, which drops into the container. **C,** The syringe is destroyed by inserting its tip into the larger opening and holding it steady with one hand while squeezing the handles together. The tip of the syringe will drop into the receptacle when it is sheared from the syringe. The remainder of the syringe is then discarded. (Courtesy Becton-Dickinson, Rutherford, N. J.)

155

of subcutaneous fat that must be penetrated and ensuring penetration into the muscle. Pressure exerted in opposite directions with the thumb and forefinger will serve this purpose (Fig. 4-15, *A*). Another method, sometimes referred to as the Z track technique, involves pulling the tissue in one direction only, so that an outline of a Z is formed (Fig. 4-15, *B*). This slides the layer of subcutaneous tissue to one side during the injection. When it is released after the injection, the tissue slides back into position. This prevents the medication from flowing into the upper layers of tissue and promotes absorption of the drug.

The needle is introduced through the skin at a 90-degree angle with a quick thrust and then advanced as necessary. It should not be advanced as far as the hub. The nurse withdraws the plunger slightly to be certain that the needle has not been placed within a blood vessel. Then the solution is injected slowly, followed by a small bubble of air previously drawn into the syringe (Fig. 4-15, *C* to *E*). The air is used to clear the needle shaft of drug that could theoretically be deposited in the overlying tissues as the needle is withdrawn. After the injection, the site should be massaged.

Massaging the site of injection for a minimum of 30 to 60 seconds reduces pain, discoloration, and induration. Massage is contraindicated by the nature of certain preparations, particularly those containing heavy metals. The manufacturer's brochure should identify this contraindication. If capillary bleeding occurs when the needle is withdrawn, the nurse should apply direct pressure to the site with a sterile sponge until the bleeding stops. Patients appreciate an explanation of the purpose of applying pressure or massaging the area. These measures reduce physical and mental discomfort to the patient and help maintain the tissues in a healthy state, thus preserving a maximum area into which future injections can be given (Table 4-2).

DESTRUCTION OF SYRINGES AND NEEDLES

After use, disposable syringes and needles are discarded. The method of discard should prevent reuse of this equipment as well as injury to those who must dispose of it. Shearing the needle from the hub and cutting off the tip of the syringe with a device that meets these objectives is illustrated in Fig. 4-16.

Questions for discussion and exploration

1. When you bring a capsule to Mrs. R., she says, "Oh, the doctor must have ordered a new drug for me!" If you are not aware that this is a new drug for Mrs. R., what might her comment indicate? What might you say if you know that this is a new drug for her?

2. To disguise the bitter taste of codeine you place the tablet inside a

gelatin capsule. Mrs. T. takes the capsule but telephones the supervisor to report that she cannot sleep because the nurse gave her the wrong pain medication. How might you have prevented this situation from developing?

3. Mrs. G. finds it impossible to swallow capsules and complains about the bitter-tasting particles of the drug lodging beneath her dentures when she chews the capsules. What possible alterations can be made in the method of administration that will make taking the drug more pleasant? What facts must you know to make your decision?

4. Mr. N. refuses to take his sleeping medication at the time you bring it to him. He tells you to set it on his bedside table and he will take it when he is ready to go to sleep. You are extremely busy carrying for six other patients who need considerable nursing care. How should you respond to his request?

5. When you bring an injection to Mrs. C.'s room, she begins to cry and tearfully says, "Not another injection. I just can't take another one." How can this individual be helped? The drug is an antibiotic.

6. Miss Y. shows you a large black and blue area near her hip where she says she was given an injection. She tells you it hurts so much that she cannot walk and that the person who gave her the injection shouldn't be allowed to ever give another to anyone. How can you safely respond to her and what can you do to make her more comfortable? What records and reports need to be made?

7. Miss Q., age 14, has been admitted to the hospital for control of her diabetes. Prepare a teaching plan that you might use to help her learn how to measure, administer, and store her insulin. What points must be emphasized in relation to insulin dosage, measurement, administration, and diet?

8. Miss Y.'s mother needs to know when and how to administer glucagon. Although the opportunity to administer this drug to her son never arises during his hospitalization, what must Mrs. Y. be taught and how?

9. Mr. Z. will be maintained on a regimen of psychotherapeutic drugs after his dismissal from the psychiatric unit. What must be and his family know about the drugs that he is taking? If Mrs. Z. comments that she wonders how they'll manage because Mr. Z. has always been reluctant to take any medicine, even aspirin, what is she indicating, and what are your responsibilities?

10. Mrs. S. is to continue treatment of vaginitis at home with the aid of a medicated suppository daily. What knowledge, understanding, and planning does she need?

11. You are asked to instill a liquid drug preparation into Mrs. G.'s bladder. Mrs. G. has an indwelling catheter in place. How would you carry out this technique, maintaining the sterility of the bladder and making certain that the drug is retained for a period of 20 minutes?

12. Mrs. K. is in the terminal phases of cancer of the spine and is receiving injections of dihydromorphinone (Dilaudid) and prometha-

zine hydrochloride (Phenergan) every 2 to 3 hours. His muscles have wasted and are lumpy from previous injections. The promethazine hydrochloride is supplied in sterile cartridge (Tubex), but the dihydromorphinone must be withdrawn from a vial. What possible sites might you use for giving both drugs? What additional factors might be considered that could promote comfort?

Selected references

Bergersen, B. S.: Pharmacology in nursing, ed. 12, St. Louis, 1973, The C. V. Mosby Co.

Brandt, P., Smith, M., Ashburn, S., and Graves, J.: IM injections in children, Amer. J. Nurs. 72:1402-1406, 1972.

Coates, F. C., and Fabrykant, M.: An insulin injection technique for preventing skin reactions, Amer. J. Nurs. 65:127-128, 1965.

Conway, B., Madelco, B., Trufant, J., and Scobic, M.: The seventh right, Amer. J. Nurs. 70:1040-1043, 1970.

Fulton, A.: Control system for medication card, Amer. J. Nurs. 71:2162, 1971.

Hanson, D. J.: Intramuscular injection injuries and complications, Amer. J. Nurs. 63: 99-101, 1963.

Havener, W. H., Saunders, W. H., Keith, C. F., and Prescott, A. W.: Nursing care in eye, ear, nose and throat disorders, ed. 3, St. Louis, 1974, The C. V. Mosby Co.

Hayes, D.: Do it yourself the Z-track way, Amer. J. Nurs. 74:1070-1071, 1974.

Kern, M. S.: New ideas about drug systems, Amer. J. Nurs. 68:1251-1253, 1968.

Lawrence, P. A.: U-100 insulin: let's make the transition possible, Amer. J. Nurs. 73: 1539, 1973.

Leary, J. A., Vessalla, D. M., and Yeaw, E. M.: Self-administered medications, Amer. J. Nurs. 71:1193-1194, 1971.

Leifer, G.: Principles and techniques in pediatric nursing, ed. 2, Philadelphia, 1972, W. B. Saunders Co.

Michael, F.: The vexing core, Amer. J. Nurs. 71:768, 1971.

Pitel, M.: The subcutaneous injection, Amer. J. Nurs. 71:76-79, 1971.

Pitel, M., and Wemett, M.: The intramuscular injection, Amer. J. Nurs. 64:104-109, 1964.

Shaffer, J. H., and Sweet, L. C.: Allergic reactions to drugs, Amer. J. Nurs. 65:100-103, 1965.

Teetelbaem, A.: Intra-arterial drug therapy, Amer. J. Nurs. 72:1634-1657, 1972.

Watkins, J. D., and Moss, F. T.: Confusion in the management of diabetes, Amer. J. Nurs. 69:521-524, 1969.

Wempe, B. M.: The new and the old intramuscular injection sites, Amer. J. Nurs. 61: 56-57, 1961.

Zitnik, R.: First you take a grapefruit, Amer. J. Nurs. 68:1285-1286, 1968.

5

Application of topical medications

Instructions concerning the kind, strength, and form of topical medications and frequency, area, and technique of their application are obtained by the nurse from the physician's orders. After the necessary dressings, equipment, and drug preparations have been assembled, the medication may be applied.

Contact with the patient during treatment gives the nurse the opportunity to demonstrate her acceptance of him and his condition. In most instances, the use of gloves and other devices that suggest self-protection should be avoided. Self-protection should be practiced if the condition being treated is infectious, if the drug is likely to be harmful to the nurse, or if the medication possesses a disagreeable odor that is difficult to remove.

A cheerful, tactful, and understanding approach is essential. The patient and his relatives are concerned about his appearance and the prolonged period of treatment required. Anxiety related to the discomfort of pruritus, insomnia, anorexia, and decreased ability to function normally adds to their burdens. Any method that helps gain the acceptance and cooperation of the patient and his relatives is of value. Teaching the patient how to live successfully with his condition should be reinforced at every opportunity. Instructions should be given carefully, and the patient's understanding of the instructions should be checked carefully. Because treatment is almost always continued at home, nurses should teach the hospitalized patient daily. Teaching is most successful when it is done concurrently with each treatment explaining the method and why the treatment is carried out in a particular way. Providing the patient with clearly written, easily understood instructions is helpful. Relatives should be included if this is possible whenever teaching is done. Patience with a slowly changing condition is important, since impatience on the part of the patient or relative may lead to a temp-

159

tation to overtreat or to use home remedies, producing disastrous results. Cotton gloves may be worn by the patient to protect sensitive or damaged skin, particularly during periods of sleep, when the patient may scratch without being aware of this until he awakens and finds the damage that has been done. Use of antihistamines, sedative, tranquilizing, or other systemic drugs as prescribed helps the patient to cope with problems that would otherwise seem insurmountable to him.

An understanding of the principles of physiology will help the nurse promote the patient's comfort. Knowledge that itching increases when the capillary bed dilates indicates careful and conscientious control of factors that influence this mechanism. Regulation of the room temperature will be determined by humidity, activity of the patient, and the method used for the application of drugs. Thus the use of wet dressings frequently dictates the need to increase room temperature. Knowledge that constriction, friction, heat, and perspiration increase itching will guide the selection and use of fabrics for dressings and clothing.

Clothing worn during hospitalization is selected for the purpose of reducing irritation of the skin. Long sleeved cotton pajamas that have been properly laundered are satisfactory for this purpose. Because elastic waist bands are likely to be irritating, men's pajamas that tie with a drawstring are preferred. Robes of any kind may be worn over the pajamas. Because they may irritate the skin condition further, other types of clothing should not be worn during hospitalization without the physician's approval.

Patients are advised not to use cosmetic preparations of any kind without the physician's permission. The ingredients in cosmetic preparations may be contributing to or even causing the condition being treated. Explanation that shaving lotions and deodorants are considered to be cosmetics is often necessary. Hypoallergenic cosmetics may be allowed when the skin is medically healed. It is essential that the patient understand that the skin may appear to be clear sometime before it is medically healed. Patients who have the plaque type of psoriasis are an exception to this rule and are allowed to use cosmetics.

External medications are usually kept in the patient's bathroom. Paper towels placed beneath the jars of ointments will prevent staining of the shelving. If medications are stored in lockers, appropriately labeled individual trays will facilitate their storage and transport. Lining the trays with paper protectors will minimize the effort needed to keep them clean.

The physician may prescribe the use of more than one form of treatment. For example, ultraviolet light therapy may be ordered to follow the removal of ointment with oil, a therapeutic bath may

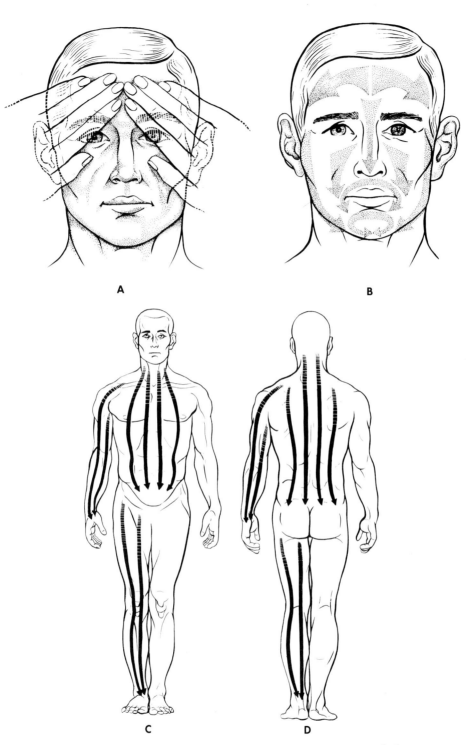

Fig. 5-1. Application of ointments. **A,** Correct position of the hands. **B,** Direction of application to the face. **C,** Direction of application to the anterior surface of the body. **D,** Direction of application to the posterior surface of the body.

161

be ordered to precede the application of ointments, or a prescription may be given to enclose in wet dressings a skin area to which a medicated cream has been applied. Various other combinations of treatment may be prescribed also. When a combination of treatments is prescribed, sequence and timing are crucial for obtaining maximum therapeutic results. For example, ointments, creams, or lotions must be applied immediately after the bath to preserve hydration of the skin. If time elapses before their application, dryness, itching, and irritation occurs due to damage to the stratum corneum; this will delay the healing process.

Ointments and creams

Ointments and creams serve as vehicles for therapeutic drugs, protective coatings, lubricators, and softeners of the skin.

After the patient has been assisted in removing clothing over the area to be treated and in assuming the desired position, the nurse places a small amount of the ointment or cream in one hand. Then it is spread to the inner aspects of both hands by gently drawing them across each other. This action not only places an equal amount of ointment on both hands but also warms it, thus facilitating even application of a thin coating that will protect the skin surface by keeping moisture in the outer layer of skin and preventing contact with air, which causes drying. Heavy applications of ointments and creams tend to build up on the skin and may be a source of itching problems. Removal of heavily applied ointments or creams requires vigorous efforts that irritate and damage the skin.

In applying the ointment or cream, long, smooth strokes that follow the direction of hair growth are used. Short, uncoordinated strokes accompanied by insufficient or excessive pressure, as well as rubbing or repetitious stroking, tend to increase itching and should be avoided. Rubbing or repetitious stroking is also avoided to prevent the introduction of ointment into the hair follicles. Each stroke is begun by placing the hands on the area to be treated in such a way that they meet and act as a single unit, with the flat portion of the hands depositing a film of ointment on the body surface (Fig. 5-1, *A*).

It is important that the nursing plan provide for a consistent technique in the application of ointments and that the nurse who applies the medication teach by example, explanations, and repeated instruction any patient who is to participate in his own treatment (Table 5-1).

After treatment, the ointment is kept in contact with the body surface by dressings. Loosely fitted cotton pajamas, laundered to re-

TABLE 5-1. Application of ointments and creams

Technique	Problem	Explanation or solution
Assist the patient as necessary to remove clothing over the area to be treated and to assume the desired position.	Medication stains clothing, bed linen, and furniture.	Have the patient stand on a disposable floor mat.
Place a small amount of ointment or cream in one hand and spread it by gently drawing the inner aspect of the other hand across it.	Uneven, heavy applications tend to cake and cause irritation; removal of heavy applications requires vigorous efforts that irritate and damage the skin.	Warming the medication in the hands facilitates even application of a thin coating.
Use long, smooth strokes that follow the direction of hair growth when applying ointments or creams.	Itching and folliculitis may occur.	Use of short, uncoordinated strokes and excessive or inadequate pressure increases discomfort. Avoiding rubbing and following the direction of hair growth prevents medication from being forced into the follicles.
Use only the flat portions of the hands and fingers when applying medication.	Abrasions of the skin may be caused if the fingertips are used.	Avoiding use of the fingertips, having short nails, and not wearing finger rings prevents damage to the skin.
Instruct the patient throughout the treatment.	Incorrect application and over-zealous treatment gives poor results and damages the skin even more.	The patient will need to continue the treatment indefinitely; knowledge and practice will assist him to carry out the treatments correctly.
Have the patient wear loosely fitted, properly laundered cotton pajamas and terry cloth scuffs after the application of ointment or cream.	A dressing is needed to keep the medication in contact with the skin. Fibers other than laundered cotton may irritate the skin.	Laundering removes fillers from clothing. Tight-fitting clothing increases irritation and constriction.
White cotton gloves may be worn if the hands are treated.	It is difficult to keep the medication on the hands and prevent soiling of personal articles.	Loosely fitted cotton gloves made of single knit material will keep the medication in contact with the hands.
White cotton stockings or socks are worn if the patient wishes to wear slippers.		Shoe dyes may be a source of irritation.

move fillers that may prove irritating to the condition being treated, fulfill the requirements of a satisfactory dressing and should be worn for 3 days without laundering. White cotton stockings and gloves or tubular gauze may be used to keep ointments and creams in contact with the skin. Terry cloth scuffs may be worn on the feet. If plastic or leather slippers are worn, cotton stockings may be necessary to protect the skin from contact dermatitis or irritation. The nurse must watch for the possibility of irritation due to shoe dye.

The usual schedule of treatment provides for two to three applications of ointments daily. If dryness occurs, additional ointment or cream applications may be indicated.

On completion of the application, wiping the excess ointment or cream from the hands with a paper towel will decrease the time needed for their removal with soap and water.

APPLYING OINTMENT OR CREAM TO THE FACE

Application of ointment or cream to small areas of the face requires the use of the flat portion of the fingers. Use of the fingertips is contraindicated, since this may cause abrasions that would predispose the skin to infection even though the nails are closely trimmed. Treatment of the face is begun at the midline, with both hands used simultaneously to apply the ointment (Fig. 5-1, A). Direction of the application to facial areas is shown in Fig. 5-1, B.

APPLYING OINTMENT OR CREAM TO TRUNK AND EXTREMITIES

In applying ointment or cream to the trunk, the first stroke is begun at the midline. If the entire anterior surface of the trunk is to be treated, this stroke is begun under the chin and extends to the genital area (Fig. 5-1, C). The second stroke is begun at the uppermost point of treatment adjacent to either side of the area to which the ointment was applied by the first stroke. This outward pattern is repeated until the anterior surface is treated. The same pattern is used to treat the posterior surface of the trunk, with the initial stroke beginning at the hairline (Fig. 5-1, D). The extremities are treated in a similar fashion. Usually two strokes are needed to treat each extremity, although this will vary, depending on the size of the extremity. The patient wears a loincloth, which allows all areas of the body to be treated except the genital area. He is usually permitted to apply medication to the genitalia after receiving instructions.

Although the position of the patient is only of relative importance in the application of ointment or cream to the trunk and extremities, having him stand erect facilitates treatment. In addition, the patient is usually pleased to avoid having his bed unnecessarily soiled by medication.

REMOVAL OF TOPICAL TREATMENT, CRUSTS, SCALES, AND DRIED SECRETIONS

Excess or dried topical treatment, crusts, scales, and dried secretions may be removed with a nonirritating solvent. Cottonseed oil is a satifactory solvent for most oil-based treatments. Other oils, such as mineral, olive, and castor oils, will serve this purpose; however, the expense, odor, and ease of removing the oil itself must be evaluated carefully.

After pouring some oil into the hands and lubricating them by rubbing them together, the nurse smooths oil onto the body area to be cleansed, using the same strokes described for the application of ointment (pages 162 to 164 and Fig. 5-1). When large areas are to be oiled, the patient may stand on the floor, which should be protected with paper mats. Liberal amounts of oil should be used, and the entire procedure is repeated as often as necessary to ensure easy and complete removal of the topical medication. Rubbing produces irritation and damage to the skin and is contraindicated.

Excess oil and topical medication are removed by gently wiping the area with a soft cloth. Used gauze that has been washed is also satisfactory. Again, the same directional strokes described previously are used. This method of removing ointments leaves on the skin a

TABLE 5-2. Removal of topical treatment, crusts, scales, and dried secretions

Technique	Problem	Solution or explanation
If large areas are to be oiled, have the patient stand on a paper mat or a layer of newspapers.	Oil tends to drip and is slippery and difficult to remove from the floor and furniture.	Standing on a mat protects the safety of the patient and others and protects the patient's belongings.
Pour cottonseed oil into the hands and rub them together.	Cool and dripping oil is aggravating; coverage of the area is necessary.	Oil is a solvent for most ointments and softens dried debris; spreading the oil lubricates the hands and warms the oil, facilitating easy, complete coverage.
Smooth the oil onto the area to be cleansed, using long, coordinated strokes that follow the directional growth of the hair.	Irritation and folliculitis can result.	Uncoordinated strokes increase irritation and itching; old medication must not be forced into the follicles by applying the oil against the direction of the hair growth.
Gently wipe the area with soft cloth or washed gauze.	The skin is easily irritated and damaged.	Rubbing and the use of a harsher material will irritate and damage the skin.
Repeat the application and removal of oil if necessary.	One treatment may be inadequate to cleanse the skin.	Additional applications of oil will further dissolve or soften the debris.

residual film of oil that is removed by the therapeutic bath. It is also used to help remove scales, crusts, and dried secretions (Table 5-2).

TRIAL APPLICATION OF OINTMENTS

The physician may test the feasibility of using a specific ointment by requesting a trial application to a small area about 1½ inches in diameter. He may specify the site to be used, usually the abdomen or the inner aspect of the forearm. In this trial application to a small area of the body, the same principles as those used for applying ointment to a large area of the body hold true. Trial applications are observed for periods of 6 to 48 hours before treatment of larger areas is prescribed. The length of observation depends on the individual's reaction.

Ideally, small jars of ointment are prepared and labeled by the pharmacist. If stock supplies must be used, the nurse will want to place a small amount of the specified ointment on a wooden spatula or tongue blade for each patient. The ointment-laden end of the spatula may be placed inside a waxed envelope or a sandwich bag, and identifying information may be recorded on the portion extending from the envelope.

Lotions

Lotions are used to protect and soothe the skin. The lotion may be prescribed for the purpose of lubricating, cooling, drying, or relieving itching. Because of the nature of the ingredients found in many lotions, application near the eyes and the mucous membranes is usually contraindicated.

Before application, most lotions must be shaken until the solution appears to be thoroughly mixed. If the lotion does not mix well within a reasonable period of time, it should be assumed that the preparation is defective, and a new supply should be obtained.

Cotton or rayon pledgets should not be used to apply lotions because the fibers tend to absorb the solute or drug, leaving primarily the solvent in contact with the area being treated. Painting the lotion onto the skin with a paintbrush has been described by various authorities. However, applying the lotion with a gentle patting or stroking motion of the hands permits control of the amount and kind of pressure used. This method appears to aid in preventing increased sensations of itching. If a drying lotion is prescribed, it will usually have a water or alcohol base and be of a watery consistency. It may be applied with a small pledget of soft gauze that does not contain fillers. Lotions with an oil base are applied in the manner described for ointments and creams. Lotions

166

should never be permitted to form a thick layer on the skin, because this is irritating and reduces evaporation. Lotions are applied at prescribed time intervals.

Dressings
WET DRESSINGS

Various types of wet dressings may be prescribed to reduce the inflammation, edema, and pruritus that accompany dermatologic conditions. In addition, they may be used to cleanse the skin and to treat infection. Before the application of wet dressings, it may be necessary to place a finely woven cloth that has been wetted with the prescribed solution over ulcerated or denuded areas. Coarsely woven gauze is not used because threads tend to adhere to the denuded area during the removal of dressings. This disturbs the epithelial tissue.

If solutions other than tap water are prescribed, the strength will be dilute. A solution that is too concentrated will produce flare of the skin condition rather than the desired resolution. The person diluting the solution must know whether sterile, tap, or distilled water is to be used. The diluted solution is warmed to the desired temperature, usually 95° to 98° F., and is poured over the dressing (Fig. 5-2, A), which has been placed in a suitable container. After the dressing has been saturated with solution, it is compressed between the hands to free it of excess moisture (Fig. 5-2, B). Although it should be thoroughly and uniformly wet, it should not drip. A dressing that contains the correct amount of solution will sound "swishy" when it is compressed or squeezed, but the moisture will not drip from it. Application of the dressing uses bandaging techniques. The dressing is applied gently, smoothly, and in a way that will prevent contact between the surfaces of the skin. Wet dressings are applied with a slight looseness because some shrinkage may occur as moisture evaporates from them.

Because evaporation of the solution produces cooling, the patient must be kept warm. Not only must the room temperature be well regulated and drafts eliminated, but the bed linen should be kept as free of moisture as possible. Placing plastic sheeting covered with a pillowcase under the part being treated and a cradle over the part will help keep both the bottom and top linen free of moisture. Measures to prevent chilling must be increased proportionately as increased body surface area is enclosed in wet dressings.

The dressing is removed, remoistened, and reapplied periodically. If continuous wet dressings are ordered, the nurse repeats the procedure every 3 hours. If the dressings dry more rapidly, they are reapplied more frequently than every 3 hours. As the moisture evapo-

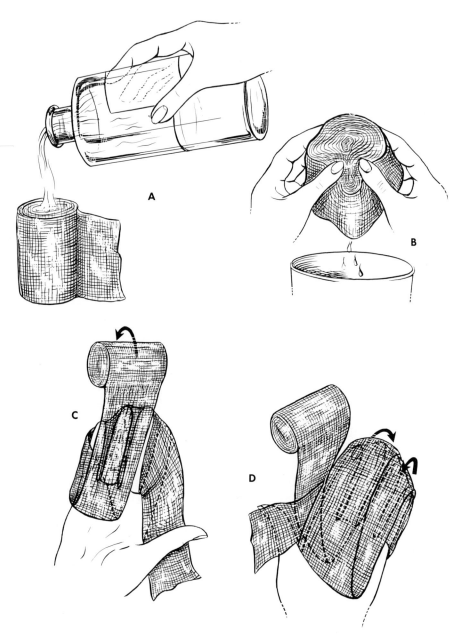

Fig. 5-2. Application of wet dressings to the upper extremity. **A,** The gauze is thoroughly saturated by pouring warm solution over it or by immersing it. **B,** The gauze is compressed between the hands to remove excess solution. Then the nurse interweaves gauze between the patient's fingers, **C,** covering his fingertips with folds of gauze, **D.**

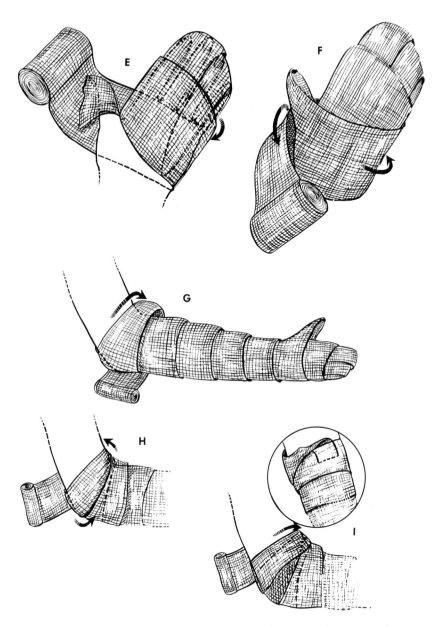

Fig. 5-2, cont'd. E, The nurse anchors the gauze that covers the fingertips with a circular turn of bandage. **F,** The thumb is encircled with gauze and the forearm is enclosed with circular turns of bandage. **G,** A circular turn of gauze is placed around the elbow. **H,** With a circular turn of bandage, the nurse anchors the lower edge of the gauze enclosing the elbow. **I,** The upper edge of gauze is anchored enclosing the elbow, the remaining portion of the extremity is encircled with gauze, and the free end of the gauze is tucked under the last circular turn to anchor the bandage.

Continued.

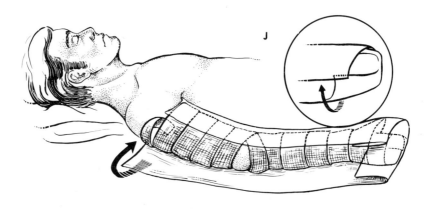

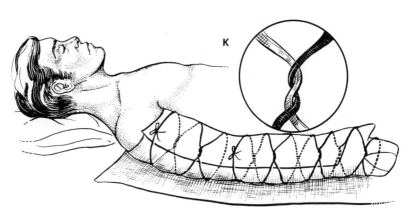

Fig. 5-2, cont'd. J, The nurse encloses the dressed extremity in a Turkish towel or a double layer of cotton flannel. Note envelope folds over the hand, which permit the patient to retain some grasping motion between his thumb and fingers. **K,** The nurse secures the cloth covering with ties, which may be fashioned from strips of roller bandage. The tie is placed around the tips and the base of the fingers to preserve the action of the thumb and to avoid bony prominences. The inset shows the method of twisting ties to permit their rapid application and removal. A protector placed under the extremity keeps the linen dry.

170

rates, the concentration of the drug contacting the skin increases. This may aggravate the condition unless the dressings are removed while they are still moist and resoaked thoroughly before being reapplied. The dressing must be moistened thoroughly if it is to be warmed adequately. Application of additional solution to the dressings with a syringe prevents the nurse from observing the reaction of the skin to the prescribed treatment. In addition, it can, unless it is skillfully done, cause maceration of the skin due to excess moisture and increased concentration of the solution. Enclosing a wet dressing in moistureproof materials, although it is sometimes desirable, results in the retention of body heat and moisture, which tends to result in maceration of the tissues, irritation of the skin, and folliculitis.

Application to extremities. To dress an entire arm, the gauze is interwoven between the patient's fingers (Fig. 5-2, C), then placed over the ends of the fingers (Fig. 5-2, D), enclosing them completely, and finally applied to the arm with circular turns. The folds placed over the fingers are anchored with the first circular turn (Fig. 5-2, E). The thumb is wrapped in a manner that allows it to move independently, permitting the patient to retain a pinching movement between the thumb and forefinger so that he can accomplish a number of activities (Fig. 5-2, F). Circular wrapping of the dressing is continued until it reaches the elbow. At this point, the nurse must take care to preserve movement of the joint (Fig. 5-2, G to I). The completed bandage is secured by tucking the free end under the last circular turn (Fig. 5-2, I, inset).

If the dressing is to be enclosed with a dry outer covering, Turkish towels or a double layer of cotton flannel may be used (Fig. 5-2, J). The nurse may secure this outer covering with the aid of ties fashioned from lengths of roller bandage 1 inch wide. Care should be taken to avoid placing knots or ties over joints (Fig. 5-2, K). Application and removal of the ties are expedited if they are twisted rather than looped (Fig. 5-2, K, inset). The use of metal fasteners such as pins is to be avoided because, it is believed, they may contribute to further irritation of the skin.

The application of wet dressings to the lower extremities is similar and is illustrated in Fig. 5-3.

Application to other parts of body. Wet dressings for the face, ears, eyes, neck, head, trunk, axilla, groin, or perineum may be prescribed. Their application is guided by the same concepts and principles discussed previously. Preparation of the solution, moistening of the dressing, and reapplication are carried out in a similar manner.

The face mask is applied in such a way that the patient can see, breathe, and drink without undue difficulty. It is tied over the fore-

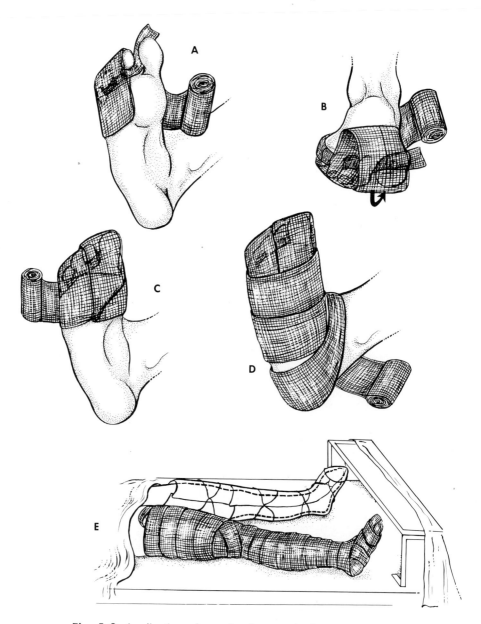

Fig. 5-3. Application of wet dressings to the lower extremity. **A,** The nurse weaves the dressing between the patient's toes. **B,** The dressing is folded over the toes, **C,** using a circular turn of dressing to anchor the folds that cover the toes. **D,** The nurse encloses the foot with circular turns of bandage. Edges of the gauze enclosing the heel are anchored with circular turns of bandage, permitting freedom of joint motion. **E,** The nurse also wraps the extremity with circular turns of bandage. Note the method of enclosing the heel and knee to permit freedom of movement. The left extremity is shown enclosed in outer wrappings. A cradle keeps the top linen free of moisture.

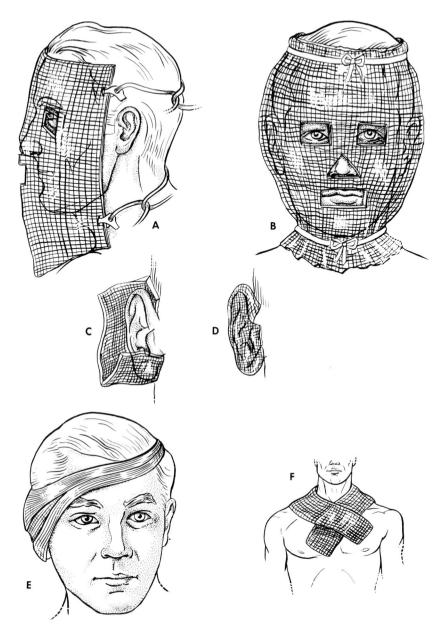

Fig. 5-4. Application of face, ear, and neck dressings. **A,** Method of securing a treated face mask posteriorly. **B,** Anterior view of the completed face mask. Anchoring the ties with bows facilitates removal. **C,** A dressing placed around the external ear. **D,** The dressing is tucked into depressions in and around the external ear. **E,** A bandage to secure the dressing on the ear. **F,** Wet dressing placed on the neck. A dry towel placed over this dressing may be secured with a safety pin. The pin must not contact the skin, however.

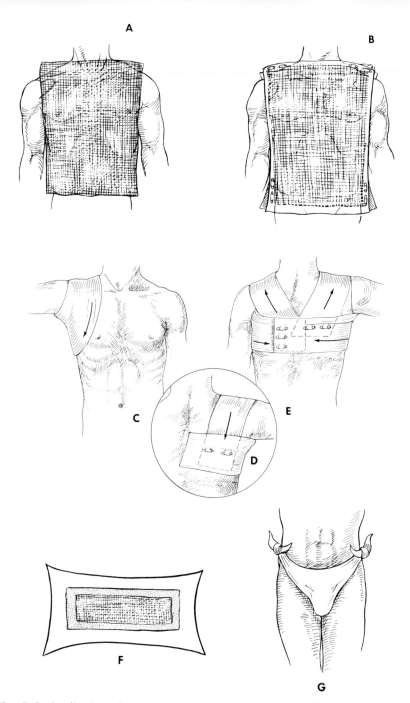

Fig. 5-5. Application of wet dressings to the upper trunk, axilla, and perineum. **A,** A wet dressing is applied to the upper trunk. **B,** The dressing is covered with dry material and is anchored by pinning the edges of the dry material. **C,** After a wet dressing is applied to the axilla, it is covered with a length of flannel, which is started near the lower scapula and brought over the shoulder and under the arm to the back. **D,** The dressing is anchored by pinning through the dry material. **E,** Both axillae are treated, and the dressing is anchored in the back with safety pins placed in the covering. **F,** A prepared perineal dressing is placed on a folded Turkish towel on a drape or four thicknesses of flannel. **G,** Completed perineal dressing tied in place.

174

head and beneath the chin (Fig. 5-4, *A* and *B*). Ear dressings must be applied carefully to keep the medication in contact with all parts of the ear. Gentle pressure is used to press the dressing into the depressions and crevices in and around the outer ear (Fig. 5-4, *C* and *D*). Ear dressings can be held in place with a bandage (Fig. 5-4, *E*). Depending on the condition of the patient, eye dressings may also be secured with bandages. Neck dressings are applied in the way a neck scarf is put on (Fig. 5-4, *F*) and are covered with a dry dressing.

Dressings applied to the trunk will remain stationary if towels or layers of cotton flannel are placed over the dressings and fastened with safety pins at the shoulder line and on both sides of the body (Fig. 5-5, *A* and *B*). Dressings applied to the axilla are kept in place with lengths of flannel (Fig. 5-5, *C* to *E*). Dressings applied to the groin and perineum are kept in contact with the area being treated with the aid of a cloth that looks like a giant-sized bikini. Usually four thicknesses of flannel or a folded Turkish towel is placed between the wet dressing and the "bikini" (Fig. 5-5, *F*). The "bikini" can be tied in place (Fig. 5-5, *G*). Other methods of securing dressings depend largely on the nurse's ingenuity.

OCCLUSIVE DRESSINGS

Occlusive dressings are placed after the prescribed medication has been applied to the area. These may consist of a thin sheet of plastic material fastened with transparent adhesive tape. The dressing should be sealed in an effort to prevent evaporation of moisture. Plastic gloves or plastic booties are practical for the hands and feet. After the glove or bootie is positioned, the upper part is taped to prevent the entry of air.

LENGTHS AND WIDTHS OF DRESSINGS

The lengths and widths of dressings needed for specific anatomic parts are shown in Table 5-3. The face mask may be prepared from 28 by 24 mesh, grade 50 gauze that is 36 inches wide. A 3-yard length of the dressing, which comes folded, is opened, folded into thirds, and then folded lengthwise to the desired size (12 by 12 inches). This folding will result in 27 thicknesses of gauze. Commonly, 20 by 12 mesh, 8-ply, grade 10 gauze is used for the extremities and the trunk. Although gauze applied to the trunk and perineum contains 16 folds or is 16 ply, a similar effect is achieved on the extremity by using 8-ply gauze, since the dressing is applied in such a way that each circular turn overlaps the previous circular turn by about half the width of the gauze. Dressings applied to the neck, upper trunk, groin, and perineum may be prepared from 20 by 12 mesh, 5-ply gauze. Folding it into thirds achieves the necessary thickness. Since the width of gauze varies with manufacturers, the

TABLE 5-3. Lengths and widths of dressings for specific parts of body

Anatomic part	Length of dressing (yards)	Width of dressing (inches)
Arm (hand to shoulder)	5	4
Axilla	2½ to 5	9
Back (entire)	5	18
Buttocks	5	18
Ears	½	5
Eye	½	4
Face	3	36
Foot	5	4
Groin and perineum	5	9
Hand	5	4
Scalp	5	9
Leg (below the knee)	5	4
Neck	5	9
Thigh	5	4
Trunk (entire)	10	18
Trunk (upper)	10 (5)	9 (18)

length needed will have to be adjusted accordingly. Materials used for dressings should be free of lint and fillers that seem to irritate the skin and increase itching. In lieu of commercially available dressings, use of bleached muslin or linen has been suggested.

Powder beds

The powder bed is used to keep powdered medications in contact with large areas of the body for a certain period of time. During this treatment, which is repeated three times daily and as necessary, the patient is virtually helpless, and the nurse must remember to provide for meeting his physiologic needs.

The foundation of the bed is made in the usual manner. However, rubber sheets and other protectors that contribute to warmth and perspiration are generally omitted, since the powder bed method of treatment is used to minimize moisture. A full-sized sheet is placed lengthwise over the foundation of the bed (Fig. 5-6, *A*) and the prescribed powder is distributed evenly over the area on which the part of the body to be treated will be resting. To prevent caking and crusting, the amount of powder used should not be excessive. Sprinkling and patting the powder will aid in its even distribution (Fig. 5-6, *B*).

The patient lies on the powdered area, and the nurse treats ap-

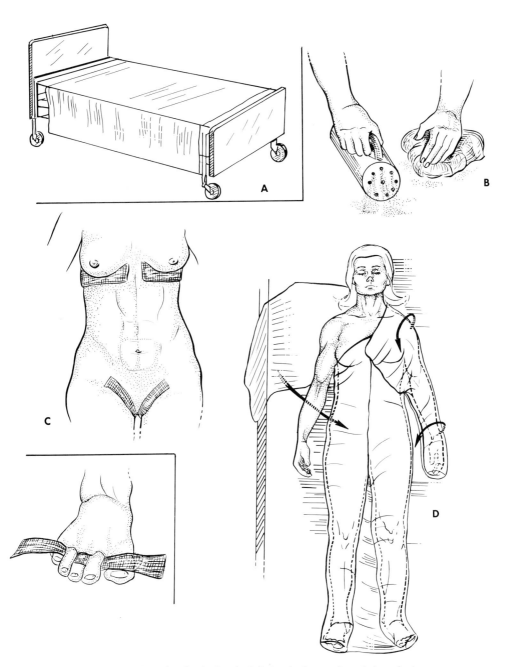

Fig. 5-6. Powder bed. **A,** A full-sized sheet placed lengthwise over the foundation of the bed. **B,** Application of powder to the sheet. **C,** Protection of apposed surfaces of the skin with gauze before the anterior surface of the body is powdered. **D,** A method of folding the sheet to keep powder in contact with the body.

177

posed surfaces of the skin with powder and protects them by double folds of soft gauze (Fig. 5-6, *C*). Such areas that need to be protected from normal body moisture include the toes, groin, intergluteal folds, inframammary region, and axillas. After providing the necessary protection, the nurse powders the anterior part of the body. Soft gauze may be used to pat the powder onto the body. Lesions exuding moisture will require additional powder. The nurse then folds the sheet over the extremities and the trunk in a manner that will keep the powder in contact with the skin but will prevent contact between body surfaces (Fig. 5-6, *D*). Half sheets may be used for treatment of the legs or the trunk only, and pillowcases may be used for treatment of the arms.

Tub baths
MEDICATED TUB BATH

After the necessary medication, materials needed by the patient and materials needed to prepare the bath are assembled; the tub is scrubbed thoroughly with a suitable cleansing agent and rinsed thoroughly. Then it is partially filled with water, and the medication is added.

Regardless of the medication ordered, the temperature of the prepared solution in the tub usually should be no less than 96° and no more than 100° F. Other temperatures for the bath solution may be prescribed. Stirring the solution with a bath thermometer will serve two functions: it will register the temperature of the solution and disperse the medication throughout the solution.

Most patients respond favorably to information and instructions regarding this form of therapy. However, it may be necessary for the nurse to reinforce explanations through positive actions. Most medicated baths are prescribed as half-hour treatments, but the duration may vary depending on the needs of the patient as determined by the physician. The possibilities of the patient falling, fainting, or adding hot water should be anticipated and prevented whenever possible.

If the bath is being used to treat conditions of the skin, the patient is asked to sit in the tub, relax, and permit the solution to bathe the lesions. In an effort to help the patient avoid further irritation of the skin, he is instructed not to rub or scrub during the bath. The nurse should explain to him that, because its use may cause further irritation, a washcloth is not provided. Furthermore, the patient should be impressed with the importance of patting the skin dry with a towel rather than rubbing it, since any action that produces friction is likely to irritate the skin condition for which he is being treated.

TABLE 5-4. Medications used in tub baths

Medication	Usual amount used*	Remarks
Potassium permanganate 1:32,000	6 Gm. (18 tablets, 5 gr., or 120 ml. of 5% solution)	Tablets placed in a waxed envelope may be pulverized with aid of tongue blades; drug is dissolved in a pitcher of water, and resulting solution is poured through several layers of gauze into bath water immediately before patient enters tub; straining of solution removes undissolved particles of drug, which will damage skin chemically; a mixture of equal parts of vinegar and hydrogen peroxide will remove residual stains from tub.
Colloidal preparations (Aveeno, Soyaloid)	4 to 6 oz. or $\frac{1}{2}$ to $\frac{3}{4}$ cup	Forcing cool water through powder will place colloid in solution; a large tea strainer permits rapid dispersion of colloid; since colloidal solutions are slippery, precautions should be used to prevent falling.
Corn starch, uncooked	$\frac{1}{2}$ lb.	If physician wishes starch solution to be cooked, a thick solution is made and heated until mixture appears translucent.
Saline	48 oz. (by volume)	Add salt while water is running; mix well.
Baking soda	$\frac{1}{4}$ lb.	Stir until soda is dissolved.
Soyadome cleanser (soybean powder emulsion with hexachlorophene)	2 oz.	Add while water is running.
Sulfur	$\frac{1}{2}$ pt.	Avoid contact of eyes, mouth, and nose with this solution; remove solution from normal skin with tap water.
Zinc sulfate	4 oz.	Dissolve crystals in 2 L. of boiling water.
Entsufon (pHisoderm)	$1\frac{1}{2}$ oz.	Disperse medication completely; other anionic surface agents may be prescribed.
Oil	$1\frac{1}{2}$ oz.	Cottonseed oil may be used. (Pharmacy may prepare this with 1 part alkyl aryl polyether alcohol (Surfactol-45) to 9 parts oil to make it water dispersable.)

*Amount listed is the amount of drug most frequently used for a conventional tub that is half filled with water. Twice the amount would be needed for larger tubs containing 30 gallons of water.

179

In special instances, however, the physician may want the patient to scrub the skin. For example, he may leave orders that the patient with psoriasis be provided with soap and a washcloth and be asked to scrub thick, dry lesions with a hand brush. Any additional topical medications that are prescribed, such as ointments, should be applied immediately after the bath.

The usual amounts of medication used in tub baths and remarks pertinent to their use are listed in Table 5-4.

CONTINUOUS TUB BATH

Occasionally the physician prescribes a continuous tub bath in tepid water or medicated solution. The tub is cleansed as described for the medicated tub bath and filled with sufficient water to ensure immersion of the patient. To ensure a constant solution temperature of between 96° and 100° F. in a tub not equipped with thermostatic controls, a thermometer is placed in each end of the tub, and the temperature is adjusted as necessary every half hour. After the tub has been filled, a canvas hammock is secured over it (Fig. 5-7, A). Specially designed tubs contain extensions to which the hammock can be fastened. The hammock is covered with a clean sheet that extends over the rim of the tub (Fig. 5-7, B). The patient is permitted to wear a loincloth, and a rubber ring or rubber pillow enclosed in a pillowcase is placed beneath his head and shoulders. He wears a harness around his chest to maintain his position and to provide for his safety when he sleeps (Fig. 5-7, B and inset). The ties of the harness are placed between the shoulder blades and are anchored to the end of the tub or to another immovable object. His chest is covered with a towel (Fig. 5-7, C) that has been saturated with the prescribed solution.

A board or tray table may be placed over the tub about 18 inches from the patient's face. Covering the patient and the board with a sheet serves to retain some heat, to ensure privacy, and to provide a surface on which may be placed items that the patient may need during this treatment, such as drinking water, a towel, and a hand-bell (Fig. 5-7, C). Contact with any electrical appliance is dangerous and must be prevented.

The patient must be observed frequently throughout the continuous tub bath. Any febrile reaction, a rapid, weak pulse, a feeling of faintness, or an increase in severity of symptoms, such as increased itching and burning, are indications that the treatment should be discontinued immediately and that the physician should be notified.

If the treatment is extended, the solution is changed completely every 4 hours. The nurse should change the linen at least twice daily and the hammock once daily.

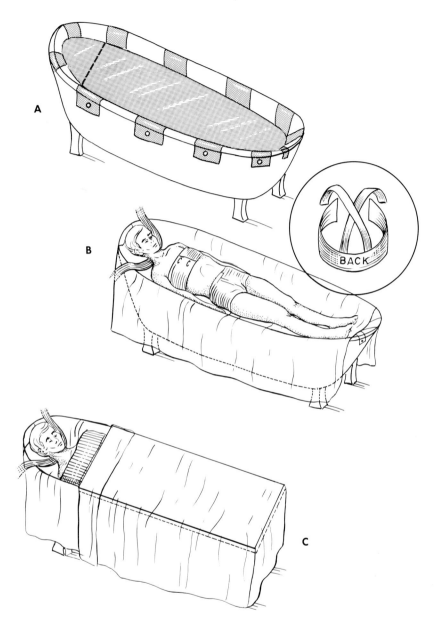

Fig. 5-7. Continuous tub bath. **A,** A canvas hammock is secured to the tub after the tub has been filled with the prescribed solution. **B,** The patient lying on the hammock that has been covered with a sheet. A waterproof pillow supports his head, and the harness around his chest is secured to the tub to maintain his position and to provide for his safety. **C,** The patient's chest is covered with a towel saturated with prescribed solution. A board is placed over the tub. A sheet is used to retain some heat, ensure the patient's privacy, and provide a surface on which materials he needs may be placed.

181

Scalp medications

The application of medications to the scalp is usually preceded by a shampoo. In most instances the shampoo can be given with the patient seated near a sink. If the patient is confined to bed, the shampoo will be facilitated by positioning him so that his head is near the edge of the bed and by improvising a drainage trough to carry away the water. Such a trough can be fashioned by rolling a rubber sheet toward both sides of the patient's head and placing the free end of the trough into a vessel that has been placed on a chair or on the floor. This method is not necessary, of course, if special equipment for a bed shampoo is available.

The nurse should follow the physician's orders in regard to agents used for both washing and rinsing. The hair is lathered twice and rinsed three times after each application of suds. It is dried with a towel, and, if indicated, a hair dryer is used. The shampoo should be done gently, taking special precautions not to traumatize the scalp with the fingernails, which must be short. Only the fleshy portion of the fingertips should be used to massage the scalp.

The nurse combs and parts the patient's hair in the middle, applies the medication in the part, and spreads it with the fingertips. A dropper may be used to apply the medication. Then the nurse repeatedly parts the hair at $\frac{1}{2}$ inch intervals and applies medication in each subsequent part until the entire scalp has been treated. Medication when properly applied will not extend more than $\frac{1}{2}$ inch onto the hair. After the entire scalp has been treated, the hair may be parted and combed in the manner the patient likes.

When hot oil treatments to the scalp are ordered, the specified oil is applied in the same manner described for the application of medications to the scalp. Then a Turkish towel that has been saturated with hot water and that has had the excess removed by wringing is wrapped around the head. At stated intervals, the towel is removed, remoistened with hot water, and reapplied.

Questions for discussion and exploration

1. Why is it important psychologically that the nurse not wear gloves when applying a topical medication to a patient?
2. Under what circumstances would the nurse wear gloves to apply an ointment? What explanation should be given to the patient?
3. What does placing some ointment in the palms of the hands and spreading it on them accomplish in terms of patient care?
4. Describe the method of applying ointment and the underlying reasons for this method.
5. Plan the teaching that you should do when: (a) applying wet dressings, (b) applying ointments, (c) removing ointments, (d) applying lotions, and (e) preparing and giving therapeutic baths.

6. Why is it important that the technique used by all nurses administering treatments to a patient with a skin condition be consistent both in method and explanation? How can this be communicated to other nurses caring for this patient?

7. What merits might washed cotton pajamas have when worn as dressings over ointments as opposed to the merits of conventional dressings in relation to (a) mobility, (b) self-care, (c) independence, (d) inspection of the lesions, and (e) diversional activities?

8. Under what circumstances would a nurse decide that an additional application of ointment is indicated? What nursing observations are helpful in reaching such a decision? Of what might the patient complain that will suggest another application of ointment is indicated?

9. What is the most effective method of removing ointments from one's hands?

10. If the patient is able to stand during application of ointment or lotion to the lower extremities, how can you protect the floor and his feet?

11. Why should ointments be applied only in the direction in which hair grows?

12. For what reason is it recommended that cotton pajamas be washed before being worn as a dressing?

13. Why might a trial application of ointment be prescribed? What should this mean in terms of nursing responsibilities?

14. Why is it usually necessary to shake a lotion before applying it?

15. Discuss possible methods of applying lotions and the advantages and disadvantages of each.

16. If Mrs. J. has wet dressings over all body surfaces, what will happen to her body heat as moisture evaporates from the dressings? How can you prevent or reduce discomforts of which she is likely to complain unless anticipatory planning is done?

17. In what diversional activities can a patient who is in wet dressings participate? If the patient has ointment applied to the extremities? If lotion has been applied?

18. If you see a patient with a neurodermatologic condition scratching his arms, what are your nursing responsibilities to him and how will you fulfill them?

19. What is the purpose of occlusive dressings, and when might you expect them to be prescribed?

20. What instructions would you expect a patient to need before a therapeutic bath? For what conditions might you expect the physician to ask that the patient scrub himself with a brush?

21. Why is it wise for the nurse working with patients who have lesions of the skin to keep her nails well trimmed? To remove finger rings?

Selected references

Bergersen, B. S.: Pharmacology in nursing, ed. 12, St. Louis, 1973, The C. V. Mosby Co.

Brunner, L., Emerson, C., Ferguson, L., and Suddarth, D.: Medical-surgical nursing, ed. 2, Philadelphia, 1970, J. B. Lippincott Co.

Corbeil, M.: Nursing process for a patient with a body image disturbance, Nurs. Clin. N. Amer. **6:**155-163, 1971.

Criep, L. H.: Dermatologic allergy: immunology, diagnosis, and management, Philadelphia, 1967, W. B. Saunders Co.

Fitzpatrick, T. B., ed.: Dermatology in general medicine, New York, 1971, McGraw-Hill Book Co., Inc.

Shafer, K. N., Sawyer, J. R., McCluskey, A. M., Beck, E. L., and Phipps, W. J.: Medical-surgical nursing, ed. 5, St. Louis, 1971, The C. V. Mosby Co.

Smith, D., Germain, C., and Gips, C.: Care of the adult patient, ed. 3, Philadelphia, 1971, J. B. Lippincott Co.

Stewart, W. D., Danto, J. L., and Maddin, S.: Synopsis of dermatology, ed. 2, St. Louis, 1970, The C. V. Mosby Co.

6
Gastric intubation and formula feedings

The patient who receives liquid feedings through a nasogastric or gastrostomy tube or by funnel feeding should have the same attention given to his mealtime as does the patient who is able to eat normally. Such feedings are necessitated by certain surgical procedures, injuries, and illnesses. The environment should be conducive to digestion, and the patient and his relatives should be encouraged to conduct themselves as they would for a normal meal; the room should be tidy and free of odors and esthetically unpleasant materials. The conversation should be pleasant.

Before tube feeding, the nurse should give oral care to the patient as a means of helping to prevent nausea. If the nurse passes the tube just before the tube feeding, the patient should be allowed to rest before the feeding is begun. If the tube is withdrawn after feeding, oral care may do much to promote comfort. Unless doing so is contraindicated, the patient should be encouraged to assist in the plans for and in the execution of these techniques.

Gastric intubation

Gastric intubation is used to administer liquid feedings to patients who are unable to eat normally, to obtain specimens for laboratory studies, to irrigate or cleanse the stomach, or to decompress it (Chapter 8). The physician, the nurse, or a skilled technician may do the intubation (Table 6-1). The patient for whom intubation for therapeutic reasons is necessary after hospitalization is taught to do the intubation himself, or a member of his family is taught to do it

TABLE 6-1. Nasogastric intubation

Technique	Problem	Solution or explanation
Select the size of tube indicated.	Excessively large tubes are unnecessarily irritating; a tube with a small lumen may be inadequate for administration of feedings, medication, or the removal of gastric contents.	A size 12 to 18 French tube is usually satisfactory; size depends on the size of the patient and the purpose of the tube.
If the tube is rubber, place it in a bowl of ice.	A limp, unlubricated tube is difficult to insert.	Chilling in ice stiffens and lubricates the rubber tube. Plastic tubes are naturally firm and slippery.
Explain to the patient what is to be done and why.	Patients who do not understand the treatment and its purpose may find it difficult or impossible to cooperate.	The patient has a right to be informed so that he will accept the treatment; this provides an opportunity to develop rapport and trust.
Position the patient.	Some positions increase the difficulty of this technique.	Initially, a natural, upright position is best.
Protect the patient's clothing.	Soiling of clothing may cause the patient anxiety and prevent him from relaxing.	A bib, apron, or towel over the chest will protect the patient's clothing.
Approximate the length of the tube that will be inserted; mark the tube if necessary.	Failure to approximate this distance may cause the practitioner anxiety.	The distance from the bridge of the nose to the tip of the xiphoid is approximately the same as the distance the tube will need to be passed to enter the stomach.
Apply lubricant to the tip of the tube by rotating it in a small amount of water-soluble lubricant.	Lubricant may interfere with cytology studies.	If cytology studies are ordered, use water or normal saline to lubricate the tube. Lubricant decreases resistance due to friction.
Hold the tube about 3 inches from the tip and place it into the nostril, advancing the tube forward and downward.	The tube tends to bend.	Control of the tube is increased as the distance between its tip and the fingers is decreased.
	The patient may tend to resist and his eyes may water.	Encourage the patient not to wince, contort his face, or pull away. Eyeglasses or contact lenses may be removed if desired.
When the tube passes into the pharynx (about 3 inches), instruct the patient to flex his neck, rest his head on his chest, and take repeated, shallow breaths.	The tube may tend to enter the mouth or trachea.	Flexing the neck helps gravity to pull the tube into the esophagus; repeated shallow breaths help to prevent the tube from being sucked into the trachea.

TABLE 6-1. Nasogastric intubation—cont'd

Technique	Problem	Solution or explanation
Advance the tube as the patient swallows.	Inhalation tends to propel the tube toward the trachea.	Swallowing interrupts inhalation and helps to propel the tube downward.
	Resistance may be felt.	Withdraw the tube a short distance and feed it forward carefully; if resistance is encountered a second time, consult a physician.
Check the placement of the tube when it has been passed to the predetermined distance.	The tube may not be in the stomach.	
1. Fluoroscope to assess the location of the tube.		Fluoroscopy is the most accurate method of determining the location of a radiopaque tube.
2. Aspirate gastric contents.	Failure to aspirate gastric contents may happen.	This may mean that the patient needs to be repositioned to bring the tube in contact with gastric secretions or that the tube may need to be advanced a bit farther.
3. Listen for the sound of air entering the stomach while injecting 5 cc. of air; use a stethoscope.		A popping or swooshing sound will be heard.
4. Place the end of the tube in water and observe for escaping air bubbles.	The tube may be in the trachea.	Rhythmic escape of air bubbles coinciding with respiration usually means that the tube is in the trachea; injection of 1 to 2 ml. of sterile normal saline will induce violent coughing.
When it has been ascertained that the tube is in the stomach, secure it with adhesive tape.	The tube tends to be displaced; pressure on the nose will cause necrosis.	Wrap a strip of tape around the tube and secure the ends of the tape to the nose; do not allow any pressure from the tube on the nose; pressure can be prevented by allowing the tube to emerge in a straight line rather than looping it back over the nose.

187

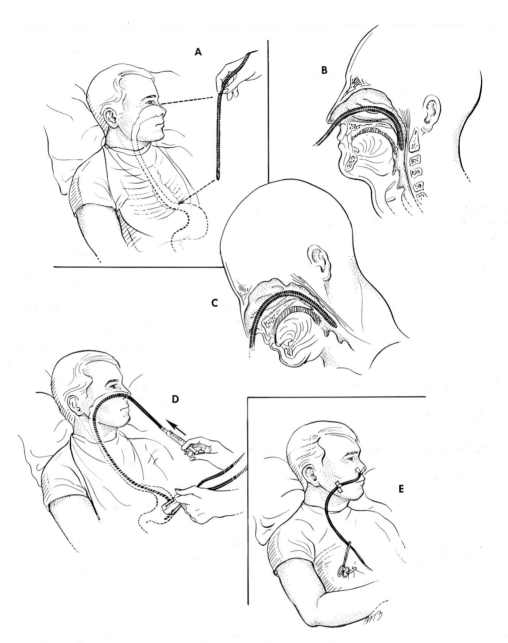

Fig. 6-1. Gastric intubation. **A,** The length of tubing needed to enter the stomach is approximated by measuring the distance from the bridge of the nose to the tip of the xiphoid process. **B,** The patient is encouraged to hold his head in a natural, upright position during the initial phase of intubation. Then the lubricated tip of the tube is placed into the nostril and advanced forward and downward. **C,** When the tube passes into the pharynx, the patient is instructed to flex his head until his chin rests on his chest, to breathe shallowly, and to swallow repeatedly. **D,** Placement of the tube is checked by listening to the sound of air entering the stomach with a stethoscope placed distal to the xiphoid process. Other methods of checking tube placement are described on pages 187, 191, and 192. **E,** The tube is taped to the nostril and clamped or connected to suction.

188

for him. If recent surgical procedure or certain types of trauma have occurred, the physician will use his specialized knowledge to introduce the tube. In some hospitals, it is required that the physician intubate the patient the first time; in a few hospitals, the nurse is not allowed to intubate the patient at all.

A gastric tube may be passed into the stomach through the nose or the mouth. The nasogastric approach is generally preferred because the gag reflex seems to be stimulated less than when the oral approach is used. The nasogastric approach is usually used when the tube is to be left in place for an extended period of time. The oral route is used when deformities such as deviation of the nasal septum or absence of the hard palate exist, when intubation is planned for a relatively short period of time, when this route is preferred by the patient, or when the tube, such as the Ewald tube, is too large to be passed through the nares.

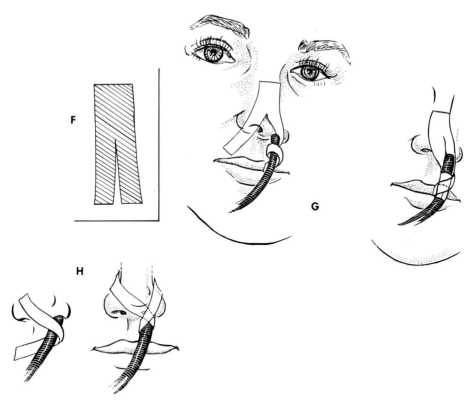

Fig. 6-1, cont'd. F, A length of adhesive tape is split for use in anchoring the tube to the nostril. **G,** The unsplit portion is affixed to the nose, one of the split portions is wrapped around the tube, and then the other portion is wrapped around the tube. **H,** A narrow strip of tape may be used to secure the tube.

The size of the tube selected is influenced by the size of the patient and the purpose of the tube. A plastic or rubber tube, French size 12 to 18, is generally used for adult patients. The type of tube used varies with the supplies available and with the length of time the tube is to be left in place. Some of the newer tubes are radiopaque. One incorporates a sump-type airway that partially suspends the tube and keeps it from direct contact with the mucosa (Fig. 10-5). The latter type prevents damage to the mucosa if suction is used and facilitates collection of specimens, since the tube does not become occluded as readily.

Rubber tubes must be chilled prior to insertion by placing them in a bowl of ice. This stiffens them, facilitating their passage, reducing friction, and lessening irritation of the mucosa. Plastic tubes are not chilled. They are naturally firm and slippery, qualities that facilitate intubation. Once the plastic tube is inserted into the upper gastrointestinal tract, the heat from the body makes it sufficiently pliable for comformance to the anatomy.

After explaining to the patient what must be done and why, the patient is placed in the desired position. A large bib, an apron, or a towel is placed over his chest to protect his clothing. Unless it is contraindicated, the patient is asked to assume a sitting position. The head of the bed may be elevated, or the patient is seated in a chair. A chair with a headrest may provide some comfort but is not essential.

The patient is encouraged to hold his head in a natural, upright position during the initial phase of intubation. If he is unable to sit up, he may lie on his back or on his right side. The latter position helps the tube to pass into the stomach. However, collection of specimens is easier if the patient is turned to his left side after the tube has been passed. Since this technique is not pleasant, it is important that the patient be positioned to promote optimum comfort.

The tube is advanced until it is placed well within the stomach. In the average-sized adult, this distance is about 45 to 55 cm. (18 to 22 inches). If the tube is not premarked, the distance the tube must be passed to enter the stomach may be approximated by measuring the length of tubing needed to extend from the bridge of the nose to the tip of the xiphoid process (Fig. 6-1, *A*).

The tip of the tube is lubricated with normal saline, water, or a water-soluble lubricant. If the latter is used, only the tip of the tube is lubricated; this is done by placing a small amount of the gel on a piece of gauze or tissue and rotating the tip of the tube in the gel to lubricate it. The tube must not be lubricated with water-soluble lubricants if samples are being obtained for cytology studies because the lubricant will interfere with visualization of cells. Oily materials such as mineral oil and petroleum jelly are not used because of the risk of lipid pneumonia developing if the tube or lubricant inadvertently enters the trachea.

NASOGASTRIC INTUBATION

The person inserting the tube graps it about 3 inches from its tip, lubricates it, and places it into the nostril, advancing it forward and downward (Fig. 6-1, *B*). During this stage of intubation the patient is encouraged not to wince, contort his face, or pull away, since these acts make passage of the tube difficult. The patient's eyes will water during this phase. Whether eyeglasses or contact lenses are removed before intubation depends largely on the desires of the patient and the preference of the person doing the intubation. When the person inserting the tube feels it pass into the pharynx, usually a distance of approximately 3 inches, the patient is instructed to flex his head until his chin rests on his chest (Fig. 6-1, *C*), to breathe shallowly, and to swallow repeatedly. Flexing the head forward helps the tube to enter the posterior pharynx rather than the mouth. If the patient is too ill to bend his head forward, an assistant may help, or pillows may be placed to help him assume and maintain this position. The tube is advanced as the patient swallows. This helps propel the tube into and down the esophagus by closing the epiglottis and increasing pharyngeal contraction and esophageal peristalsis. Swallowing interrupts inhalation temporarily, and shallow breathing minimizes the possibility of the tube being sucked into the trachea. The tube is advanced by feeding it forward with each swallow. If excessive gagging occurs, the advancement of the tube may be interrupted temporarily. The patient should be instructed to pant until this sensation passes. If resistance is met, the tube should not be advanced forcibly. The tube is withdrawn a short distance and carefully fed forward. If resistance is again encountered, a physician should be consulted.

Checking placement of tube. When the tube has been passed to the predetermined distance, its placement should be checked to be certain that it is in the stomach. The most accurate method of determining the exact placement of the radiopaque tube is with fluoroscopic visualization. In lieu of such equipment, other methods of checking placement, such as a syringe to aspirate gastric contents, are used. Failure to aspirate gastric contents, however, does not indicate conclusively that the tube is not in the stomach. It indicates only that the tube is not in contact with gastric contents. Changing the position of the patient or advancing the tube farther may bring the tube in contact with the contents of the stomach. A position useful for this purpose is a left side-lying one. However, in some cases effective use of the left side-lying position requires slight elevation of the head of the bed.

The left side-lying position helps the collecting end of the tube to gravitate toward the greater curvature of the stomach where the contents pool when the patient is in this position. Another method of determining that the tube is in the stomach is to place the distal (free) end of the tube in a container of water and evaluate the rhythm of escaping air bubbles. Although some air may be released initially from the stomach, continued rhythmic escape of air bubbles coinciding with the respiratory rate of the patient probably means that the tube has entered the trachea. If the tube is passed through the larynx, the patient will be unable to speak or hum. If it has passed into the lower trachea, contact with the carina tracheae will induce violent coughing. Injection of 1 to 2 ml. of sterile normal saline will stimulate violent coughing if the tube is in the upper respiratory tract. Another method of testing placement in the stomach is injection of a small amount (approximately 5 ml.) of air through the tube. Then placement of the tube is checked by listening to the sound of air entering the stomach, with a stethoscope or one's ear placed over the stomach. A swooshing or popping sound is heard as the air enters the stomach (Fig. 6-1, D).

Securing tube. After the tube is in place, it is secured with tape (Fig. 6-1, E). Either adhesive, masking, or nonallergenic tape may be used. The method of securing the tube should not cause pressure on the tissues or obstruct vision. Pressure on the nose can cause necrosis if allowed to persist. One method of securing the nasogastric tube is to prepare a piece of tape, ½ inch wide and 2½ to 3 inches long, by splitting it lengthwise to its midpoint or a little farther (Fig. 6-1, F). The unsplit portion of the tape is affixed to the nose, and the divided lengths are wrapped around the portion of the tube proximal to the nose (Fig. 6-1, G). Another more simple method that seems to work well is to wrap a narrow strip of tape around the tube and attach the loose ends of the tape to the nose (Fig. 6-1, H).

ORAL INTUBATION

When the tube is introduced through the mouth, the technique is essentially the same as that described for nasogastric intubation, with a few exceptions. The tube is placed over the center and the back of the tongue (Fig. 6-2, A). The patient is instructed to suck on it as he might suck on a straw, and to swallow it as he might swallow a piece of spaghetti. When the tube has been passed about 6 inches, it is placed in the left buccal area, between the teeth and the cheek, to reduce gagging (Fig. 6-2, B). Then it is advanced as the patient swallows. Dentures that fit well need not be removed for intubation. They are helpful in maintaining the orally inserted tube between the teeth and the cheek. If excessive gagging occurs, the tube may be

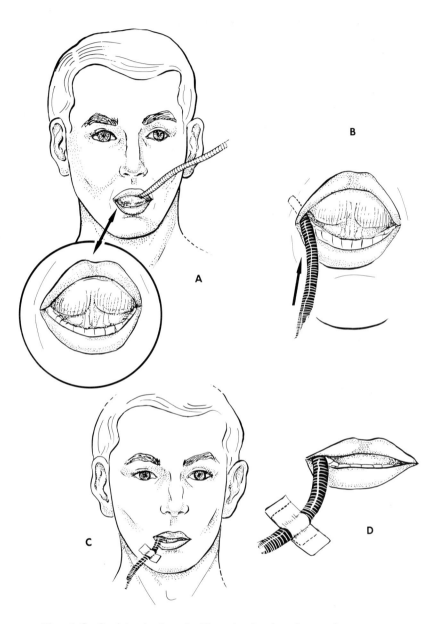

Fig. 6-2. Oral intubation. **A,** The tube is placed over the center and back of the tongue. **B,** When the tube has passed about 6 inches, it is positioned in the left buccal area between the teeth and the cheek to reduce gagging. **C** and **D,** The tube is anchored to the chin with two pieces of tape, placing the first piece over the tube so that the two sides of the tape meet behind the tube and fixing the free ends of the tape to the chin. The second piece of tape is slightly longer than the first and is placed over the first to anchor it more securely.

curling in the back of the throat. This is observed readily by looking into the patient's mouth. Anesthetic agents to relieve gagging should be used only with the physician's approval.

Checking placement of tube. Placement of the tube is checked as described under nasogastric intubation.

Anchoring tube. If the tube has been passed through the mouth, it is anchored to the chin with two pieces of tape. The first piece, about 1½ inches long, is placed over the tube so that the two sides of the tape meet behind the tube, and the free ends of the tape are fixed to the chin. Another piece of tape, slightly longer than the first, is placed over the first piece to anchor it more securely (Fig. 6-2, *C* and *D*). The tube can then be clamped and its end covered and secured to the patient's clothing until a feeding is given. If the patient is ambulatory, he may prefer to drape the tube around his neck. If a sump tube is used, the end of the sump part can simply be placed over the connector, rather than clamping the tube (Fig. 10-5, *C*).

IRRITATION RELATED TO INTUBATION

Permitting the patient to rest for a time after passing the tube allows him to adjust to its presence and to overcome feelings of gagging and nausea that may occur during intubation. The presence of the tube in the nasopharynx may cause irritation that can be eased with any of several methods. A physician's prescription is required for the use of drugs that are applied locally or swallowed. Lozenges, a liquid antacid preparation, and anesthetic sprays or gels may be allowed. Antacids coat the mucosal lining of the pharynx, relieving irritation, and anesthetic agents relieve sensation in the area. Any of the nonsystemic antacid gels or creams seem to give some relief. Lidocaine (Xylocaine) spray, 2%, lidocaine viscous, and Cetacaine are commonly used anesthetic agents.

While the tube is in place the patient tends to breathe through his mouth, thus drying the mucous membranes. In addition, the salivary glands are stimulated less than when one eats normally. Meticulous oral hygiene is indicated for the patient's comfort and to prevent complications such as parotiditis. Lemon and glycerin mixtures coat the membranes as well as cleanse them. Allowing the patient to suck on sour candy stimulates salivation and helps to keep the ducts of the salivary glands patent. Occasional rinsing of the mouth with mouthwashes or water may be soothing; however, frequent rinsing seems to increase dryness and thirst.

REMOVAL OF TUBE

To prevent liquid within the tube from escaping and being aspirated, the tube is clamped before it is removed (Fig. 6-3, *A*). If

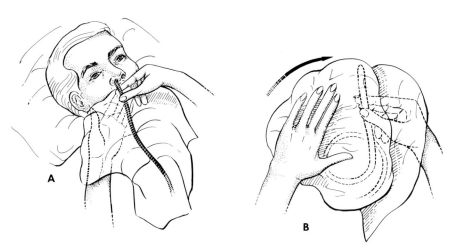

Fig. 6-3. Removal of the tube. **A,** The clamped tube is drawn through a towel held in a manner so that the tube is wiped of secretions as it is pulled through the towel. **B,** The tube is wrapped in a towel and discarded.

a sump-type gastric tube is used, the end of the airway slipped securely over the end of the tube will serve this purpose. A mechanical clamp is preferable to pinching the tube or bending the tube over itself because this permits the person removing the tube to use both hands for this activity and to concentrate on encouraging the patient in cooperating. It also ensures that the tube will remain clamped during removal.

Any tape that was used to anchor the tube is removed, and a towel is placed beneath the tube. If the person removing the tube is right-handed, it is convenient to hold the towel by placing the left hand beneath it in such a manner that the tube will be wiped of secretions as it is pulled through the towel. The patient is instructed to take a deep breath and to exhale slowly; exhalation helps to prevent aspiration of liquids or even inhalation of the tube. During exhalation, the tube is pulled out with one continuous, rapid motion. The tip of the tube is caught with the towel, which is used to cover the tube (Fig. 6-3, *B*). If the person removing the tube wishes, he may place the tube within the towel or simply turn away from the patient momentarily while he discards the tube. Disposable tubes are discarded; tubes that are to be reused must be washed well, rinsed thoroughly, and sterilized.

Tube feeding

The physician prescribes the amount, frequency, and kind of feeding that is to be administered through the tube. The formula for tube feeding can be prepared in advance and stored in the refrigerator. At feeding time, the nurse pours the specified amount of formula into a graduated measure and places it in a basin of warm water (Fig. 6-4, *A*). The temperature of the water should be such that the formula is warmed without producing coagulation. Warming the formula by letting it stand at room temperature for any length of time is a questionable practice because the ingredients and nature of most tube feeding formulas provide an excellent medium for bacterial growth.

After determining that the tube is in the stomach (pages 187, 191, and 192), the nurse pours the formula into a gavage container suspended from an intravenous standard (Fig. 6-4, *B*). The tubing is freed of air, clamped, and connected to the gastric tube (Fig. 6-4, *C*). The patient should, of course, be in a sitting position. When this is not possible, he may be turned on his right side. Suction apparatus should be available if the patient being tube fed is unresponsive or unconscious.

The nurse regulates the rate of flow of the feeding by adjusting the clamp. The flow should be relatively slow to minimize unpleasant sensations that occur when formula passes rapidly through the nasopharyngeal portion of the tube. Ideally, 30 to 45 minutes are required to administer 200 to 300 ml. of liquid formula. Rapid introduction of tube feedings, especially when the caloric content is high, is generally undesirable because of the increased incidence of diarrhea that occurs when this is done.

The formula is followed by a specific amount of water that rinses the tube and prevents coagulation of the formula within the tube. The volume of water used is unlikely to be greater than the volume of any given feeding. The occurrence of nausea or vomiting during feeding may indicate intolerance of the rate of administration, the volume, or the formula itself. Table 6-2 summarizes this technique.

Drugs may be administered by pouring liquid medicine into the gavage container with the formula or water, or by pouring it directly into the tube through a funnel or the barrel of a large syringe that has been connected to the tube. If the form of medication ordered is not suitable for this method of administration, the physician should be consulted, and the pharmacist should be requested to prepare a medication that can be administered safely and accurately through the gavage tube. When the feeding has been completed, the equipment used for gavage must be cleansed thoroughly or discarded.

Infant gavage differs from adult gavage in the volume of the feeding and in the specifications and preparation of the formula. Often a funnel or the barrel of a syringe is attached to the tube, the formula is poured into it, and its rate of flow is regulated by gravity.

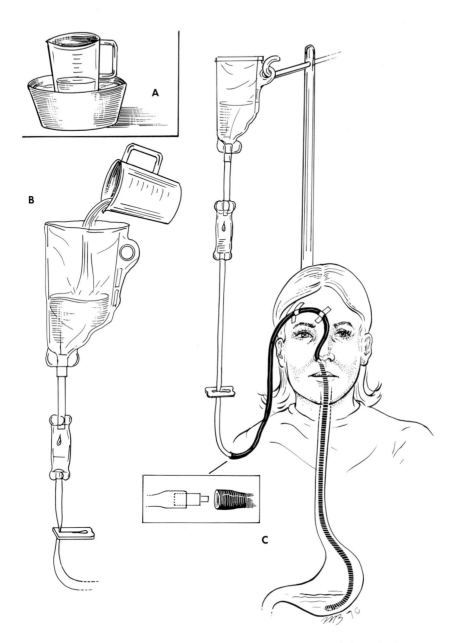

Fig. 6-4. Tube feeding. **A,** A measured amount of formula is warmed in a basin of water. **B,** Formula is poured into the gavage container. **C,** After the tubing is freed of air, clamped, and connected to the gastric tube, the rate of flow is regulated. The inset shows one method of joining the tubes. (Courtesy Travenol Laboratories, Inc., Deerfield, Ill.)

TABLE 6-2. Tube feeding

Technique	Problem	Explanation or solution
Pour specified amount and kind of formula into a graduated measure.	Administration of an incorrect type or amount of formula is dangerous to the welfare of the patient.	The physician prescribes the amount and kind of formula and the frequency with which it is to be given.
Place graduated measure of formula into a basin of warm water for a few minutes.	Hot water coagulates protein and encourages microbial growth.	Normally, fluids are warmed by the body before reaching the stomach.
Place the patient in a sitting position; if this is not possible, elevate the head of the bed and turn the patient on the right side.	Formula can be aspirated into the respiratory tract.	The cardiac sphincter is relaxed by the presence of the tube; the patient may not be able to use the normal mechanisms for preventing aspiration.
Pour formula into gavage container and free the tubing leading from the container of air.	Formula may escape from the tube if the clamp is difficult to control.	Hold the end of the tube over the graduated measure; bend the tubing over itself or pinch it shut manually if this is possible.
Attach the gavage tubing to the nasogastric tube and adjust the flow of the formula.	Rapid flow may be uncomfortable and may cause side effects; slow flow may interfere with being able to give the prescribed amount over a period of 24 hours.	Rapid flow may cause an unpleasant sensation in the nasopharynx and is likely to cause diarrhea.
As soon as the last of the formula has emptied into the tubing, place the specified amount of water into the gavage container.	The formula may coagulate and obstruct the nasogastric tube.	The volume of water is unlikely to exceed the amount of the feeding prescribed; water clears the tube of formula.
Clamp the tubes and disconnect them; cover the end of the nasogastric tube with gauze and leave the patient in a sitting position for an hour or longer.	Gastric contents may return through an unclamped tube; contents may flow around the tube and be aspirated.	It takes about an hour for the fluid to leave the stomach; maintaining the patient in a sitting or semisitting position for this period of time helps to prevent aspiration of gastric contents.

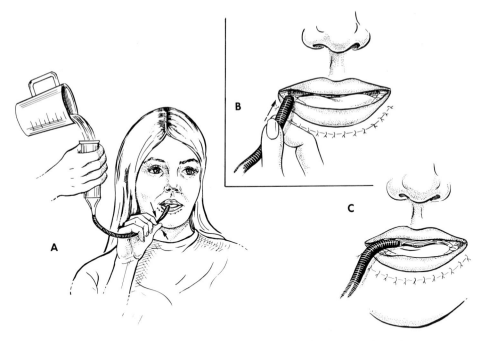

Fig. 6-5. Funnel feeding. **A,** After the tube is connected to the funnel and is placed, the patient regulates the flow of feeding with the fingers and tongue. **B,** The tube is inserted distal to surgical repair. **C,** The tube is directed so that the liquid is placed near the back of the patient's tongue.

The rate of flow is therefore influenced by the distance between the tip of the tube and the tip of the funnel.

Funnel feeding

When mastication and movements of the lips are contraindicated, liquids may be given orally with the aid of a funnel to which a length of rubber tubing has been attached (Fig. 6-5, *A*). The tubing is placed in the patient's mouth at a point distal to any surgical repair, usually at one corner of his mouth (Fig. 6-5, *B*), and directed so that the liquid is placed near the back of the patient's tongue (Fig. 6-5, *C*). The patient, even an infant, quickly learns to control the flow of liquid feeding with sucking actions and the position of his tongue. If this method is used to feed a young or weak infant, a rubber bulb attached to the syringe may be necessary. The rubber bulb must be compressed gently, slowly, and continuously to control the rate of flow and prevent the introduction of air.

199

Infant feeders

Tiny infants who do not have the strength to suck may be fed with the aid of an infant feeder. Such a feeder resembles a bulb syringe with an elongated nipple. Again, the pressure used to squeeze the bulb must be slow and gentle if the infant is to be kept from strangling.

Questions for discussion and exploration

1. If a patient who is intubated is found to be achlorhydric, what foods or drugs might be given to him to stimulate the secretion of hydrochloric acid?
2. What disease is ruled out if the patient secretes hydrochloric acid either with or without stimulation?
3. What are some of the factors (cultural, economic, religious, emotional, esthetic) that influence the acceptance of a diet or its components?
4. What are some of the causes and symptoms of nausea?
5. How do people react when nausea and vomiting occur? Why?
6. What are some of the nursing and medical measures used to relieve nausea and vomiting?
7. Under what circumstances is vomiting beneficial to the patient? How can vomiting be induced?
8. If the patient with a gastric tube gags easily and complains of a sore throat, what might you as a nurse do to lessen these problems?
9. When you walk into a room and find that the nasogastric tube in a patient has been looped back and up and taped to the nose and forehead, what should you look for? Why? What nursing action is indicated and why?
10. If you answer a patient's call and find him with a nasogastric tube in place and doing one of the following, think through the possible causes, methods of evaluating this situation, and appropriate nursing action for each:
    a. Patient is wretching
    b. Patient is vomiting
    c. Patient is coughing
    d. Patient seems to be choking and is pulling at the tube
    e. Tube is obviously slipping out of the nose
11. If the physician asks that a nasogastric tube be removed, how is this done? Discuss the rationale for the method you described.

Selected references

Bockus, H. L.: Gastroenterology, ed. 2, Philadelphia, 1963, W. B. Saunders Co., vol. 1.

Davenport, R. R.: Tube feeding for long-term patients, Amer. J. Nurs. 64:121-123, 1964.

Davidsohn, I., and Henry, J., editors: Todd-Sanford clinical diagnosis by laboratory methods, ed. 15, Philadelphia, 1974, W. B. Saunders Co.

Fason, M. F.: Controlling bacterial growth in tube feeding, Amer. J. Nurs. 67:1246-1247, 1967.

Freidrich, H. N.: Oral feeding by food pump, Amer. J. Nurs. 62:62-64, 1962.

Larson, C. B., and Gould, M.: Orthopedic nursing, ed. 8, St. Louis, 1974, The C. V. Mosby Co.

Larson, D. L., Karzel, R., and Cameron, H.: Intestinal intubation with the aid of a magnetic tube, Surg. Gynec. Obstet. 115:503-504, 1962.

Marlow, D. R.: Textbook of pediatric nursing, ed. 4, Philadelphia, 1973, W. B. Saunders Co.

Smith, A. V.: Nasogastric tube feedings, Amer. J. Nurs. 57:1451-1452, 1957.

Williams, S. R.: Nutrition and diet therapy, ed. 2, St. Louis, 1973, The C. V. Mosby Co.

7

Intravenous fluid therapy

Selection of suitable equipment for venipuncture is guided by detailed information about the planned therapy. It is helpful to know the types of fluids that will be infused, whether the infusion is to be continuous or intermittent, the anticipated length of time over which therapy will extend, and the predicted need for blood transfusions. It is useful to know whether medications are to be administered and what the action of these drugs is on the cardiovascular system. Knowledge that a drug is irritating to the vein or the heart will guide the selection of equipment and the rate of flow of solution.

Preparation for venipuncture

After obtaining the necessary equipment, the site of venipuncture is selected and prepared. The site of choice is usually in the arm. For short procedures such as a single-dose injection or withdrawal of a blood sample, the most conveniently located vein, frequently an antecubital vein, may be used. If therapy is to extend for a long period of time, it is preferable to choose a vein that is naturally splinted by long bones such as the ulna and the radius. The veins are distended by the application of pressure that permits arterial flow into the extremity but blocks the venous outflow. The use of a sphygmomanometer for this purpose is superior to the use of a tourniquet. The blood pressure cuff is applied as high on the upper arm as possible to preserve accessibility of the antecubital veins. A pressure setting of 100 mm. of mercury should cause engorgement of the veins of most patients within 60 to 90 seconds (Fig. 7-1). When they are palpated, veins feel similar to flexible, hollow tubes.

If the venous pattern is not visible or palpable after a reasonable period of time, the nurse may apply hot packs. Hot packs applied to distend the veins should enclose the entire hand, the forearm, and extend well above the elbow for maximum effectiveness (Fig. 11-7). The hot, moist pack is enclosed in plastic or another waterproof material to retain the heat and then is wrapped with a Turkish towel secured with bandage or safety pins. If a heating pad that can safely be placed in contact with moisture is available, it is placed directly over the hot, moist pack, wrapped securely around it, and covered with a towel to hold it in place. When a heating pad is used, pins are not used because of the dangers of puncturing the heating element. The hot, moist pack should be left in place for a minimum of 20 minutes and preferably for 30 minutes to ensure maximum

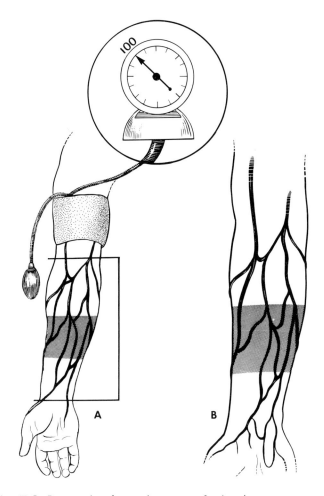

Fig. 7-1. Preparation for venipuncture. **A,** A sphygmomanometer is applied to the upper arm and inflated to distend the veins. **B,** An average pattern of superficial veins. The preferred area for fluid therapy is shaded.

distention of the veins. The skin must not be treated with oil before applying hot, moist packs to distend the veins because this increases the difficulty of venipuncture.

A right-handed person grasps the extremity with the left hand so that the thumb rests on the skin at a point approximately 2 inches distal to the selected site of venipuncture and exerts tension toward

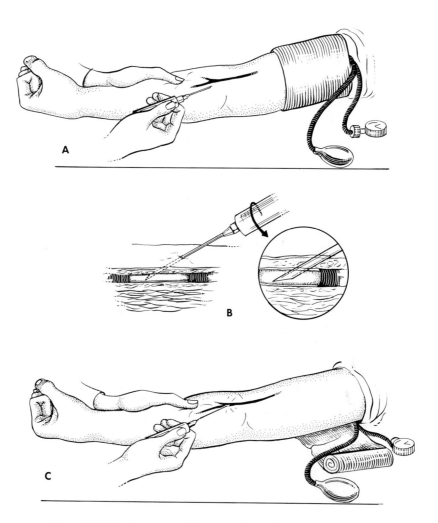

Fig. 7-2. Venipuncture with a steel needle. **A,** Tension of the thumb, distal to the site of venipuncture, stretches the skin and stabilizes the vein. The needle, attached to a syringe, is inserted through the skin adjacent to the vein. **B,** The needle is held at a little less than a 45-degree angle for penetration of the skin. When the needle enters the vein, the bevel is rotated to prevent puncture of the posterior wall of the vessel. **C,** The needle and syringe are lowered nearly parallel to the skin for advancement into the vein.

the hand. This tension minimizes the difficulty experienced when superficial veins retract or curl away from the needle point and is helpful if it is maintained until the needle is in its final position within the vein (Figs. 7-2, *A* and *C*, and 7-3, *A, B, D,* and *F*). Prior to puncturing the skin, the nurse cleanses the site with a suitable antiseptic such as 70% alcohol.

Venipuncture with a steel needle

To perform venipuncture with a steel needle (Table 7-1), one seldom needs to use a needle larger than 20 gauge. The needle is attached to the syringe and is inserted through the skin adjacent to the vein (Fig. 7-2, *A*), holding the syringe at a little less than a 45-degree angle (Fig. 7-2, *B*). As soon as the needle has penetrated through the skin, the syringe is lowered to a position almost parallel to the skin, and the needle is advanced into the vein (Fig. 7-2, *C*). It is extremely important that direct contact with the patient's extremity be maintained while manipulating the syringe to avoid losing the vein or inadvertently puncturing the posterior wall of the vessel. As soon as the needle enters the vein, the bevel is rotated to prevent puncture of the posterior wall of the vessel (Fig. 7-2, *B*).

If the purpose of venipuncture is to obtain a sample of blood, this is done before the pressure applied to the extremity by the blood pressure cuff is released. When the sample has been obtained, the tourniquet is released, the needle is removed, and pressure is applied to the puncture site with a sterile compress until the bleeding subsides. When the purpose of venipuncture is to infuse a single bottle of fluid or blood, the needle and tubing are affixed to the arm with adhesive tape, the tourniquet is released, and the tubing is connected to the needle. The method of taping the steel needle to the arm is similar to that illustrated in Fig. 7-4, *B* and *C*, for securing the plastic needle. A small piece of tape (Fig. 7-4, *B, 3*) is placed beneath the hub of the needle, and a longer piece of tape is placed over the top of the hub and applied to the skin on either side of the hub (Fig. 7-4, *C*). This stabilizes the needle.

Venipuncture with a plastic needle

The plastic needle is one of the various devices available for prolonged intravenous therapy. Some plastic needles are intended for single use only and are considered disposable. Others can be reassembled, sterilized, and reused. Plastic stylets to fit these needles are available and may be used when intermittent infusions are in-

TABLE 7-1. Venipuncture with a steel needle (for obtaining a blood sample or for giving a single dose of medication)

Technique	Problem	Solution or explanation
Select the necessary equipment.		A 20-gauge needle, alcohol wipes, and a sphygmomanometer or tourniquet are needed.
Locate a fairly large, convenient vein.	A vein that is small or difficult to reach cannot be punctured easily and satisfactorily.	Usually an antecubital vein is satisfactory.
Apply pressure above the site for 60 to 90 seconds before beginning venipuncture; pressure is left on during venipuncture; a blood pressure cuff inflated to 100 mm. of mercury is satisfactory.	The cuff will interfere with the technique if it is applied too near the site of venipuncture; if it is too inflated, it may occlude venous flow.	The cuff interferes with venous return; the blood that is unable to return distends the veins.
If necessary, apply hot packs around the hand, forearm, and upper arm for 20 minutes; during this time, release the tourniquet and reapply it when venipuncture is to be carried out.	The venous pattern may not be visible or palpable.	Heat brings more blood to the area and helps to distend the veins.
Grasp the extremity with the left hand so that the thumb rests on the skin about 2 inches distal to the site of venipuncture and exert tension toward the hand.	Superficial veins tend to retract or curl away from the needle point.	Tension on the skin stabilizes the vein.
Cleanse the site of venipuncture.	Organisms may be introduced and cause infection.	Frictional cleansing with an antiseptic removes organisms from the skin.
Holding the syringe a little lower than a 45-degree angle, insert the needle into the skin adjacent to the vein; when the needle has penetrated the skin, lower the syringe so it is almost parallel to the skin and advance the needle into the vein; when the needle enters the vein, turn its bevel downward.	The vein may be lost, or its posterior wall may be penetrated.	Maintaining tension on the skin will usually prevent loss of the vein; rotating the bevel of the needle helps to prevent puncture of the posterior wall of the vein.
Aspirate to obtain a sample of blood if this is the purpose of venipuncture.	The wall of the vein may collapse, making it impossible to obtain a sample even though the needle is in the vein.	Aspiration with the syringe should be done slowly and gently to prevent this from happening.
Remove the tourniquet or deflate the blood pressure cuff.	The extremity may become mottled, cyanotic, or numb.	Restoration of circulation supplies the tissues with oxygen and blood.
Remove the needle, cleanse the site, and apply pressure with a small bandage or dressing.	Bleeding from the site occurs whenever a vein is penetrated.	Cleansing helps to prevent infection. The dressing acts as a barrier to organisms in the environment; direct pressure will stop bleeding from a superficial vein.

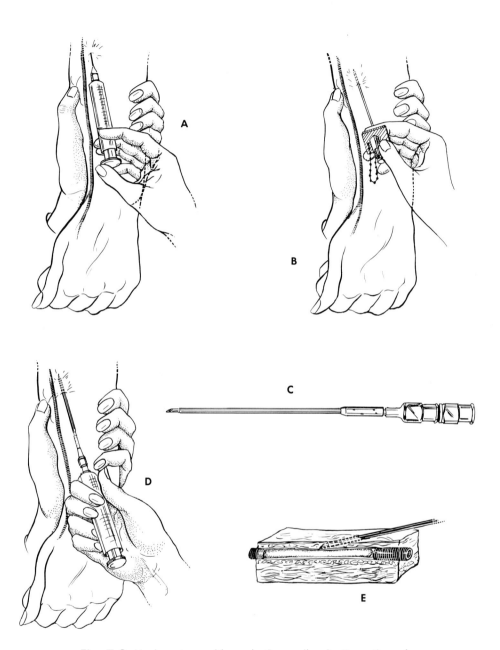

Fig. 7-3. Venipuncture with a plastic needle. **A,** Formation of a skin wheal with a local anesthetic agent. **B,** A pathway for the plastic needle is formed by puncturing the skin with a large-bore steel needle. **C,** Plastic needle, Jelco I. V. catheter placement unit. **D,** The plastic needle is attached to a syringe for introduction through the preformed channel. **E,** Cross section showing a needle being introduced through the channel.

Continued.

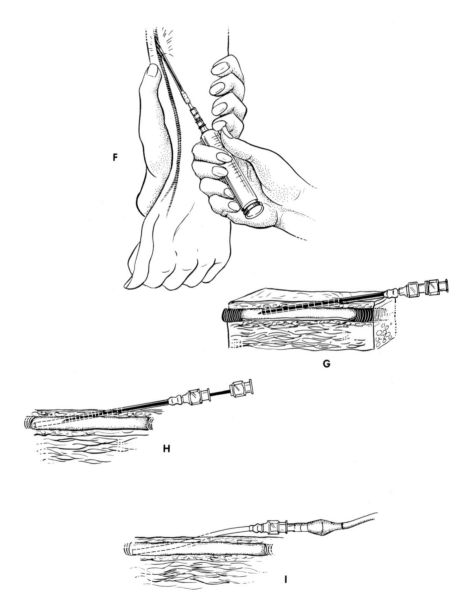

Fig. 7-3, cont'd. F, The plastic needle is introduced into the vein. **G,** Cross section of a needle entering the vein. **H,** When the plastic part of the needle has entered the vein, the styletted steel needle is withdrawn about 0.5 cm. The needle is then advanced to its final position. **I,** After the plastic needle has been advanced to its final position, the styletted steel needle is withdrawn before administration of fluids. (Courtesy Jelco Laboratories, Raritan, N. J.)

dicated. Each of the plastic needles encases a conventional steel needle that facilitates the introduction of the device. The tip of the steel needle extends a few millimeters beyond the tip of the plastic needle (Fig. 7-3, C).

The technique of introducing the plastic needle into the vein differs somewhat from the technique described for venipuncture with a steel needle. Although the demonstration of the vein and the preparation of the site are the same, the site should be selected carefully, because the plastic needle is used when prolonged infusion is desired. The introduction of the plastic needle is painful enough to make the use of a local anesthetic agent mandatory. A skin wheal that is approximately ½ inch in diameter should be raised at the site selected for venipuncture (Fig. 7-3, A). Care to prevent the local anesthetic agent from entering the bloodstream should be exercised.

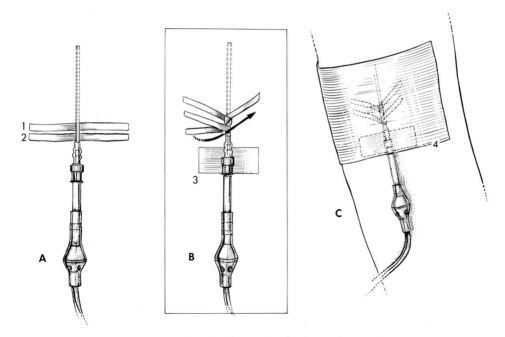

Fig. 7-4. Securing the plastic needle. **A,** Approximate placement of narrow strips of tape. The first tape is anchored before the second one is placed. The tape must adhere to the distal end of the plastic needle. **B,** Method of fastening tape to the needle and skin. Tape beneath the hub is placed with its adhesive side up. Its adherence to overlying tape prevents movement of the needle, which may contribute to separation and loss of the plastic tube. Tape should not interfere with injection into the needle. **C,** A large piece of tape completes stabilization of the needle. It is labeled to show the date of insertion and that a plastic needle is in place.

Introduction of the plastic needle is made easier if a pathway for the plastic needle is provided by puncture of the skin with a large-bore steel needle such as a Lewisohn needle (Fig. 7-3, *B*). The diameter of the steel needle used to create the pathway should equal the diameter of the plastic needle that will be introduced. Care to avoid injury to the vein with this needle is necessary. Venipuncture with the plastic needle is performed by introducing the plastic needle through this preformed channel (Fig. 7-3, *D* and *E*). When the plastic needle has entered the vein (Fig. 7-3, *F* and *G*), the styletted steel needle is withdrawn about 0.5 cm. (Fig. 7-3, *H*). The plastic needle is then advanced as far as possible into the vein, and the styletted steel needle is removed entirely (Fig. 7-3, *I*).

SECURING THE PLASTIC NEEDLE

A method of securing the plastic needle is shown in Fig. 7-4. Two narrow strips of tape circle the distal portion of the needle and are taped to the skin in a modified V pattern (Fig. 7-4, *A* and *B*). These tapes prevent slippage and loss of the plastic tube. Separation of the plastic tube from the hub occurs infrequently. The described method of anchoring the needle prevents loss of the plastic tube within the vein if such separation occurs. Two additional strips of tape are used to prevent the hub from sliding sideways. The smaller strip of tape is placed under the hub (Fig. 7-4, *B*) so that it can adhere to the hub and to the larger strip of tape that is placed over it (Fig. 7-4, *C*). The tape will adhere better if excess hair is removed

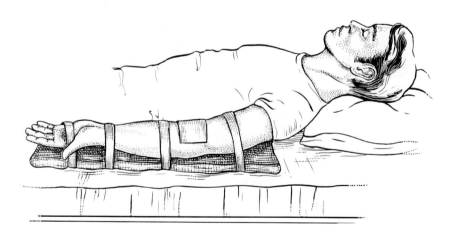

Fig. 7-5. Application of splints. The arm board should extend well beyond movable joints (elbow and wrist). Its use is necessary when the site of venipuncture is not splinted naturally by long bones. Bands used to secure the arm board should be snug, but not constricting.

from the site beforehand. If the plastic tube becomes detached from the hub and floats in the vein, the person discovering this must prevent the tube from traveling through the circulatory system. A tourniquet, preferably a blood pressure cuff, will serve this purpose. The physician must be notified immediately so that he can remove the tube without delay. Radiographs are useful in locating the tube, which is radiopaque.

Use of veins in the hand

Occasionally one may be tempted to use protruding veins of the hand for venipuncture. Results of the use of this site have been unsatisfactory. Often these veins are more brittle than veins of the lower arm, particularly in older people. Because an undue amount of motion of the hand is unavoidable, hematomas develop frequently; they are particularly painful in this area.

Application of splints

Splinting the arm can be avoided in many instances. If it is necessary because of the site of venipuncture, the arm board should be well padded and applied carefully. It is applied to the back of the forearm and should extend from the lower part of the upper arm to the back of the hand, immobilizing both the elbow and wrist (Fig. 7-5).

Administration of solutions by intravenous infusion

To administer fluids intravenously, the nurse needs to obtain the designated solution and an appropriate length of tubing fitted with a drip chamber, needle adaptor, an adaptor to connect the tubing to the reservoir of solution, and a clamp to regulate the flow of solution. It is always advisable to administer fluids with a filter. Use of a filter is mandatory when whole blood is being administered. The filter used must be chosen according to the fluid being administered.

Disposable connecting tubing designed with all of these features is available from manufacturers of solutions for intravenous infusion. The tubing is attached to the reservoir of solution, the solution is suspended several feet above the site of venipuncture, and the drip chamber is partially filled by squeezing it. The tubing and the filter, if one is incorporated into the administration tubing, is freed of air by filling it with solution, the flow of solution is interrupted with a clamp, and the tubing is connected to the needle. In keeping with the physician's orders, the rate of flow is adjusted by regulating the clamp on the tubing, positioning the site of injection, and altering the height of the container of solution.

The method of connecting the tubing to the bottle varies with the equipment. If the container of solution is fitted with a rubber stopper sealed with a thin rubber covering, it is important that the covering diaphragm be removed before the tubing adaptor is inserted into the stopper. The adaptor is placed securely into the larger of the openings, not the smaller airway opening. If the container of solution incorporates an entry port into its design, the spike adaptor of the intravenous administration tubing is inserted into the entry port until it penetrates the seal. The adaptor is then twisted until it is securely in place. Asepsis should be maintained throughout this technique (Figs. 7-6 to 7-9).

If the container is fitted with a solid rubber stopper, the adaptor from the tubing is inserted through the center of the stopper at a 90-degree angle (Fig. 7-6, F). Any other angle or the turning of the adaptor during insertion may cause coring of the stopper and is, therefore, contraindicated. If an air filter is contained in the tubing, closing the clamp on the tubing before suspending the solution will facilitate filling of the drip chamber to the desired level.

The rate of flow of the solution can be determined by using the following formula:

$$\frac{\text{No. of milliliters of solution} \times \text{No. of drops/ml.}}{\text{No. of hours over which solution is to be administered} \times 60 \ (\text{min.})} = \text{Drops/min.}$$

The number of drops per milliliter delivered varies with the manufacturer and the equipment used. The labels should be consulted to learn the approximate number of drops per milliliter delivered by a particular system. Direct observation of the rate of flow is necessary because of the number of factors that may cause the flow rate to vary.

ATTACHING A SECOND CONTAINER OF SOLUTION USING Y TUBING

A second container of solution can be attached to the primary container of solution. Although the bottles of solution may be attached in a series with a short length of tubing (Fig. 7-6, M and N), it is preferable to attach two bottles with a Y connector that permits the two solutions to be administered either simultaneously or intermittently (Figs. 7-7 and 7-9, H). The method of attachment is similar regardless of the equipment available. Sterile Y tubing complete with adaptors to fit the containers of solution is available. An adaptor is attached to each bottle of solution in the manner described previously. Both bottles of solution are suspended, and air is re-

Text continued on p. 217.

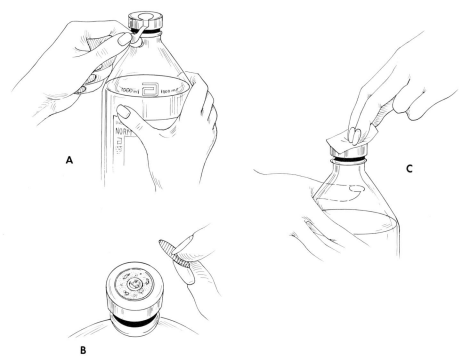

A

B

C

Continued.

Fig. 7-6. Administration of fluids from containers fitted with solid rubber stoppers. **A,** The metal seal is removed from the bottle. **B,** The metal disk covering the stopper in the bottle is removed. **C,** The stopper is cleansed with an antiseptic, usually 70% alcohol. **D,** The administration tubing is unpackaged, and the clamp on the tubing is closed. **E,** The insertion pin of the tubing, located above the drip chamber, is exposed. **F,** The pin on the administration tubing is inserted into the center of the stopper by pushing it straight down through the marked circular area on the stopper. The pin must not be angled or twisted if coring of the stopper is to be avoided. **G,** The solution is suspended, and the drip chamber is partially filled. **H,** The clamp is opened to free the tubing of air. **I,** After the tubing is freed of air, it is attached to the venipuncture needle. This may be done before or after venipuncture is performed. **J,** Medication can be added with a syringe and needle through the stopper before the tubing is attached to the bottle. **K,** Medication may be added through the medication port after the tubing is attached. **L,** Medication may be added through the medication port after the solution is suspended. **M,** A secondary bottle of solution may be added to the primary bottle by attaching a short length of tubing into the primary air inlet. For this, the air filter must be removed from the primary bottle. **N,** After attaching the secondary bottle of solution, the clamp on the short length of connecting tubing is opened fully. The rate of flow is adjusted as necessary with the clamp on the primary tubing. (Courtesy Abbott Laboratories, North Chicago, Ill.)

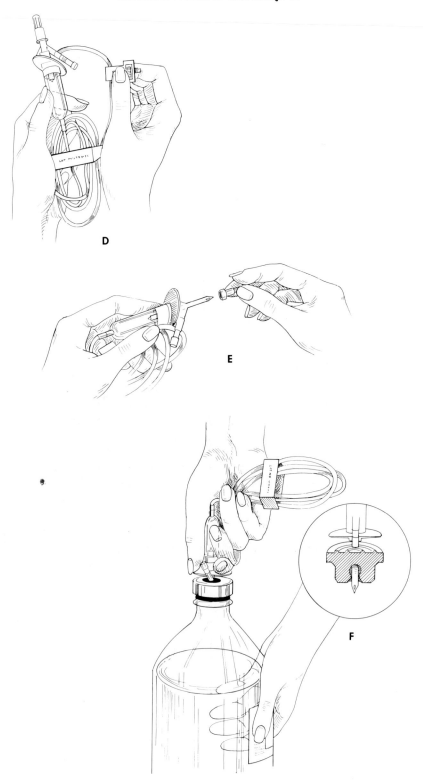

Fig. 7-6, cont'd. For legend see p. 213.

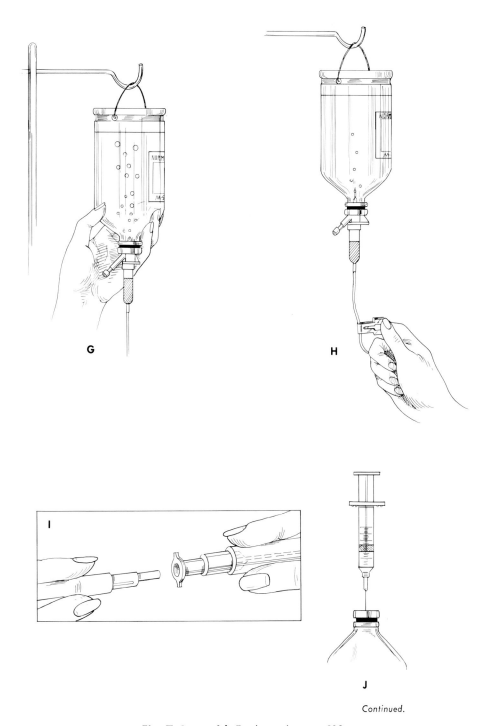

G

H

I

J

Continued.

Fig. 7-6, cont'd. For legend see p. 213.

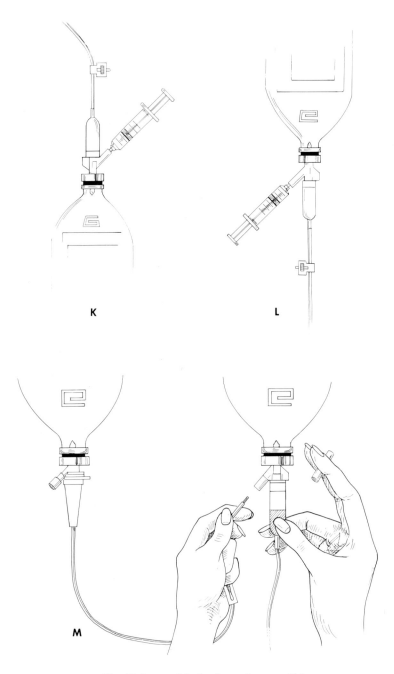

K   L

M

Fig. 7-6, cont'd. For legend see p. 213.

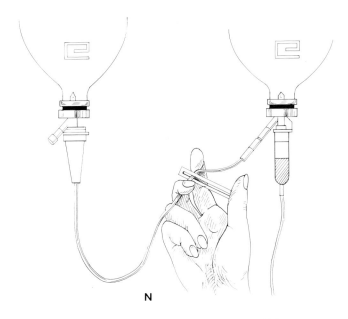

N

Fig. 7-6, cont'd. For legend see p. 213.

moved from the tubing. The two solutions will tend to mix, depending on the position of the clamps on the tubing and the height and specific gravities of the solutions. Mixing of the solutions can be prevented by closing the clamp on one extension of the Y tubing or by using special tubing and a hanger designed for this purpose (Fig. 7-7).

ADDITION OF MEDICATIONS AND ATTACHMENT OF TUBING

Medications may be administered simultaneously as part of the intravenous infusion solution or separately through the needle that has been placed in a vein. Before administering any drug intravenously, precautions are taken to be certain that the preparation available is suitable for intravenous administration. Preparations that are unsterile or that have an oil base are not suitable. The medication must be compatible with the intravenous solution and with any other drugs that are to be added to the same solution. For this information, the nurse should consult reliable sources.

To administer the medication separately, the rubber inset of the tubing near the needle is cleansed with an antiseptic, the flow of solution is interrupted, and the drug is injected by piercing the rubber inset with a small needle, frequently 25 gauge, attached to the drug-filled syringe. It is important to observe for the presence of air bubbles in the tubing and for solution leaking from the tub-

217

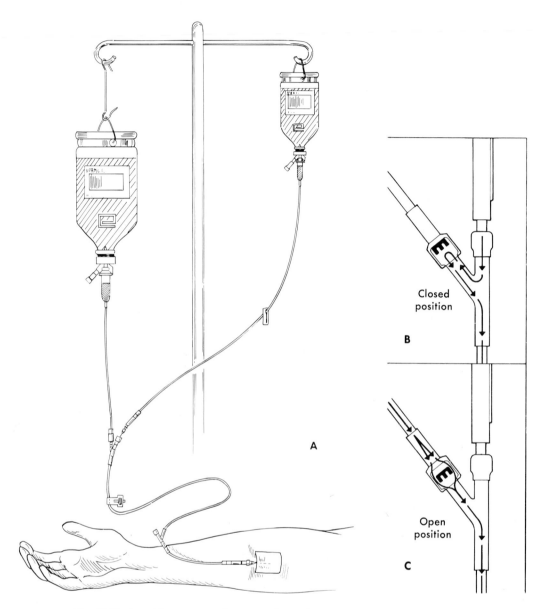

Fig. 7-7. Attaching a secondary container of additive solution, including drugs.
A, The additive solution is suspended, its tubing is cleared of air, and its clamp
is closed. After the injection site is cleansed with antiseptic, the needle on the
tubing from the secondary container is inserted into the injection site on the primary tubing. The primary solution is suspended lower than the additive solution
with a special hanger. The rate of flow is adjusted by the clamp on the primary
tubing. **B,** Closed valve showing direction of flow. When the additive solution is
attached, tapping the injection site on the tubing lightly helps to ensure that the
backcheck valve is seated properly. The higher pressure of the secondary solution
forces the valve closed until all of the additive solution has been administered. **C,**
Open valve showing direction of flow. When the additive solution has been administered, the equalization of pressure in the containers allows the valve to open,
allowing the solution from the primary container to flow.

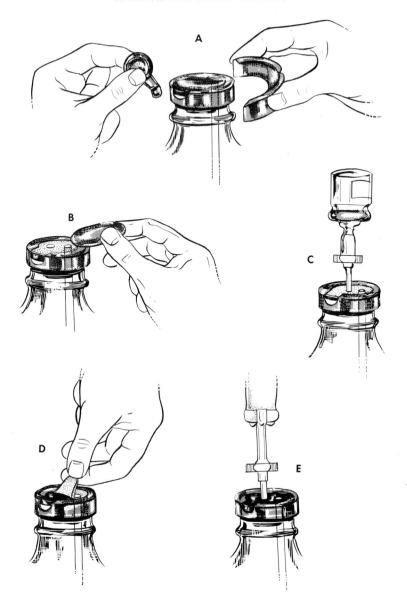

Continued.

Fig. 7-8. Administration of intravenous fluids with a metal seal and rubber diaphragm covering. **A,** The metal seal covering the bottle is removed. **B,** The metal cover is removed. **C,** Medication is added through the rubber seal or diaphragm, using a special medication vial. Injection must not be placed into the airway. **D,** The rubber seal is removed. **E,** The adaptor on the intravenous administration tubing is inserted. **F,** The bottle of solution is suspended, and the tubing remains clamped until the adaptor for the needle is uncovered. **G,** The drip chamber is squeezed and released to partially fill it. The tubing is freed of air by permitting fluid to fill it completely. **H,** The tubing is attached to the needle. **I,** The arrow points to self-sealing sites for injection into the flashball. (Courtesy Baxter Laboratories, Inc., Morton Grove, Ill.)

219

ing. If the rubber inset in the tubing does not seal itself, air can be pulled into the tubing by the flow of the solution, resulting in an air embolus. The use of large-bore needles is undesirable; these tend to remove a core of rubber and cause leakage to occur. Various mechanical devices facilitating the injection of drugs are available as a part of different brands of tubing.

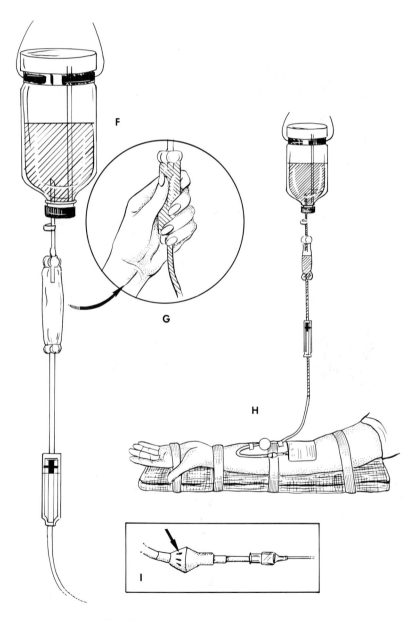

Fig. 7-8, cont'd. For legend see p. 219.

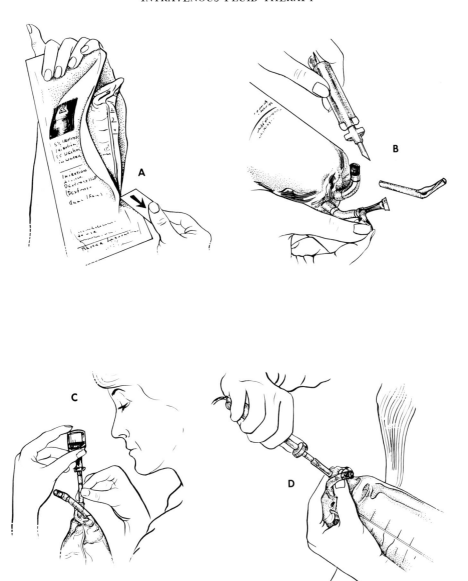

Fig. 7-9. Administration of intravenous solution in plastic containers (Viaflex solution packs). **A,** The container of solution is removed from its protective covering by tearing the wrapper along a premarked line. **B,** The protective coverings are removed from the adaptor spike and the port into which it will be inserted. These parts must be kept sterile. **C,** Medication contained in vials may be added to the solution before the adaptor spike of the intravenous tubing is uncovered and inserted into the port. Some vials are pumped with a device that is built into the vial to force the medication into the intravenous solution; others require that the bag of solution be compressed and released alternately to draw the medication into the bag. When no medication is to be added, this step is omitted. **D,** After adding the medication, the adaptor spike of the intravenous tubing is inserted into the port of the plastic solution pack.

Continued.

221

The method of adding drugs to the solution will vary with the type of equipment used and the time at which the drug is added to the solution. In some institutions, medication is added to the intravenous solution by the pharmacist. If the container of solution is fitted with a solid rubber stopper, the drug can be injected directly though the stopper before the administration tubing is attached to the container (Fig. 7-6, *J*). If the bottle is fitted with a rubber stop-

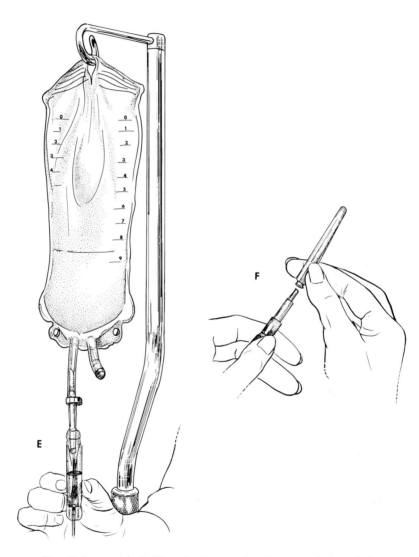

Fig. 7-9, cont'd. E, The plastic container is suspended, and the drip chamber is squeezed and released to partially fill it. **F,** The nurse removes the covering from the adaptor that connects the tubing to the needle, and then clears the tubing of air by filling it with fluid.

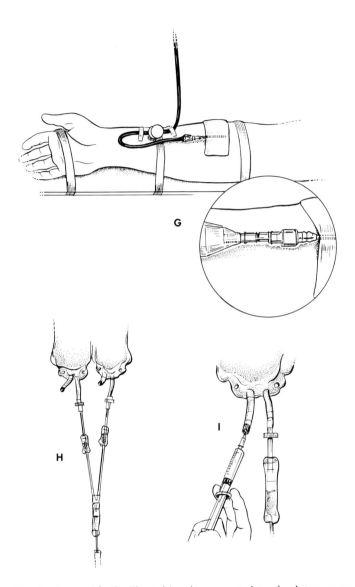

Fig. 7-9, cont'd. G, The tubing is connected to the intravenous needle or catheter. **H,** A Y tubing may be used to connect two containers of solution. These may be administered alternately or simultaneously by regulating the flow of solution with the clamps on the tubings above the drip chamber. Solutions that are to be administered simultaneously must be compatible with each other. **I,** Medication may be injected into the solution before or after the container has been suspended. The covering over the port through which the medication is injected must be cleansed with a suitable antiseptic before the sterile needle is inserted. (Courtesy Baxter Laboratories, Morton Grove, Ill.)

per sealed with a thin sheet of rubber, the drug can be injected through the rubber diaphragm into the opening intended for the insertion of the tubing adaptor (Fig. 7-8, *C*). The bottle of tubing is suspended, and the tubing is freed of air and attached to the needle (Figs. 7-6, *I,* 7-8, *H,* and 7-9, *F* and *G*).

ADMINISTRATION TUBING FOR SECONDARY CONTAINER OF SOLUTION

Administration tubing designed for the addition of a secondary container of solution is available. This tubing is attached to the container of primary solution, which is then suspended below the level of the secondary container. A hanger is supplied with the tubing for this purpose. Next, the tubing from the secondary container is freed of air, the container is suspended, and the needle on the secondary tubing is inserted into the previously cleansed medication site located on the administration tubing leading from the primary container. The rate of flow is adjusted. The secondary container will empty first. A valve in the tubing from the primary solution will prevent the secondary solution from backing up into the primary solution; as soon as the secondary container has emptied, the valve permits the primary solution to flow (Fig. 7-7).

Fig. 7-8 shows administration of intravenous fluids with a thin rubber seal type of covering. After the metal seal covering the bottle and the metal cover are removed, medication is added through the rubber seal, using a special medication vial (Fig. 7-8, *A* to *C*). This special medication vial can also be used for the administration of fluids supplied in plastic containers shown in Fig. 7-9, *C*. The medication vial is equipped with a special adaptor to fit the opening in the bottle's stopper. As a precaution against overdosage and contamination, it is left in place until the rubber seal is removed. Addition of the drug must be made with the aid of a syringe after breaking the rubber seal. It is important with this type of bottle that the drug be introduced through the correct opening, since functioning of the reservoir is dependent on patency of the airway. The airway will be blocked or dislodged if the drug is inserted through it. If the container is fitted with an air filter, the filter can be removed, even after the container has been suspended, and a syringe filled with medication can be inserted into this opening (Fig. 7-6, *K* and *L*). The syringe is not fitted with a needle. After the drug has been injected, the syringe is removed and the air filter is replaced; the solution should be swirled to ensure complete mixing of the drug with the solution.

After adding medication to intravenous fluid supplied with a metal seal type of covering, the rubber seal is removed, the adaptor on the intravenous tubing is inserted, and the bottle of solution is suspended. The tubing is freed of air by permitting fluid to fill it completely, squeezing the drip chamber and releasing it to partially fill it. The tubing is attached to the needle (Fig. 7-8, *D* to *H*). Fig. 7-8, *I*, illustrates the arrow pointing to self-sealing sites for injection into the flashball.

Fig. 7-9 shows administration of intravenous solution in plastic containers. The container of solution is removed from its protective covering by tearing the wrapper along a premarked line. Then the protective covering is removed from the adaptor spike and the port into which it will be inserted, seeing to it that these parts are kept sterile (Fig. 7-9, *A* and *B*). If the container of solution is equipped with an entry port and a port for administering medication, either of two methods may be used. The spike of preparations that come equipped with it may be inserted into the entry port and the bag of solution squeezed to force air into the medication vial, then released to allow the medication to flow into the bag of solution (Fig. 7-9, *C*). Some vials incorporate a pumping device that can be used to force the solution into the bag (Fig. 7-8, *C*).

After adding the medication, the nurse inserts the adaptor spike of the intravenous tubing into the port of the plastic solution pack and suspends the plastic container, squeezing and releasing the drip chamber to partially fill it (Fig. 7-9, *D* and *E*). After removing the covering from the adaptor that connects the tubing to the needle, the tubing is cleared of air by filling it with fluid. The tubing is connected to the intravenous needle or catheter, as shown in Fig. 7-9, *F* and *G*. A **Y** tubing may be used to connect the two containers of solution, and they may be administered alternately or simultaneously by regulating the flow of solution with the clamps on the tubings above the drip chamber (Fig. 7-9, *H*). The nurse must see to it that any solutions administered simultaneously are compatible with each other.

Medication can be added to the solution through the medication port with a needle and syringe either before or after the bag of solution has been suspended (Fig. 7-9, *I*). The surface of the medication port should be cleansed with an antiseptic solution such as 70% alcohol to preserve asepsis. To determine the amount of solution remaining in the bag, grasp the sides of the bag and pull gently in opposite directions. The upper, empty part of the bag will collapse, and a fairly accurate reading can be obtained. Flow rate can be maintained during ambulation or transport by exerting gentle, steady pressure on the bag instead of suspending the bag.

IN-LINE DEVICES

In-line devices are used to deliver small amounts of solution and medication.

In-line burette. A burette may be placed in the line between the

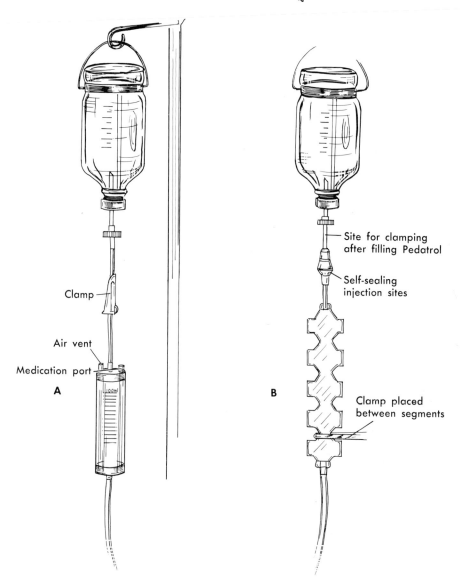

Clamp

Air vent

Medication port

A

Site for clamping
after filling Pedatrol

Self-sealing
injection sites

Clamp placed
between segments

B

Fig. 7-10. In-line devices for administration of small amounts of solution and medications. **A,** In-line burette (Buretrol) for intravenous administration of measured amounts of fluid or medication. Clamp above burette is used to regulate flow of solution from the bottle to the burette. Medication may be injected through the medication port after cleansing it with a suitable antiseptic. **B,** The Pedatrol may be used to control the amount of fluid administered. When filled, each section contains approximately 10 ml. of solution. A clamp may be placed above any section to ensure that no more than the amount of solution below the clamp will be administered in a given period of time. Segments below the level of the clamp will collapse at the same rate that the solution leaves them. Medication can be injected into the solution through the self-sealing injection sites provided in the flashball. The site must be cleansed with a suitable antiseptic before the medication is introduced. (Courtesy Travenol Laboratories, Inc., Deerfield, Ill.)

container of solution and the intravenous administration tubing, as illustrated in Fig. 7-10, *A*. The clamp above the burette regulates the flow of solution into the burette, and the nurse may close it when the burette is being used to administer medication diluted with a small amount of solution. When the burette is used, the administration tubing must be freed of air, as described previously. Medication is injected into the burette through the self-sealing rubber covering the medication port. It must be cleansed with a suitable antiseptic agent prior to inserting the needle. A size 20- or 22-gauge needle is recommended because a larger needle may prevent the rubber from sealing itself and may lead to contamination. The rate of flow of solution is regulated by the clamp on the administration tubing leading from the burette to the needle used for intravenous infusion.

Pedatrol. A Pedatrol is placed in the line between the container of solution and the administration tubing (Fig. 7-10, *B*). Again, the administration tubing must be freed of air. The Pedatrol is used to deliver a controlled volume of solution. Each segment of the Pedatrol will hold approximately 10 ml. of solution, and the entire Pedatrol will hold 50 ml. of solution. The amount of solution permitted to leave the Pedatrol is controlled by placing a clamp between the desired segments on the tubing between the Pedatrol and the flashball, or just above the flashball. Medication can be added through the self-sealing injection sites in the flashball. For this purpose the tubing above the flashball may be clamped. This is used primarily in pediatric nursing when the amount of solution administered must be carefully controlled.

CHANGING INTRAVENOUS ADMINISTRATION TUBING

It is necessary to change intravenous administration tubing if it has been used too long, if the filter becomes obstructed, or if the tubing becomes contaminated. Some institutions have established policies that require the tubing to be changed on a regular basis.

The Center for Disease Control (Atlanta) recommends that the administration tubing be changed at 24-hour intervals. The system for recording changes of the administration tubing varies. This record may be kept on the patient's chart or in the cardex, or the tubing itself may be labeled. A combination of these methods is sometimes used.

Changing the tubing is easiest to do if two persons work together and if the change can be planned to coincide with the addition of a new container of solution. The new container of solution is prepared as described previously; depending on its design, the administration tubing is connected to it and freed of air. During this time, the other person loosens the tubing from the needle. When the new container and solution are ready, the person who is removing the adaptor of the old tubing from the needle clamps the tubing and maintains a gentle pressure at the end of the indwelling needle. This prevents blood from flowing out of the needle when the tubing is changed. The old tubing is removed, and the adaptor of the new tubing is placed in the needle. The actual changing of the tubing at the point of connection to the needle should be done rather quickly, and asepsis must be preserved. It is somewhat more difficult for one person to change tubing for the administration of intravenous infusions.

POSSIBLE MECHANICAL DIFFICULTIES

At frequent intervals, the nurse should determine that the intravenous infusion is functioning properly. If the needle has been properly positioned within the vein and has been well secured, it is unlikely that infiltration will occur. However, the flow of solution may be slowed or stopped by mechanical difficulties as well as by infiltration of solution into the tissues due to puncture of the vessel wall by the needle. Mechanical difficulties most frequently encountered include obstruction of the tubing, obstruction of the filter, obstruction of the airway leading into the reservoir of fluid, and obstruction of the needle. Kinking of the tubing is readily located by observation and is easily corrected. If the container has an air filter, it may need to be removed and inspected. Tubing containing an in-line filter should be changed when enough particulate matter has been filtered out to slow the flow appreciably. Flow of the solution may be obstructed if the bevel of the needle is occluded by the wall of the vein. Rotation of the needle will correct this.

Clogging of the needle can be prevented by flushing solution through the needle at half-hour intervals. If the solution flows freely, the needle is probably in the vein. If the entire length of the needle can be palpated within the vein, infiltration has not occurred. Fluid infiltrating the interstitial space tends to obscure palpation of the needle.

Another method of checking the placement of the needle is to clamp the administration tubing, detach it from the needle, and observe blood flow. If blood flows back, the needle is in the vein. If no blood flows back, either the needle is outside the vein or the vein is collapsed. In the latter case, outflow of blood will be produced if the needle is in the vein with a blood pressure cuff applied to the upper part of the arm and inflated to approximately 70 mm. of mercury. Other methods such as lowering the bottle below the venipuncture site in hopes of obtaining return of blood into the tubing are not dependable. It is extremely difficult to aspirate blood with a plastic syringe because this must be done slowly and gently;

TABLE 7-2. Care of the venipuncture site

Technique	Problem	Solution or explanation
Remove the bandage over the needle and cleanse the site with 70% alcohol or the prescribed germicide; proceed from the site outward using sterile applicators.	Organisms may invade the tissues around the site or the blood stream.	Frequent cleansing removes organisms; cleansing from the site outward carries organisms away from the puncture wound.
Apply prescribed disinfectant, antibiotic, or both.	Iodine is irritating to the skin.	Wiping the area with alcohol will remove much of the iodine when such solutions are prescribed.
Apply a sterile dressing over the site of venipuncture.	Organisms may contact the site directly or indirectly.	The dressing serves as a barrier between the site and the environment.

more rapid aspiration tends to pull the walls of the vein over the end of the needle. This occludes the lumen of the needle even though it may be placed properly. However, if a glass syringe is used, the force of the blood will move the plunger back. To be effective, the inside of the barrel and the outside of the plunger must be wet with sterile solution.

CARE OF THE VENIPUNCTURE SITE

Care of the venipuncture site is intended to prevent microorganisms from entering the body though the opening made by venipuncture. Site care is performed daily, as frequently as is stipulated by institutional policy, or as prescribed by the physician.

The area is cleansed, proceeding from the site of venipuncture outward. This may be done with 70% alcohol and sterile applicators. Next, a disinfectant such as a solution of 2% iodine in 70% alcohol or an antibiotic such as polymyxin B (Neosporin) is applied to the site. When both an antiseptic and an antibiotic are used, the disinfectant should be allowed to dry before the antibiotic is applied. The site is then covered with a small sterile dressing, which is taped in place (Table 7-2).

TERMINATION OF AN INFUSION

Termination of an infusion is begun by clamping the tubing through which the solution is flowing. Next, the tape fixing the needle and the tubing to the skin is loosened (Fig. 7-11, *A*). The needle must be held firmly while the tape is removed to prevent unnecessary trauma to the vein and the surrounding tissues. While the nurse holds a sterile pledget or an alcohol sponge over the site of insertion with one hand, the other hand is used to slowly withdraw the needle, carefully keeping the needle parallel with the skin (Fig. 7-11, *B*). As soon as the needle has been removed, pressure is applied to the site with a sterile pledget or alcohol sponge for the period of time necessary to stop bleeding from the wound. The pledget can be secured with a strip of adhesive tape if desired, or a Band-Aid may be applied to the puncture site (Table 7-3).

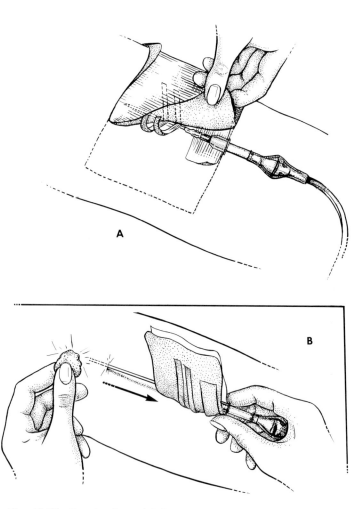

Fig. 7-11. Termination of infusion. **A,** To discontinue an intravenous infusion, tape adhering to the skin is loosened but not removed from the needle. **B,** The needle is withdrawn and direct pressure applied to the site with a sterile pledget until bleeding stops.

TABLE 7-3. Termination of an intravenous infusion

Technique	Problem	Solution or explanation
Clamp the tubing leading from the intravenous solution.	Without clamping, solution will continue to flow.	Clamping the tubing prevents this; patients appreciate not having their clothing or linen soiled.
Loosen the tape that fixes the tubing and needle to the skin.	Trauma may occur to the tissues and skin.	Holding the needle firmly prevents it from being moved while the tape is loosened.
Hold a sterile alcohol sponge over the site without applying pressure and withdraw the needle slowly.	Discomfort may occur.	Slow withdrawal of a needle held parallel to the skin causes least discomfort; application of pressure with the alcohol sponge while the needle is being withdrawn will increase discomfort.
Apply pressure to the site with the sterile sponge after the needle is withdrawn.	Bleeding occurs after the needle is removed.	Direct pressure stops the bleeding.
Apply a small bandage to the site using a small amount of pressure.	Infection can occur; bleeding can recur.	The bandage is a barrier to organisms; pressure prevents bleeding.

Measurement of central venous pressure

Central venous pressure may be measured at frequent intervals for varying periods of time with the aid of an indwelling plastic catheter or needle and a simple venous pressure set. This set is basically an intravenous set with a calibrated open-end sidearm that is used as the pressure manometer. The physician positions the needle or catheter within the vein and sets the level of the manometer scale and tubing on the intravenous stand. When a needle is used, the physician places it in the external jugular vein. It is preferable to insert a small catheter into the antecubital vein and advance it about 24 inches so that the tip of the catheter is placed close to the right atrium.

The nurse may assist the physician with this technique. The venous pressure set is attached to the container of solution in the manner described for connecting tubing for intravenous infusion. The stopcock on the venous pressure set is closed, the solution is suspended, and the drip chamber is squeezed and released to partially fill it with solution. The manometer scale, marked in centimeters, is taped to the intravenous stand in such a way that the zero mark on the scale is at the level of the right atrium of the patient's heart. This level is half the distance from the sternum to the skin of the back when the patient is in a recumbent position. The side-arm tube should be taut, and an intravenous stand attached to the bed should be used to keep the level of the scale constant if the height of the entire bed is changed (Fig. 7-12, A). Accurate readings can be obtained only if the zero mark on the manometer scale is level with the patient's right atrium. The patient must be in a recumbent position (Fig. 7-12, A).

To fill the intravenous tubing with fluid, the stopcock is turned so that the extensions from the stopcock, which are across from each

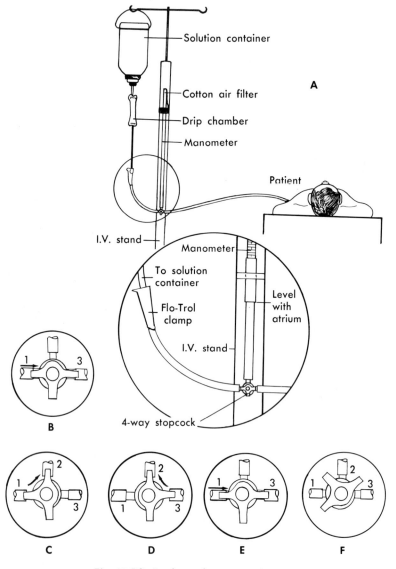

Fig. 7-12. For legend see opposite page.

other, are aligned with the intravenous tubing. The third projection points downward and away from the manometer (Fig. 7-12, *B*). This position permits fluid to flow through the intravenous tubing only and prevents fluid from entering the manometer. Filling the intravenous tubing before attempting to fill the manometer prevents air bubbles from getting into the solution in the manometer. Next, the sidearm manometer is filled to a level of 10 to 15 cm. by turning the stopcock so that its adjacent projections align with the tubing leading from the reservoir of solution and with the manometer (Fig. 7-12, *C*). Because central venous pressure is measured in relation to atmospheric pressure, solution should not be permitted to contact the air filter at the top of the manometer if one is incorporated into the design. It is advisable to retain at least an inch of space between the column of solution and the filter. Next, the protective cover-

Fig. 7-12. Measurement of venous pressure. **A,** Venous pressure set in use. Fluid flows from the container to the patient when venous pressure is not being measured. The calibrated scale on the sidearm manometer is used to read venous pressure. For the reading, the patient must be in a recumbent position with the zero mark on the manometer scale level with the patient's right atrium. **B,** To fill the intravenous tubing, the four-way stopcock is turned so that the extensions from the stopcock are aligned with the intravenous tubing only (*1* and *3*). The extensions on the stopcock may be thought of as showing the direction of flow. The tubing is then attached to the indwelling catheter or needle. **C,** To fill the manometer, the stopcock is turned so that one extension is aligned with the tubing leading from the container of intravenous solution, *1,* and the other extension is aligned with the tubing leading to the manometer, *2.* **D,** To read venous pressure, the stopcock is turned so that one extension is aligned with the tubing leading to the manometer, *2,* and the other extension is aligned with the tubing leading from the patient, *3.* The level of solution in the manometer is pushed down by air pressure on the column of fluid in opposition to the venous pressure from the patient. The level of solution in the manometer settles and pulsates at the level of venous pressure. The venous pressure reading is taken, recorded, evaluated, and used to alter the nursing care of the patient. **E,** To maintain patency of the intravenous needle or catheter, the stopcock is turned so that the two extensions are aligned with the tubing leading from the bottle, *1,* to the patient, *3.* **F,** The flow of solution is stopped in all directions when the stopcock is positioned so that the extensions are not aligned with the tubing or the manometer. (Courtesy Baxter Laboratories, Inc., Morton Grove, Ill.; Travenol Laboratories, Inc., Deerfield, Ill.)

ing over the needle adaptor on the intravenous tubing is removed, and the adaptor is inserted into the indwelling catheter or needle. The rate of flow of the solution should be sufficient to maintain patency of the indwelling catheter or needle and may, therefore, be slow.

To measure central venous pressure, the stopcock is turned so that one extension is aligned with the tubing leading to the manometer, and the other extension is aligned with the tubing leading from the patient (Fig. 7-12, *D*). The level of the solution in the manometer tube will settle and pulsate at the level of the central venous pressure. The stopcock is turned so that the two extensions are aligned with the tubing leading from the bottle to the patient to maintain patency of the intravenous needle or catheter (Fig. 7-12, *E*). To continue intravenous infusion between readings, the stopcock is repositioned. The flow of solution is stopped when the extensions from the stopcock are not aligned with the tubing or the manometer (Fig. 7-12, *F*).

Central venous pressure readings are recorded on the patient's chart. The physician should be informed of significant changes or trends in venous pressure. Unless the physician specifies otherwise, it is assumed that a venous pressure reading between 5 and 20 cm. of water is reasonably safe.

Venous pressure is used in the diagnosis and treatment of inadequate circulation. High venous pressure in the presence of hypotension suggests myocardial insufficiency, which may be treated with cardiotonic drugs. Low venous pressure suggests low circulating blood volume or peripheral vasodilatation, conditions treated by increasing the blood volume. Intelligent observation can prevent the venous pressure from rising above the desired reading and can avoid infusion of excessive amounts of blood or fluids.

Questions for discussion and exploration

1. What factors determine the choice of needles or catheters used for intravenous infusion?
2. What sites can be used for venipuncture? What factors influence the selection of a particular site?
3. What are the advantages of using a sphygmomanometer instead of a narrow tourniquet?
4. What is the importance of applying manual traction distal to the site of venipuncture?
5. What is the value of maintaining contact with the extremity during venipuncture?
6. Why is the tourniquet not released until a blood sample is obtained, and why must it be released before infusion is begun?
7. If you notice that an intravenous infusion is leaking and on palpation discover that the plastic part of the needle has come apart from

the hub and is felt a few inches away from the site of venipuncture, what nursing action is indicated?

8. What is the purpose of a splint, when should it be used, and how must it be applied to serve its purpose?

9. Calculate the rate of flow in drops per minute when 800 ml. of solution is to be administered in 6½ hours and the manufacturer's information states that the solution provides approximately 10 drops per minute.

10. As you enter Mrs. G.'s room, you notice that her intravenous solution is not running. She complains that her arm hurts. What information do you need and what will you do to determine if the intravenous needle is in place, to determine why it is not working, and to make Mrs. G. comfortable?

11. Jack E. is upset about having intravenous infusions for several days. He complains bitterly and threatens to discontinue the intravenous infusion himself. You know that he has been bleeding in the gastrointestinal tract and that the "needle" is really an intravenous catheter. What approach might you use with him?

12. When the physician orders a penicillin preparation to be added to an intravenous solution, how will you learn if the preparation ordered is compatible with the solution being administered? If it is not compatible, what is your nursing responsibility?

13. Jane R., age 17, is admitted in a poor nutritional state. When the physician orders hyperalimentation solution to be given intravenously, what are the nurse's responsibilities?

14. When assisting Mr. D, a postoperative patient, to ambulate, you notice that the intravenous solution is running poorly and that blood is visible in the tubing proximal to the needle. What nursing action is indicated?

15. When blood transfusions are given, nursing care and patient activity may be limited to essential care only. Why? What are the signs and symptoms of an adverse reaction to a transfusion, and what nursing action is indicated for each?

16. By what methods can you check the placement of a needle in the vein?

17. Of what value are central venous pressure readings to the physician?

18. What errors in technique can cause erroneous readings of central venous pressure?

Selected references

Adriani, J.: Techniques and procedures of anesthesia, ed. 4, Springfield, Ill., 1972, Charles C Thomas, Publisher.

Adriani, J.: Venipuncture, Amer. J. Nurs. **62**:66-70, 1962.

Betson, C., and Use, L.: Central venous pressure, Amer. J. Nurs. **69**:1466-1468, 1969.

Child, J., Collins, D., and Collins, J.: Blood therapy, Amer. J. Nurs. **72**:1602-1605, 1972.

Chow, R.: Innovations in IV equipment, Amer. J. Nurs. **62**:80-81, 1962.

Crouch, M. L., and Gibson, S. T.: Blood therapy, Amer. J. Nurs. **62**:71-76, 1962.

Donn, R.: Intravenous admixture incompatibility, Amer. J. Nurs. **71**:325, 1971.

Grant, J. N., Moir, E., and Fago, M.: Parenteral hyperalimentation, Amer. J. Nurs. **69**: 2392-2395, 1969.

Grant, J.: Patient care in parenteral hyperalimentation, Nurs. Clin. N. Amer. 8:165-181, 1973.

Haselman, J.: Teaching principles of intravenous therapy, J. Nurs. Educ. 2:21-23, 34-42, 1963.

Humphrey, N., Wright, P., and Swanson, A.: Parenteral hyperalimentation for children, Amer. J. Nurs. 72:286-288, 1972.

Imperiale, M., and Krebs, T.: The intravenous therapy nurses, Amer. J. Nurs. 61:53-54, 1961.

Massa, D. J., Lundy, J. S., Faulconer, A., Jr., and Ridley, R. W.: A plastic needle, Proc. Mayo Clin. 25:413-415, 1950.

Metheny, N., and Snively, W. D.: Nurse's handbook of fluid therapy, ed. 2, Philadelphia, 1974, J. B. Lippincott Co.

Michel, F.: The vexing core, Amer. J. Nurs. 71:768, 1971.

Moffitt, E. A., and Sessler, A. D.: The circulation in anaesthesia, Canad. Anaesth. Soc. J. 11:173-181, 1964.

Parsa, M., Thornton, B., and Ferrer, J.: Central venous alimentation, Amer. J. Nurs. 72:2042-2047, 1972.

Programmed instruction: Intravenous infusion of vasopressors, Amer. J. Nurs. 65:129-152, 1965.

Russell, M. W., and Maier, W. P.: The ABC's of C.V.P. measurement, RN 69:34-35; 68-69, 1969.

Shanck, A.H.: The nurse in an intravenous therapy program, Amer. J. Nurs. 57:1012-1013, 1957.

Voda, A.: Body water dynamics, Amer. J. Nurs. 70:2594-2601, 1970.

Wilmore, D. W.: The future of intravenous therapy, Amer. J. Nurs. 71:2334-2338, 1971.

Wilson, J. N., and Owens, J. C.: Pitfalls in monitoring central venous pressure, Hosp. Med. 6:86-93, April, 1970.

8
Elimination

Assistance, instruction, encouragement, and explanation of the planned care must accompany techniques used to promote elimination. The nurse must assure the patient by words, actions, attitude, and facial expression that elimination of waste material is a normal, healthy process.

Intestinal decompression

When peristalsis is lacking or when intestinal obstruction occurs, a gastrointestinal tube may be used to remove gaseous and liquid materials. This treatment, called decompression therapy, is used to relieve abdominal distention and distress.

The nurse should recognize that swallowing a tube is not pleasant even under the best conditions. Preparation of the tube is similar to that described for gastric intubation (pages 191 to 194). Frequently a Miller-Abbott intestinal tube is used. Before insertion, its balloon should be tested for capacity and leakage; then all air should be aspirated from the balloon. The lubricated tube is passed through the nostril into the gastrointestinal tract by the physician, who will give instructions about positioning the patient, advancing the tube periodically, and irrigating the tube.

When the tube has been passed to the pylorus, the patient is usually positioned on his right side for 2 hours. During this time, the patient may not have a pillow, and the foot of the bed is elevated about 12 inches. This position allows gravity to aid the balloon in its passage through the pylorus. At this time, duodenal drainage should return. Fluoroscopy or films may be used to determine the exact location of the tube. Periodic advancement will be ordered after the tube has been passed into the intestinal tract. The rate of advancement may be as much as 6 inches an hour.

Each time the tube is advanced, the patient should be told what is to be done and what is expected of him. Unless it is contraindicated, the patient is placed in a high Fowler's position for advancement of the tube. The nostrils and the proximal portion of the tube are lubricated, and the patient is asked to swallow at the exact time that the tube is advanced. If it is allowed, the patient is given sips of water or small amounts of melted ice to aid in swallowing the tube. Intake is restricted whenever fluid and electrolyte balance or obstruction is a problem, however. If the patient is unable to swallow, it is helpful to stroke the area from the upper end of the sternum to the chin, advancing the tube as the larynx rises.

During the period that the tube is being advanced, it can be anchored within a piece of split rubber tubing about 1½ inches long, which is taped to the forehead. The tube is threaded through the split tubing to obtain the necessary slack prior to each advancement. When the tube has been passed to the desired location, it is taped securely to prevent its continued propulsion by peristalsis. The tube is then attached to an intermittent suction unit (Chapter 9). Periodic irrigation of the tube may be ordered (Chapter 10).

Enemas

Enemas introduce solution into the rectum for cleansing or therapeutic purposes. Commercially prepared, disposable enemas may be used, or the solution may be prepared just prior to use.

The purpose of the prescribed enema must be explained to the patient. If the enema is to be retained rather than expelled, this must be explained carefully to gain the patient's cooperation. Often an oil retention enema is followed several hours later by a cleansing enema.

The patient is assisted as necessary to assume the desired position. The bed is protected with disposable pads or waterproof material covered with a cloth.

Depending on the purpose of the enema, the patient may be encouraged to retain the solution for 10 minutes or longer. Remaining on his side or back will enable the patient to retain the solution longer than if he sits up or stands. The latter positions cause the solution to collect in the rectum and stimulate the desire to defecate. Unless it is contraindicated, the patient is allowed to expel the enema into the toilet.

If a large amount of solution is not expelled within a reasonable length of time, the physician may ask that another enema be given in the hope that additional solution will stimulate peristalsis. The retained solution may be drained through a rectal tube also. To siphon the retained solution, the lubricated rectal tube is inserted 4 to 5 inches, then lowered into a receptacle that is about 18 inches below the level of the bed. When gravity fails to drain the retained solution, the rectal tube is filled with fluid and inserted, a small amount of fluid is allowed to enter the rectum, the rectal tube is lowered as previously described, and, if contact with the retained solution has been made, the siphonage will cause the retained fluid to flow. If contact is not made, the procedure is repeated. Regardless of the method used, the draining rectal tube must be held in place until the flow is complete.

Results of the enema should be observed and recorded. Notations for a cleansing enema should include the type of enema given, the amount of solution administered, the patient's tolerance of the procedure, the color, consistency, and amount of evacuation, and other pertinent information. This information is useful in assessing how well the purposes for the enema were met and if orders for additional enemas might be indicated. Observation of abnormal characteristics of the stool should be noted and reported. Observation of a significant amount of bright red blood in the stool may be an indication that enemas should be discontinued until further orders are obtained. The amount of blood would guide the nurse in choosing appropriate means of assessing the patient's status and in determining further actions. If the returns of the last in a series of cleansing enemas given before colon surgery contain stool, the surgeon may decide that additional enemas are needed.

COMMERCIALLY PREPARED ENEMAS

A variety of disposable enemas are available commercially. These are supplied with the manufacturer's directions for preparation and administration of each product. Left lateral positioning of the patient is used unless another position is indicated. The patient is instructed to retain the solution for a short period of time. Results are usually obtained within 10 minutes.

For one type of disposable enema (Fig. 8-1), the protective covering is removed from the rectal tube, and the tip of the tube is lubricated and inserted into the rectum for a distance of about 6 inches. Then the plastic container is compressed to force the fluid into the rectum.

Another type of disposable enema is illustrated in Fig. 8-2. Pressure is exerted on the portion of the tube proximal to the bead. This expels the bead from the tube into the bag and permits the solution to flow through the tube. Dislodgment of the bead can be done before the rectal tube is inserted (Fig. 8-2, B). The cover is removed from the tip of the rectal tube with a rotating motion, which distributes the lubricant contained in the cover onto the tip of the rectal tube (Fig. 8-2, C). The guard can be moved to a position on the tube to mark the distance the tube is to be inserted

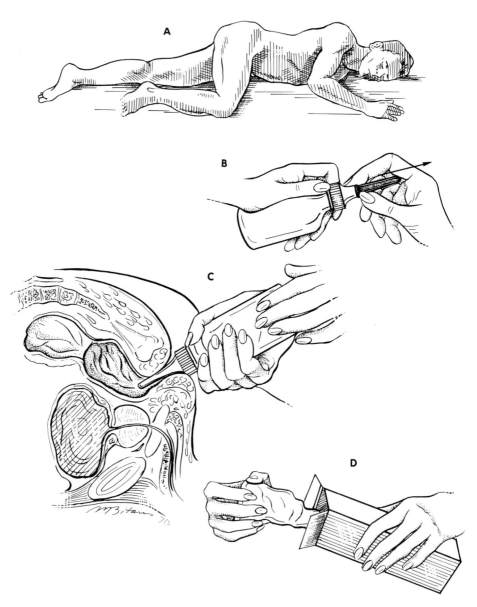

Fig. 8-1. Administration of a disposable enema (Fleet enema). **A,** The nurse places the patient in a left lateral position unless the knee-chest position has been specified. **B,** The protective covering is removed from the rectal tube, and the tube is lubricated with a lubricant contained in this cover. **C,** Then the lubricated rectal tube is inserted into the rectum and the solution is injected by compressing the plastic container. **D,** The used container may be replaced in its original container for its disposal. (Courtesy C. B. Fleet Co., Inc., Lynchburg, Va.)

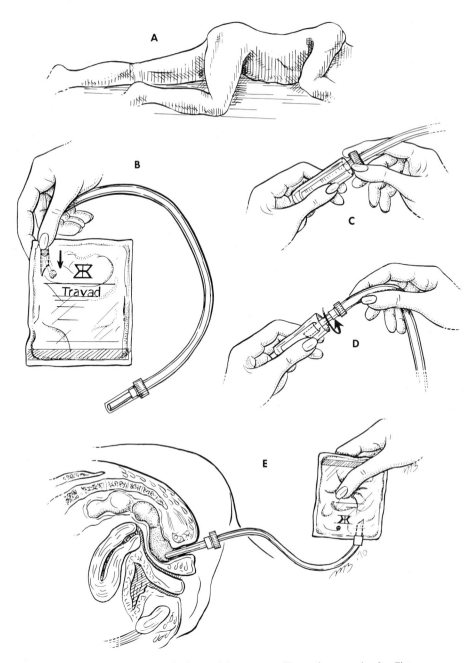

Fig. 8-2. Administration of disposable enema (Travad enema). **A,** The nurse places the patient in a left lateral position. **B,** The orange bead is expelled from the tube into the bag by exerting pressure on the tube proximal to the bead. This can be done either before or after the rectal tube has been inserted. Dislodgment of the bead permits the solution to flow through the tube. **C,** The Measur-Gard protector cover is removed from the tip of the container with a rotating motion. This distributes lubricant in the container onto the tip of the rectal tube. **D,** The guard may be moved to a position on the tube that represents the distance the rectal tube is to be inserted. **E,** After the tube has been inserted, the bag is compressed until the desired amount of fluid has been administered. The used equipment may be replaced in its original package for disposal. (Courtesy Travenol Laboratories, Inc., Deerfield, Ill.)

TABLE 8-1. Enema with reusable equipment

Technique	Problem	Solution or explanation
The necessary equipment includes an 18- to 20-gauge French catheter, a 2 to 3-foot length of tubing, an enema can, the solution, and a thermometer.	Viewing the equipment and its preparation may cause the patient unnecessary anxiety.	Enema equipment and solution are prepared away from the patient's view.
The temperature of the solution is commonly 100° to 105° F. or less.	The nerve endings in the rectum are sensitive to change in temperature; changes in temperature stimulate peristalsis.	Since solutions warmer than 105° to 115° F. are damaging to the mucous membranes, and since cold solutions cause the muscles to contract, a temperature of from 100° to 105° F. is needed.
The patient is told the purpose of the enema and informed that some discomfort may occur.	The enema may cause spasms of the colonic muscles.	Stop the flow of solution temporarily. Understanding the need for treatment fosters cooperation with the nurse.
The patient is assisted to a lateral, dorsal (with hips elevated), or knee-chest position.	The position and direction of the large intestine will influence the distance that the solution will flow.	The patient should be placed in a position that will facilitate evacuation.
After expelling the air from the tubing, the tip of the catheter is lubricated.	Friction traumatizes the mucous membranes and stimulates contraction of the anal sphincter.	Lubrication decreases friction between the catheter and the mucous membranes; this allows the catheter to be introduced more easily.
The patient is instructed to bear down and the catheter is inserted 4 to 8 inches, depending on the purpose of the enema.	Perforation of the wall of the intestine at the splenic flexure must be prevented.	The rectum is 7 to 8 inches long, and the anus is about 1 inch long. Rotation of the catheter may prevent involuntary contraction of the sphincter.
If the catheter does not advance easily, it is withdrawn slightly and advanced, allowing a small amount of solution to flow during advancement.	Solution cannot flow freely if the eye of the catheter is obstructed.	Fecal impactions are removed manually before administering the enema. Redirecting the eye of the catheter may circumvent the obstruction. The force of the solution may displace folds of the mucous membranes.
The solution flows from a level approximately 18 inches above the level of the hips. A maximum of 500 to 1000 ml. of solution is given to an adult.	Rapid administration of the solution increases discomfort and decreases ability to retain or accept the solution.	The height of the solution determines the rate of flow. The musculature of the colon will determine its capacity, which is often 750 to 2000 ml.
The catheter is withdrawn, and pressure is applied over the anus.	The urge to defecate may interfere with retention of the solution.	External pressure on the anus helps the patient to retain the solution.

TABLE 8-1. Enema with reusable equipment—cont'd

Technique	Problem	Solution or explanation
The patient is instructed to retain the solution for a period of time.	The chemical and physical action of the solutions that soften fecal material is dependent on how long the solution is retained.	The length of time the solution should be retained depends on the amount and kind of solution and the individual.
Unless it is contraindicated, the patient assumes a sitting position to expel the enema.	Evacuation of the lower bowel is aided by the use of the abdominal and perineal muscles.	Contraction of the abdominal and perineal muscles is influenced by position and habit.
A signal cord and toilet tissue are left within the patient's reach, and his signal is answered promptly.	The effort of expelling the enema may be exhausting, and the procedure may be embarrassing to the patient.	Independence, privacy, and assurance of assistance are most important.
The equipment is cleansed first with cold water, then with warm soapy water and sterilized.	Protein is coagulated by heat.	Washing the equipment with cold water interferes with the transfer of organisms.

(Fig. 8-2, *D*). Then the bag is squeezed to force the solution into the rectum (Fig. 8-2, *E*).

With either type of disposable enema, it may be advantageous to roll the plastic container as solution is administered. This prevents aspiration of the solution as the solution container re-expands. The used equipment can be placed in the supply package for its disposal.

PREPARATION OF EQUIPMENT AND SOLUTIONS FOR ENEMAS

Unless commercial disposable enemas are used, the equipment and solution are prepared in a service area before taking them to the nursing care center. The amount of preparation that must be done by the nurse will vary with the institution. In some, the equipment is supplied and the nurse must select and assemble the necessary supplies. In other institutions, the equipment is supplied after have been assembled in central supply. The nurse may need to make the necessary kind, strength, and amount of solution, or it may be supplied in its prepared form.

Funnel method. When a small amount of solution (8 ounces or less) is to be given, a rectal tube attached to a funnel may be used. The prepared solution is poured into the funnel after the rectal tube is inserted. If it is preferred, a clamp may be placed on the rectal tube so that it can be cleared of air before insertion.

Irrigating container method. For the administration of larger amounts of solution, an irrigating can or container is used. A 2- to

TABLE 8-2. Enema solutions*

Name of enema	Type	Ingredients	Additional information
Alum	Astringent	Alum, 2 Gm. (30 gr.) Water, 500 ml. (1 pt.)	If enema is not expelled after 30 minutes, siphon solution from colon with a rectal tube.
Glycerin and water	Carminative	Glycerin, 30 to 90 ml. (1 to 3 oz.) Water, 500 ml. (1 pt.)	This is sometimes referred to as a G and W enema.
		or	
		Glycerin, 30 ml. (1 oz.) Water, 90 ml. (3 oz.)	This is referred to as a "cup" enema.
Milk and molasses	Carminative	Equal amounts of milk and molasses: 90-250 ml. (3-8 oz.) of each	Warm milk to 110° F.; add molasses, followed by a cleansing enema.
1-2-3	Carminative	Magnesium sulfate, 30 Gm. (1 oz.) or 50% solution (1 oz.) Glycerin, 60 ml. (2 oz.) Water, 90 ml. (3 oz.)	Dissolve magnesium sulfate in boiling water; add glycerin and cool to 105° F.
Peroxide	Cleansing	Hydrogen peroxide, 15 ml. (½ oz.) Water, 500 ml. (1 pt.)	Insert rectal tube after 10 minutes.
Oil retention	Softening	Mineral, cottonseed, or olive oil, 120-240 ml. (4-8 oz.)	This solution is to be retained indefinitely; it may be followed by a cleansing enema.
Saline, physiologic	Cleansing	Salt, 4 Gm. (1 tsp.) Water, 500 ml. (1 pt.)	
Soapsuds	Cleansing	Soap solution, 30 ml. (1 oz.)	
		or	
		Powdered soap, 1 tbsp. Water, 1000 ml.	
Soda	Cleansing	Sodium bicarbonate, 20 Gm. (5 tsp.) Water, 1000 ml.	

*Temperature of the solution on administration should be 105° F. The total amount of solution may be increased or decreased as necessary, if the proportions of the contents remain the same.

TABLE 8-2. Enema solutions—cont'd

Name of enema	Type	Ingredients	Additional information
Starch	Emollient, vehicle for medications	Starch, 4 Gm. (1 tsp.) Water, 8 oz.	Mix starch with 2 oz. of cold water; slowly add 6 oz. of boiling water; add prescribed medication; administer solution slowly with a small catheter (12- to 14-gauge French). Instruct patient to retain solution.
Tap water	Cleansing	Water, 1000 ml.	
Turpentine	Carminative	Turpentine, 4 ml. Soap solution, 30 ml. Water, 500 ml.	Stir well; turpentine is irritating to mucous membranes; follow with a cleansing enema.

3-foot length of tubing, on which a clamp, pinchcock, or shutoff valve has been placed is attached to the irrigating container. The tubing is connected to the rectal tube with an adaptor. Commonly, an 18- to 22-gauge French rectal tube is used for cleansing enemas. A larger size may be used for viscous solution; a smaller size may be used for retention enemas. The larger the diameter of the rectal tube used for the administration of the enema, the greater will be the stimulation of the sphincters and the more rapid will be the flow of the solution.

The tubing and catheter may be coiled loosely around the container and placed on a tray that contains lubricant, tissue, and protective pads. The prescribed amount and kind of solution is prepared and poured into the irrigation container. Table 8-2 lists the ingredients of various enemas.

Temperature of the solution must be tested with a thermometer. It should never exceed 110° F.; commonly 100° to 105° F. is the temperature used. If the solution is too warm, it may injure the intestinal mucosa; if it is too cool, it may cause cramping.

Positioning the patient will be influenced by his condition and the results desired. If the patient is able to lie on his left side to receive the enema, the solution will flow more easily through the rectum and into the sigmoid and descending colon. Alternatively, the patient may lie on his right side.

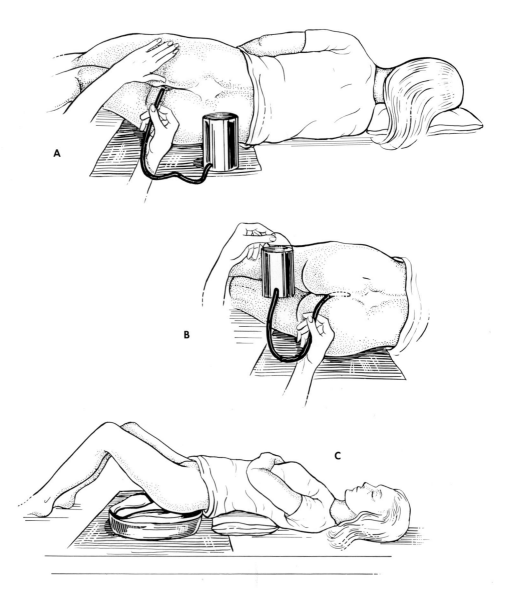

Fig. 8-3. Three-maneuver enema. **A,** The patient assumes the right lateral position for administration of the solution. **B,** The nurse administers the solution. **C,** The hips are elevated as the patient is turned; evacuation occurs with the hips at a higher level than the chest, shoulders, and head. The lumbar area is supported with a pillow or lumbar pad.

A flat, back-lying position with the legs flexed is useful if the patient is unable to control the anal sphincter. This may occur in the unconscious person or in those who have had an injury to the sphincter. When this position is used, the nurse inserts the catheter after placing the bedpan. A rubber glove is used to protect the hand holding the rectal tube during administration of the solution. Supporting the lumbar region with pillows or a folded bath blanket may add some comfort to this position.

The knee-chest position, prescribed occasionally, must be used cautiously if the patient is weak, debilitated, or elderly. Unless the mattress is completely protected and the bed can be lowered, it may be desirable to place a large foam rubber mat covered with a cloth on the floor of the bathroom, asking the patient to assume the knee-chest position on this mat. It is imperative that complete privacy be provided and that the patient's safety is ensured when this position is used.

If the three-maneuver enema is used to eliminate or reduce the need for several cleansing enemas, the patient assums a right lateral position for administration of the solution (Fig. 8-3, *A* and *B*). The hips of the patient are elevated as he is rolled onto his back. Evacuation occurs with the hips elevated higher than the level of the chest, shoulders, and head (Fig. 8-3, *C*). A pillow under the back and a small pillow beneath the head may provide some comfort for the patient when this position is used.

ADMINISTERING THE ENEMA SOLUTION

Whenever the solution is to be retained or when a considerable length of tubing is used as described for the irrigating container method, air is displaced from the tubing by filling it with the enema solution. This is done by momentarily releasing the clamp on the tubing. A receptacle should be used to catch any escaping solution. Small amounts of air are not believed to be harmful; larger amounts increase pressure and may interfere with the patient's ability to accept and retain the desired amount of solution. Beginning at the tip of the catheter, lubrication is applied for about 2 to 3 inches. The patient is asked to bear down to relax the anal sphincter during insertion of the catheter. The catheter or rectal tube is inserted about 4 to 6 inches for cleansing enemas and approximately 6 to 8 inches for retention enemas. Insertion beyond this distance or forcing the catheter may injure the wall of the colon. If the catheter cannot be advanced easily, it may be in contact with a fecal mass or folds of tissue. If the catheter is withdrawn slightly, then eased forward while permitting the solution to flow slowly, the colon will be distended by the fluid. This removes the folds of tissues and allows the solution to flow around the fecal mass.

The solution is administered slowly by elevating the container about 18 inches above the level of the hips. More rapid administration stimulates peristalsis and increases pressure, causing intestinal cramping and reduced ability to retain the solution. These symptoms may be relieved by interrupting the flow of solution temporarily, by lowering the container to slow the rate of flow, or by lowering the container below the level of the patient to permit gases to escape from the colon. Breathing slowly and deeply through the mouth several times also helps to relieve the urge to defecate and may enable the patient to receive more solution.

The amount of solution that is needed to stimulate defecation and that can be tolerated varies with each individual. If, after accepting a reasonable amount of solution and using measures to relieve discomfort, the patient indicates inability to tolerate additional solution, the flow is stopped, the catheter is withdrawn, and pressure is applied to the anal area with tissues. The latter helps to minimize spasms of the sphincter. Unless it is contraindicated, the patient is assisted to the bathroom to expel the enema. Table 8-1 summarizes the technique for administering an enema.

Rectal tube

When discomfort is related to flatus or liquids in the rectum that the patient is unable to expel voluntarily, the physician may order a rectal tube. Frequently the rectal tube is used in conjunction with drugs such as glycerin suppositories. A physician's order is required because certain pathologic problems and surgical procedures contraindicate the use of a rectal tube.

The rectal tube is lubricated and inserted as described for enemas. Usually it is left in place 20 minutes. A longer period of time tends to produce spasms of the anal sphincter, which may ultimately cause relaxation of the sphincter. Infrequently it may be necessary to tape the tube to the buttocks to anchor it. Provision for drainage is essential.

Disposable units, consisting of a rectal tube connected to a flatus bag, are available (Fig. 8-4, A). The lubricated tip of the tube is inserted, and the flatus bag rests on the bed (Fig. 8-4, B). The rectal tube may be placed into a vented drainage container (Fig. 8-4, C). If the container is suspended from the bed, placing a measured amount of water in it will cause "bubbling" when flatus escapes (Fig. 8-4, D), thus giving some indication of the effectiveness of this measure. When a tube is inserted into a colostomy for similar reasons, the length of time it is allowed to remain in place may be somewhat longer because the stoma has no sphincter.

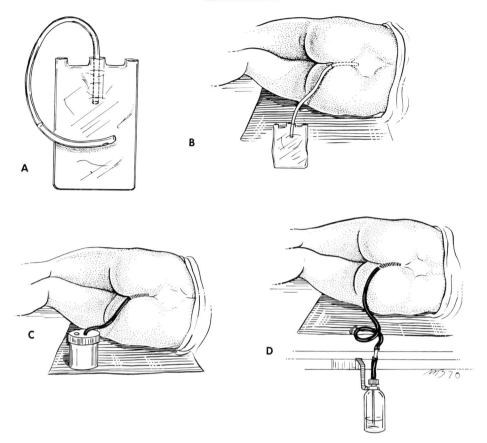

Fig. 8-4. Rectal tube. **A,** Kenwood flatus bag. Projections on either side of the rectal tube are air vents. **B,** The lubricated tip of flatus bag is inserted, and the flatus bag rests on the bed. (Courtesy Will Ross, Inc., Milwaukee, Wis.) **C,** The rectal tube drains into a vented container. **D,** The rectal tube drains into a vented bottle suspended from the bed. Escaping gas causes the water to bubble.

Fecal impaction

Every effort should be taken to prevent fecal impaction from occurring. Preventive measures, including adequate fluid intake, exercise, diet, laxatives, and cleansing enemas, are especially important for elderly persons and for those patients receiving drugs known to be constipating. Thus laxatives and enemas are often prescribed after the use of barium sulfate.

If contents harden within the colon, obstruction of varying degrees results. Then diarrhea, which characteristically has a foul odor, may pass around the fecal mass and cause fecal incontinence. It can occur within a 24-hour period. In addition to diarrhea, the patient may complain of rectal pain and inability to defecate. Ignoring symptoms at this stage can result in serious imbalance of fluids and electrolytes.

Early medical treatment of fecal impaction includes administration of medicated suppositories, oil retention enemas, or both. This treatment should be followed by a cleansing enema. Subsequent cleansing enemas may be ordered if necessary.

Late treatment of fecal impaction involves digital manipulation to break and remove the obstruction mass. For this procedure, the patient assumes a Sims' position. Protective pads should be placed beneath the patient's buttocks. A bedpan is convenient for receiving the fecal material as it is removed. The nurse or the physician wears a clean rubber glove, lubricates the forefinger well, and uses it to break up and remove the obstructing fecal mass. After removal of the impaction, the area should be cleansed and the patient should be allowed to rest, since this procedure causes considerable discomfort.

Abdominal stomas

Rehabilitation of the patient with an abdominal stoma is dependent on his acceptance of this method of elimination and on the development of a basic but satisfactory self-care program. To promote such rehabilitation, it is necessary for the nurse to develop a positive approach that combines acceptance, compassion, firmness, knowledge, and skill.

By the time the patient is dismissed from the hospital, he should be able to care for his stoma and be aware of agencies available to help him. Information concerning "ostomy" clubs and surgical supply houses is useful.

Generally, the patient who has learned to care for his stoma adapts the procedure to meet his own needs. This, as well as participation in planning his care, should be encouraged.

SKIN CARE

Fig. 8-5, *A*, shows a common anatomic location of a stoma. Discharge from an abdominal stoma contains material irritating to the skin. Efforts to keep the surrounding skin and adjacent incision clean, dry, and protected are important in preventing odor, irritation, excoriation, and infection (Fig. 8-5, *B*). Intensity of care and selection of techniques are influenced by the fluid state and nature of the drainage. Thus provision for drainage and methods of skin care are similar for an ileostomy, draining fistula, urinary diversion, and liquid drainage from a colostomy.

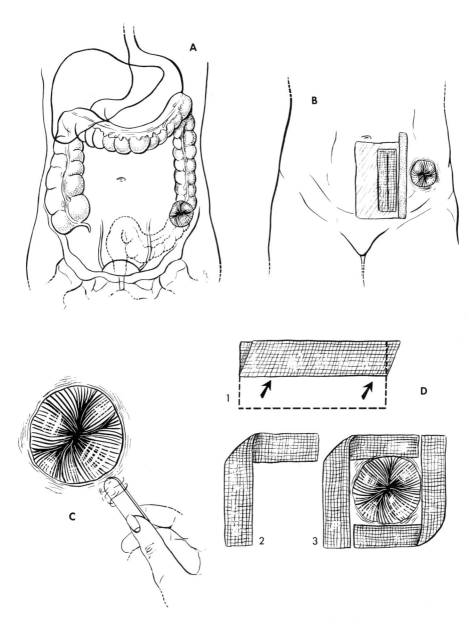

Fig. 8-5. Colostomy dressings. **A,** Anatomic location of a stoma. **B,** The adjacent incision is protected from contamination with a "dam" made of waterproof material. A strip of waterproof tape seals the material to the skin. **C,** After cleansing and drying of the area around the stoma, the prescribed ointment is applied. **D,** Gauze strips are folded and placed around the stoma.

Continued.

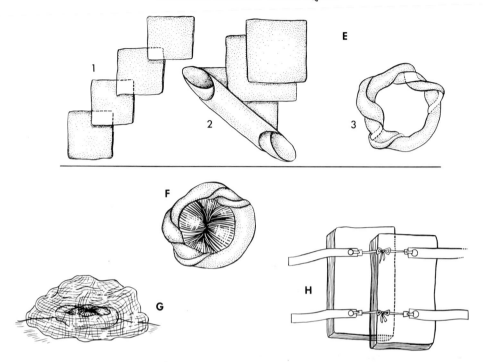

Fig. 8-5, cont'd. E, Layers of Cellucotton are used to form a circular dressing, popularly called a doughnut dressing. After the material is formed into a roll, the ends are interlocked with a twisting motion. **F,** The circular dressing is placed around the stoma. **G,** The stoma is covered with layers of gauze, then with fluffed Cellucotton. **H,** The dressing is completed with large abdominal dressing pads held in place by Montgomery straps.

The skin will remain healthy only if it is kept clean and dry. Mild soap and water is used to sponge the skin until it is clean. The soap must be removed by thorough rinsing and the skin blotted dry.

TREATMENT OF SKIN IRRITATION

Irritation of the skin may be treated by sprinkling karaya powder over it. This powder has some adhesive properties, and sprays can be applied over it. Karaya paste may be used, or the skin can be moistened with water or antacid over which the karaya powder is sprinkled. Allowing the antacid to stand for several hours and then pouring off the top liquid is one method of obtaining an antacid paste. Another method is to boil the antacid solution to concentrate it by evaporating the liquid. A commercial preparation of karaya and aluminum hydroxide gel, Neo-Karaya, is available commercially. Other protective agents are available.

Skin that is excoriated may be exposed to air for 20 to 30 minutes after cleansing. Either lights or a warm air blower should be placed at least 18 inches away from the stoma. The light bulb used should be no larger than 60 watts. During either of these treatments, the stoma must be covered with gauze to protect it.

Usually, the patient is positioned on his side, and a piece of rather heavy plastic is placed under the lower edge of the stoma to shield the skin and to funnel drainage into a basin. A towel or other cloth material placed between the plastic and the skin adds to patient comfort.

To heal unusually large areas of excoriation, it may be necessary to place the patient on a Foster reversible bed, Stryker turning frame, or a CircOlectric bed and turn him onto his abdomen to permit drainage to drop from the stoma into a basin without contacting the skin. These turning devices are discussed in Chapter 2.

COLOSTOMY DRESSINGS

Generally, dressings are used only when an appliance cannot be fitted around the stoma. The size of the stoma and the presence of clamps or a large rod, also called a bridge, may prevent the use of an appliance over a loop colostomy until it has been matured by the surgeon. Otherwise, the surgeon may place an appliance with a rod to hold up the loop immediately after surgery. When this is done, disposable bags are used.

When dressings must be used, the skin around the stoma is protected with a protective agent such as vaseline dressings or petroleum jelly and gauze dressings (Fig. 8-5, *C* and *D*). Absorbent pads, available with a precut, centered opening may be used to prevent pressure on the stoma. A doughnut dressing (Fig. 8-5, *E* and *F*) fashioned from absorbent material encloses the stoma and protects it. It also acts as a dam to prevent drainage from flowing over the skin. A single layer of gauze is placed over the stoma itself, and then layers of absorbent material are placed over the gauze. Separating and fluffing the layers of Cellucotton, which is available with or without a moisture-resistant backing, increases its absorbency. Large abdominal pads or dressings held in place with Montgomery straps, commonly called tie tapes, complete the dressings (Fig. 8-5, *G* and *H*).

COLOSTOMY IRRIGATION

The purpose of colostomy irrigation is to regulate the discharge of fecal contents and flatus. Selection of the time for irrigation should be determined by the patient's pattern of daily activities. Preference for pre-breakfast or evening irrigation is common. Initially, irrigations are done daily. After control is established, irrigation every other day or every third day may give satisfactory results.

The size of the catheter used for irrigation may vary depending on the size of the stoma. A 24- to 26-gauge French catheter is usually suitable for irrigation of an adult's stoma. Tap water or physiologic saline is used for routine irrigation. Occasionally a mild soapsuds enema or a medicated solution such as 2% neomycin solution may be prescribed. Variations in the amount of solution used have been reported. Commonly, 1000 ml. of cool to lukewarm solution (100° to 105° F.) is prepared and used in the amount needed for satisfactory results. For some persons, this may require as little as 500 ml.; others report needing to use 2000 ml. of solution or more.

Various types of irrigating appliances are available. In some, the catheter is introduced through an opening in the drainage sleeve. The opening may be designed to seal itself when the catheter is withdrawn, or it may need to be plugged (Fig. 8-6, *A* to *C*). In others, the top of the drainage bag is opened during irrigation, then sealed during evacuation (Fig. 8-6, *D*). Another type necessitates pulling the dome or ring of the appliance away from the body during irrigation. If an irrigating appliance is not used, a large basin can be held against the abdomen to collect the returns, or a trough can be fashioned of waterproof material and taped to the skin.

Irrigation is convenient if the patient sits on the toilet or on a chair facing the toilet during irrigation. This position allows the returns to flow directly into the toilet. Irrigation for a patient confined to bed can be carried out by having him lie on his side near the edge of the bed. The bed should be well-protected, and the drainage sleeve of the appliance is placed into a large receptacle. Bedside irrigation requires careful planning, since it is difficult to leave the bedside once the irrigation has begun.

The patient is taught that the irrigation container should be about 1½ to 2 feet above the stoma, which will allow the solution to flow by gravity. It might also be stated that the irrigation container should be shoulder level when the patient is seated. The catheter should be cleared of air by allowing solution to flow through it. It is lubricated well and is introduced through an irrigating appliance into the stoma and advanced for 2 to 6 inches. It must never be advanced forcibly; any resistance that is encountered is treated as described for enemas (page 247). Excessive backflow of irrigating solution can usually be corrected by advancing the catheter a bit farther.

Often the returns are complete within 45 to 60 minutes. Many find that the end of the drainage sleeve can be closed after about 15 minutes and the appliance worn for the remaining period of time, during which the patient may resume other activities. When the appliance is removed, the abdomen is washed and dried, and a stoma pad, dressing, or drainage bag is placed over the stoma. A

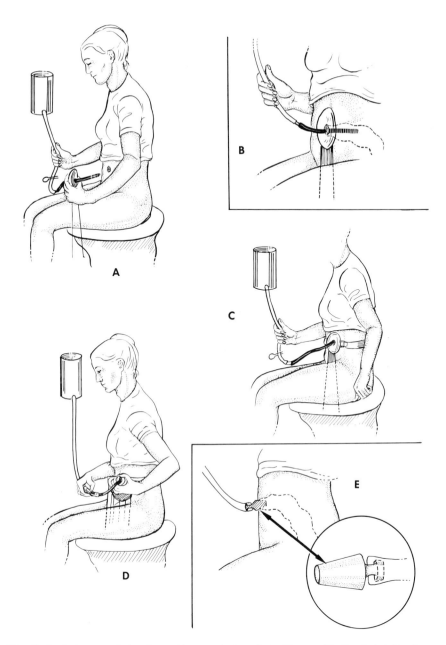

Fig. 8-6. Colostomy irrigation with a catheter, **A** to **D**, or with the Laird tip, **E**. **A**, The catheter is introduced through an opening in the irrigating appliance. After the desired amount of solution has been introduced, the opening through which the catheter was introduced is sealed. **B**, Cross section shows the catheter inserted and the irrigation appliance in use. **C**, The container of irrigating solution is placed at shoulder level or approximately 1½ to 2 feet above the stoma. **D**, The catheter may be introduced through the open top of the appliance. **E**, The Laird tip may be used to irrigate a colostomy without using an irrigating appliance. The size of the tip is individually selected and should fit into the stoma so that it acts like a cork. A properly fitted tip extends about ¼ inch on the outside of the stoma and must never be so small that it could slip into the colon. After the irrigation is complete, the tip is removed, and the returns flow through a drainage sleeve or into a receptacle held beneath the stoma. The inset shows an enlarged view of the Laird tip attached to tubing. (Courtesy John F. Greer Co., Oakland, Calif.)

drainage bag is used until the colostomy is regulated. Once regulated, the colostomate may find that a small piece of gauze dressing is adequate. The dressing may be held in place with a girdle, colostomy belt, or strips of tape. Some persons prefer to place a facial tissue treated with a lubricant, if the stoma is discharging minimal amounts of mucus. A small appliance designed for this purpose is available commercially.

Irrigator tips. Instead of a catheter, an irrigator tip may be used for irrigation. The conical shape of the tip serves to prevent penetration of the colon, to dilate the stoma, and to hold the irrigating solution in the colon, thus allowing it to fill more readily. If the tip is available in a variety of sizes, the size should be selected so that after insertion only a small portion of the tip protrudes from the stoma (Fig. 8-6, *E*). It must, however, be large enough to prevent it from slipping completely into the colon. Another design, also cone-shaped, is about 3 inches long and can be used for irrigation of most colostomies. A smaller tip will be required for small children. The lubricated tip, connected to tubing leading from the irrigation container, is inserted through the stoma for irrigation.

Use of an irrigator tip may be unsatisfactory if the stoma protrudes for some distance because the lumen of the colon is likely to be smaller inside the abdomen than it is on the outside of the abdominal wall. Generally, a tip is not used to irrigate a newly created colostomy. It is not used until healing has occurred. A tip is not used to irrigate a stoma that is flush with the skin.

Three-way irrigation. A three-way irrigation is done for persons who have either a temporary loop colostomy or a double-barrel colostomy. Each stoma or opening and the rectum are irrigated until clear returns are obtained. The following sequence is suggested: (1) proximal loop, (2) distal loop, and (3) rectum. This sequence is used because drainage from irrigation of the proximal loop may enter the distal loop, and drainage from the distal loop may enter the rectum. During the rectal irrigation, which is like an enema, solution may escape from the distal stoma. Provision for collection of drainage from the distal stoma is necessary. An irrigator appliance may be used during the irrigation of the proximal and distal loops.

The informed patient will know which stoma or opening leads to the proximal and which leads to the distal end of the colon. Knowledge of the usual arrangement of stomas or openings is useful when a three-way irrigation is ordered. If it is in the transverse colon, the stoma for the proximal loop is usually located on the patient's right. If the descending colon is involved, the upper stoma enters the proximal loop. The lower stoma enters the proximal loop when the sigmoid colon is involved.

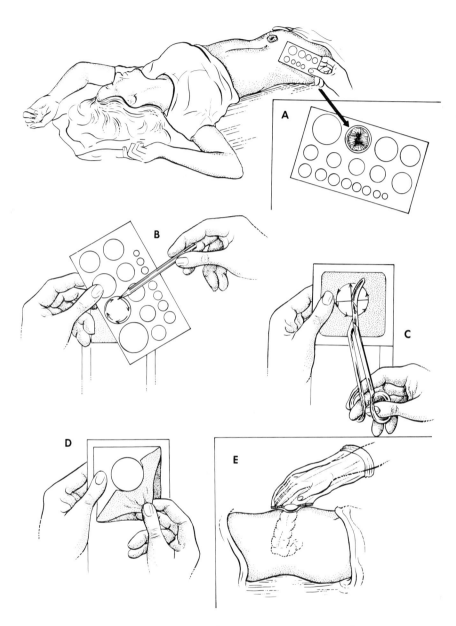

Fig. 8-7. Temporary drainage bags. **A,** A measuring guide is used to determine the size of the opening in the drainage bag. A safety margin of 1/8 inch around the stoma is allowed. **B,** The measuring guide is used to mark the desired size of opening. **C,** The opening is enlarged by first cutting diagonally. The opening is completed by cutting along the marked circle. **D,** The adhesive surface is exposed by removing the backing. A stoma seal may be applied. **E,** The adhesive surface of the bag is applied.

Continued.

257

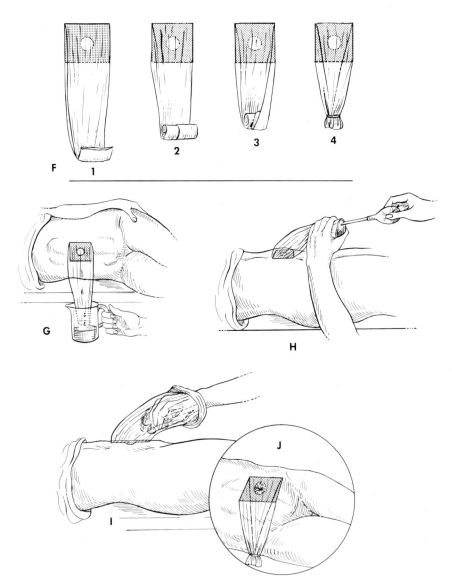

Fig. 8-7, cont'd. F, Air is removed from the bag, which is closed by folding it up at least twice, then toward the center. The seal is secured with a rubber band. **G,** The bag is emptied whenever necessary. **H,** The bag applied over the colonic stoma is rinsed with warm water. **I,** The lower part of the bag is dried. **J,** The bag is resealed.

DRAINAGE BAGS FOR INTESTINAL STOMAS

There is no need to apply a drainage bag over a regulated colostomy except during episodes of diarrhea, after irrigation, or for the security of the patient. Temporary drainage bags may be applied to a colostomy or an ileostomy immediately after surgery. Later, a permanent appliance is fitted over an ileostomy or an unregulated colostomy.

A measuring gauge is used to determine the correct size of opening for the temporary drainage bag or the face plate of the permanent appliance (Fig. 8-7, *A*). The guide is a series of sized rings or cut-out circles (Fig. 8-7, *A, inset*) and is available from surgical supply houses. It may be used to mark the temporary drainage bag prior to making or enlarging the opening (Fig. 8-7, *B*). The ideal size opening for an intestinal stoma provides a space of $\frac{1}{8}$ inch between the aperature of the bag and the exterior aspect of the stoma.* This safety margin is necessary because the stoma opens and expands as peristalsis occurs. Fitting an appliance too close to the stoma may result in complications such as interference with healing, the development of fistulae, or impairment of circulation to the stoma.

The skin must be clean and thoroughly dry before the appliance or drainage bag is placed. A rolled 4- by 4-inch gauze can be placed over the stoma to keep the area dry. This acts as an absorbent wick and is replaced as it becomes wet. A double-faced adhesive disk may be used to seal the appliance to the skin. Hypoallergenic disks are available; these are convenient to use, easy to apply, and do not require the use of cementing agents or solvents. Skin reactions and irritations are reduced. A karaya ring can be used to seal the space between the stoma and the appliance. The moistened side of the karaya ring is placed against the skin and the appliance is placed on top of the ring. Some prefer to use a commercial cement, a spray adhesive, or tincture of benzoin to increase adherence. When two coatings of tincture of benzoin are used to increase adherence and to protect the skin, it is important that the first coating is dry before applying the second coating.

Temporary drainage bags. The following method may be used to apply a temporary drainage bag after the skin has been cleansed and dried (Table 8-3). The adhesive surface on the bag is exposed (Fig. 8-7, *D*). If it is desired, a double-faced adhesive disk is applied to the adhesive surface of the bag. The opening of the bag is centered over the stoma and gentle pressure is used to seal the bag around the

---

*Urinary appliances are fitted with a space of $\frac{1}{16}$ inch between the stoma and the appliance. The urinary stoma is flush with the skin and does not expand as does the intestinal stoma.

TABLE 8-3. Application of temporary drainage bags for intestinal stomas

Technique	Problem	Explanation or solution
Use a measuring gauge to determine the correct size of opening for the bag; mark and cut the opening.	Interference with healing or circulation to the stoma may occur; fistulae may develop.	An intestinal stoma opens and expands as peristalsis occurs, requiring a space of ⅛ inch.
Cleanse the skin with soap and water, rinse, and pat dry.	The adhesive may not form a tight bond with the skin.	A clean, dry skin is less likely to become irritated, excoriated, infectious, or odoriferous. Fecal drainage is irritating to the skin. A rolled 4- by 4-inch gauze placed perpendicularly over the stoma and changed as necessary will keep the area dry.
If the skin is already irritated, (1) treat with lights placed at least 18 inches away from the stoma for 20 to 30 minutes, or (2) see text for more vigorous treatment.	The skin may be irritated before the bag is applied. The skin may be irritated further if light bulbs are larger than 60 watts.	Radiant energy evaporates moisture and brings more circulating blood to the area; both promote healing. The stoma must be covered with gauze to prevent excessive drying of the mucous membrane.
Expose the adhesive surface of the bag, and, if it is desired, apply a hypoallergenic double-faced disk to the adhesive surface.	The skin may be further irritated by the application and removal of the adhesive portion of the bag.	Hypoallergenic disks are less irritating to the skin than other adhesive materials.
Center the opening in the bag over the stoma and seal it smoothly to the skin with firm, gentle pressure, working outward from the opening.	Drainage may seep beneath the bag, destroying the seal and irritating the skin.	Placing one hand inside the bag to seal it to the skin and gradually working outward from the edges of the opening helps to prevent this.
Remove all but a small amount of air from the bag; pleat the bag, and close and fasten its distal end securely.	The thin plastic tends to adhere to the stoma.	A small amount of air in the bag helps to prevent this.

stoma, gradually working in an outward direction until the entire adhesive surface is sealed smoothly to the skin (Fig. 8-7, *E*). A tight seal is essential if drainage is to be prevented from seeping beneath the bag and destroying the seal as well as damaging the skin. All but a small amount of air is removed from the bag, which is then pleated, closed, and fastened securely at its distal end with a rubber band or a clamp (Fig. 8-7, *F*).

Permanent appliances. Several permanent appliances are available for use over an ileostomy. The design may allow the faceplate to be reused, or the faceplate may need to be discarded when the bag is discarded. Each time the appliance is changed, the faceplate may be removed, and the skin is washed and dried. The use of a solvent to remove the faceplate may be indicated. This will depend on the method that was used to attach the faceplate. As a rule, solvent is not necessary when a stoma seal or tincture of benzoin has been used. An adhesive agent, either a disk, liquid, or cement, may be used to increase adherence.

A double-faced adhesive disk may be placed on the back of the faceplate, which is centered over the stoma and adhered firmly to the skin by pressing on it. Strips of nonallergenic tape may be placed over the corners of the faceplate to make it more secure. The collection bag is stretched over the rim of the faceplate, secured, and closed. For added security, a belt may be attached to the faceplate.

DILATING THE INTESTINAL STOMA

Patients are taught to dilate the stoma manually when this is ordered by the physician. For this, either finger cots or a glove may be used to protect the fingers from fecal contamination. The lubricated finger is eased into the opening of the stoma and rotated gently as it is advanced further into the colon. The choice of finger used depends on the size of the stoma. Usually, dilation is begun by using the little finger first and progressing to the index and middle fingers only if the stoma will admit them easily. Occasionally a commercial dilator is used to dilate the stoma.

CONTROL OF ODOR

Cleanliness is essential in controlling odor. Each time an ileostomy or colostomy bag is emptied, it should be rinsed thoroughly with cool water. Hot water coagulates protein, making cleansing difficult; if hot water is used in latex bags, the permeability to odor will be increased. The bag may be rinsed with a deodorant solution or a commercial antibacterial solution if it is desired. Patients have reported good results from placing one of the following in the bottom of the stoma bag: commercially available deodorant, a piece of cotton saturated with rubbing alcohol or mouthwash, bicarbonate of soda (baking soda), a chlorine tablet (4.6 grains), aspirin (0.6 Gm., or 10 grains), charcoal tablets, charcoal obtained by crushing a charcoal briquette, vinegar, sodium benzoate, or ordinary room deodorant. The patient must be taught that these substances are irritating to the mucus membrane and must not contact the stoma. Due to the potential danger of contact with the stoma, the use of alcohol or aspirin is avoided for children who have need for a deodorant.

Agents that act as deodorants when taken orally are medications and should be used only with the physician's approval. Common prescriptions are bismuth subgallate or bismuth subcarbonate, 0.6 Gm. or ½ tsp. three times each day.

Methods of controlling room odor vary. The advent of air conditioning has decreased this problem. Commercial room deodorants may be used; choice varies with individual preference. Methyl salicylate into which a wick has been placed to hasten its evaporation is sometimes used in controlling severe odors associated with fecal fistulae and grossly infected wounds.

Questions for discussion and exploration

1. If the physician plans to start intestinal decompression, what supplies should you have at the bedside?
2. What are your responsibilities in preparing the patient for insertion of a gastrointestinal tube? In advancing it? In preventing or relieving irritation of the nostril?
3. What responsibilities does the nurse have in preventing fecal impaction from occurring?
4. How does an enema ordered to cleanse the rectum differ from an enema used to cleanse the colon, that is: (a) distance tube is inserted, (b) amount of solution used, and (c) position of the patient?
5. Discuss the nurse's role in helping the patient being prepared for reentry into normal living after (a) colostomy, (b) ileostomy, and (c) ileal bladder (ileal conduit).
6. Mr. Y. has been told that a stoma is necessary. What information should be given to him to help him accept his diagnosis and the need for intervention and to prevent postoperative discouragement?
7. Prepare a teaching plan for a patient who is admitted to the hospital for surgery that will result in colostomy.
8. To help Mr. A., a patient with chronic ulcerative colitis who is facing an ileostomy, you might decide to ask a person with an ileostomy to visit him. List criteria you would use to select the visitor so that this would be a positive experience. How would this differ if the patient were a young mother?
9. What is the nurse's role in helping the patient with a stoma maintain family relationships?
10. In what way might a busy executive with a stoma need to modify his living patterns? How might a homemaker modify her patterns of living? How could a college freshman modify his patterns?
11. What are some methods that a patient might use to control odor?
12. Mr. Z. asks how soon he'll be permitted to return to work after a colostomy. What facts must you know to answer his question honestly?
13. What information do you need to obtain in order to teach a patient colostomy care? Why?
14. Why is gentleness in cleansing and dressing a stoma emphasized?
15. How would you adapt a hospital procedure for irrigating a colostomy to the patient on complete bedrest? How would you adapt the irrigation procedure for use in the patient's bathroom at home?

16. Mr. K. complains of his stoma being "inappropriately noisy." What ways might he deal with this problem and still remain active in society?

17. While bathing Mrs. J., she states that she always takes an enema daily if she has not had a bowel movement before 10 A.M. What therapeutic reaction could you make to this statement?

Selected references

Barnes, M. R.: Clean colons without enemas, Amer. J. Nurs. 69:2128-2129, 1969.

Care of your colostomy, a source book of information, New York, 1964, American Cancer Society, Inc.

Colostomy, ileotsomy and ureterostomy care, Cleveland, 1971, American Cancer Society, Inc., Cuyahoga Unit, Ohio Division.

Dericks, V. C.: Rehabilitation of patients with ileostomy, Amer. J. Nurs. 61:48-51, 1961.

Dubois, E. C.: Hints on the management of a colostomy, Amer. J. Nurs. 55:71-72, 1955.

Gibbs, G. E., and White, M.: Stomal care, Amer. J. Nurs. 72:268-271, 1972.

Goligher, J. C., deDomal, F. T., Watts, J. McK., Watkinson, G., and Morson, B. C.: Ulcerative colitis, Baltimore, 1969, The Williams & Wilkins Co.

Gutowski, F.: Ostomy procedure: nursing care before and after, Amer. J. Nurs. 72: 262-267, 1972.

Hammer, L. G., Sawyer, J. G., Sister Monica, and McKnight, J.: The three-maneuver enema, Amer. J. Nurs. 62:72-73, 1962.

Happenie, S. D.: Colostomy, a second chance, Springfield, Ill., 1968, Charles C Thomas, Publisher.

Horowisz, M.: Profiles in OPD: a rectal and colon service, Amer. J. Nurs. 71:114-116, 1971.

Lenneberg, E., and Mendelssohn, A. N.: Colostomies, a guide, Washington, D.C., 1971, United Ostomy Association.

Vukovich, V., and Grubb, R. D.: Care of the ostomy patient, St. Louis, 1973, The C. V. Mosby Co.

9

Drainage and suction

Drains may be placed in various anatomic locations to remove fluids or air. The purpose and location of the drain determine whether its placement is a medical or nursing function. Therefore, when an incision is necessary, the surgeon places the drain. If the drain is inserted through a normal orifice, the nurse may be permitted to introduce the drain. However, a nurse does not insert a drain without a physician's order.

Knowledge of whether insertion of the drain requires aseptic technique is essential. Sterile technique is used if the area is normally sterile. Clean technique may be permitted if the area is not normally sterile. Strict aseptic technique is used for urethral catheterization, but clean technique is usually permitted for gastrointestinal decompression.

After a drain is in place, care to ensure its patency and to keep it free of tension is essential. The drain is anchored to prevent dislodgment and provide comfort. Flow of drainage depends on gravity, pressure, capillary attraction, or suction. The purpose and location of the drain, the kind, amount, and viscosity of drainage, the pathologic condition, the anatomic location, and the preferences of the attending physician influence the methods used to promote the flow of drainage.

All drainage systems should be observed frequently to ascertain that criteria necessary for satisfactory function are met. It is helpful to develop the habit of observing all aspects of the drainage system whenever one is seen to be in use. A commonly encountered problem, loose connections between drainage tubes, can be corrected by tightening the connections or by replacing parts; applying a water soluble lubricant to the connection point provides a temporary seal. Other problems include disconnection of suction machines from the source of electricity or lack of patency of the drains.

Drainage of the urinary bladder

Voluntary micturition should be promoted when it is indicated. Unless it is contraindicated, the patient is encouraged to assume the normal position for voiding. A sitting position is usual for female patients; male patients who are unable to ambulate may be allowed to stand beside their bed. Not infrequently the female patient needs to be guided in leaning forward slightly to relax the urethral sphincter. Micturition is further promoted by ensuring privacy, using a positive approach, and using comfort measures such as warming the bedpan. It is desirable to permit the patient to use bathroom facilities whenever possible. A collecting basin placed in the bowl of the toilet is used whenever a record of output is necessary. Other measures such as the sound of running water may help some patients void.

Responsibilities for and judgments concerning urethral catheterization are frequently delegated to the nurse who performs catheterization of the female patient. Commonly, a male nurse, a urology technician, or the physician catheterizes the male patient. Ureteral catheterization is performed by the physician.

Catheterization is indicated in the presence of obstruction or paralysis, in the absence of voluntary micturition, after surgery or trauma involving contiguous pelvic organs, and as an aid to clinical evaluation. Careful observation and evaluation, in light of the physician's order, of the individual's fluid intake and output, bladder distention, and discomfort are imperative.

Traumatic catheterization predisposes the urinary tract to infection. If difficulty is encountered in passing the catheter, the physician should be consulted.

Anomalies and certain surgical procedures may obscure the female urethra. Normally the meatus is located between the clitoris and the vagina. It must be exposed and identified. If the orifice is not in the usual anatomic location, it may be found lateral to the usual location. After gynecologic procedures, edema and swelling may obscure the orifice. After radical vulvectomy, identification of the meatus can be exceedingly difficult because it may be located beneath a fold of tissue, and the nurse may need to consult the surgeon to learn its location.

Urethral catheterization of the male and female patient uses the same principles and similar equipment. However, the method of packaging equipment and supplies modifies the technique.

The indications for urethral catheterization, the need for intermittent or continuous drainage of the bladder, and the size and condition of the urethra influence the selection of the catheter. For catheterization of the male, a coudé catheter or a finely woven silk

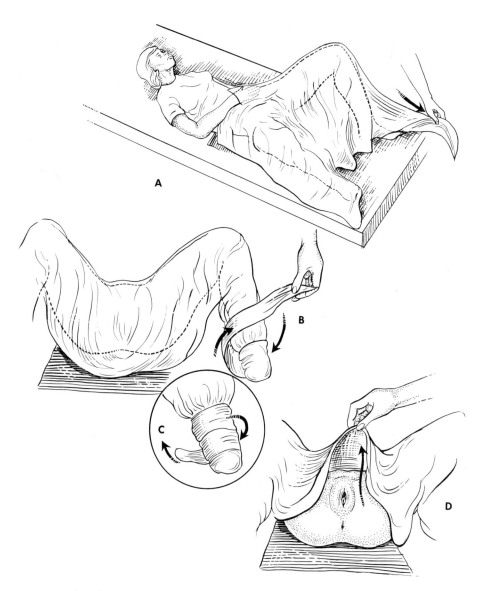

Fig. 9-1. Draping the perineal area. **A,** A sheet, placed diagonally over the patient, is arranged to cover the legs and feet. The corner of the sheet is straightened preparatory to wrapping the foot. **B,** Wrapping the foot. **C,** The foot rests on a corner of the drape, anchoring it. **D,** The perineal area is exposed by lifting the corner of the drape.

catheter may be used. Special skill is needed to introduce metal or glass catheters. The introduction of retention catheters necessitating the use of a stylet is a physician's responsibility. If the catheter is to be retained, one with an inflatable bag is likely to be selected. Sediment is less likely to collect around catheters treated with silicone; patency of these catheters is maintained longer than patency of latex catheters. A straight catheter, French size 12 to 16, is usually selected if the purpose of catheterization is to relieve retention, obtain a sterile specimen, or instill medication.

When the purpose of catheterization is to relieve distention, it is usual to clamp the catheter after 1000 ml. of urine has been removed and to seek further orders from the physician before the bladder is emptied completely. Removal of an amount in excess of 1000 ml. of urine predisposes the bladder to trauma and may cause complications such as shock and chills.

FEMALE CATHETERIZATION

Before positioning the patient, privacy must be provided and the purpose of the technique must be explained to the patient. The patient who trusts the nurse performing the technique and who understands that the catheter is inserted into the bladder to remove urine for a designated purpose is more able to cooperate. Referring to the catheter as a small tube and telling the patient that the catheter will be in the bladder temporarily often relieve undue apprehension. In addition, assuring privacy through adequate draping and screening avoids discomfort and anxiety due to unnecessary exposure. Explaining that passing the catheter does not produce pain but may cause some temporary discomfort may also be helpful.

Ideally, the patient is positioned on a gynecology table. If this is not possible, the patient is positioned in a back-lying position with her knees flexed and legs abducted (Fig. 9-2, A). This locates the bladder above the level of the meatus, permitting urine to escape through the catheter by gravity. Draping the patient is done as described in Fig. 9-1. If a sterile protector is placed beneath the patient's hips at this time, only the outermost corners of the protector may be touched. The drape may also be placed after gloving.

After washing her hands well with soap and water, the nurse puts on sterile gloves (Figs. 1-1 and 1-5). If the protector is to be placed beneath the patient's hips at this time, it is held so that the edge of the drape nearest to the patient is draped over the gloved hands. A sterile perineal drape may then be placed over the genitalia. The right-handed nurse uses the thumb and forefinger of the left hand to separate the labia minora and to retract the tissue slightly upward to expose the meatus (Fig. 9-2, B). The meatus and the surrounding area are cleansed with a suitable solution. A solution of benzal-

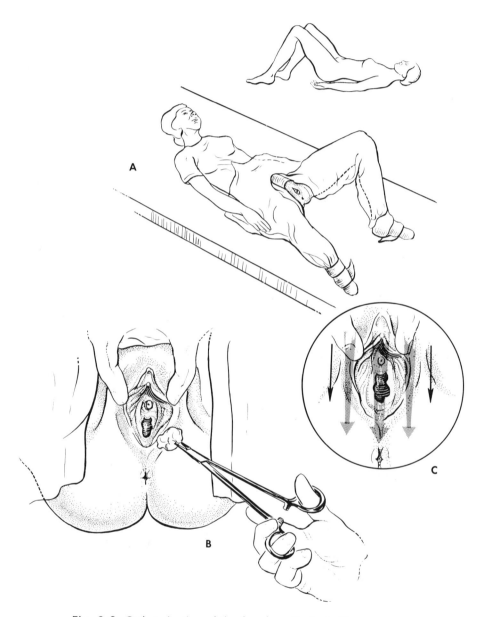

Fig. 9-2. Catheterization of the female patient. **A,** The nurse positions and drapes the patient. **B,** The labia minora are separated with the left thumb and forefinger and cleansed. **C,** Cleansing proceeds downward and outward.

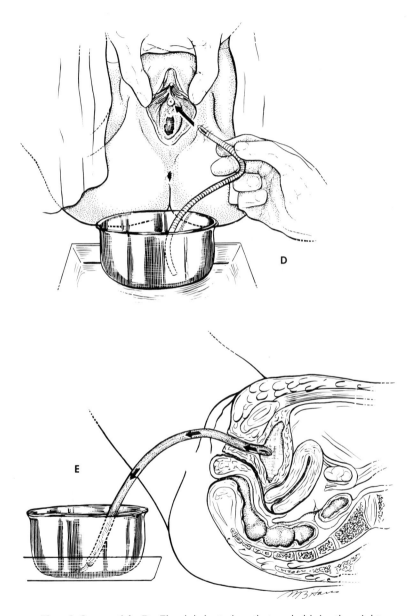

Fig. 9-2, cont'd. D, The lubricated catheter, held in the right gloved hand, is inserted. The free end of the catheter rests in a sterile receptacle. **E,** The catheter, inserted through the urethra into the bladder, drains into a sterile receptacle.

TABLE 9-1. Female catheterization

Technique	Problem	Explanation or solution
Explain the purpose of the technique.	The patient may be apprehensive.	The person who understands the purpose of this technique is more able to cooperate.
Obtain the necessary equipment.		If disposable equipment is not available, a French size 12-16 catheter is used.
Position the patient is a back-lying (dorsal recumbent) position with the knees flexed and the legs abducted.	Adequate exposure of the area may be difficult unless positioning is used.	This locates the bladder above the level of the meatus and will permit drainage of the bladder.
Drape the patient.	If the patient is not relaxed, it is difficult to cleanse the area and to insert the catheter.	Embarrassment causes tenseness; a feeling of exposure and chilling interferes with relaxation.
Direct a bright light at the meatus.	The meatus is sometimes difficult to see.	Additional light directed at the area is helpful and may remove interfering shadows.
Wash and dry the hands well, and open the catheterization tray.	Organisms from the hands may contaminate the catheterization set.	Clean hands are less likely to contain organisms.
Place a sterile protective pad beneath the hips by holding it by its edges.*	Contamination from the environment may occur.	The pad provides a sterile field.
Put on sterile gloves.	Even though the hands have been washed, some organisms remain.	Sterile gloves act as a barrier between organisms on the hands and sterile materials.
Place the catheterization tray on the sterile field between the patient's thighs.	Contamination of the tray can occur.	A sterile field on which the sterile tray is placed after removing it from its wrapper helps to prevent contamination.
Place a sterile drape over the genital area.	The gloves may be contaminated if the body is touched.	The drape provides a sterile field; the opening in the drape is centered over the labia.
With the thumb and forefinger, retract the tissue and separate the labia minora.	Inadequate exposure and cleansing will allow organisms from the genitalia to be introduced into the urethra.	Cleansing removes organisms.
Cleanse the area from the anterior to the posterior using one pledget for each stroke and discarding each pledget before beginning another stroke; three or more cleansing strokes are used; use a sterile forceps to hold the pledgets.	Contamination from the anal area can be transferred to the genitalia. Contamination of the glove that will hold the catheter can occur.	Downward strokes and a fresh sterile pledget for each stroke prevent transference of contamination. Use of a sterile forceps to hold pledgets maintains the sterility of the glove.

*The sterile pad may be placed after gloving by folding the pad over the sterile gloves.

TABLE 9-1. Female catheterization—cont'd

Technique	Problem	Explanation or solution
Look for the meatus during cleansing.	The meatus may be difficult to identify.	This allows an opportunity to locate the meatus, which may separate slightly during cleansing.
Keeping the labia separated, pick up the catheter about 1½ inches from its tip.	The catheter is flexible and may tend to coil.	Grasping the catheter near its tip allows good control.
Lubricate the tip of the catheter.	Friction increases resistance to the introduction of the catheter into the urethra.	Lubrication decreases friction and trauma; trauma is thought to be almost as harmful as the use of unsterile technique.
Divert the patient's attention and insert the catheter a distance of about 3 inches until urine begins to flow.	Worry about the discomfort and tenseness increases the difficulty of insertion.	Asking the patient to take a deep breath, engaging her in conversation, or asking her to focus on a specific point in the room fosters relaxation.
Hold the catheter in place until urine ceases to flow; massage the bladder gently.	The catheter will tend to slide out of the bladder. Massage aids in emptying the bladder.	Reinsertion of the catheter is unnecessarily traumatic and causes additional expense.
When urine ceases to flow withdraw the catheter slowly.	The bladder may not be completely empty; withdrawing the catheter may be uncomfortable.	Slow withdrawal permits the catheter to contact urine lying above the eye of the catheter; rapid removal of the catheter may be traumatic to the urethra.
Use a sterile sponge to apply gentle pressure to the meatus, remove any lubricant, and dry the area; help the patient to a comfortable position.	The patient will be somewhat tired and uncomfortable.	Comfort measures are appreciated by most patients.

konium chloride, pHisoHex, or green soap, followed by sterile normal saline or sterile water might be used. The solution is applied with saturated sterile pledgets or gauze sponges held with sterile forceps. The downward direction of cleansing must proceed from the anterior to the posterior, thereby preventing contamination of the perineal area with organisms normally found in the anal area. Cleansing proceeds outward (Fig. 9-2, C). A fresh sponge is used for each cleansing stroke. During cleansing, the meatus may separate slightly, aiding in its identification.

After the area is cleansed, the labia must be kept separated. A sterile collecting basin is placed near the area. The catheter is picked up in the right hand, its tip is lubricated 1 to 1½ inches, and it is moved to the work area, where the distal end of the catheter is placed into the sterile collecting basin. Asking the patient to take a deep breath may cause slight dilation of the meatus. The lubricated tip of the catheter is inserted through the meatus and urethra into the bladder (Fig. 9-2, *D*), at which time urine will flow through the catheter into the basin (Fig. 9-2, *E*). The fact that the urethra is 1½ to 2½ inches long and that the opening in the straight catheter is about ½ inch from the tip of the catheter indicates that the catheter will be inserted a total distance of 2 to 3 inches; then it is advanced about ½ inch farther.

The catheter must be held in place throughout the drainage period. When urine ceases to flow, the bladder is massaged and the catheter is withdrawn slowly to permit complete drainage of the bladder. Immediately after removal of the catheter, a sterile sponge is used to apply gentle pressure to the meatus and to remove lubricant from the area. After the area has been dried, the patient is made as comfortable as possible. Notation of the amount, color, odor, and other important characteristics of the urine should be made. The used equipment is washed and sterilized unless disposable equipment is used. Table 9-1 summarizes the technique of female catheterization.

MALE CATHETERIZATION

The purposes and principles of male catheterization do not differ from those of female catheterization. A protective pad is placed beneath the patient's hips after draping him. The nurse washes his hands well, puts on sterile gloves, and centers the opening of a sterile perineal drape over the penis. The penis is held between the thumb and forefinger. If it is present, the foreskin is retracted. The meatus and surrounding area are cleansed using pledgets saturated with a suitable cleansing agent or antiseptic solution. Cleansing begins at the meatus and proceeds outward. Another sterile pledget is used for each cleansing stroke. The penis is elevated, and gentle traction is applied to position it perpendicular to the body; this straightens the urethra. The lubricated catheter is inserted through the meatus and advanced until slight resistance is encountered, about 5 to 6 inches. The patient is instructed to breathe deeply if he is able to cooperate; otherwise, waiting momentarily will allow the sphincter to relax, and the catheter is advanced. When urine begins to flow, the catheter is advanced about ½ inch farther. When urine ceases to flow, the catheter is removed, and the area is cleansed of lubricant. Table 9-2 summarizes the technique of male catheterization.

TABLE 9-2. Male catheterization

Technique	Problem	Explanation or solution
Explain the procedure to the patient.	Anxiety, fear, and tension may increase the difficulty of catheterization.	Knowledge allays apprehension; an explanation is given by the nurse if the catheterization is to be done by the physician or by a urology technician.
Help the patient to assume a flat, back-lying position with the knees slightly apart; fanfold the linen to his knees, and fanfold the gown onto his chest.	Inadequate exposure of the area contributes to contamination.	This position allows the bladder to drain and promotes muscular relaxation.
Wash the hands and dry them well.	Organisms from the hands can be a source of contamination.	Washing removes bacteria.
Open the sterile disposable catheterization tray and put on sterile gloves.	Some organisms may remain on the hands and become contaminants.	Sterile gloves protect the patient from organisms remaining on the hands.
Place a sterile drape with a center-cut opening over the penis, or place a sterile towel beneath the penis.	Organisms from the patient or the environment may contaminate the equipment used.	A sterile field will prevent the accidental contamination of the catheter.
Hold the penis between the thumb and forefinger and cleanse it from the meatus outward; retract the foreskin during cleansing.	Adequate cleansing will prevent the introduction of organisms into the urethra.	Slight pressure on the penis causes the meatus to open slightly. Retraction of the foreskin exposes the meatus for cleansing.
With gentle traction, elevate the penis until it is perpendicular to the body.	The catheter may be difficult to pass.	This straightens the urethra as much as is anatomically possible.
Lubricate the catheter, insert it, and advance it until resistance is felt.	Resistance may be felt almost immediately.	A twisting motion applied to the catheter as it is advanced will aid in slipping it past folds of mucosa or through the pouches.
Ask the patient to take deep breaths and retract the penis further; lower it slightly and advance the catheter with short, pushing motions.	Reflex contracture of perineal musculature may occur.	This aids in passing the catheter through the pouch in the lower wall of the urethra; deep breaths help relax muscles.
Advance the catheter until urine begins to flow; then advance it about ½ inch farther (for an approximate total distance of 7 to 10 inches). Hold the catheter in place while the bladder drains; for this the penis is lowered to a more natural position.	The catheter will tend to glide out of the bladder.	Reinsertion of the catheter is unnecessary, traumatic, and expensive. Lowering the penis allows the force of gravity to drain the urine.
When urine ceases to flow, withdraw the catheter slowly, cleanse the area, and assist the patient to be as comfortable as is possible.	The patient will be somewhat tired and uncomfortable.	Comfort measures are appreciated by the patient.

RETENTION CATHETER

When continuous or intermittent bladder drainage is necessary, a catheter with an inflatable bag may be used. The previously described technique is used to cleanse the area and insert the catheter. The catheter is inserted beyond the distal portion of the uninflated balloon, approximately 3 to 4 inches in female patients (Fig. 9-3, *A*). In male patients, the catheter is advanced about 7 to 10 inches or about 1 inch after urine begins to flow. When the bladder has been emptied, the bag is inflated.

Catheters are available with inflatable balloons of varying sizes; the size of the balloon determines the amount of solution or air that is needed for inflation. The amount needed is usually imprinted on the distal extension of the catheter through which the balloon is inflated.

Several basic types of balloon catheters are available, each requiring a somewhat different method of inflation and closure (Fig. 9-3, *B*). Sterile solution or air may be injected through an open sidearm, which is then folded over itself and fastened with a clamp, rubber band, or fishline. A similar catheter is inflated by penetrating a seal in the end of the sidearm; this may require the use of a needle, or it may require the introduction of the tip of the syringe to inject the solution. Another type inflates itself when a prepositioned clamp is loosened. A metal clamp may be used to compress the catheter.

The catheter is connected to sterile drainage tubing that extends into a sterile drainage receptacle (Fig. 9-3, *C*). This may be done after catheterization; use of completely preassembled catheterization equipment is preferable. Taping the catheter to the patient's thigh prevents tension on it and prevents unnecessary discomfort (Fig. 9-3, *D*). However, there should be no undue tension placed on the catheter when it is taped to the patient. The drainage tubing is secured to the foundation of the bed in such a way as to ensure gravity drainage. The tubing is placed over the top of the thigh to prevent its occlusion by the weight of the patient; on rare occasions other positioning of the tubing may be used. Both the catheter and the tubing should be inspected periodically to prevent compression or kinking that may obstruct flow. The receptacle may be suspended from the bedframe (Fig. 9-3, *E*). Teaching the patient how to adjust the drainage tubing will increase his mobility. If he is ambulatory, teaching him to manipulate the drainage tubing and container will help him to achieve increased independence. Helping him to understand the principles of gravity drainage will assist him in realizing the importance of keeping the drainage tubing and the drainage receptacle lower than the bladder at all times.

Generally, an indwelling catheter is not disconnected, clamped,

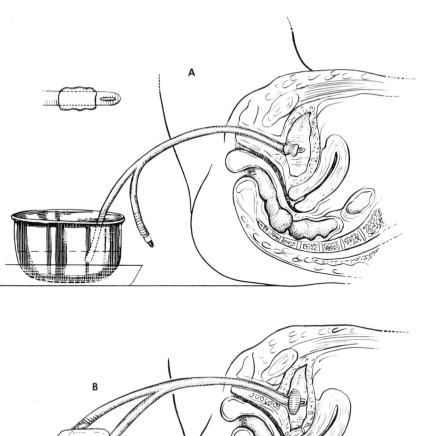

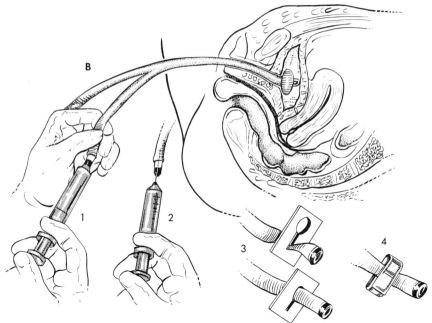

Fig. 9-3. Insertion of a retention catheter with an inflatable bag. **A,** The catheter with an inflatable bag is inserted. The enlarged view shows the relationship of the deflated bag to the eye of the catheter. **B,** Methods of inflating the bag: *1,* the tip of the filled syringe is placed directly into the sidearm extension, the solution is injected, and the sidearm is folded over itself and clamped; *2,* solution is injected through a needle or the tip of a syringe that pierces the self-sealing end of the sidearm; *3,* the prepositioned clamp is released from the sidearm of a self-inflating type of catheter; *4,* a metal clamp may be used to compress the catheter.

Continued.

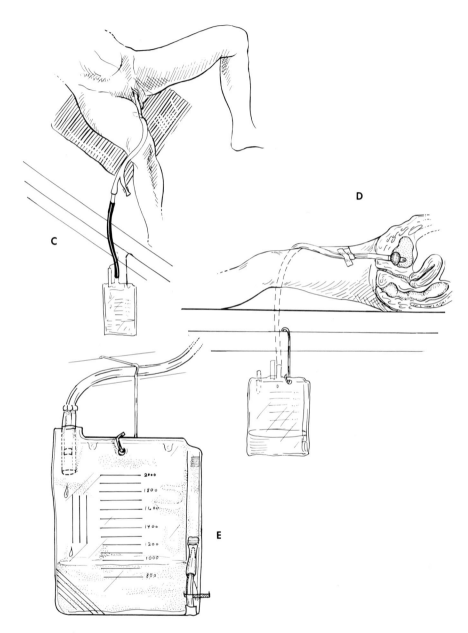

Fig. 9-3, cont'd. C, The catheter is connected to sterile tubing that extends into a sterile container, providing straight drainage. **D,** The catheter is taped to the inner aspect of the thigh. **E,** The drainage container may be suspended from the side of the bed. (Courtesy Baxter Laboratories, Inc., Morton Grove, Ill.; Travenol Laboratories, Inc., Deerfield, Ill.)

or irrigated without the permission of the attending physician. Sitz baths may be given without contamination if the catheter remains connected to the drainage apparatus. Irrigation of catheters is discussed in Chapter 10. If the catheter is to be disconnected from the drainage tubing for a period of time, it is clamped, and the juncture is cleansed with an antiseptic. Then it is disconnected and protected with a sterile covering. A sterile plastic catheter plug may be placed into the end of the catheter, and a sterile drainage tube protector may be placed over the end of the drainage tube. Catheter plugs should be used only once; reuse of the same plug creates a septic condition and increases the incidence of infection. If the ends of the catheter and tubing are to be covered with sterile gauze, then previously sterilized packages containing gauze sponges, rubber bands, and a clamp may be supplied for this purpose.

In an attempt to reduce infection, the point of juncture between the catheter and the meatus may be cleansed at least once daily for male patients and twice daily for female patients. Gentle hygienic cleansing is almost never contraindicated, and it is particularly important to cleanse the area well when the patient is unable to do so. An antiseptic medication in ointment, aerosol, or liquid form may be prescribed to be applied after each cleansing. As a part of routine catheter care, the juncture between the catheter and tubing may be cleansed with a suitable antiseptic solution such as 70% alcohol.

COLLECTION OF URINE SPECIMENS

Clean voided specimens (midstream, clean-catch urine specimens). Increased use of clean voided specimens for laboratory studies has reduced the frequency of catheterization. Before the specimen is collected, the patient's bladder should contain a fair amount of urine, and factors contributing to contamination should be reduced to a minimum. For this reason, the nurse should direct the female patient to insert a tampon if a vaginal discharge is present, should cleanse the meatus and adjacent tissues, and should direct her to pass at least an ounce of urine to cleanse the urethra before the specimen is collected.

If a special table is available, the nurse positions the patient on it. The back of the table is raised so that the patient is in a sitting position with her feet in stirrups and her legs abducted. If such a table is not available, cleansing is done while the patient is seated on the toilet with her legs well apart. Throughout the entire cleansing and until the specimen has been collected, the labia must be held apart. Cleansing is done as for catheterization. A solution of 1:3 pHisoHex and water or another suitable agent is used. Each cleansing stroke begins above the meatus and proceeds toward the

277

anal area. Opinions vary on whether cleansing should begin at the midline and proceed outward or whether it should begin at the inner aspect of the labia majora and proceed to the midline. A single sterile sponge is used for each cleansing stroke. After this, the area is cleansed again with sterile sponges and sterile normal saline or sterile water. After the specimen is collected, the area is dried with sterile sponges in single-directional strokes.

The nurse instructs the patient to void forcefully without permitting the labia to close. After the patient has passed an ounce or more of urine, the nurse collects the specimen by catching the stream of urine in a sterile collecting container. During the catch, it is important that the flow be sufficient to force the stream away from the tissues and directly into the bottle. Gentle retraction of the tissues may be helpful in directing the stream. As soon as the nurse has collected the specimen it is capped, using sterile precautions, labeled, and placed in the refrigerator or cultured immediately. If the patient wishes, she may finish voiding as soon as the specimen has been collected.

Collection of a midstream specimen from the male patient is based on similar principles. Many patients can be taught to carry out this technique satisfactorily; otherwise, a urology technologist, male nurse, or the physician assists the patient.

The area is cleansed with a circular motion, beginning at the meatus and working away from it. Sufficient urine, at least 2 ounces, is passed to cleanse the urethra, and the stream is stopped momentarily and directed into the container. As soon as the specimen has been collected, urination should be stopped. Complete emptying of the male bladder is accompanied by possible contamination of the specimen with prostatic fluid; therefore it is important that the bladder contain a fair amount of urine before the specimen is collected. After collection of the specimen, the bladder can be emptied completely.

Catheterized specimens. If the purpose of catheterization is to obtain a sterile specimen for culture, the patient's bladder should contain a fair amount of urine. Ideally, he should void an amount sufficient to cleanse the urethra immediately prior to the cleansing of the surrounding area and insertion of the catheter. It is desirable that the female patient pass an ounce or more of urine; the male patient should pass at least 2 ounces.

CONTINUOUS IRRIGATION AND DRAINAGE

Continuous irrigation and drainage of the bladder is used in selected cases. Sterile irrigating solution flows into the bladder at a specified rate, often 30 to 60 drops per minute. The height of the siphon tube regulates the amount of intravesical pressure. If straight

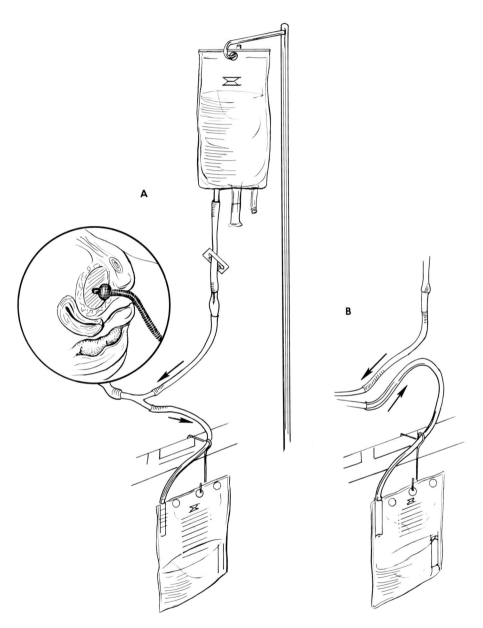

Fig. 9-4. Irrigation and drainage. **A,** Solution flows into and drains out of the bladder continuously. **B,** Modified tidal drainage results when the tube draining the bladder is elevated. This tube must not be arched without instructions from the physician. (Courtesy Baxter Laboratories, Inc., Morton Grove, Ill.; Travenol Laboratories, Inc., Deerfield, Ill.)

drainage is used to empty the bladder continuously, the drain leading from the catheter must be below the level of the bladder and must be arranged so that drainage by gravity is possible (Fig. 9-4, *A*). Increased intravesical pressure is produced when the drainage tube is arched (Fig. 9-4, *B*). This produces a modified type of tidal drainage that should not be used without direction from the physician. If straight drainage apparatus is used for this purpose, the physician determines the height of the siphon tube.

TIDAL DRAINAGE

After certain types of trauma to the bladder, tidal drainage may be used to empty it periodically. This mechanically controlled method of bladder drainage is used to promote bladder function. It is used to increase muscle tone and to reduce hypertonicity of the bladder that would cause it to empty frequently.

In addition to equipment used to catheterize with a three-way retention catheter, the nurse needs a sterile tidal drainage set, sterile solution, and an intravenous standard from which the solution is suspended. After inserting and inflating the retention catheter, the nurse places its distal end in a sterile basin or connects it to straight drainage until the tidal drainage apparatus is assembled.

The nurse assists the physician as necessary by placing the intravenous standard beside the bed or attaching it to the bed. The collecting receptacle may be hung from the bed; if a bottle is used, it may be placed on the floor. Strict aseptic technique is used in assembling the apparatus. All parts of the apparatus except the upper end of the manometer, when one is used, are connected. During assembly of the equipment, open ends of tubes may be covered with sterile gauze or sealed with a sterile catheter plug and drainage tube protector to prevent their contamination. Disposable tubing sealed with temporary coverings that ensure sterility is available. The siphon tube is clamped, and the prescribed solution is used to expel air from the drainage set. The siphon loop must be filled with solution to prime it. When the tube that leads to the catheter is filled with solution and therefore free of air, the flow is interrupted, and the tube is connected to the catheter. The rate of flow is regulated according to the physician's orders, often at 30 to 50 drops per minute. The height of the siphon tube is selected by the physician and will need adjusting when the bed is raised or lowered unless the loop is attached to a pole incorporated into the design of the bed.

Throughout this treatment, the nurse must be certain that all tubing is kept patent and free of kinks and pressure. Approximately 3000 ml. of irrigating solution may be used in a 24-hour period unless doing so is contraindicated. It is imperative that disten-

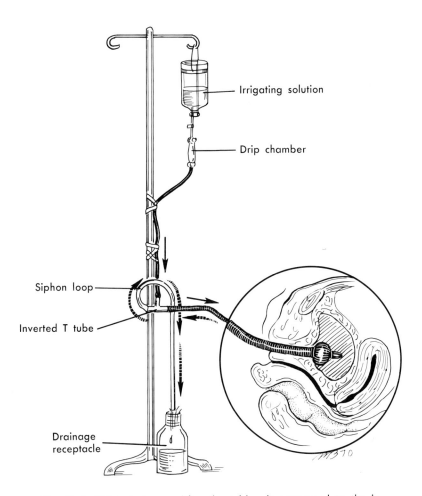

Fig. 9-5. Tidal drainage. After the tubing is connected to the irrigating solution and filled with solution to clear it of air, it is connected to the indwelling urinary catheter. The siphon loop must be filled with solution to prime it. The inverted T tube is level with the symphysis pubis, and the height of the siphon loop, often about 10 cm., is set by the physician. When intravesical pressure is equal to that in the siphon loop, siphon action begins and will continue until the contents in the bladder have emptied into the drainage receptacle. The rate of flow of the irrigating solution is prescribed by the physician. When periodic determination of pH of the urine is used to determine the rate at which the irrigating fluid should flow, the sample for testing should be obtained directly from the catheter. When possible, tidal drainage apparatus should be suspended from an intravenous pole that is attached to the bed.

tion of the bladder and the length of the cycle be observed and noted. Usually the bladder is expected to empty every 2 to 3 hours. The nurse adds additional irrigating solution when necessary.

When tidal drainage is interrupted for purposes such as ambulation, the nurse connects the catheter to straight drainage or clamps it in accordance with the physician's orders. If the catheter is to be disconnected, a sterile equipment set containing a basin, a clamp, gauze sponges or catheter plug and drainage tube protector, and a sterile towel are needed. The catheter and connecting tubing are disconnected and held over the basin to drain; both are placed on the sterile towel until the catheter is clamped. The ends of the catheter and the tubing are covered with gauze sponges and secured with rubber bands or sealed with a sterile catheter plug and drainage tube protector.

Intravesical pressure can be measured if the tidal drainage apparatus incorporates a manometer and scale. The nurse or physician fastens the calibrated scale to the intravenous standard with the zero mark parallel to the level of the bladder. The siphon tube leading from the bladder is clamped; a predetermined amount of solution is allowed to enter the bladder, and the resulting pressure is measured by reading the mark on the scale that parallels the level of fluid in the manometer. The siphon tube is unclamped, and the pressure is recorded (Fig. 9-5).

Biliary drainage

If the common bile duct is entered surgically, the surgeon inserts a T tube to splint the duct and maintain its patency. The tube should be kept sterile, and a drainage system should be provided. A simple method of providing for straight drainage that permits independent activity consists of attaching a disposable but sterile collecting bag to the T tube. Bags containing a valve that prevents drainage from reentering the drainage tube are available. The bag may be folded and secured to the patient's binder or to the uppermost layer of dressings by safety pins passed through slits incorporated into the design of the bag for this purpose (Fig. 9-6, *A*). The bile bag can be secured with adjustable latex belts and special buttons supplied with the bag or it may be pinned to adhesive tabs affixed to the abdomen. Unless dressings are present, a piece of gauze (4 by 4 inches) may be placed between the bag and the skin for additional comfort. The bile bag may be folded as shown in Fig. 9-6, *A,* or unfolded as shown in Fig. 9-6, *B*. Preparatory to emptying the bag into a graduated measure, the distal end of

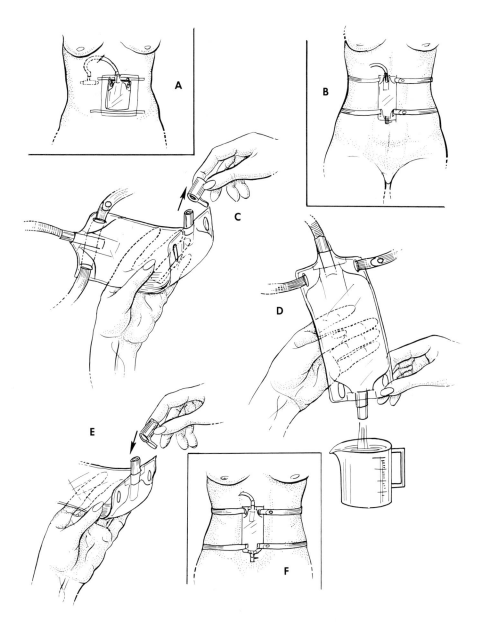

Fig. 9-6. Biliary drainage (Bardic bile bag). **A,** The bile bag may be folded and pinned to the patient's binder or to the uppermost layer of dressings with safety pins passed through the slits incorporated into the design of the bag. **B,** The bile bag can be secured with adjustable latex belts and special buttons supplied with the bag. It may be folded as shown in **A** or unfolded as shown. **C,** Preparatory to emptying the bag, its distal end is elevated to prevent escape of drainage, and the cap is removed. **D,** The contents of the bag are drained into a graduated measure. The hand beneath the bag supports it and positions it to aid in draining the contents from the bag. **E,** After the bag is emptied, the cap is replaced. **F,** The bag is again secured in a position that prevents tension on the T tube and facilitates gravity drainage. (Courtesy C. R. Bard, Inc., Murray Hill, N. J.)

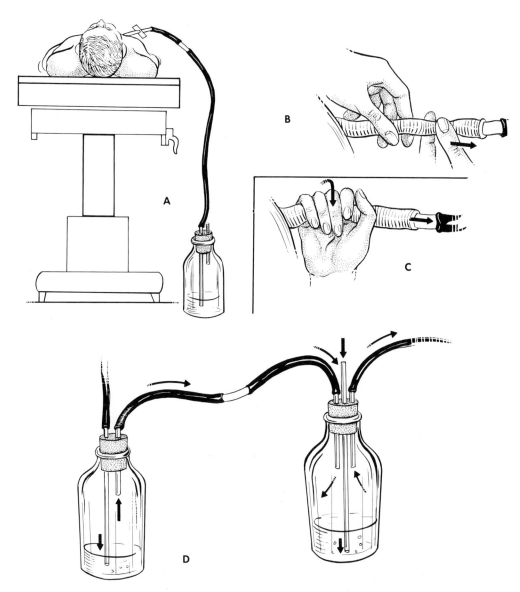

Fig. 9-7. Chest drainage. **A,** Water-seal drainage. **B,** Stripping a drain. **C,** Milking a drain. **D,** Regulated suction. The depth of the tube below the level of the water in the bottle on the right determines the amount of negative pressure that can result from suction. **E,** Combination water manometer and underwater seal used for water-seal drainage only or combined with suction. (Courtesy Ohio Chemical & Surgical Equipment Co., Madison, Wis.)

the bag is elevated to prevent escape of drainage, and the cap is removed (Fig. 9-6, *C* and *D*). After the bag is emptied, the cap is replaced; the bag is again secured in a position that prevents tension on the T tube and facilitates gravity drainage (Fig. 9-6, *E* and *F*). The amount, color, and odor of the bile are observed and recorded. Occasionally it is necessary to empty the bag more frequently than every 3 to 4 hours. This depends on the amount of the bile escaping into the bag and the size of the bag used.

Chest drainage

After surgery, it is extremely important that air not enter the drainage tube leading from the chest cavity, that patency of the drains be maintained, and that an acceptable method of drainage be used. Orders aimed at maintaining patency of the drain may include periodic stripping (Fig. 9-7, *B*) and milking (Fig. 9-7, *C*) of the chest catheter.

Precautionary measures such as taping the tubing to the chest wall, sealing all connection points, and fastening the electric plug of the suction machine to the outlet with waterproof adhesive tape

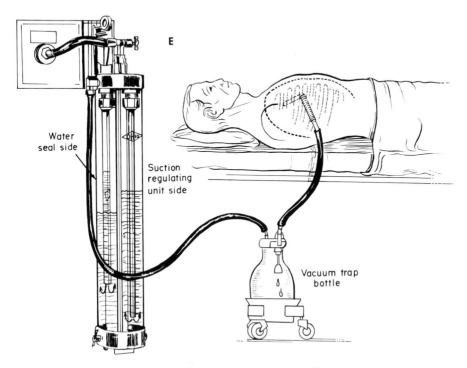

Fig. 9-7, cont'd. For legend see opposite page.

help to prevent accidental interruption of the system. When they are used, bottles should be taped to the floor with vertical strips of adhesive tape to prevent them from tipping, which will destroy the water seal. In addition, a pair of clamps should be readily available, because if the system is interrupted for any reason, the nurse must clamp the chest catheters immediately unless written orders specify otherwise. The nurse should place the clamp on the catheter close to its point of entry through the chest wall. A second clamp placed distal to the first is used as a precautionary measure. Kelly clamps or hemostats are used because they can be applied quickly. The inside surfaces of the blades should be free of sharp points or teeth that could damage the tubing. When the chest drainage system is functioning well, some fluctuation of drainage in the drainage tube can be observed with each respiration; a wide fluctuation of drainage in the tube may indicate leakage.

If the fluctuation of drainage or the amount of suction becomes less or greater than the prescribed range, the physician will wish to be notified at once. Often, more than a borderline fluctuation outside the prescribed range is considered an indication for clamping the chest tubes immediately. If the gauge consists of a side-arm manometer, the area directly behind the permissible range of fluctuation can be shaded or colored to facilitate visualization. Any material of contrasting color may be applied; however, it must not interfere in any way with the reading of the manometer.

If the chest tube is dislodged accidentally, the nurse must immediately seal the site through which the tube entered the chest. This can be done by forming an airtight seal with the hand, a piece of adhesive tape, or several layers of petroleum jelly gauze placed over the site and held with gentle pressure. Although these methods carry some risk of contamination, failure to seal the drain site immediately will permit air to enter the pleural cavity, causing pneumothorax.

WATER-SEAL DRAINAGE

Water-seal drainage consists of a bottle fitted with a 2-hole stopper through which tightly fitted tubes extend. One tube is short and acts as an escape route for air in the bottle (Fig. 9-7, A). The other tube, which is connected to the drain, extends 1 to 2 inches below the surface of water previously placed in the bottle. The use of sterile equipment and water lessens the possibility of accending infection. The water acts as a seal or valve, permitting air or fluid to escape into the bottle and preventing its entry into the chest cavity. The bottle is placed on a level lower than the cavity being drained, often on or near the floor, to permit gravity to drain fluid into the bottle. The bottle must not be elevated, or siphonage of its contents into the chest will occur. Measures to prevent the bottle from being tipped, which would break the water seal, include a special holder or taping the bottle to the floor.

To maintain effective water-seal drainage, the drain must be placed carefully, the water seal and air escape must be maintained, and the tubing must be arranged so that straight drainage is possible. If the bottle is to be changed, the chest tube must be double-clamped. However, the bottle is not changed, disconnected, or discontinued without a physician's order. The amount of drainage that occurs within a specified time period may be marked on a piece of adhesive tape placed on the bottle.

REGULATED SUCTION

Sometimes suction is reduced by connecting a water-seal drainage bottle between the patient's drain and the suction apparatus. The number of bottles connected in a series will determine the degree to which suction will be reduced (Fig. 9-7, *D*). This is referred to as regulated, cut-down, or bubble suction.

MACHINES USING PRINCIPLES OF WATER-SEAL DRAINAGE AND ELECTRIC SUCTION

Machines that incorporate water-seal drainage and principles of electric suction are available. In some, an electrically driven motor heats the air within the system to a preset level, expanding it and forcing it into the atmosphere. At prescribed intervals the cycle is interrupted and the air remaining cools, producing a partial vacuum that results in mild suction. As suction is created, the level of the liquid in the manometer rises, indicating the amount of suction. The weight of the liquid used in the manometer influences the amount of suction possible. Thus use of mercury permits more suction than does use of an equal amount of water.

A combination water manometer and underwater seal that can be used for water-seal drainage only or be combined with suction is available (Fig. 9-7, *E*). The drainage bottle containing a vacuum trap is placed on the floor, and the combination manometer and underwater seal is mounted on the wall near the source of suction. This arrangement facilitates observations and eliminates problems encountered when all equipment is placed on the floor. After the equipment is prepared and checked for proper functioning, the nurse connects it to the chest catheter. The clamp on the catheter is then opened slowly and the rate of bubbling is observed at the lower end of the manometer, which is adjusted as necessary. Directions of the manufacturer should be consulted for details concerning the operation and repair of this equipment.

PLEUR-EVAC

The Pleur-evac (Fig. 9-8) is a one-piece plastic, sterile, disposable unit that can be used instead of one-, two-, or three-bottle underwater-seal drainage systems. A suction chamber, suction control chamber, water seal, and collecting chambers are incorporated into its design. In addition to directions supplied with the unit, sequentially numbered directions are printed on the unit itself. Space for marking the levels of drainage in the collecting chambers is provided on the unit. The unit may be suspended from the bedframe or stretcher, placed in its disposable floor stand, or transported with the patient. It must be kept below the level of the patient's chest at all times. It must also be maintained in a fairly upright

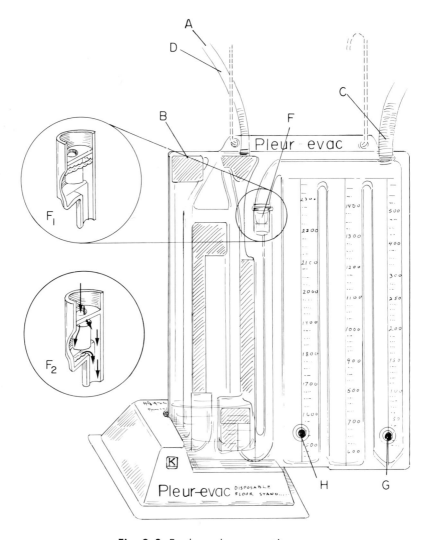

Fig. 9-8. For legend see opposite page.

position, although it can be tipped slightly without destroying the underwater-seal. During transport or ambulation, the unit is disconnected from suction; however, the tube leading to the suction must not be occluded, nor are the chest tubes clamped. The end of the tube leading to suction may be covered with sterile gauze. When the patient has a second chest tube, a second sterile unit is attached. Additional information may be obtained from the manufacturer.

Electric suction pumps

Several electrically operated suction machines are available. Among these are the Gomco thermotic drainage pump and the Emerson suction machine. Satisfactory operation of these machines depends on establishing and maintaining airtight connections be-

---

Fig. 9-8. Pleur-evac. A, First, the water-seal chamber is filled to the prescribed level through the 1-foot tubing. Commonly it is filled to the 2 cm. level for adults, which requires the addition of 95 ml. of water. B, Second, the suction control chamber is filled to the prescribed level, often 15 to 18 or 20 cm. For the 15 cm. level, 300 ml. of sterile water is needed; for the 20 cm. level, 450 ml. is needed. C, Third, the tubing from the collection chamber is connected to the patient's chest catheter. D, Fourth, the tubing leading from the water-seal chamber is connected to suction when it is prescribed. When suction is not prescribed, this tube is left open to the atmosphere. Fifth, the suction is started and increased until bubbling appears. Continuous suction is set above the pressure on the suction control; commonly this is between 20 and 30 cm. An air muffler, which must have a hole in it, may be inserted into the suction chamber, B, to decrease noise from the suction. F, The float valve prevents backflow. F_1, The water seal closes when the patient inhales with excessive negative pressure. F_2, The water-seal float valve opens when the patient inhales. G and H, Self-sealing diaphragms are accessible from the back of the unit. G, Specimens for laboratory examination may be aspirated with a 15-gauge or smaller needle attached to a syringe. Usually an 18-gauge needle is satisfactory. *The needle must be attached to the syringe before insertion into the diaphragm.* Aseptic technique is required. H, If the valve sticks, the chest tube is clamped, and a needle is inserted through the diaphragm to correct the problem. If all of the chambers contain drainage, air may be withdrawn by inserting a needle through the diaphragm. For this, the chest tube must be clamped also. (Courtesy Krale Laboratories, Queens Village, N. Y.)

tween the drains and the drainage bottle, connecting the machine to a source of electricity, and maintaining patency of the drainage system.

Questions for discussion and exploration

1. When Mr. T. is returned to his room from surgery, you are the only nurse present to help the nonprofessional personnel transfer him from the surgical cart to his bed. Before this is done, you have a responsibility to make certain that any drains inserted into him will not be displaced. How will you determine this (a) if his chart is not available? (b) if his chart is available?

2. In the preceding situation, if an orderly insists that speed is urgent because he must return to the surgical suite, what is your obligation to the patient? How might you tactfully handle this situation?

3. If drains are in place, what are your responsibilities in relation to each of the following and why?
   a. Urinary catheter intended for straight drainage
   b. Urinary catheter intended for tidal drainage
   c. Gastrointestinal tube
   d. Penrose and cigarette drains
   e. Biliary drainage
   f. Chest drains
   g. Straight drain placed in the hepatic duct
   h. T tube placed in remaining stump of duodenum for decompression purposes

4. Mrs. K. has not voided for 12 hours. How can you systematically determine whether her bladder is distended?

5. What can you do to assist Mrs. K. to void voluntarily?

6. Mr. Q. states that he feels like he must urinate but cannot do so while lying on his back. What factors will determine whether he will be allowed to stand by his bedside or walk to the bathroom? If he has recently returned from surgery and is too weak to stand by himself, how could you handle this situation?

7. If the physician orders "up to void" for a surgical patient who has chest tubes in place, think through the steps you would follow if the patient is (a) 15-year-old boy weighing 180 pounds, (b) a 35-year-old man weighing 165 pounds, (c) a 60-year-old man weighing 165 pounds, or (d) an 80-year-old lady weighing 98 pounds.

8. What observations should you make routinely in relation to the drains listed in question 3?

9. Write out a plan of teaching and action for situations in which you are asked to obtain a clean-catch specimen from a female patient.

10. How would you alter the preceding plan for (a) a child or (b) an adult male patient?

11. In passing the room of a patient with drains, if you observe the following, what action should you take and why?
    a. Drainage in the receptacle on the floor is red
    b. Drainage in the reservoir is about to overflow

c. Suction machine is not functioning

d. Patient is manipulating drain

12. What systematic, routine observations should you make related to a patient who has drainage of any type?

Selected references

Birum, L., and Zimmerman, D.: Catheter plugs as a source of infection, Amer. J. Nurs. 71:2150-2152, 1971.

Delehanty, L., and Stravino, U.: Achieving bladder control, Amer. J. Nurs. 70:312-316, 1970.

Dittbrenner, Sister Marilynn, and Herbert, W. M.: Regimen for a thoracotomy patient, Amer. J. Nurs. 67:2072-2075, 1967.

Drummond, E. E., and Anderson, M. L.: Gastrointestinal suction, Amer. J. Nurs. 63:109-113, 1963.

Fuerst, E. V., Wolff, L. V., and Weitzel, M. H.: Fundamentals of nursing, ed. 5, Philadelphia, 1974, J. B. Lippincott Co.

Hunt, E. L., and Magee, M. J.: Collecting urine specimens, Amer. J. Nurs. 57:1323-1324, 1957.

Linden, R., and Keane, A. J.: The catheter team, Amer. J. Nurs. 64:128-132, 1964.

Mackinnon, H. A.: Urinary drainage: the problem of asepsis, Amer. J. Nurs. 65:112, 1965.

McGrath, D., and Kruger, B. K.: Chest suction using mercury instead of water, Amer. J. Nurs. 62:72-73, 1962.

Morgan, C. V., and Orcutt, T. W.: The care and feeding of chest tubes, Amer. J. Nurs. 72:305-308, 1972.

Murray, B., Elmore, J., and Sawyer, J.: The patient has an ileoconduit, Amer. J. Nurs. 71:1560-1565, 1971.

Revolution in chest drainage, RN 68:50-51, March, 1968.

Sagath, E. E.: Using a pleural pump postoperatively, Amer. J. Nurs. 62:102-103, 1962.

Santora, D.: Preventing hospital-acquired urinary infection, Amer. J. Nurs. 66:790-794, 1966.

Saxon, J.: Techniques for bowel and bladder training, Amer. J. Nurs. 62:69-71, 1962.

Tudor, L.: Bladder and bowel retraining, Amer. J. Nurs. 70:2391-2393, 1970.

Williams, T. J., and Julian, C. G.: Tidal drainage in the postoperative bladder, Amer. J. Obstet. Gynec. 83:1313-1317, 1962.

Winter, C. C., and Barker, M. R.: Nursing care of patients with urologic diseases, ed. 3, St. Louis, 1972, The C. V. Mosby Co.

10
Irrigations

Irrigation may be used to maintain patency of drains or to cleanse, soothe, and medicate wounds, body areas, channels and cavities. A physician's order is necessary for most irrigations. If the purpose of the irrigation is to be achieved, the following information should be known: (1) the reason for the irrigation, (2) the specific area or drain to be irrigated and its size, (3) the need for clean or sterile technique, (4) the kind, strength, and amount of solution, (5) the amount and kind of pressure to be used for introducing the solution, (6) the method of removing the solution after irrigation, (7) the frequency of irrigation, and (8) the equipment needed.

As a guide, clean technique is usually permitted if the area being irrigated is normally contacted by air or food. Sterile technique is used when solution enters an area normally considered to be sterile. With either technique, care must be exercised to prevent the introduction of contaminants.

The solution prescribed is usually dilute. Often a physiologic strength is prescribed. The amount used varies with the nature and purpose of the irrigation.

As a general rule, only gentle pressure is used to introduce solutions internally. Because the height of the irrigating solution above the area being irrigated determines the force of gravity, height can be used to control the amount of pressure used. The force and rapidity with which it is applied to the bulb or the plunger of a syringe will influence the amount of pressure and rate at which the solution will be introduced. The amount of pressure used is directly related to the pathophysiology of the tissues involved and their relationship to other anatomic structures. The main indication for increased pressure occurs when irrigation is used to cleanse an infected wound of accumulated secretions, enabling it to heal by granulation.

If undue pressure is necessary to introduce the solution or if its instillation produces discomfort, the nurse should interrupt the irrigation and consult the physician.

The method of removing the solution varies with the nature of the irrigation. When fluid and electrolyte balance is precarious, the physician may ask that the solution be aspirated with a syringe immediately after instillation. This must be done gently to avoid trauma to the tissues. In some instances, the nurse may remove the solution by reestablishing suction or gravity drainage. In either case, it is important to observe whether the solution returns. If solution does not return, the drain may be blocked by a mucous plug. Measures to dislodge it, such as milking or stripping the drain, may be necessary, or the drain may need to be changed. The nurse must ask the physician for permission to do this; some drains are placed only by the physician. With some irrigations, the solution is allowed to return by itself. The rate is influenced by the force of gravity and deviations in pressure.

Irrigation of the eye

Irrigation of the eyelids and conjunctival sac serves to cleanse and soothe the tissues. Its need is indicated by the presence of discharges, inflammation, infection, or superficial irritation. Prior to irrigation, the nurse should protect the bed beneath the patient's head from drainage. Accumulated secretions may be removed gently with moistened pledgets.

The irrigating solution is allowed to flow over the area from a distance no greater than 4 inches. An undine, irrigating bottle, soft-bulb syringe, or eyedropper may be used. The patient is positioned with his head turned in the direction of the eye that is to be irrigated (Fig. 10-1, *A*). This can be accomplished whether he is lying in bed or seated in a chair. This position and seeing to it that the solution flows from the inner canthus to the outer canthus of the eye prevent contamination of the opposite eye (Fig. 10-1, *B* and *C*).

Knowledge that the eye is sensitive to touch and temperature guides the nurse in this technique. Unless it is contraindicated, the prescribed solution should be lukewarm, that is, between 95° and 100° F. The nurse holds the eyelids apart without exerting pressure on the eye itself, and asks the patient to look toward the top of his head. This prevents the solution from flowing onto the sensitive cornea, which not only causes discomfort but also squinting, an activity that can be damaging to the eye that has been treated surgically. The hand separating the lids may be rested on the underlying skeletal structures surrounding the eye (Fig. 10-1, *B*). The patient is permitted to assist by holding the pledgets or the basin used to collect the irrigating return and by retracting the lower eyelid to expose the conjunctival sac (Fig. 10-1, *C*).

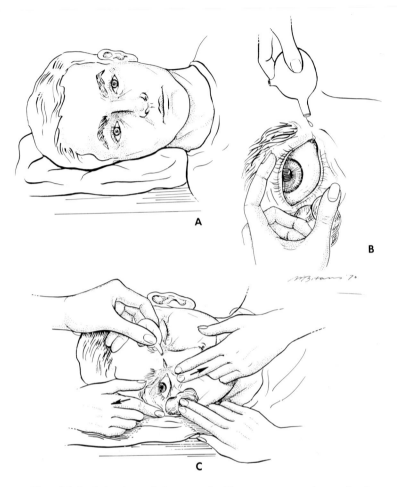

Fig. 10-1. Irrigation of the eye. **A,** The nurse turns the patient's head toward the eye that is to be irrigated. **B,** Solution flows from the inner canthus to the outer canthus of the eye. The irrigator is held less than 4 inches away from the eye. **C,** The patient may assist by retracting the lower eyelid and collecting irrigating solution with absorbent material.

Irrigation of the ear

Irrigations with water, 2% to 4% boric acid solution, 0.8% bicarbonate of soda (1 tsp. to 500 ml.), or normal saline are used to cleanse the external auditory canal.

Although the patient may lie down for this technique, it is preferable to seat him and protect the area to which solution might escape with a suitable drape. The nurse assists the patient in tilting his head slightly in the direction of the ear that is to be irrigated. The patient is permitted to hold the basin into which returning solution flows (Fig. 10-2, *A*).

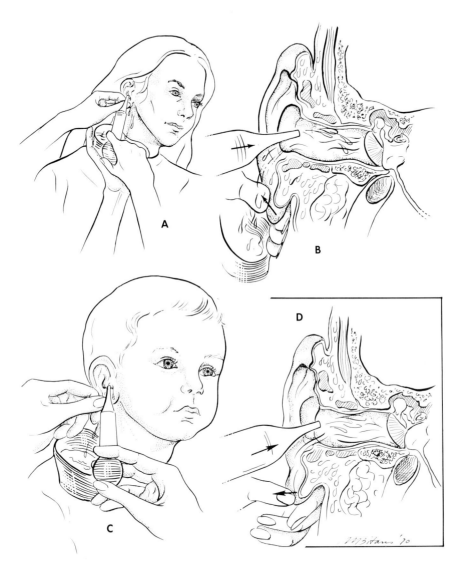

Fig. 10-2. Irrigation of the ear. **A,** The method of exposing the external ear canal in an adult. The nurse tilts the patient's head toward the ear being treated. The patient holds the basin for collecting solution as it returns. **B,** Front view showing retraction of external ear and direction of solution against the side of the canal. **C,** Exposure of the external ear canal in a child. **D,** Front view showing retraction of child's ear and direction of solution against the side of the canal.

To expose the auditory canal, the nurse gently pulls the earlobe of an adult upward and backward (Fig. 10-2, *A* and *B*) and that of a child downward and backward (Fig. 10-2, *C* and *D*). If it is desired, the auricle of the ear rather than the lobe may be manipulated in the same direction.

Because the injection of cool solutions produces discomfort, the temperature of the prescribed solution should be 105° to 108° F. The flow of solution is directed toward the side of the canal (Fig. 10-2, *B* and *D*). It should not be injected forcefully or directed toward the eardrum because doing so causes discomfort and can, in some instances, create additional problems. If pain or dizziness occurs, the irrigation should be interrupted until further instructions can be obtained from the physician.

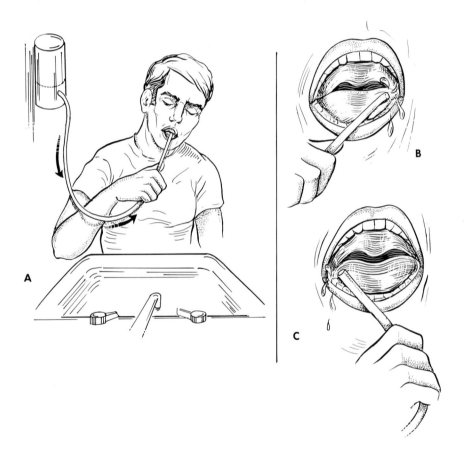

Fig. 10-3. Irrigation of the mouth and throat. **A,** The patient holds his head over a sink. Solution flows from a height slightly above the level of the mouth. The patient is permitted to direct the flow of solution. **B,** Solution is directed toward the area being treated. **C,** Solution is not directed at the uvula or the base of the tongue.

Irrigation of the mouth and throat

Occasionally, irrigation is used to remove secretions and to relieve inflammation in the throat or to cleanse an oral wound. The kind and strength of solution prescribed is prepared. The permissible temperature ranges between 100° and 120° F. and is altered according to the patient's tolerance for heat.

The patient is positioned with his head tilted forward over the sink or collecting basin. The desired rate of flow of the irrigating solution is achieved by holding the container just slightly above his mouth (Fig. 10-3, A). A rapid rate of flow may stimulate the gag reflex or may produce discomfort due to irritation.

The patient may direct the irrigating solution against the affected part. He will be more comfortable if the solution is not directed toward his uvula or the base of his tongue. Breathing through his nose will also facilitate this irrigation. Deep breathing should be discouraged because it can cause aspiration of solution. If necessary, the nurse or the patient can clamp the tubing intermittently for his comfort. Having the patient tilt his head first to one side and then to the other during this procedure will improve irrigation results (Fig. 10-3, B and C).

Drainage tubes
IRRIGATION OF GASTROINTESTINAL TUBES

When the irrigation of a nasogastric or gastrointestinal tube such as the Levin or Miller-Abbott tube is ordered, the prescribed frequency may extend from 1- to 8-hour intervals. Knowledge that irrigation is sometimes undesirable emphasizes the importance of obtaining a physician's order. Although other dilute solutions are sometimes ordered, it is common to use 20 to 60 ml. of normal saline solution for each irrigation. This solution is used in an attempt to replace chloride ions that are removed with irrigation and suction. It can be made by dissolving 4 Gm. (1 tsp.) of sodium chloride in 500 ml. of water. Clean technique is usually permitted.

The nurse fills an Asepto syringe or a calibrated syringe fitted with an adaptor with the designated amount and kind of solution and then frees it of air. If a T connector is placed between the gastrointestinal tube and the tube leading to suction (Fig. 10-4, A), the tip of the syringe is inserted into the short length of tubing that extends from the T connector. The nurse directs the syringe slightly downward and rests it in the palm of one hand. The thumb and forefinger of the same hand occlude the extension tube (Fig. 10-4, B). With the other hand the clamp on the extension tube is transferred to the tubing that leads to the suction apparatus. The clamp

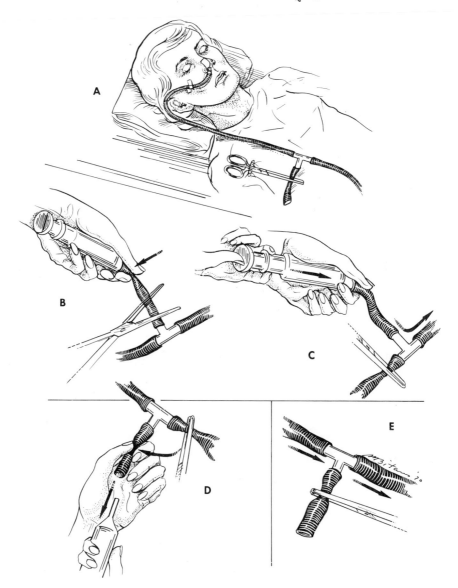

Fig. 10-4. Irrigation of gastrointestinal tubes. **A,** A T connector is in place between the gastrointestinal tube and the tube leading to suction. The short length of tubing extending from the T connector is clamped. **B,** A syringe filled with the designated solution is inserted into the extension tubing and rested in the palm of the hand while the thumb and forefinger occlude the extension tube during transfer of the forceps. **C,** The forceps is placed on the tubing leading to suction. The thumb and forefinger are used to secure the extension tubing over the tip of the syringe. Solution is injected into the gastrointestinal tube. **D,** The extension tubing is occluded with thumb and forefinger for removal of the syringe and transfer of the clamp. **E,** The clamp is reapplied to the extension tubing, reestablishing suction.

TABLE 10-1. Irrigation of the nasogastric tube

Technique	Problem	Explantion or solution
Ascertain the frequency of irrigation and the amount and kind of solution to be used; determine if the irrigating solution is to be aspirated after its instillation.	Irrigation washes electrolytes from the stomach. Some physicians will wish the solution aspirated, others will not desire this.	A physician's order is necessary; frequency of irrigation is usually at 1- to 8-hour intervals; 20 to 60 ml. of normal saline is usually ordered. Sodium chloride helps to prevent the loss of electrolytes. Aspiration may be indicated if electrolyte balance is precarious or if distention is a problem.
Obtain the necessary equipment and solution.	The use of unclean equipment or an incorrect kind or amount of solution is hazardous.	Normal saline is prepared with 4 Gm. (1 tsp.) of salt in 500 ml. of water.
Fill the syringe with the designated amount and kind of solution, and free the syringe of air.	Instillation of an incorrect solution may be hazardous; air may contribute to discomfort.	Use of a solution that is not physiologic in strength may damage the tissues; prescribed solutions should be dilute if tissue damage is to be avoided.
Disconnect the gastrointestinal tube from suction and insert the syringe into its distal end; if a T connector is located between the tube and the suction, clamp the suction tubing, and insert the syringe into the short tubing that extends from the T connector.	The sound of suction when the tubes are disconnected may frighten the patient.	Before disconnecting the tube, tell the patient that a loud suctioning noise will occur. Unless the suction is interrupted, the irrigation solution will be drawn into the suction rather than being instilled through the nasogastric tube.
Instill the solution slowly and gently.	The patient may complain of an uncomfortable sensation in his nasopharynx.	Slow, gentle instillation minimizes this sensation; forceful irrigation is contraindicated after gastric surgery.
If ordered, aspirate the solution.	Retained solution and secretions may cause discomfort and may be hazardous to the patient.	Aspiration and reestablishment of suction keeps the stomach relatively free of contents.
Remove the syringe and reconnect the tube to suction.	Tension on the tubing may cause discomfort.	Careful handling of the tube will prevent this.

is placed relatively close to the connector, since the solution will flow to this point. The thumb and forefinger that have been pinching the extension tubing are now free to secure this tubing over the tip of the syringe (Fig. 10-4, C). The solution is instilled slowly and gently; semirotation of the plunger may be helpful in controlling this rate. The patient may feel the solution flow through the nasopharyngeal portion of the tube. If ordered, the solution is aspirated immediately by slowly drawing back on the plunger. To reestablish suction, the nurse occludes the extension tubing with the thumb and index finger, removes the syringe (Fig. 10-4, *D*), and transfers the clamp back to the extension tube (Fig. 10-4, *E*).

If a straight connector is in place, the nurse must separate the tube from the connector and insert the syringe into the free end of the gastrointestinal tube. If the tube leading to suction is clamped before the tubing is separated, air will not be pulled into the suction apparatus. When a motor-driven suction machine is used, clamping the tube prevents air from rushing into the vacuum and creating a

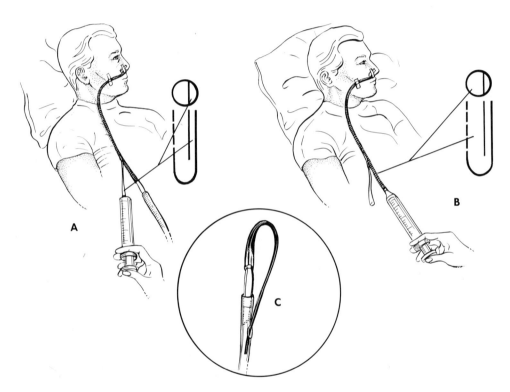

Fig. 10-5. Irrigation of the Salem sump tube. **A,** The tube may be irrigated through the funnel end of the air vent lumen without disconnecting the tube from suction. Cross section shows the part of the tube that is being irrigated. **B,** The stomach may be irrigated by introducing the irrigant through the main part of the tube after it has been disconnected from suction. Cross section shows the part of the tube through which the solution enters the stomach. **C,** The funnel end of the air vent lumen can be placed over the connector placed in the distal end of the tube, when suction is to be interrupted for a time. This eliminates the need for clamps. During ambulation, the tube can be draped around the back of the patient's neck or secured to his gown. (Courtesy Sherwood Medical Industries, Inc., St. Louis, Mo.)

noise that may startle or annoy the patient. With certain types of suction, such as the three-bottle suction, this may save considerable time because once the siphonage mechanism is interrupted, suction must be re-created.

When a balloon type of gastrointestinal tube is used, care must be exercised so that irrigating fluid is not introduced into the balloon. This is a matter of becoming familiar with the various types of tubes and the markings used to indicate which extension lends to the balloon.

The Salem sump tube may be irrigated through the funnel end of the air vent lumen without disconnecting the tube from suction. The part of the tube being irrigated is shown in the cross section in Fig. 10-5, *A*. The stomach may be irrigated by introducing the irrigant through the main part of the tube after it has been disconnected from suction, and Fig. 10-5, *B*, shows in the cross section the part of the tube through which the solution enters the stomach. When suction is to be interrupted for a time, the funnel end of the air vent lumen can be placed over the connector placed in the distal end of the tube, thus eliminating the need for clamps (Fig. 10-5, *C*). The tube can be draped around the back of the patient's neck or secured to his gown during ambulation.

IRRIGATION OF URETHRAL CATHETERS

The closed system of irrigating retention catheters is described on pages 278 to 280. This method may be applied continually or intermittently. For example, the surgeon may ask that continuous drainage and irrigation be used in the immediate postoperative period after transurethral resection. If an anterior-posterior repair has been done, tidal drainage may be used on a fairly continuous basis, but the physician may allow it to be interrupted during ambulation. (See pages 280 to 282.)

Internal irrigation of the catheter, achieved with adequate intake, is preferable to manual irrigation, which involves separating the catheter from the drainage tube and is accompanied by risk of introducing contaminants. However, when patency is questionable, irrigation with sterile solution and equipment may be ordered. If the urine is clear, it is not usually necessary to irrigate retention catheters more than once or twice daily. Catheters left in place for long periods of time are changed at regular intervals, often every week. Use of silicone-coated catheters seems to reduce the problem of sediment collecting around the catheter and blocking the flow of urine. The presence of large amounts of macroscopic materials, such as shreds of mucus or purulent material, indicates the need to irrigate more frequently or even continuously. Physiologic saline, 2% boric acid, or other dilute solutions are used. Either a syringe or a funnel may be used to introduce the solution into the catheter.

The nurse places the irrigation set on a sterile field between the patient's thighs. If the equipment is packaged individually, the inside of the wrapper provides a sterile area. After carefully disconnecting the catheter, its free end is placed in the sterile basin, and the open end of the drainage tube is placed on the sterile wrapper (Fig. 10-6,

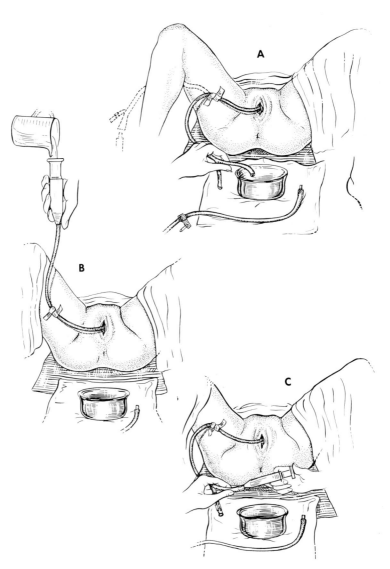

Fig. 10-6. Irrigation of a urethral catheter. **A,** The catheter is disconnected from the drainage apparatus. The drainage tubing lies on the sterile field, and the catheter drains into a sterile basin. **B,** Instillation of sterile solution using a funnel through which solution is poured. **C,** Instillation of irrigating solution with a syringe.

A), thus minimizing the possibility of contamination. The solution may be poured into a sterile funnel attached to the catheter (Fig. 10-6, *B*). Air pressure and gravity cause the solution to flow into the bladder. If a syringe is used, the solution should be injected slowly (Fig. 10-6, *C*). Approximately 30 to 60 ml. of solution is introduced. The irrigating solution is drained from the bladder by disconnecting the syringe or funnel and permitting the solution to flow into the basin. The irrigation is usually repeated until the return is clear. The nurse in charge should be notified if the solution does not return. This may indicate that the eye of the catheter is blocked. Sometimes catheter blockage can be corrected by milking the catheter to dislodge mucus; the catheter may need to be changed.

SURGICALLY INSERTED DRAINS

Irrigation of surgically inserted drains requires skillful technique, together with special knowledge of the exact anatomic location of the drain and of the condition of the surrounding tissues. Often, when such an irrigation is indicated, a doctor assumes this responsibility. Needed supplies will probably include a sterile solution of normal saline, a sterile 10 ml. syringe, and sterile gloves.

Wounds

Nursing responsibility for wound irrigation varies. In general, nurses are permitted to irrigate wounds known to be infected or contaminated. Because of the problems involved, a wound that enters the peritoneal cavity is usually irrigated by the physician.

The nature of the wound is evaluated by the physician, who decides if a catheter is to be inserted, the direction and depth of its insertion, the solution to be used, its strength, and the frequency of irrigation. This information should be a part of the nursing care plan and should be altered as the condition of the wound changes.

Solutions prescribed, which are usually dilute, include 2% hydrogen peroxide, 0.5% sodium hypochlorite (modified Dakin's solution), physiologic saline, antibiotic solutions, and proteolytic enzyme solutions. The amount of solution used varies with the size of the wound and the amount and kind of drainage present. The wound is usually irrigated until the return flow appears to be clear. Thus the amount of solution used may vary. An amount of 120 to 200 ml. or more is often needed to irrigate an abdominal wound.

It is more comfortable for the patient if the solution is at room temperature or warmer. The temperature of the solution must not exceed 39° to 40° C. (103° to 105° F.). *Heating is contraindicated if increased temperature destroys or releases the active ingredients.*

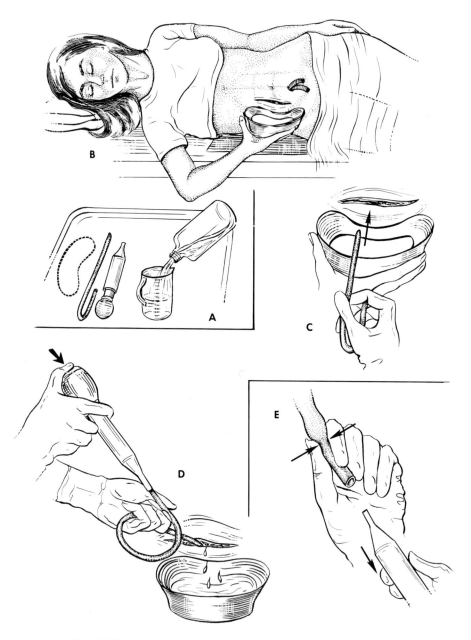

Fig. 10-7. Anterior wound irrigation. **A,** Solution is poured into a graduated measure. **B,** The patient, in side-lying position, holds a collecting basin beneath the wound. Proper positioning prevents contamination of the drain site above the wound. **C,** The gloved hand directs the catheter into the wound. **D,** The wound is irrigated by instilling solution with a syringe. **E,** The catheter is occluded while the syringe is detached from it for refilling. This prevents aspiration of contaminated solution.

Reliable sources should be consulted for information related to the properties of specific solutions.

ANTERIOR WOUND IRRIGATION

For anterior wound irrigation, the nurse needs the prescribed solution, some type of bed protector, and a sterile irrigation tray (Fig. 10-7, *A*) containing a graduated measure, a catheter, a kidney basin, a syringe, and forceps or latex gloves.

After the dressing is removed and placed in a waxed bag or wrapped in several layers of newspaper, the nurse assists the patient in assuming a side-lying position. The side to which the patient turns will depend on the presence of other wounds and drain sites and on his physical comfort (Fig. 10-7, *B*).

Immediately before opening the tray, the nurse's hands must be thoroughly washed. If the nurse is working alone, the prescribed solution is poured into the graduate measure first (Fig. 10-7, *A*), gauging the amount needed by the appearance of the wound. Unless the solution has been warmed previously or unless its action depends on antibiotic or enzyme activity, the graduate measure containing the solution may be placed in a basin of warm water. The kidney basin is removed from the tray and held snugly against the abdomen below the wound. This can be done by the patient, if he is able, or by an assistant (Fig. 10-7, *B*).

The catheter is handled with sterile forceps or sterile gloves. It is guided gently into the wound until it reaches the desired depth (Fig. 10-7, *C*). If resistance is encountered, the catheter is not advanced forcibly but is withdrawn slightly and redirected. The filled syringe is attached to the catheter, and the solution is instilled (Fig. 10-7, *D*). Unless forceful instillation is desirable, irrigation should be gentle. When the syringe is empty, the catheter is pinched to prevent accidental aspiration of the irrigation return while the syringe is being disconnected. These steps are repeated until the returning solution is clear. If a catheter is not to be inserted, the solution is sprayed directly onto the wound until it appears clean.

At the completion of the irrigation, the area is dried with sterile sponges. Drying begins at the wound and proceeds away from it. After this, abdominal lights (page 325) or dry, sterile dressings (pages 336 and 337) are applied. Notations concerning the amount of solution used, the nature of the irrigation returns, and other pertinent observations are recorded.

POSTERIOR WOUND IRRIGATION

Similar equipment, technique, and positioning can be used to irrigate wounds after posterior resection. If the wound is close to the perineal area, folded Cellucotton or gauze will prevent irrigating

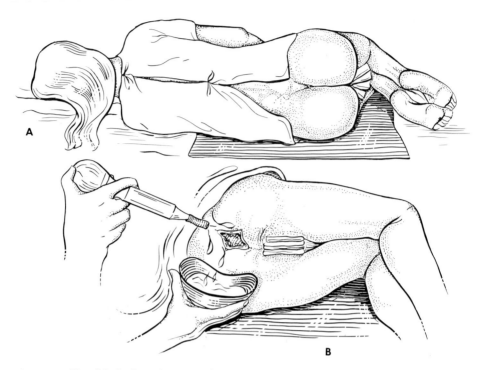

Fig. 10-8. Posterior wound irrigation. **A,** A patient prepared for posterior wound irrigation. Folded material is used to prevent solution from flowing over the perineal area. **B,** A syringe fitted with a short length of rubber tubing is used to irrigate the wound. A basin collects solution as it returns.

solution from flowing over the perineal area (Fig. 10-8, *A*). A catheter is not usually needed, but the syringe may be fitted with a short length of rubber tubing (Fig. 10-8, *B*). The gluteal tissues may be retracted by the patient or taped to maintain exposure of the wound.

The nurse should report any evidence of adhesion formation and, if instructed, interrupt this process by wiping these areas with a sterile cotton applicator.

ANAL SPRAYS

After rectal procedures such as hemorrhoidectomy, the physician may order anal sprays for cleansing and comfort. The nurse positions the patient in a side-lying or Sims' position and instructs him to retract the upper buttock with his hand so that adequate exposure is obtained (Fig. 10-9, *A*). When the patient does the retracting himself, little if any discomfort occurs. The presence of a cotton wick, medications, or dressings in or over the anal area indicates that further orders are necessary before proceeding with the irrigation.

A 60 ml. syringe is filled with warmed solution. This is sprayed

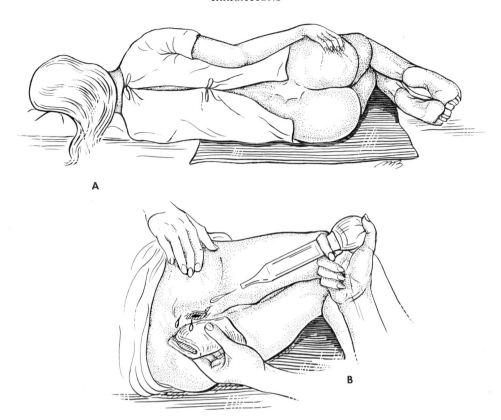

Fig. 10-9. Anal spray. **A,** The patient assumes a side-lying position and retracts the upper buttock with his hand to expose the anal area. **B,** The nurse sprays warm solution against the wound. Absorbent material is used to collect returning solution.

gently against the wound and absorbed by several layers of Cellu-cotton held gently against the tissues distal to the wound (Fig. 10-9, *B*).

ANAL IRRIGATIONS

After hemorrhoidectomy or other rectal procedures, the physician may prescribe anal irrigation. This can be carried out by the patient if the nurse instructs and assists him as necessary. Most patients prefer to do this technique themselves and are able to do so with coaching.

One method requires an irrigating container, tubing, connector, clamp, and an 18-gauge French catheter. These are assembled in the same way as is equipment used for enemas. Approximately 400 ml. of tap water is placed in the irrigating container. Temperature of the water should not be greater than 105° F.

Anal irrigation is carried out in the bathroom with the patient

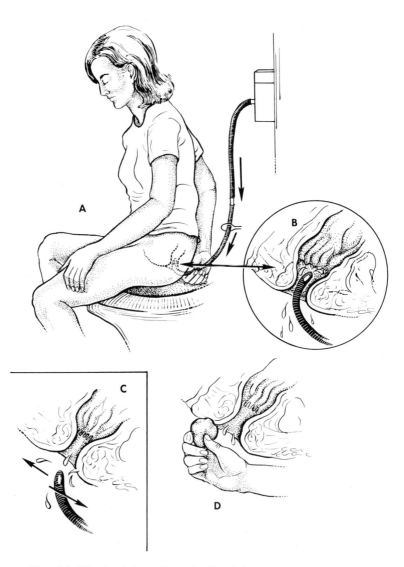

Fig. 10-10. Anal irrigation. **A,** The irrigating container is suspended about 2 feet above the anus. The patient, seated on a toilet, is permitted to insert the well-lubricated catheter. **B,** The catheter is inserted 1 to 1½ inches so that solution returns as rapidly as it enters. **C,** The remaining solution is directed toward the external anal area from a distance of 1 to 1½ inches. **D,** The area is patted dry with absorbent pledgets.

seated on the toilet. Therefore this treatment is not done until the patient is ambulatory. The irrigating container is suspended about 2 feet above the level of the anal area, the tubing is freed of air, and the catheter is lubricated generously with a water-soluble lubricant and inserted 1 to 1½ inches (Fig. 10-10, *A* and *B*). Further insertion or rapid injection of the fluid produces an enema effect, which is undesirable because the purpose of the irrigation is to cleanse the anal area. If the solution is administered correctly, it will return at the same rate at which it enters the internal anal area.

After 200 to 300 ml. of the solution has been used to irrigate the internal anal area, the catheter is withdrawn, and the remaining solution is used to irrigate the external area (Fig. 10-10, *C*). For this part of the procedure, the tip of the catheter is held about 1 to 1½ inches away from the anal area. After the anal irrigation is completed, the anal area is gently patted with absorbent pledgets to dry it (Fig. 10-10, *D*).

Perineal care

The physician may prescribe perineal cleansing after certain surgical and obstetric procedures. It is used at prescribed intervals and after defecation or urination. Until the patient can perform this procedure herself, the nurse must do it for her. This provides an opportunity to teach the technique and to stress the underlying principles used.

Regardless of the method used, the cleansing should always proceed from the vulva toward the anal area and from the midline outward. After each cleansing stroke, the used pledget or disposable washcloth is discarded. This prevents transfer of fecal contaminants to the urethra, vagina, and perineal wounds. The number of pledgets or cloths used should be guided by the purpose, which is to cleanse the area.

STERILE PERINEAL CARE

Regardless of the exact technique used to cleanse the perineum, a sterile basin, pitcher, or graduated measure containing 300 to 500 ml. of solution, forceps or gloves, and pledgets are needed. After the patient is assisted in assuming the desired position and draped, she is placed on a bedpan if the solution is to be poured over the vulva; otherwise, a disposable pad is placed beneath the buttocks. A waxed bag or several layers of newspaper are placed in a convenient location for receiving the soiled pledgets. Throughout the technique, privacy should be ensured. If desired, the procedure is begun by pouring approximately 200 to 300 ml. of solution over the vulva (Fig. 10-11, *A*). Moistened pledgets held with sterile forceps or gloved hand are used to cleanse the area further (Fig. 10-11, *B*). The area is then dried using sterile pledgets, the bedpan, if used, is removed, and the patient is turned to one side for cleansing and drying of the posterior area (Fig. 10-11, *C*). The direction of the cleansing and drying must always prevent contamination of the perineal area.

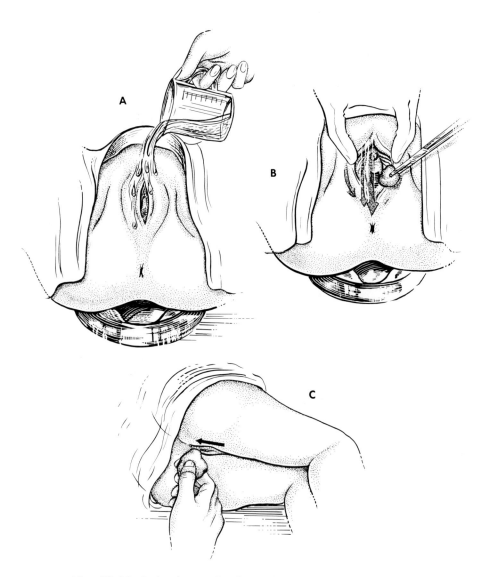

Fig. 10-11. Perineal care. **A,** The patient is placed on a bedpan and solution poured over the vulva. **B,** The nurse uses sterile pledgets to cleanse and dry the area. Arrows show direction of cleansing. **C,** After the bedpan is removed, the nurse dries the posterior area.

TABLE 10-2. Clean perineal care (female) using disposable washcloths

Technique	Problem	Explanation or solution
Explain the purpose of this technique; inform the patient of the underlying principles as cleansing is carried out.	The patient may be apprehensive; incorrectly managed self-care contributes to urinary tract infections.	Understanding allays anxiety; knowledge is basic to correct application of principles.
Bring the necessary supplies to the bedside.	Interruptions due to lack of adequate supply of materials mean delay and may cause the patient some embarrassment and unnecessary tension.	A clean basin containing warm water, a supply of disposable washcloths, soap, and a bath blanket are needed.
Assist the patient to a dorsal recumbent position (back-lying with knees flexed and legs apart) and drape her.	Inadequate exposure makes cleansing difficult. The patient may feel tense, embarrassed, or chilly.	Adequate exposure is essential to thorough cleansing. Draping offers privacy and promotes relaxation and comfort.
After placing several disposable washcloths in the basin of warm water, remove one, squeeze excess water from it, and cleanse the area from the anterior portion of the vulva toward the anus; discard each cloth after one downward cleansing stroke, and repeat this process until the area is clean.	Contamination of the perineal area with fecal organisms can occur.	Using one cloth for each downward stroke prevents transfer of organisms to the area. The number of cleansing strokes and thus the number of cloths needed varies with the amount of discharge or soilage.
With moistened disposable cloths, remove residual soap with downward strokes.	Soap is irritating to some persons; soap that is allowed to remain on the skin becomes an irritant.	Soap is not used for persons with sensitive skin; rinsing the area cleanses the skin of soap.
Dry the area, using disposable washcloths and one downward stroke per cloth.	Moisture may be irritating and infection may occur.	A dry area is less likely to become irritated; moisture is essential for bacterial growth.
Turn the patient to her side and cleanse the posterior area, again using one cloth per stroke and working directionally away from the vaginal area.	Organisms from the anal area may cause infection.	Cleansing away from the vaginal area helps to prevent infection by reducing the likelihood of contamination.
Dry the area and make the patient as comfortable as possible.	Vaginal discharges may cause discomfort due to soiled clothing or linen.	Place a clean disposable protective pad beneath the patient's buttocks; a perineal pad may be applied in some cases. (Perineal pads are thought to be irritating and may not be allowed.)

CLEAN PERINEAL CARE

For clean perineal care, disposable washcloths are placed in a clean basin of warm water. The patient is draped as described previously. For each cleansing stroke, a disposable washcloth is removed from the basin, soap is applied to it, if desired, and the area is cleansed, proceeding always from the anterior to the posterior. Fresh washcloths are used to remove the soap; then the area is dried using a separate cloth for each drying stroke. The patient is turned to one side, and the posterior area is cleansed and dried. The patient is commonly taught to carry out this technique as soon as she is able. Usually the patient is taught to cleanse herself while seated on the toilet. The principles of using one cloth for each stroke, always cleansing from front to back, and never moving the cloth back and forth are stressed so that the patient will avoid contaminating the urethral and vaginal areas. Table 10-2 summarizes the technique of clean perineal care.

Vaginal irrigation

Vaginal irrigation differs from a douche in that the former introduces solution under low pressure, and the latter introduces solution under increased pressure. Usually the patient is positioned as described for catheterization (Fig. 10-12, *A*). In some cases, the procedure may be carried out in the bathroom with the patient seated on the toilet.

Necessary equipment may be assembled on a tray for transport. This includes an irrigating container, tubing, a clamp, and a douche tip. Temperature of the solution should not be greater than 105° F. (40.6° C.). Water or other nonirritating solutions may be prescribed. Amounts of solute needed to prepare 1 L. of commonly prescribed solutions are 2 tsp. of bicarbonate of soda, 2 tsp. of salt, or 1 tbsp. of vinegar.

Prior to the irrigation, the patient is asked to empty her bladder because a full bladder may cause discomfort and interfere with irrigation. The vulva is cleansed as described for perineal care or by allowing about 150 ml. of the solution to flow over the area (Fig. 10-12, *B*). The vaginal irrigator, commonly called a douche tip, is inserted into the vagina to a depth of $1\frac{1}{2}$ to 2 inches (Fig. 10-12, *C*). Unless it is contraindicated, the patient is permitted to insert the douche tip. The bottom of the irrigation container is held about 30 cm. (1 foot) above the vaginal orifice while the solution flows into the vagina.

If the patient is unable to ambulate, the irrigation may be done after a bedpan is placed. The position of the patient is illustrated in

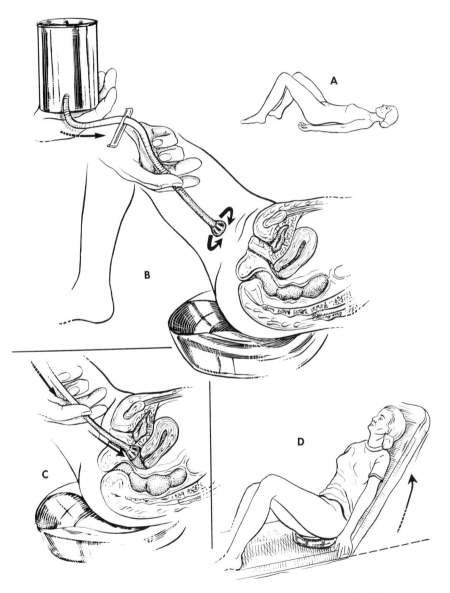

Fig. 10-12. Vaginal irrigation. **A,** Position of the patient. **B,** Solution is used to cleanse the vulva. **C,** Solution flows into the vagina through a vaginal irrigator that has been inserted to a depth of 1½ to 2 inches. **D,** Elevating the head of the bed hastens the rate at which solution is returned.

313

Fig. 10-12, *A;* the patient is draped, and the irrigation is carried out. After the irrigation, the patient is allowed to assume a sitting position, unless sitting is contraindicated, to hasten the return flow of the solution.

Questions for discussion and exploration

1. What are the various purposes that irrigations may serve?
2. What information should the nurse have to accomplish the purpose of the irrigation ordered?
3. What may happen if high pressure is used to introduce irrigating solution into (a) a nasogastric tube, (b) a wound catheter, and (c) a urethral catheter?
4. Why is it important to start solution flowing close to the inner canthus of the eye and then move the irrigating solution slowly to the desirable distance from the eye to obtain some force?
5. Why is it uncomfortable to have solution directed at the cornea of the eye?
6. Why should solution not be directed toward the cornea of the eye after surgery on the eye? What will the patient probably do, and what might the results of his action be?
7. Why should solution not be injected forcefully toward the eardrum? Of what might the patient complain if the solution is cold?
8. In carrying out a vaginal irrigation or douche to cleanse and medicate vaginal tissues, what should the nurse do if the returns obtained are bloody? On what information should her reasoning be based?
9. When anal irrigation is prescribed after a hemorrhoidectomy, what is the maximum distance that the catheter is to be inserted? What happens if the catheter is inserted beyond the dentate margin and into the rectum, and why might this be a temptation for the patient?
10. What is the patient who is having oral irrigations likely to complain of if the irrigating container is placed too high above the oral cavity?
11. If an infected wound is being irrigated, how important is it to have the equipment, solution, and technique used sterile? What is your reasoning?
12. If, during a wound irrigation, the patient complains of severe pain as the solution is introduced, what nursing action is indicated?

Selected references

Herbut, H.: Clean perineal care, Amer. J. Nurs. 56:1124, 1956.

Montague, J. F.: Better care for patients with rectal ailments, Amer. J. Nurs. **65**:83, 1965.

Havener, W. H., Saunders, W. H., Keith, C. F., and Prescott, A. W.: Nursing care in eye, ear, nose, and throat disorders, ed. 3, St. Louis, 1974, The C. V. Mosby Co.

Shafer, K. N., Sawyer, J. R., McCluskey, A. M., Beck, E. L., and Phipps, W. H.: Medical-surgical nursing, ed. 5, St. Louis, 1971, The C. V. Mosby Co.

Wallace, G., and Hayter, J.: Karaya for chronic skin ulcers, Amer. J. Nurs. **74**:1094-1098, 1974.

Winter, C. C., and Barker, M. R.: Nursing care of patients with urologic diseases, ed. 3, St. Louis, 1972, The C. V. Mosby Co.

11

Moisture and heat control

Local and systemic factors influence the need for increased heat, cold, moisture, or dryness, and the physiologic response to them is complex. If these agents are used in the presence of wounds, the transfer of microorganisms, the promotion of drainage, and the cellular response must be considered.

Factors known to alter tissue response are to be observed and evaluated in light of the expected effect. Any evidence of skin reactions, particularly those preceding the destruction of skin, is likely to be significant. It is known that impaired peripheral circulation, abnormal body weight, edema, thyroid dysfunction, general state of health, fatigue, muscular activity, extremes in age, and sensory perception alter tissue response. Individual tolerance to heat, cold, and moisture also varies. Although therapeutic applications are prescribed, the nurse is permitted to use reasonable measures to promote comfort unless definite contraindications are present.

The therapeutic order is likely to specify the area to be treated, the duration and frequency of treatment, and the general method of application. Temperature may be prescribed; otherwise, a safe temperature range is used.

Pressure should not be used to force such applications against a wound. Rather, the normal contour of the area to be treated, positioning, and auxiliary devices are used to keep the applications in place.

Cold applications

Cold may be applied for a local or a systemic effect. Local vaso-constriction of the superficial blood vessels, decreased flow of blood, lowered tissue metabolic activity, and decreased tissue temperature result from the application of cold for short periods of time. Locally, cold inhibits inflammation, suppuration, and microbial activity in the early stages of an infection. It may be used to control bleeding. It is also used to prevent or to control edema after sprains, contusions, and muscle strains. It may be used to increase the comfort level of the patient as well. Decreasing the blood supply locally will increase the supply to other areas of the body. Prolonged application of cold produces vasodilatation. For this reason, local applications are usually of short duration and are repeated at specified time intervals.

Tolerance to cold varies with the individual, the size of the area being treated, and the coldness of the application. As a rule, tissue damage and discomfort do not occur when cold is applied to small areas for a short time. Cold applications for long periods of time must be well controlled and supervised. The skin should be observed for signs of adverse reaction such as blue to purple mottled skin. Redness precedes freezing and should not be disregarded. Pallor, gray discoloration, or the appearance of blisters is ominous. If any of the preceding signs are observed, the treatment should be discontinued, and the physician should be notified.

ALCOHOL SPONGE BATHS

Alcohol sponge baths are used to lower elevated body temperature. The rapid evaporation of moisture from the body surfaces dissipates heat to the external environment. The room temperature should be lowered, if possible, to assist the process of lowering an elevated temperature. For this method of cooling, a washcloth, four bath towels, a bath blanket, and a basin containing 25% to 50% alcohol are needed. Although plain water may be used to sponge the patient, the use of a tepid solution of alcohol seems to reduce the reflex stimulation evidenced by shivering.

The patient is covered with a cotton bath blanket, the top linen is folded to the foot of the bed, and a towel placed beneath the part to be sponged. If the bath is to last 25 to 30 minutes, the minimum time believed necessary for physiologic adjustment, each extremity is sponged for 5 minutes, and the entire back, including the buttocks, is sponged for 5 to 10 minutes. Only the part being sponged is exposed. If turning the patient is contraindicated, the mattress can be depressed with one hand and the other hand slipped beneath the patient to sponge the trunk and buttocks (Fig. 11-1).

To further increase the effectiveness of sponging the patient, cloths moistened with the solution or ice bags may be placed in the axillae and over the groin areas. Both contain large, superficial blood vessels. Application of an ice cap to the patient's head pro-

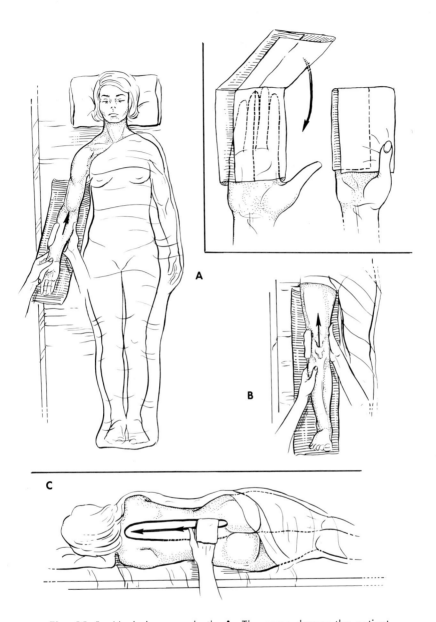

Fig. 11-1. Alcohol sponge bath. **A,** The nurse drapes the patient with a cotton bath blanket, folds the top linen to the foot of the bed, and places a towel beneath the part being sponged. Each extremity is sponged for 5 minutes with alcohol solution. The inset shows a method of wrapping the washcloth around the hand that makes it possible to work quickly and control the washcloth. **B,** Only the extremity being sponged is exposed. **C,** The nurse may sponge the posterior area for 5 to 10 minutes after turning the patient to one side. If the patient is not to be turned, depression of the mattress permits the hand to contact the posterior area.

vides additional comfort. One may also be allowed to apply a warm water bottle to the feet to promote comfort. If, during the sponge bath, the skin feels cold, it may be rubbed. The bath should be continued until the desired effects are obtained.

Observation of the patient during and after treatment includes taking the vital signs before the treatment is begun and 15 minutes after it is completed. Thereafter, the vital signs are taken at frequent intervals, depending on the trend and actual readings obtained. If the temperature is not lowered or continues to rise, the physician should be notified so that more vigorous treatment may be prescribed. Changes that may indicate impending heart failure such as rapid, weak pulse, change in respirations, or cyanosis of the lips or nail beds should be reported to the physician immediately.

HYPOTHERMIA BLANKETS

Several hypothermia machines are available. These are used to provide prolonged or profound cooling. Prolonged cooling is used in certain neurologic conditions, and profound cooling accompanies selected surgical procedures.

These machines circulate a liquid, specified by the manufacturer, from a reservoir through tubing contained within a thin, mattress-like pad, commonly referred to as a hypothermia blanket. The tubing through which the cooling fluid circulates must not be allowed to become kinked because this will interrupt its flow. The tubing kinks most readily near its juncture with the blanket. Directions supplied by the manufacturer should be consulted for details of operating the machine.

Orders concerning the rapidity of cooling, the desired body temperature, the area to be cooled, and the duration of the treatment are obtained from the physician. Unless the order states that the treatment is to be discontinued at a specific temperature, knowledge that the patient's temperature usually decreases 2° F. after discontinuance of cooling will guide the nurse in knowing when the treatment is to be stopped. In the clinical nursing situation, consideration should be given to both the patient and his family. The amount and kind of explanation given to the patient are influenced by his state of consciousness and his awareness of this therapy. Even though the patient appears to be unconscious, it is possible that he may have some sensory perception. Considerable support is likely to be needed by the family.

Individual response to cooling by a hypothermia blanket necessitates careful observation of the patient. Shivering, a response that increases body temperature, thereby decreasing the effectiveness of the treatment, may occur. It is usually observed initially in the chest muscles, which appear to quiver. Shivering is seen less frequently when the level of consciousness is decreased. To combat shivering, drug therapy may be ordered. Nursing responsibility for administration of the drugs necessarily varies with the prescribed drug, dose, and method of administration. In addition, the

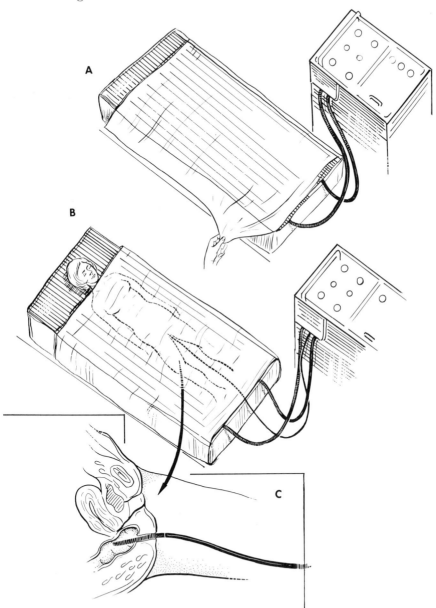

Fig. 11-2. Hypothermia. **A,** After the hypothermia blanket is placed on the bed, it is covered with a sheet. **B,** The patient lies on the covered hypothermia blanket and is covered with a top sheet. **C,** Cross section showing rectal probe used to monitor the body temperature.

effects of drugs are altered because the rates of their absorption, destruction, and elimination are delayed when body temperature is lowered.

Although the patient may be placed directly onto the hypothermia blanket, it is usual to protect the skin by placing a sheet between the patient and the blanket (Fig. 11-2, *A*). A thin coat of oil or lanolin may be applied to the skin as protection against frostbite if the body temperature is to be lowered profoundly. It is common to place one hypothermia blanket beneath the patient, cover it with a sheet tucked under the mattress, place the patient on the sheet, and cover him with a second sheet (Fig. 11-2, *B*). A drawsheet placed lengthwise serves this purpose. If the patient is to be enclosed in hypothermia blankets, a second one is placed over the sheet covering the patient. The blankets may be fastened together with ties or a zipper. Pins are avoided because they puncture the blanket and cause loss of the coolant, destroying the effectiveness of the blanket. Use of additional covers in contraindicated because they produce warmth and defeat the purpose of the treatment.

Monitoring the body temperature involves use of a rectal probe inserted approximately 2 inches and taped in place before arrangement of the top sheet (Fig. 11-2, *C*). The probe is attached to an electric thermometer that is part of the machine. Some units combine this with a thermostatic device that coordinates the temperature of the cooling agent with the desired temperature of the patient. If the thermostat is adjusted manually, the temperature of the coolant often needs to be 15° to 20° F. cooler than the desired body temperature. This will vary with the desired rate of lowering the body temperature.

LOCAL APPLICATION OF COLD

A small hypothermia blanket, ice bags, or moist, cold compresses may be used to apply cold to small areas. Specific instructions concerning the method to be used may be given, or the nurse may be permitted to use her own discretion. This is influenced largely by whether the application is used for comfort measures or as a part of planned therapy.

Hypothermia blankets. Hypothermia devices are operated in accordance with the manufacturer's directions and the prescribed temperature. As with the large blankets, a layer of cloth should be placed between the cooling blanket and the skin. The method of securing the blanket in place varies with the design and the area treated. If the blanket cannot be secured satisfactorily with the self-contained ties or fasteners, it can be enclosed in a cloth wrapper that can be secured. For example, the blanket applied to

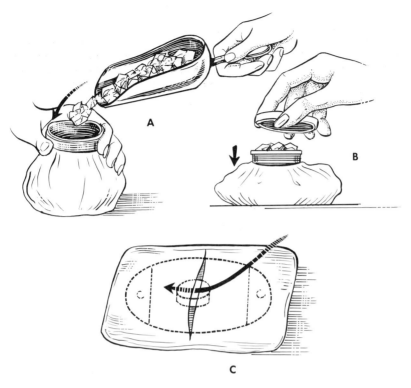

Fig. 11-3. Ice bags. **A,** An ice bag is filled with crushed or shaved ice. **B,** The bag is pressed against a flat surface to remove air and is sealed. **C,** The bag is enclosed with flannel.

an extremity can be kept in place by wrapping it with a towel and tying the towel in place with a roller bandage. Pins must not be placed in the blanket, and tape should not be applied to it.

Ice bags. Several types of ice bags, caps, and bottles are available commercially. They can also be created from plastic bags, which can be sealed with tape.

The container is filled half to two-thirds full of crushed or shaved ice (Fig. 11-3, *A*). Before sealing the container, residual air, which decreases thermal conductivity, is removed by pressing the bag against a flat surface such as a tabletop (Fig. 11-3, *B*). After the container is sealed, it is covered with flannel, which helps to absorb moisture that condenses on the outside of the bag as heat is removed from a body area (Fig. 11-3, *C*). The cover is replaced with a dry one each time the bag is refilled (Table 11-1). Refilling may be necessary at hourly intervals or oftener, depending on the environmental temperature, local heat, and the size of the container. It is thought that the most benefit is obtained by applying an ice bag for 30 to 60 minutes followed by an hour of rest, then repeating this sequence.

TABLE 11-1. Preparation of an ice bag

Technique	Problem	Solution or explanation
Fill an ice bag half to two thirds full of crushed or shaved ice.	The bag may not conform to the area being treated.	Select the type of ice bag according to the area to be treated. A partially filled ice bag can be molded to the contour of the body. Cold is dissipated more quickly when small pieces of ice are used.
Remove residual air from the bag and seal the bag.	Residual air interferes with thermal conductivity.	Pressing the bag against a flat surface will expel most air; the bag is sealed before removing it from the flat surface.
Dry the outside of the bag, and cover it with flannel.	The covering may become moist, causing discomfort and increased penetration of the coldness.	Flannel absorbs moisture that results from condensation; moist cold application is more penetrating than dry cold. Change the flannel covering each time the bag is filled.

Moist, cold compresses. Moist, cold compresses provide another method of applying cold to a small area. These are fashioned by folding gauze, washcloths, towels, or other material to the size of the area treated. The compress is immersed in ice water, freed of excess moisture, and placed on the designated area. The compresses are changed according to the rate at which the body warms them, often every minute or two. The patient may indicate that the compress has warmed and needs to be changed, or he may be allowed to change them himself. The usual duration of treatment is 15 to 20 minutes; this is generally repeated every 2 to 3 hours. Preparing the ice water with large pieces of ice reduces the rate of its melting and the possibility of transferring pieces of ice to the skin. An ice bag may be applied over the compress to keep it cold for a longer period of time.

Applications of heat

Heat serves to increase the temperature of the tissues, resulting in vasodilatation, decreased viscosity of the blood, and increased circulation and flow of lymph. As the cutaneous vessels dilate, the flow through them and capillary pressure increase, resulting in transudation. The rate of waste removal is improved by increased cellular metabolism. Phagocytosis increases in the presence of inflammation. Sedation, decreased pain, decreased muscle tension, and decreased congestion also occur.

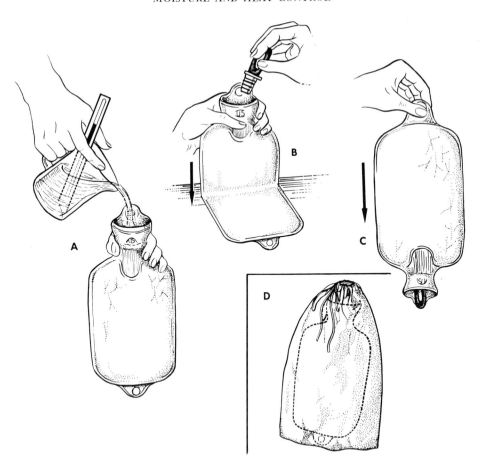

Fig. 11-4. Hot water bottle. **A,** After the temperature of the water has been tested, the bottle is filled about two thirds full. **B,** Air is removed from the bottle, which is then sealed. **C,** The seal is tested for leakage. **D,** The bottle is enclosed in a cloth cover.

The effects of local heat applications are highest in the skin. Maximum effects occur within 20 to 30 minutes. Application for more than 1 hour causes vasoconstriction and may result in thermal injury. During the treatment, the patient will feel warmth but should not be uncomfortable. When the treatment is finished, the skin may be warm and will appear pink and moist. If the skin is mottled for some time after the treatment, the degree of heat needs to be decreased or the distance from its source increased.

Although heat treatment is therapeutic, caution is necessary for persons with impaired circulation or sensation, the old or young, unconscious persons, and others who are not able to respond appropriately. Initially, heat is not used in the treatment of acute inflammation or trauma. It is not used when malignancy is present.

Before applying heat to large areas of the body, the cardiovascular, respiratory, and renal systems should be evaluated.

Local heat may be applied with hot water bottles, heating pads, moist compresses, baths, soaks, lights, or hyperthermia pads. Its use is relatively safe for persons with normal response to sensation and normal circulation. The patient should be encouraged to report

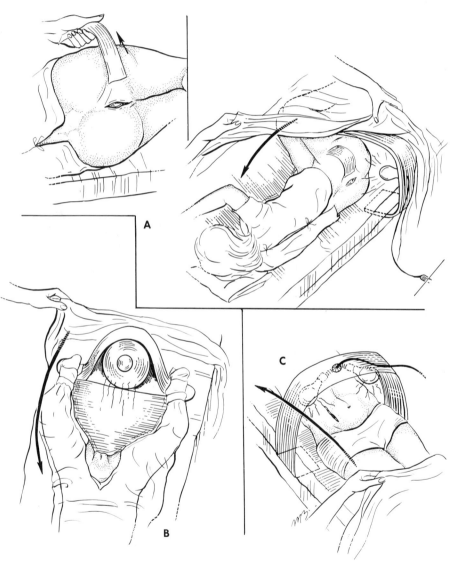

Fig. 11-5. Lights. **A,** Application of lights to a posterior wound. Inset shows a method of exposing the wound. Adhesive tape is used to retract the upper buttock during treatment. **B,** Method of applying perineal lights. **C,** Method of applying abdominal lights.

immediately any application that feels too warm. Dry heat will be tolerated better than moist heat because water is a better conductor and slows evaporation. Usually a physician's order is required for any heat treatment because it can cause injury and because it produces physiologic changes.

HOT WATER BOTTLES

Heat is applied with a hot water bottle in accordance with hospital policy and the physician's order. The temperature should not exceed 120° F. (49° C.), unless a higher temperature is specifically ordered by the physician. Specialized knowledge is needed to determine when the application of a higher temperature is safe.

The temperature of the water is tested with a thermometer before filling the hot water bottle two-thirds full (Fig. 11-4, *A*). Residual air is removed from the bottle, which is then sealed, tested for leakage, and enclosed in a cloth cover (Fig. 11-4, *B* to *D*). Sometimes the hot water bottle is applied directly to the involved area; it may also be used to prolong the effectiveness of warm, moist dressings.

LIGHTS

Light bulbs incorporated into frames or on standards may be used to apply dry heat (Fig. 11-5). The size, number, and kind of light bulbs and the distance between the source of light and the exposed tissue affect the amount of heat applied. Twenty-five-watt bulbs may be placed 14 inches from the area. Forty- or 60-watt light bulbs are used if the distance to the treated area is about 18 inches. Larger bulbs should be placed 24 to 30 inches from the area being treated. The amount and type of covering applied over the cradle during treatment will influence heat loss due to convection. When rather intense sources of heat are used, wounds, scars, and stomas should be covered because of their lack of sensation.

Usually heat is applied with lights for 20 to 30 minutes. However, the first treatment may be for only half of this time.

HOT PACKS

After selecting cloth material of an appropriate size for the area to be treated, the nurse may use one of several methods to prepare it with moisture and heat. The exact technique of application depends on the method of preparation. Similarly, the frequency of changing the application also varies.

Autoclave method. After moistening wool material with water, wringing it to free it of excess moisture, and folding it to a size slightly larger than the area to be treated, the nurse lays it in a

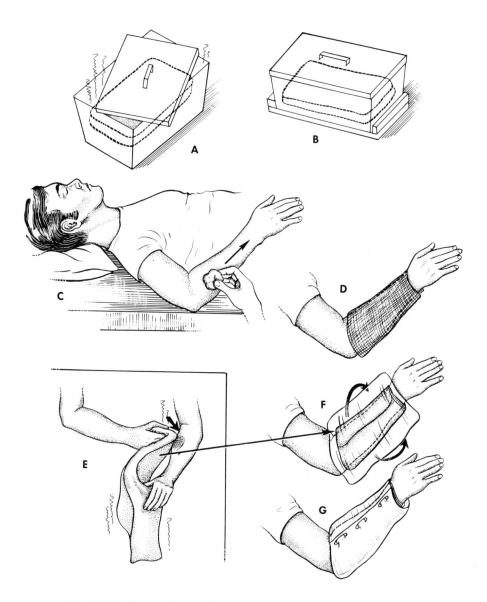

Fig. 11-6. Hot packs, autoclave method. **A,** Moist hot packs are placed in a metal container preparatory to heating. **B,** Method of transporting a metal container containing hot packs. **C,** Unless it is contraindicated, the nurse applies a thin coat of mineral oil to protect the skin. **D,** A layer or two of gauze placed over the area to be treated increases protection. **E,** The temperature of the hot pack is tested on the wrist or forearm or with a thermometer. **F,** After the hot pack is applied, it is covered with moistureproof material. **G,** Additional material covering the pack helps retain the heat.

metal container equipped with a cover and places it in the auto-clave (Fig. 11-6, *A*). As soon as the pressure gauge registers 15 pounds, the nurse removes the container. Otherwise, the wool fibers harden, changing the texture, odor, and heat retention of the material. The cover is placed on the container while it is carried to the nursing care center (Fig. 11-6, *B*). For this purpose, it is convenient to use a heavy board, constructed to prevent the container from slipping during transport.

Unless a wound is present or the hot packs are being applied to distend the veins for venipuncture, a thin coat of mineral oil is used to protect the skin (Fig. 11-6, *C*). A layer or two of gauze is placed over the area for the same purpose (Fig. 11-6, *D*). In the presence of a wound, a dry, sterile dressing is placed over the wound, and the surrounding skin is treated with oil and gauze. A sheet of plastic is placed over the wound dressing to keep it dry, thus preventing contamination.

The nurse removes the wool material, which is likely to be hot, from the container and exposes it to air as necessary to dissipate the excess heat. Its temperature may be tested with a thermometer or on the wrist or forearm (Fig. 11-6, *E*). If the latter method is used, the nurse applies the hot pack slowly enough to permit the patient to decide whether he finds this temperature comfortable. If he thinks the hot pack is too warm, it should be removed immediately.

After the hot pack is applied, it is covered with moistureproof material (Fig. 11-6, *F*). Additional material covering the pack helps retain the heat (Fig. 11-6, *G*). If continuous application is ordered, the packs are changed every 2 hours or more often. Maximum effectiveness is thought to occur when the packs are changed at 5- to 10-minute intervals for 30 minutes.

Hot water method. Moist heat may be applied by the hot water method using wool material heated in a hot water bath or with folded towels that have been moistened with hot water and wrung fairly dry (Fig. 11-7, *A* to *C*). The nurse can protect her hands from excess heat by the method used to fold and wring the material or by using a stupe wringer. When the material is prepared by running hot water over it, the skin may not need to be treated with mineral oil and gauze before its application because the temperature of the hot pack is less than when the autoclave method is used. Hot packs prepared in this way will need to be changed frequently, often every 30 to 60 minutes unless external heat is applied.

Use of oil is definitely contraindicated if the purpose of the hot packs is to distend the veins prior to venipuncture. When used for this purpose, the hot pack should extend well beyond the chosen site for venipuncture. Thus, if a vein in the forearm is to be used,

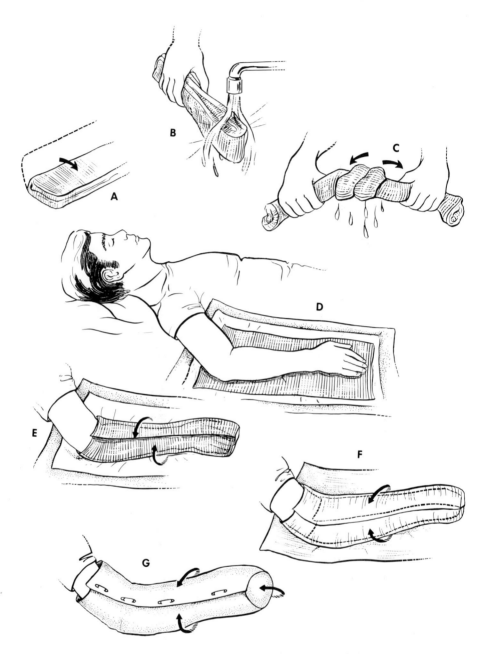

Fig. 11-7. Hot packs, hot water method. **A,** Method of folding a Turkish towel. **B,** Method of holding the towel during application of hot water. **C,** Method of wringing excess moisture from the towel. **D,** Area beneath the extremity protected with a Turkish towel and waterproof material. The hot pack is placed under the extremity. **E,** Hot pack wrapped around the extremity. **F,** Waterproof material wrapped around the hot pack. **G,** Dry Turkish towel used to stabilize the pack and to retain heat.

328

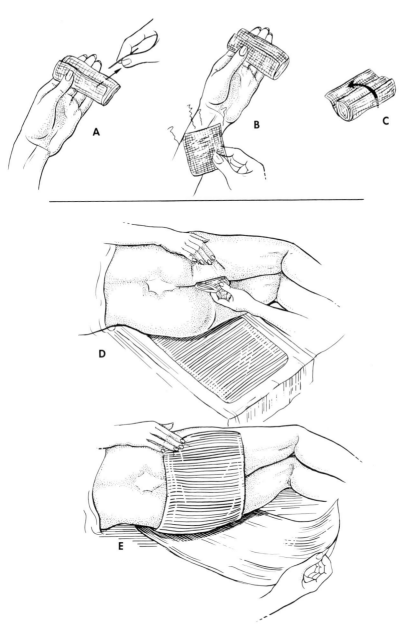

Fig. 11-8. Hot packs, preshaped for the anal area. **A,** After the preshaped dressing is heated, its fastener is removed. **B,** The outer dressing is removed to test its temperature. **C,** The cooled outer dressing is replaced around the heat-retaining core. **D,** The patient retracts his upper buttock during placement of the dressing. **E,** After a hyperthermia blanket or a special heating pad is in place, a large towel is used to maintain its position.

the hot pack should enclose the entire forearm, the hand, and the elbow (Fig. 11-7, *D* to *G*).

Compresses can be preshaped to fit a specific area. For example, the nurse might shape hot packs that are to be applied to the anal area into a small roll. If the dressing is to be clean, rather than sterile, a 4- by 4-inch dressing can be rolled and then enclosed within another dressing. This permits the nurse to remove the outside dressing when testing the temperature, while the inner dressing acts as a heat-retaining core. The outer dressing is cooled as necessary, then replaced around the core and applied to the wound. After a hyperthermia blanket or a special heating pad is in place, a large towel is used to maintain its position (Fig. 11-8).

WARM, MOIST, STERILE COMPRESSES

It is usual to apply these compresses four times a day. The schedule chosen should not interfere with the patient's rest. This, of course, requires knowledge of his rest and sleep patterns. After a specified length of time, often an hour, the compresses are removed, and dry sterile dressings are applied. The exact method of preparing the compresses varies with the area to which they are to be applied and the available equipment.

Method 1. Prepared packs of cotton-filled 4- by 8-inch dressings are satisfactory for treating incisions. They are prepared by enclosing four dressings within a fifth dressing (Fig. 11-9, *A*). The number of packs needed varies with each incision. Thus two to three packs might be needed to treat some abdominal incisions.

The nurse moistens the packs, wrings them as dry as possible, fluffs them, and arranges them in a dressing kettle (Fig. 11-9, *B* to *E*). The folded edges of the packs are placed so that they can be grasped securely with transfer forceps. The lid of the kettle should contain an opening for the forceps so that they are sterilized with the dressings. These are autoclaved for 15 minutes at 250° F.

The nurse tests the temperature of the compresses with a thermometer if the patient has diabetes or a vascular condition. In these cases, the temperature should never exceed 105° F. In all instances the nurse should apply the dressing slowly, until it is known that the patient tolerates the temperature satisfactorily (Fig. 11-9, *F*). Applying the first pack so that it initially touches tissue distal to the incision permits temporary removal, if necessary, until it has cooled sufficiently. If this is done carefully, contamination can be avoided.

The nurse covers the moist compresses with dry, sterile dressings, moistureproof material, and additional reinforcement dressings (Fig. 11-9, *G* to *I*). The method of securing these dressings varies. An abdominal binder or tie tapes may be used when an abdominal incision is involved.

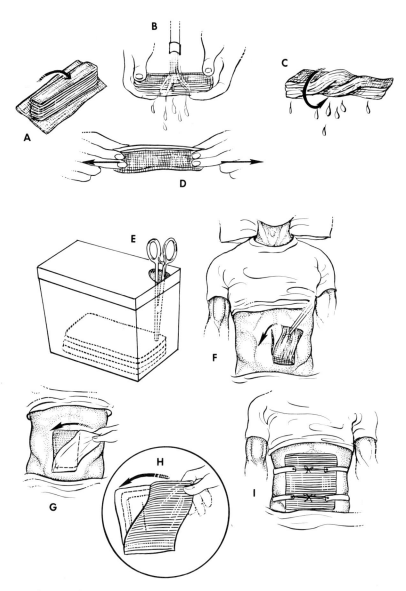

Fig. 11-9. Warm, moist, sterile compresses. **A,** The folded dressings are placed inside the open dressing, thus forming a pack of dressings. **B,** The dressing pack is moistened. **C,** Excess moisture is removed. **D,** Method of fluffing the pack. **E,** Packs are placed in a kettle with dressing forceps for autoclaving. **F,** The dressing is applied slowly until it is certain that the patient tolerates its temperature. **G,** Additional dry, sterile dressings cover the moist dressings. **H,** The dry dressings are covered with moistureproof material. **I,** Reinforcement dressings are applied and stabilized with Montgomery straps or an abdominal binder.

Method 2. A less desirable method involves sterilizing the dressings by boiling or steaming them for 15 minutes. Maintenance of sterility by this method requires considerable effort and skill. The nurse uses sterile forceps to wring the moisture from the dressings and to fluff and apply them.

APPLICATION OF HEAT WITH AN AQUAMATIC K-PAD OR K-MODULE

An Aquamatic K-pad (Fig. 11-10, *A* and *B*) or module (Fig. 11-10, *C*) may be used to maintain the desired temperature of dry or moist heat continuously. Both consist of a control unit and a pad through which water circulates. After filling the control unit with distilled water, the K-pad is connected to the unit by turning the knurled sleeves, located at the end of the bifurcated K-pad tubing, onto the outlets of the unit (Fig. 11-10, *A*). The size of the pad used will depend on the size of the area to be treated. Both the control unit and the pad should be placed on the same level for effective operation of the unit. After filling, the control unit is tilted slowly from side to side and end to end to allow air bubbles to escape. The cap on the reservoir is then loosened a quarter turn, and the temperature of the unit is set as prescribed. The unit is connected to electricity for at least 2 minutes to allow the pad to fill with heated water. During this time, the moist or dry application is prepared.

When dry heat is prescribed, the pad may be placed inside a pillow case for application to the skin. After application to the specified area, ties made of 1- or 2-inch roller gauze or of twill tape are used to tie it in place. Excess tubing may be coiled onto the bed to prevent it from hanging below the level of the unit (Fig. 11-10, *F*). Allowing the tubing to hang down below the level of the unit or the pad will disrupt efficient functioning of the unit.

When moist heat is prescribed, material for the moist compress and a plastic covering, if desired, are needed. After moistening the compress with hot water, it may be enclosed in the plastic for transport to the bedside. Excess moisture should be removed from the compress. The compress is placed over the part to be treated, and the K-pad is applied (Fig. 11-10, *D* and *E*). If desired, the compress may be enclosed in plastic before applying the K-pad. The pad may be either enclosed in a pillow case or wrapped with a towel and held in place with ties (Fig. 11-10, *F*). Pins must not be used because puncturing the pad will cause it to leak.

Precautions that should be followed during the use of this equipment include careful attention to the skin, observation of the temperature control unit and tubing, and placement of the unit on the same level as the pad. The tubing must not be allowed to kink, since this will interfere with circulation of the water. The skin must be inspected at designated intervals. In some institutions, the compress and pad are removed at designated intervals for a specified period of time in an effort to prevent skin damage. Often the pad is removed for 30 minutes three times a day to allow the skin to rest. This, like controlling the temperature, is especially important for patients with poor circulation or decreased sensation, children, and debilitated or incapacitated persons (Table 11-2).

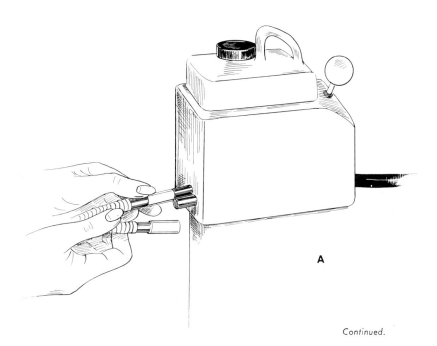

A

Continued.

Fig. 11-10. Use of the Aquamatic K-pad and the Aquamatic K-module. **A,** Back view of the Aquamatic K-pad control unit showing the attachment of the tubing that leads from the control unit to the K-pad. Note the key, which is inserted through a rubber stopper and turned to set the desired temperature. **B,** Front view of the Aquamatic K-pad control unit. The key used to set the temperature is inserted through the center of the round rubber stopper. The temperature at which the unit is set is indicated on the arc-like gauge above the key placement. **C,** Front view of the Aquamatic K-module unit. Note the attachment of the tubing and the key for setting the temperature. **D,** The moistened, warm compress is applied to the designated area. It may be enclosed in plastic, if desired. **E,** The K-pad is applied over the warm, moist compress. Placement is planned to prevent the tubing from being kinked. **F,** A Turkish towel is wrapped around the K-pad, and ties are used to hold the compress and pad in place. Alternatively, the K-pad may be fastened by lacing the ties through holes incorporated into the edges of the K-pad. The use of pins is contraindicated. Note the excess tubing coiled on the bed.

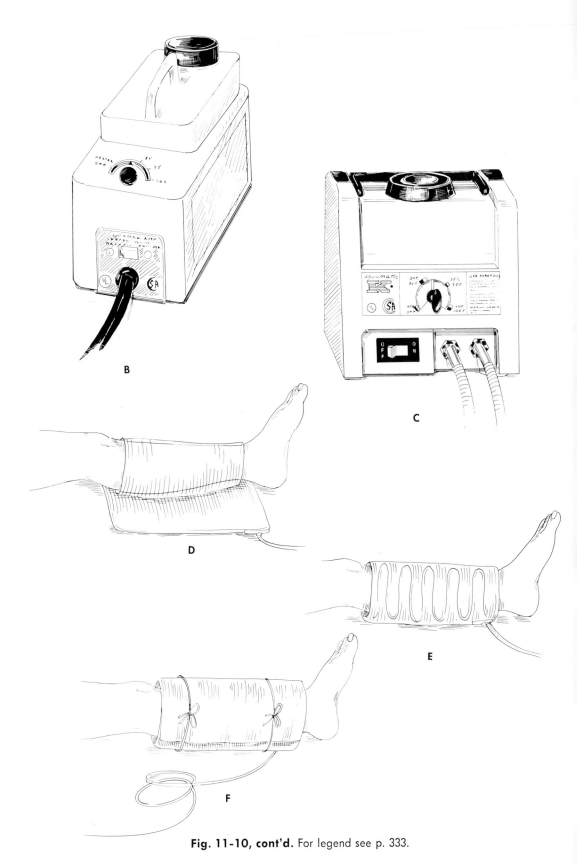

B

C

D

E

F

Fig. 11-10, cont'd. For legend see p. 333.

TABLE 11-2. Application of heat with an Aquamatic K-pad or K-module

Technique	Problem	Solution or explanation
Fill the control unit to the designated point with distilled water, replace the cover, and open it a quarter turn; connect the heating pad to the unit and the unit to electricity; move the electrical switch on the unit to the "on" position	The unit may not operate properly unless it is prepared correctly.	Distilled water prevents accumulation of minerals in the unit; opening the cap a quarter turn allows for escape of air. Various size heating pads are available.
Adjust the temperature setting on the unit and lock it in by removing the key.	Unless the key is removed, other persons may use it to change the temperature.	Usually the prescribed temperature is 105° F. or lower. An improperly heated pad may fail to provide adequate heat, or it may damage tissues with excessive heat.
Observe the pad to be sure that it is filling.	An improperly positioned unit or tubing or kinked tubing may interfere with proper filling of the pad.	The coils bulge as the pad fills. The unit should be on the same level as the pad, and tubing is coiled to prevent it from hanging lower than either the unit or the pad; check for kinking of the tubing, especially at the point at which it is fastened to the pad.
When the pad has filled completely, tip the unit gently from side to side and from end to end.	Residual air in the unit decreases its efficiency and may be hazardous.	Tipping the unit allows air bubbles to escape.
Prepare and apply a moist or dry application for the area to be treated; for a dry application, place the pad inside a pillow case; for a moist application, enclose it with plastic if desired.	The effect of the treatment may differ from that prescribed. Moist heat is more penetrating than dry heat.	The physician will specify if moist or dry heat is to be used; this depends on the nature of the problem and the physiologic changes desired as a result of the treatment. Water increases conduction of heat and slows evaporation; dry heat is tolerated better than moist heat.
Apply the smoothest surface of the pad to fit the contour of the area designated for treatment.	Air may be trapped between the pad and the skin.	Fitting the pad to the contour of the body decreases dead space between the pad and the skin; applying the smoothest side of the pad to the skin further decreases dead space.
A towel may be placed around the K-pad and held in place with ties.	A punctured or cracked pad is useless.	Avoid the use of pins; either tape or cloth ties will prevent puncture of the pad; proper storage of the pad will prevent it from cracking.
Remove the pad and inspect the skin at designated intervals.	Heat may cause skin damage particularly in children, debilitated or incapacitated patients, and those with poor circulation, decreased sensation, or decreased response to sensation.	Prolonged application of heat causes vasoconstriction and may result in thermal injury; prolonged mottling of the skin suggests that the temperature is excessively high.

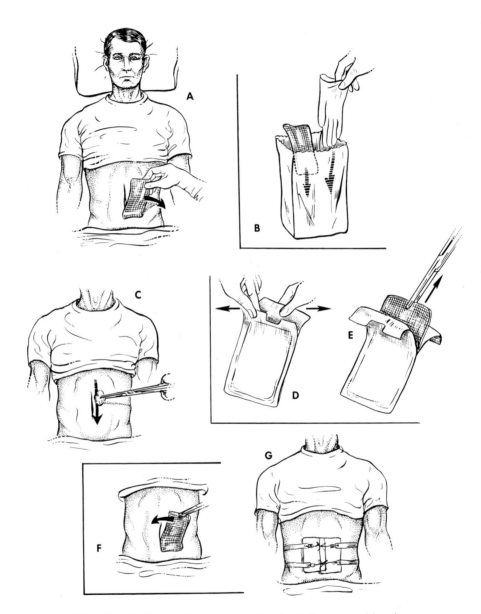

Fig. 11-11. Dry sterile dressings. **A,** A sterile disposable glove offers protection during removal of contaminated dressing. **B,** The soiled dressing and the glove are discarded. **C,** The wound is cleansed, if necessary, using sterile materials. **D,** Method of opening an individually packaged dressing. **E,** The dressing is removed from the wrapper with sterile forceps. **F,** A dressing being applied with sterile forceps. **G,** Completed dressing.

336

Dry sterile dressings

Dry sterile dressings serve to protect wounds from contamination and to absorb drainage. Selection of the type, thickness, size, and absorbency of dressings will be influenced by the nature of the wound, its anatomic location, and the amount and kind of drainage present.

The physician's approval should be obtained before these dressings are changed. Often they may not be disturbed unless evidence of excess drainage or hemorrhage occurs. Even then, the nurse may be asked to reinforce rather than change the dressings. For this it may be permissible to replace the upper layers of a large dressing. The urgency of transmitting information concerning the quantity and kind of drainage present will differ with each situation.

Some physicians prefer to do the initial dressing change. Should this procedure be delegated, the nurse needs to know if drains are present because their placement must not be disturbed. The drains may adhere to the dressings. If this happens, the use of precautions that will prevent any displacement of the drains is mandatory.

It is imperative to maintain the sterility of the dressing by using sterile forceps or gloves (Fig. 11-11). It is also possible to maintain sterility through careful manipulation of the wrapper if dressings are packaged individually. Wearing a gown and mask to prevent contamination of the wound is recommended.

Questions for discussion and exploration

1. Presence of which conditions would indicate that either heat or cold need to be applied with additional caution?
2. With what symptoms is the use of hot water bottles or other forms of local heat contraindicated?
3. What nursing observations indicate that the skin is reacting adversely to (a) heat? (b) cold?
4. For what conditions or symptoms would you expect hypothermia to be used?
5. What explanations should be given to the family and the patient when hypothermia is ordered?
6. When the patient is treated with hypothermia, he may begin to shiver. What is the cause, result, and treatment of shivering?
7. What must be done to prevent the skin from breaking down when hypothermia is used for a prolonged period of time?
8. Hypothermia blankets may lower the temperature of the patient within an hour or two. If the temperature of the patient drops profoundly within a 15-minute period, what would you check and why?
9. Why do some authorities recommend that the patient be placed directly in contact with the blanket instead of placing a sheet between the patient and the blanket? What modifications must be made in

the care of the patient if the blanket is placed in direct contact with the patient?

10. What is meant by regional hypothermia? What are some examples of how hypothermia is applied regionally?

11. How might hypothermia be used to combat gastrointestinal bleeding?

12. Think through a plan for changing sterile dressings. The plan should include (a) nursing approach to the patient, (b) anticipation of supplies needed, (c) placement of supplies for your convenience but protection of them from contamination, (d) direction of removing dressing, (e) observations of drainage and wound, (f) how to learn if drains are present, (g) how to manage a dressing that is adhering to drains or wound or both, and (h) the advisability of gowning and masking.

13. Although you have just changed the dressings, an undesirable odor persists and is noticeable. What are some of the possible origins of the odor, and what nursing action would be indicated?

14. If the tie tapes holding the dressing in place need to be changed, how can you remove the old ones with minimal trauma to the patient? Where should clean tie tapes be applied in relation to the sites from which the old ones were removed? How would you apply the tie tapes to prevent placing any of the tissues under pressure?

Selected references

Beaumont, E.: Hypo/hyperthermia equipment, Nursing 74:34-41, April, 1974.

Devney, A., and Kingsbury, B.: Hypothermia in fact and fantasy, Amer. J. Nurs. 72:1424-1425, 1972.

Fernandez, J. P., and others: Rapid active rewarming in accidental hypothermia, J.A.M.A. 212:153-156, 1970.

Havener, W. H., Saunders, W. H., Keith, C. F., and Prescott, A. W.: Nursing care in eye, ear, nose, and throat disorders, ed. 3, St. Louis, 1974, The C. V. Mosby Co.

Hickey, M. C.: Hypothermia, Amer. J. Nurs. 65:116-122, 1965.

Isler, C.: Hypothermia in action, RN 25:36-47, 1962.

Larson, C. B., and Gould, M.: Orthopedic nursing, ed. 8, St. Louis, 1974, The C. V. Mosby Co.

Michenfelder, J., Terry, H., Daw, E., and Uehlein, A.: Induced hypothermia: physiologic effects, indications, and techniques, Surg. Clin. N. Amer. 45:889-897, 1965.

Nugent, G. R.: Prolonged hypothermia, Amer. J. Nurs. 60:967-969, 1960.

Seldon, N. S.: Sterile warm wet compresses, Amer. J. Nurs. 59:982-984, 1959.

Shafer, K. N., Sawyer, J. R., McCluskey, A. M., Beck, E. L., and Phipps, W. H.: Medical-surgical nursing, ed. 5, St. Louis, 1971, The C. V. Mosby Co.

Sheridan, B. A.: After hemorrhoidectomy; postoperative nursing care, Amer. J. Nurs. 63:90-91, 1963.

Suddarth, D. S.: Individual dressing packs, Amer. J. Nurs. 60:991-992, 1960.

Williams, M. E.: Chilled water mattress, Amer. J. Nurs. 70:2377, 1970.

12

Emergency action

The prevention, early recognition, and immediate treatment of emergencies are important nursing responsibilities. With adequate preparation, the nurse or other trained person can do much to preserve function and save lives. Observation and assessment of the patient's condition are helpful in determining the action indicated and in obtaining medical assistance before an acute emergency develops. The simple action of turning the patient's head to one side or otherwise positioning the lower jaw to remove the tongue from the airway may, if done when stertorous breathing or increased efforts to inhale are noted, prevent a respiratory emergency from developing. This is especially important when the patient is too exhausted to move or is unable to move.

Principles commonly used in nursing can be applied in emergency situations. For example, the principles of moving patients can be used to transfer victims in emergencies. Principles of providing support, understanding, and guidance to patients and relatives during the stress that accompanies illness can be applied in emergency situations also. However, the welfare of the patient is of primary importance during an acute emergency. When sufficient personnel are available or when the emergency is under control, relatives must be given explanations, guidance, and support. As the patient regains consciousness, he needs help to retain or regain his ability to function.

Cardiopulmonary resuscitation

Cardiopulmonary emergencies usually follow some form of accident or occur secondary to disease. A common example is myocardial infarction secondary to arteriosclerosis. Inadequate ventilation allowed to persist long enough to produce myocardial hypoxia may lead to cardiac arrest. This is seen in the early postoperative period or after generous doses of drugs, such as the opiates, that depress the central nervous system. In these instances, accidental death can be prevented simply by assisting the patient to maintain an adequate ventilatory exchange until he is able to do this spontaneously.

When resuscitation is successful and the victim survives, it is almost always due to the immediate action of the person discovering him. Therefore hospitals should expend the necessary time and effort to train a first line of defense. This means that all floor personnel, regardless of their position or education, should be trained to act promptly in such situations. This training should include lectures, demonstrations, and an opportunity to practice the techniques. Manikins designed for such practice are available. Artificial ventilation can be practiced on live persons; cardiac massage should be practiced only on a manikin.

All floor personnel should have a clear understanding of the sequential steps that must be carried out when confronted with a situation demanding either rescue breathing or cardiopulmonary resuscitation. The following steps are suggested as being helpful:

1. Appraise the victim's physical status and determine whether cardiopulmonary resuscitation is indicated.
2. If cardiopulmonary resuscitation is indicated, start ventilation and external cardiac massage promptly.
3. Call the resuscitation team or the attending physician or both for definitive treatment.

Determination of the physical status of the victim is concerned with observations of any spontaneous respiration, assessment of circulatory status, and assessment of possible central nervous system damage by observing the pupils of the eyes.

If the patient shows any attempt at spontaneous respiration, he should be assisted immediately with artificial ventilation. If the patient is still attempting to breathe, one should assume that some circulatory function still exists. Restoration of an adequate ventilatory volume may be the only measure necessary to overcome this situation.

The rescuer assesses circulatory status by palpating the carotid artery. When circulatory function is poor or nonexistent, it is important to place the palpating fingers directly on the artery. The rescuer approaches the common carotid artery from the front and slides three fingers between the side of the wall of the larynx and the sternocleidomastoid muscle, pulling this muscle to the side (Fig. 12-1). If no pulse is felt, it is assumed that cardiac arrest is present.

Hypoxic effects on the central nervous system can be assessed by examining the pupils of the eyes. When cerebral function ceases, the pupils begin dilating immediately and are dilated completely in about 45 seconds. After the pupils are maximally dilated, they will continue to contract when exposed to light for approximately 3 more

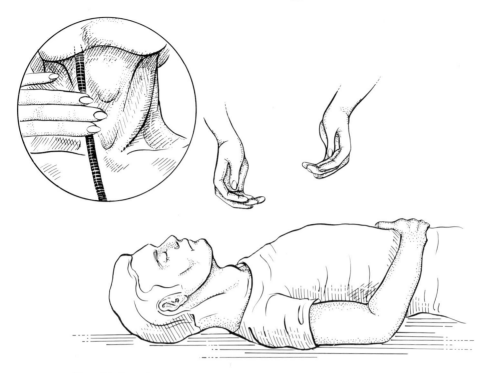

Fig. 12-1. Palpation of the carotid artery. The rescuer palpates the common carotid artery by approaching it from the front and sliding three fingers between the side of the wall of the larynx and the sternocleidomastoid muscle, pulling this muscle to the side.

minutes. After 4 minutes elapse, the pupils become centrally fixed, remain dilated, and fail to react when exposed to a bright light. An attempt to observe both pupils simultaneously should always be made. It is helpful for the physician to know if the pupils vary in size; variance in size indicates a cerebrovascular accident or central nervous system lesions. Deviation or movement of the pupils indicates a light stage of unconsciousness and means that resuscitation is likely to be successful.

The aim of resuscitation is to *maintain life,* and it is indicated for the purpose of restoring the victim to a useful life when this is possible. Resuscitation is not indicated when cardiopulmonary arrest represents the termination of an irreversible disease process such as advanced malignancy. In these situations, the decision not to follow resuscitation procedures should be made and communicated to appropriate personnel before the time when clinical death occurs.

Institution of resuscitation follows the ABC's of resuscitation, in that order. This means that one must restore first the air passages, *A,* second the breathing, *B,* and third the circulation, *C.* Table 12-1

TABLE 12-1. Cardiopulmonary resuscitation (one rescuer)

Technique	Problem	Explanation or solution
Observe for respiration and palpate for carotid pulse.	The pulse and respiration may be absent; if either is absent, arrest of the other system will occur shortly.	Absence of either pulse or respiration are indications for immediate resuscitation.
Observe both pupils.	The eyes may be dilated, pinpoint, reactive or unreactive to light, unequal in size, fixed, deviated, or moving.	The pupils dilate completely within 45 seconds after cessation of cerebral function. After about 4 minutes, pupils become centrally fixed, dilated, and fail to react to light due to cerebral anoxia; cerebral damage is probably present. Variance in the size of the pupils assists the physician in the diagnosis and treatment of an underlying pathologic condition. Deviation or movement of the eyes indicates a light stage of unconsciousness and the probability of successful resuscitation.
Note the exact time.	Resuscitation efforts may be discontinued too soon or prolonged beyond the time necessary if the physician does not have this information.	This information gives the physician some indication of the effectiveness of the efforts and the period of time for which efforts should be continued.
Remove loose dentures, foreign materials, or vomitus from the mouth and pharynx.	Obstruction of the airway will prevent successful resuscitation.	Inspect the area, grasp foreign objects to remove them, and wipe vomitus from the mouth. A clear airway is essential for successful resuscitation.
Position the patient on a firm surface.	Cardiac massage may be ineffective due to inability to compress the heart.	A board ½ inch thick and 2½ feet square is placed beneath the thorax, or the patient is positioned on the floor.
Blow three or four deep breaths into the patient's lungs after positioning him correctly.	The blood may not be oxygenated.	Blowing into the patient's lungs increases the amount of oxygen in the blood.
	The tongue may obstruct the airway.	Place one hand under the neck and lift or pull the lower jaw into a jutting position; maintain this position to keep the tongue from obstructing the airway.
	Air may escape from the nose.	Seal the nose with fingers, or, if possible, seal both nose and mouth with your mouth.

TABLE 12-1. Cardiopulmonary resuscitation (one rescuer)—cont'd

Technique	Problem	Explanation or solution
Observe the chest during inflation.	The chest may not expand.	Failure of the chest to expand means that the air is not reaching the victim's lungs; air may be escaping, or an obstruction may be present; recheck for obstruction and reposition the head and jaw.
If the stomach becomes inflated, turn the patient's head to one side, and press with the flat of the hand on the area above the patient's umbilicus; reposition the head and jaw, and continue to inflate the lungs.	If the stomach is inflated, vomiting may occur.	Pressing releases the air from the stomach; turning the head to one side helps to prevent aspiration during vomiting.
Observe for deflation of the chest before blowing the next breath into the patient's lungs.	Exchange of gases cannot occur without exhalation.	Exhalation occurs passively and may take more time than one might estimate; overinflation is especially disastrous in children.
Apply external cardiac compression: take a position at a right angle to the patient's chest; place the heel of the right hand on the lower third of the body of the sternum with the left hand over it; apply pressure to depress the sternum 1½ to 2 inches, and release the pressure.	Improper placement of the hands may injure tissues.	Maintain the position of the hands between compressions; position makes this technique less tiring to the rescuer. Compress and release the chest at a regular rate of approximately 80 times a minute.
Interrupt cardiac massage every 30 seconds to blow three or four deep breaths into the patient's lungs.	The blood is not oxygenated in the absence of respiration.	This supplies some oxygen to the victim.

summarizes cardiopulmonary resuscitation when only one rescuer is available.

RESTORATION OF AIRWAY AND RESCUE BREATHING

The obstruction of the upper airways is caused most commonly by the base of the tongue, which falls down and lies on the posterior wall of the pharynx (Fig. 12-2, *A*). In younger persons this type of obstruction can be relieved by hyperextending the neck (Fig. 12-2, *B*). In older persons or in those with neck injury, hyperextending the neck may not be possible. Then the rescuer lifts the lower jaw forward into a jutting position until the lower teeth extend well in front of the upper teeth, positioning the head to remove the tongue from the airway (Fig. 12-4, *C*).

The nasal pathways must be occluded with pressure by the thumb and index finger for effective mouth-to-mouth breathing, as shown in Fig. 12-2, *C* to *F*. The rescuer seals his mouth over the mouth of the victim, and his exhalation is used to inflate the victim's lungs (Fig. 12-2, *E*). The rescuer seals the mouth with his index finger and seals his mouth over the victim's nose for the inhalation phase of mouth-to-nose breathing (Fig. 12-3, *A*) when this method is used. The jaw must be maintained in the jutting position while the rescuer removes his mouth from the victim's nose or mouth and observes passive exhalation (Figs. 12-2, *F,* and 12-3, *B*).

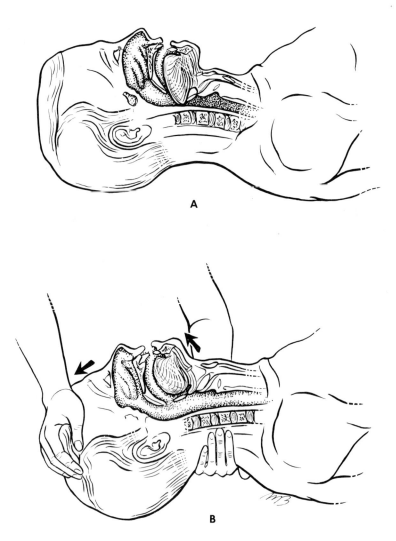

Fig. 12-2. Mouth-to-mouth breathing. **A,** Position of victim showing tongue pulled down by gravity and occluding the air passages. **B,** Hyperextension of the neck elevates the lower jaw, to which the tongue is attached, and opens the airway.

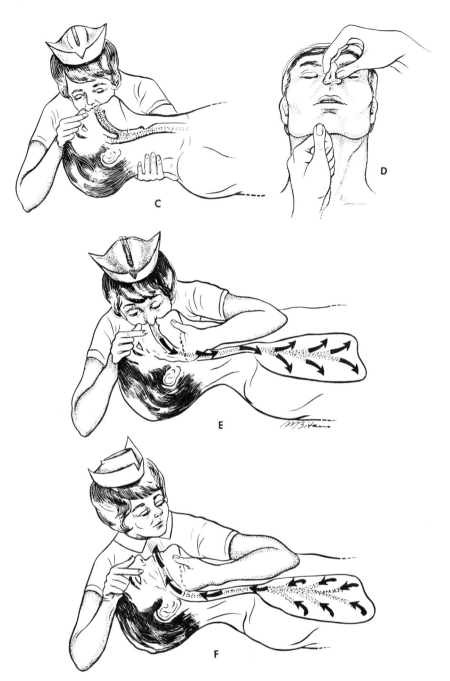

Fig. 12-2, cont'd. C, The nose is sealed with the thumb and index finger; then the rescuer seals his mouth over the mouth of the victim for inhalation. Note that the position of the victim's head is maintained in order to keep the airway open. **D,** An alternative method of maintaining the position of the victim's head. Pressure exerted on the forehead and the jaw is used to maintain hyperextension of the neck. The nostrils are occluded with the thumb and index finger of the hand that is exerting pressure on the forehead. **E,** The rescuer inflates the victim's lungs with his exhalation. **F,** The rescuer observes the chest and listens for passive exhalation.

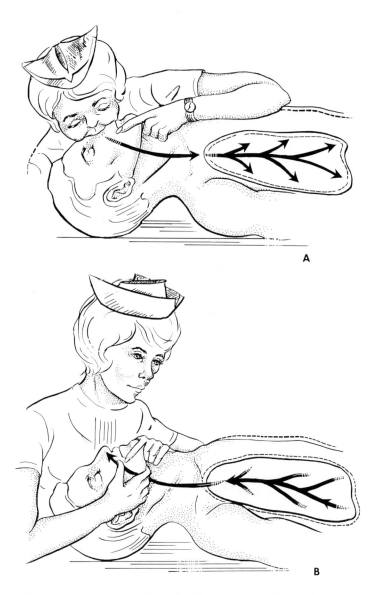

Fig. 12-3. Mouth-to-nose breathing. **A,** The rescuer positions the victim's head to remove the tongue from the airway, seals the victim's mouth with the index finger, and seals his mouth over the nose of the victim for the inhalation phase. **B,** The rescuer maintains the jaw in the jutting position while removing his mouth from the victim's nose and observing passive exhalation. The rescuer repeats these steps alternately until the victim is able to breathe spontaneously.

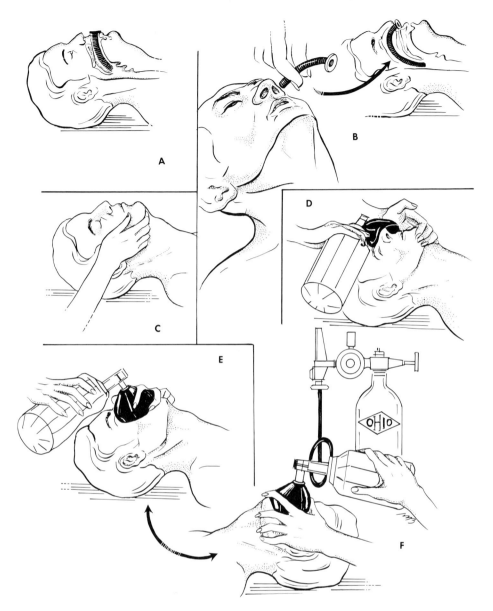

Fig. 12-4. Use of the Hope self-inflating portable resuscitator. **A,** An oropharyn-geal airway in place helps to keep the tongue forward but does not guarantee an open airway. As the patient regains consciousness, this airway may stimulate gagging, vomiting, or biting. **B,** Placement of a nasopharyngeal airway. The tube is inserted downward through the widest part of the nose. If any resistance is encountered, the other nostril should be used. This airway must be inserted gently to avoid damage to the vessels in the nose, resulting in hemorrhage as circulation is restored. **C,** The fingertips of the rescuer are placed on the angles of the jaw, which is pulled forward until the lower teeth extend over the upper teeth. **D,** The position of the jaw is maintained with one hand while using the other hand to fit the narrowest part of the mask into the deepest depression at the bridge of the nose. **E,** The mask is brought forward over the mouth, using care not to exert pressure on the eyes. The thumb and index finger are wrapped around the mask to hold it firmly in place. **F,** The remaining fingers of the same hand are used to maintain the position of the jaw. The other hand compresses the bag to augment spontaneous inspiration and then releases the bag until exhalation is complete. All portable resuscitators should be connected to oxygen if available. (Courtesy Ohio Medical Products, Division of Air Reduction Co., Inc., Madison, Wis.)

Before ventilation is started, the rescuer must remove loose dentures or foreign bodies that may cause obstruction. If stomach contents have been regurgitated into the pharynx, he must remove them also. Maintenance of open air passages may be difficult for the inexperienced. The insertion of an oropharyngeal airway (Fig. 12-4, *A*) may be helpful, but this device alone is not designed to maintain open air passages. A nasopharyngeal airway inserted carefully through the widest part of the nose may be more helpful (Fig. 12-4, *B*).

Either mouth-to-mouth (Fig. 12-2) or mouth-to-nose rescue breathing (Fig. 12-3) may be employed for adequate ventilation. These techniques provide a form of intermittent positive pressure ventilation. Their effectiveness depends on a leakproof system that does not allow air flow into spaces other than the lungs. The victim's exhalation is purely passive and is checked by watching deflation of the chest (Figs. 12-2, *F*, and 12-3, *B*). Tight clothing around the neck, which causes significant obstruction of the airway, or unnecessary pressure on the thorax or abdomen may interfere with inflation of the lungs.

Although mouth-to-mouth and mouth-to-nose breathing are effective and have helped save lives, the exhaled air of the rescuer used to ventilate the victim is relatively poor in oxygen content and relatively rich in carbon dioxide. These factors are not in the best interest of the victim, and it is preferable to employ fresh air for each breath with a simple nonrebreathing technique. A self-inflating portable resuscitator is used for this purpose (Fig. 12-4). The resuscitator should be connected to oxygen if it is available.

USE OF A PORTABLE RESUSCITATOR

When a portable resuscitator is used, the position of the patient is the same as that described for mouth-to-mouth and mouth-to-nose breathing (Fig. 12-4, *C* to *F*). This position may be improved somewhat by elevating the shoulders with a blanket folded to a thickness of about 2 inches.

If an oropharyngeal airway is used, the rescuer must position it properly (Fig. 12-4, *A*). It may stimulate gagging and can be occluded by the patient biting on it. These reflexes return as the patient regains consciousness. If a nasopharyngeal airway is available, it can be introduced by bending the tip of the nose upward and pushing the tube downward through the widest part of the nose (Fig. 12-4, *B*). If any resistance is encountered, the other nostril should be used. Forcible advancement of the airway is likely to damage blood vessels, resulting in nasal hemorrhage as the circulation is restored. As a guide, a soft latex tube, size 32 French, is used for the adult female patient, and size 34 French is used for the adult male patient.

The experienced person will probably find it convenient to position the head in the following manner. Place the tips of the index and middle fingers on the angle of the lower jaw, and pull it forward until the lower teeth extend well over the upper teeth (Fig. 12-4, C). Move the fingers around the edge of the lower jaw. Be careful not to press on the soft tissues but yet maintain the position of the jaw. Fit the narrowest part of the mask into the deepest depression at the bridge of the nose (Fig. 12-4, D) and bring the mask forward over the mouth (Fig. 12-4, E). Wrap the thumb and index finger around the mask to hold it firmly in place, maintaining the position of the jaw with the remaining fingers of the same hand (Fig. 12-4, F). Use the other hand to compress the bag for inhalation. Then release the bag until passive exhalation occurs (Fig. 12-4, F). Squeezing the bag should coincide with any spontaneous efforts to inhale. If the bag is compressed rapidly and vigorously, air turbulence rather than entry of air into the lungs will occur.

If the chest does not rise and the bag does not empty when squeezed, an obstruction is present. Correction of the obstruction by removal of secretions, loosening the gown, and repositioning has been discussed previously. If the bag empties but the chest does not rise, air may be leaking between the mask and the face. This must be corrected by refitting the mask. Leakage that forces gases to flow over the eyes must not be allowed to persist because it may cause irreversible damage to vision. Continuous care must be exercised when a portable resuscitator is used so that the eyes are not damaged by exertion of pressure on them. It should always be assumed that the victim may be wearing contact lenses. These need not be removed if the mask is positioned properly.

RESCUE BREATHING FOR INFANTS AND CHILDREN

Rescue breathing is done for infants and children in a manner similar to that for adults. The volume of air used to inflate the lungs of infants will be less than that for an adult, but the pressure needed to inflate the lungs of an infant will be greater than that for an adult. The volume of air needed for children can be determined best by observing the inflation of the chest.

If the stomach rises during inflation, manual pressure is exerted on the abdomen to remove the air. Regurgitation may result, and therefore the head should be turned to the side before pressing on the abdomen. If regurgitation occurs, secretions must be removed before the patient is repositioned and rescue breathing is continued. There is usually no need for an oropharyngeal or nasopharyngeal airway.

RESCUE BREATHING THROUGH A STOMA

If the patient is to be ventilated through a stoma, the rescuer should elevate his shoulders slightly and align his head with his body. His head should not be turned to either side, since doing so may change the shape of the stoma and occlude the airway. The airway is suctioned through the stoma (pages 115 to 117). It is not necessary to remove obstructions above the stoma or to occlude the mouth and nose before administering ventilation through a stoma.

If the tracheostomy tube is fitted with an inflatable balloon, inflation of the balloon will seal the space between the tube and the wall of the trachea, increasing the effectiveness of ventilation. (See pages 119 and 120 for the technique of inflating a cuffed tracheostomy tube.)

The patient with a permanent stoma may not be wearing a tube in it. If a tube is in place, the inner cannula should be removed. If a breathing machine fitted with adaptors for the tube is readly available, it should be connected to the outer cannula. As soon as air exchange is occurring freely, secretions must be aspirated from the airway. If a breathing machine is not available immediately, the mask of a portable resuscitator is positioned to adjust to the contour of the neck. A seal between the mask and the neck is obtained by removing the plug from the mask, if it is of an inflatable type, or by packing a damp cloth around the mask. If equipment is not available, mouth-to-stoma breathing is used. The rescuer takes a deep breath, seals his mouth around the stoma, and inflates the patient's lungs by exhalation.

If it is known that the patient has a permanent stoma that has healed, there should be no hesitation about removing the cannula from the trachea. This is done by breaking the chain or cutting the cloth tapes that hold the cannula in place. *Removal of the outer cannula from the trachea of a patient with a fresh, temporary stoma will result in occlusion of the stoma within a matter of minutes.*

Restoring cardiac function
EXTERNAL CARDIAC MASSAGE

External cardiac massage must begin soon after cardiac arrest occurs, because irreversible brain damage begins within 3 to 5 minutes. The patient with cardiac arrest loses consciousness suddenly, becomes cyanotic rapidly, ceases to breathe, and has no pulse. Cardiac massage is sometimes indicated when the heart is beating so faintly and rapidly that adequate circulation is not maintained.

The patient should be positioned on a firm surface as described for mouth-to-mouth resuscitation. A board $\frac{1}{2}$ inch thick and $2\frac{1}{2}$ feet square, placed directly under his thorax, is ideal. If such a board is not readily available, a closet shelf or a serving tray turned up-side down on the bed will provide a firm surface, or the patient may be placed on the floor.

If alone, the rescuer should use mouth-to-mouth resuscitation to blow three or four deep breaths into the patient's lungs to oxygenate the blood before beginning external cardiac massage. Until a trained person is available to apply continuous recue breathing, cardiac massage must be interrupted every 30 seconds to blow four deep breaths into the lungs. This interruption reduces the effectiveness of cardiopulmonary resuscitation significantly. Another trained person should be called as quickly as possible.

The rescuer positions himself at a right angle to the patient's chest, with the major portion of his body above the level of the patient's chest. If the bed cannot be lowered or if a footstool is not available, this position can be achieved by kneeling on the bed. The sternum is located by palpation (Fig. 12-5, *A*).

The right-handed rescuer places the heel of his right hand *on the lower third of the body of the sternum*. The heel of the left hand is positioned on top of the right hand and at a right angle to it. The fingers of both hands should be interlaced, straight, or slightly hy-perextended to prevent trauma to adjacent tissues (Fig. 12-5, *B*). Finger rings may also produce trauma.

Enough pressure is applied to depress the sternum 1½ to 2 inches, then the pressure is released (Fig. 12-5, *C*). Placement of the hands on the sternum should be maintained during the recoil period, simultaneously allowing the heart to fill with blood. The rhythm of alternately applying and releasing pressure should occur at a regular rate of approximately 60 times a minute when a second person is available for cardiopulmonary resuscitation. If only one person is available, the recommended rate of cardiac compression is 80 times a minute. If the technique is effective, the carotid or femoral pulse will become palpable. A blood pressure cuff placed on the upper arm should register 100 mm. of mercury with each compression. The rescuer continues resuscitation until the physician relieves him of this responsibility.

If the physician is resuscitating the patient, he may ask the nurse or another trained person to check his timing and the effectiveness of cardiac massage or to relieve him while he performs other tasks. The nurse should direct others to bring needed equipment and supplies to the bedside. A special cart equipped with supplies, solutions, and needed equipment should be maintained in a convenient location within the hospital area. Supplies needed immediately frequently include an electrocardiograph, an external defibrillator, and 1 ml. of aqueous epinephrine (Adrenalin) in a syringe fitted with an intracardiac needle, usually a 22-gauge needle 3½ inches long.

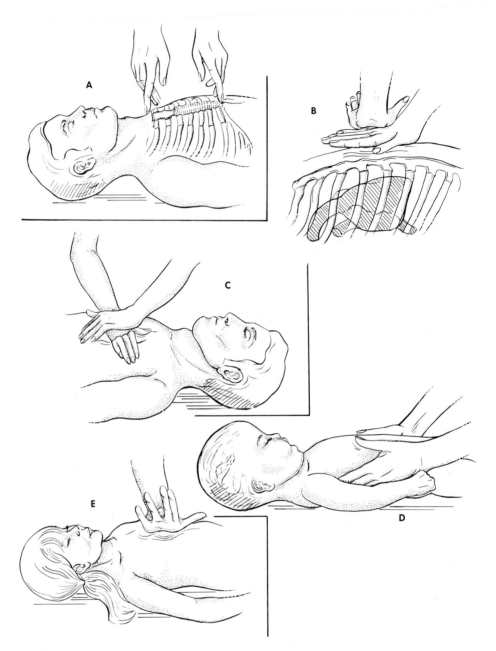

Fig. 12-5. External cardiac massage. **A,** The sternum is located by palpation. **B,** Back view of the rescuer's hands. The righthanded person places the heel of the right hand on the lower third of the body of the sternum. The left hand is placed on top of the right hand and at a right angle to it. The fingers are straight or slightly hyperextended. **C,** With the hands in position on the lower third of the body of the sternum, pressure is applied and released alternately. This placement of the hands is maintained during the resting phase to conserve energy and to avoid any need to reposition the hands. **D,** The rescuer may reach around the chest of a small infant and use the thumbs to depress the sternum. If preferred, the index and middle fingers may be used. **E,** The sternum of an older child is depressed with the heel of one hand only.

Epinephrine stimulates the myocardium and the conduction tissue, electrocardiography monitors the heart, and defibrillation converts fibrillation to effective contraction of the heart. Injectable solutions of 10% calcium gluconate and sodium bicarbonate (approximately 1 mEq. of drug per milliliter of solution) should be readily available to combat electrolyte imbalance. Other drugs, solutions, and equipment needed are discussed by Jude and Elam.

Before using the defibrillator, a special electrode paste is applied to the electrodes to prevent severe burns of the skin. The patient's arms and legs may be restrained with drawsheets to prevent injury as a result of reflex action. All electrical equipment is removed from the patient except one set of electrocardiograph leads from a machine that is built with special insulators. All persons must stand well away from the patient and his bed to avoid conduction of the electric current to themselves. Contact with the current could shock the normally functioning heart into asystole (cardiac arrest). If asked to hold the electrodes, the nurse must touch only the handles of the electrodes.

External cardiac massage applied to children. Modification of the amount of pressure exerted on the sternum of the infant is achieved by using the index and middle fingers, or the thumbs only (Fig. 12-5, *D*). For the child 1 year old or older, pressure may be applied with the heel of one hand (Fig. 12-5, *E*).

Control of hemorrhage

The flow of blood to an area is limited by restricting activity, elevating the part, and applying direct pressure. If signs and symptoms of shock are present, the patient may be placed in a supine position with his legs elevated at approximately a 45-degree angle to the pelvis. The knees should be straight and the pelvis slightly higher than the chest. The head may be supported with a pillow. This is believed to be more useful in the treatment of cardiogenic or neurogenic shock than the traditional Trendelenburg position for aiding the supply of blood to the brain.

The Trendelenburg position may be used in the treatment of hypovolemic shock. For this position, the foot of the bed is elevated to place the body on an inclined plane, and a pillow is placed under the patient's head. This increases the flow of blood to the brain and venous return to the heart. Placing a pillow under the left shoulder and turning the patient to the right side facilitates the filling of the right atrium and maintenance of the airway. This position is usually contraindicated when head, neck, or chest injuries are present.

In addition, the patient should be supplied with increased concen-

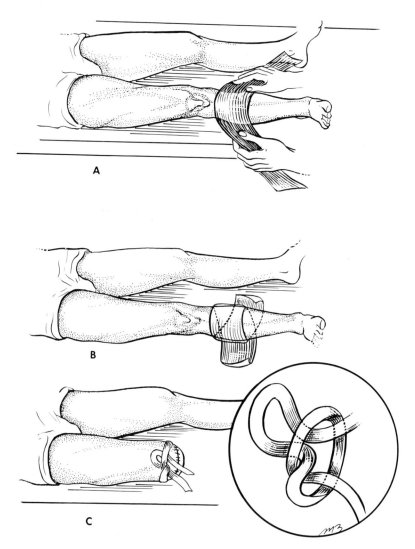

Fig. 12-6. Control of hemorrhage. **A,** Pressure is applied to the wound with a bandage over a dressing on the wound. **B,** Preparation for securing the bandage with pressure. **C,** Application of a tourniquet proximal to the site of hemorrhage. A tourniquet is used with knowledge that the limb may have to be sacrificed. The surgeon may leave instructions for its use if hemorrhage occurs after amputation. The inset shows a method of applying a tourniquet that provides for easy removal.

trations of oxygen. Central venous pressure is used to measure the need for and response to fluid replacement. Efforts to supply external warmth are no longer commonly practiced. Additional warmth increases metabolism and the need for oxygen.

The physician must be notified whenever evidence of shock is detected so that measures to correct the cause can be instituted. The action planned by the physician will depend on the cause of the shock. The nurse should anticipate the need for replacement fluids, intravenous therapy, vasopressor drugs, ventilatory assistance, and equipment for monitoring central venous pressure, blood pressure, and urinary output.

DIRECT PRESSURE

Applying a thick, sterile compress with manual pressure is a simple method of controlling most bleeding (Fig. 12-6, *A* and *B*). Pressure is exerted in such a way that the edges of the wound are brought together rather than forced apart. Sustained pressure can be achieved with a pressure dressing secured with bandage, tape, or elastic tape. An inflatable plastic splint or bandage can be used to apply uniform pressure to an extremity.

Frequent inspection for signs of continued bleeding is necessary. A hematoma that forms beneath an elastic bandage may not be visible, but it will feel spongy when palpated.

TOURNIQUET

If a physician is available, a tourniquet should not be used without his order. In the absence of a physician, a tourniquet may be applied to save a life, recognizing that the limb may be sacrificed as a result. A tourniquet should always be attached to the head of the bed so that it is readily available immediately after an amputation. It should be applied as closely as possible to the source of the bleeding (Fig. 12-6, *C*).

Tourniquets applied to occlude arterial circulation should be at least 2 inches wide to avoid damage to the underlying tissues, blood vessels, and nerves. After a tourniquet has been applied, it should be released only when medical assistance is available to control the hemorrhage and to restore blood volume. If a tourniquet is applied, medical assistance should be obtained without delay. A tourniquet is rarely needed because bleeding can usually be controlled by other means.

PRESSURE POINTS

Firm manual pressure on the main artery supplying the wound is used when direct pressure fails to control bleeding. This method is particularly useful in the control of nosebleed (Fig. 12-7). Certain

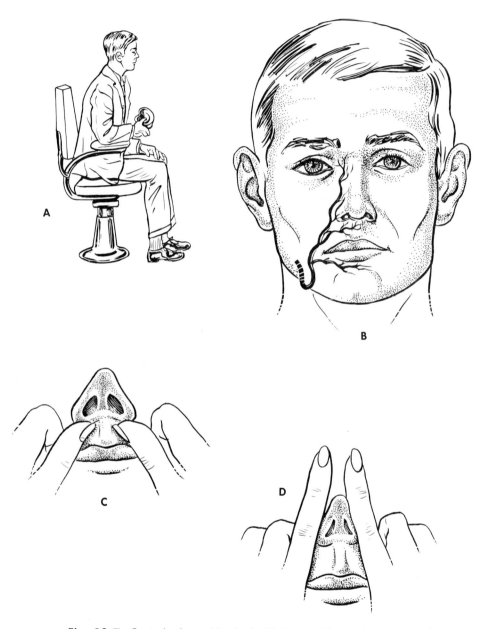

Fig. 12-7. Control of nosebleed. **A,** Sitting position reduces the flow of blood to the head and nose. The forward position of the head prevents swallowing of blood. **B,** Anatomic location of blood vessels supplying the nose. **C,** A common method of occluding the main artery supplying the nose. **D,** An alternative method of occluding the artery and its branches.

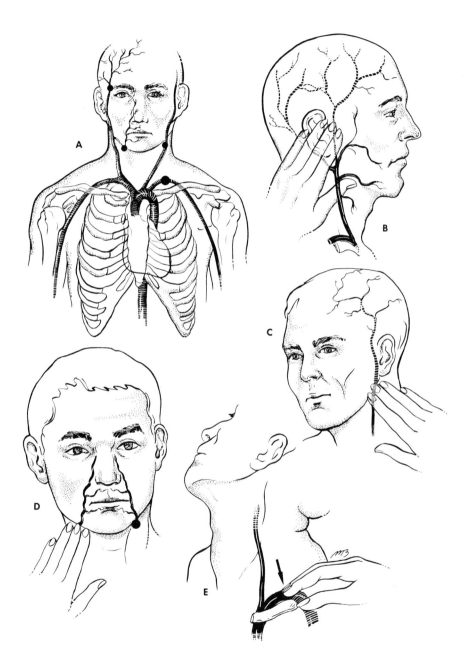

Fig. 12-8. Use of pressure points to control bleeding. **A,** Anatomic location of major blood vessels and pressure points. **B,** Pressure to stop scalp bleeding. **C,** Head and neck. **D,** Face. **E,** Chest wall and armpit.

Continued.

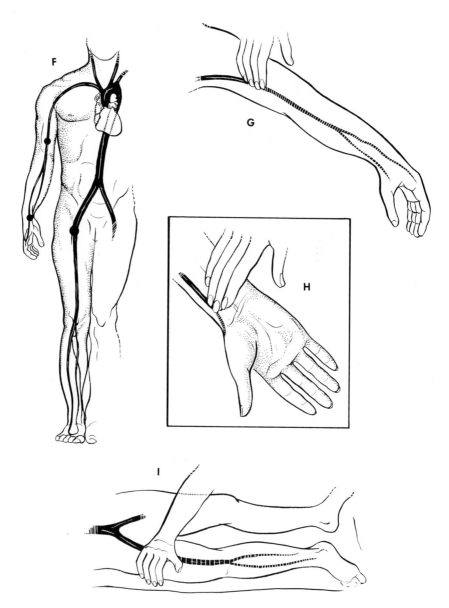

Fig. 12-8, cont'd. F, Anatomic location of blood vessels and pressure points. **G,** Pressure to stop bleeding of the upper arm. **H,** Wrist. **I,** Leg.

points commonly referred to as pressure points are used to control bleeding (Fig. 12-8). These same points can be used to obtain pulses.

Wound disruption

If a patient complains of a sensation of something giving way or leaking in the area of the wound, inspection for bleeding, dehiscence, or evisceration is indicated. If dehiscence is apparent, the nurse should alleviate the tension on the wound by positioning. The patient with an abdominal wound should lie supine with his knees flexed. The nurse should place a sterile dressing over the wound and apply pressure in an effort to prevent evisceration. A binder applied snugly is thought to be helpful. Evisceration is treated immediately by placing the patient in the supine position with the knees flexed and covering the protruding viscera with a sterile dressing moistened with sterile normal saline. The physician should be notified at once.

Eye injury

Immediate treatment is indicated whenever foreign material contacts the eye accidentally. After contact with acid or alkali the eyes

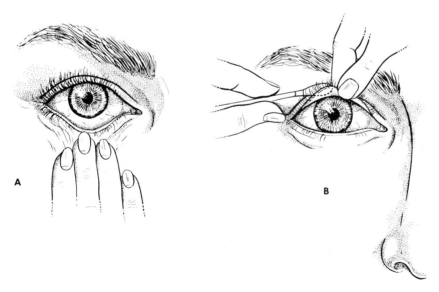

Fig. 12-9. Preserving sight. **A,** Traction on the tissues distal to the eye exposes the inner aspect of the lower eyelid. **B,** The upper eyelid being everted. The index finger may be used instead of a swab.

should be flushed with copious amounts of clean water. In an emergency, a person can flush the eye by holding his head over a drinking fountain, with the injured eye nearest the flow of water and the eyelids separated. Gently flowing water from a faucet or a clean container will suffice. The direction of flow should be from the inner angle of the eye to the outer angle (pages 293 and 294).

It may be necessary to evert the eyelid to remove a foreign object from the eye (Fig. 12-9). A cotton-tipped applicator, not much larger than the foreign object, moistened with normal saline or sterile water is used. Gentle swabbing or rotation of the applicator is used to remove a foreign object. If the object is on the cornea or appears to be embedded, the eye should be bandaged and medical treatment obtained at once. Any evidence of hemorrhage or loss of vision should be evaluated by a physician.

Questions for discussion and exploration

1. As you walk by a room you notice that a patient is snoring loudly and exerting effort to inhale. What may this indicate? What action should you take?
2. You are on your way to obtain some sterile supplies for a doctor who is waiting in his patient's room. Suddenly Mrs. X. runs into the hallway screaming, "He's dead!" List the actions you would take, the order in which you would carry them out, and the reasons for each action.
3. You see the relatives of Mr. X., who is being resuscitated, standing in the hallway near the door of his room, wringing their hands and crying. You are free to initiate supportive action. What can you say or do to help them and the other patients in the nursing unit?
4. When you are helping a postoperative patient to cough productively, he eviscerates. What must you do? In what order? Why?
5. A neighbor's child comes to you after being hit in the eye with a mud ball. What first aid can you initiate? On what basis will you decide whether he should be seen by a physician?
6. You come on an accident on your way home from vacation. One person has blood spurting from the popliteal area, another appears not to be breathing, and a third has blood on his forehead and an obvious fracture of the left arm. What will your actions be?
7. When you take a specimen to the laboratory, you learn that a technician has just gotten a chemical in her eye. She is holding her eye and saying, "I can't see!" What is the first thing you can do to help her? What is the rationale for your thinking?
8. List and discuss methods of preventing accidents (a) in your hospital and (b) in your home.
9. Mrs. Y. exhibits evidence of shock shortly after you have given her an injection of meperidine. What are the signs and symptoms of shock? What action must you take immediately?
10. If irreversible symptoms leading to death occur, what is your role in

relation to the patient? The relatives? What are your feelings about death?

Selected references

Abramson, H.: editor: Resuscitation of the newborn infant and related emergency procedures, ed. 3, St. Louis, 1973, The C. V. Mosby Co.

Barber, J. M., Stokes, L. G., and Billings, D. Mc. G.: Adult and child care, a client approach to nursing, St. Louis, 1973, The C. V. Mosby Co.

Beland, I.: Clinical nursing: pathophysiological and psychosocial approaches, ed. 2, New York, 1970, The Macmillan Co.

Bergersen, B. S.: Pharmacology in nursing, ed. 12, St. Louis, 1973, The C. V. Mosby Co.

Bordicks, K. J.: Patterns of shock, New York, 1965, The Macmillan Co.

Cahill, D.: The nurse's role in closed-chest cardiac resuscitation, Amer. J. Nurs. 65:84-88, 1965.

Craven, R. F.: I died for a few seconds, Amer. J. Nurs. 72:718-719, 1972.

Emergency intervention by the nurse, Monograph 1, New York, 1962, American Nurses' Association.

Feely, E. M.: The new graduate in cardiopulmonary resuscitation, Amer. J. Nurs. 70:1304-1307, 1970.

Feldman, S., and Ellis, H.: Principles of resuscitation, Philadelphia, 1967, F. A. Davis Co.

First aid for laryngectomees, New York, 1962, American Cancer Society, International Association of Laryngectomees.

Henderson, J.: Emergency medical guide, ed. 3, New York, 1973, McGraw-Hill Book Co.

Horgan, P.: The nurse's guide to rescue breathing, R.N. 60:35-45, 1960.

Instructor's manual in cardiopulmonary resuscitation, New York, 1965, American Heart Association.

Jude, J. R., and Elam, J. O.: Fundamentals of cardiopulmonary resuscitation, Philadelphia, 1965, F. A. Davis Co.

Lister, J.: Nursing intervention in anaphylactic shock, Amer. J. Nurs. 72:720-721, 1972.

Modell, W., editor: Drugs of choice, 1974-1975, St. Louis, 1974, The C. V. Mosby Co.

Nett, L., and Petty, T.: Acute respiratory failure, Amer. J. Nurs. 67:1847-1853, 1967.

Schneewind, J. H.: Medical and surgical emergencies, ed. 3, Chicago, 1973, Year Book Medical Publishers, Inc.

Schwerman, E., Schwartau, N., Thompson, C., and Didier, E.: The pharmacist as a member of the cardiopulmonary resuscitation team, Drug. Intel. Clin. Pharm. 7:298-308, 1973.

Simeone, F. A.: The nature of shock, Parts I and II, Amer. J. Nurs. 66:1287-1294, 1966.

Standard first aid and personal safety, New York, 1973, Doubleday & Co., Inc. (American Red Cross.)

Standards of cardiopulmonary resuscitation (CPR) and emergency cardiac care (ECC), J.A.M.A. 227 (supp):833-868, 1974.

Stephenson, H. E.: Cardiac arrest and resuscitation, ed. 4, St. Louis, 1974, The C. V. Mosby Co.

Sun, R. L.: Trendelenburg's position in hypovolemic shock, Amer. J. Nurs. 71:1758-1759, 1971.

Vallari, R. M.: Mobile unit for cardiac arrest, Nurs. Outlook 64:39, 1964.

von Morpurgo, D., and Gauder, P. J.: Coordinated action in cardiac arrest, Amer. J. Nurs. 62:91-93, 1962.

Wagner, M. M.: Assessment of patients with multiple injuries, Amer. J. Nurs. 72:1822-1827, 1972.

Webb, K. J.: Early assessment of orthopedic injuries, Amer. J. Nurs. 74:1048-1052, 1974.

White, J.: Closed chest cardiac massage, Amer. J. Nurs. 61:57-59, 1961.

Zoll, P. M., and others: Use of external electric cardiac pacemaker in cardiac arrest, J.A.M.A. 159:1428-1431, 1955.

Glossary

Listed at the left are the symbols used in this glossary to indicate pronunciation. Listed at the right are common words using the sounds, which are indicated by boldface letters.

ă	**h**a**t**
ā	**h**a**y**
âr	**p**a**re**
ä	**f**a**ther**
b	**b**id
ch	**ch**ild
d	**d**id, wille**d**
ĕ	w**e**t
ē	s**ee**
f	**f**ine, **ph**ase
g	**g**et
h	**h**it
hw	**wh**at
ĭ	s**i**t
ī	l**ie**, b**y**
îr	**p**ier
j	**j**ump, fu**dge**
k	**k**ick, **c**ot, pi**que**
l	**l**id
m	**m**ore
n	**n**ot
ng	si**ng**
ŏ	l**o**t, t**o**rrid
ō	w**o**e, s**o**ar
ô	c**au**ght, l**aw**, f**or**
oi	n**oi**se
o͝o	l**oo**k

362

o͞o	toot
ou	snout
p	pot
r	rear
s	sister
sh	shop, dash
t	top, rapped
th-	thick
th	that
ŭ	nut
ū	mute
ûr	urgent, stern, firm, heard, word
v	vane
w	wish
y	yoke
z	zenith, xylophone
zh	leisure, garage, visual
ə	around, item, circus, edible, gallop
ər	bitter

A

abdominal (ăb-dŏm′ə-nəl) area of the body between the diaphragm and the pelvis.

abduction (ăb-dŭk′shən) drawing away from the midline of the body.

abrasion (ə-brā′zhən) injury produced by scraping away some skin or mucous membrane.

activity (ăk-tĭv′ə-të) motion; optimum activity refers to most favorable amount.

adaptor (ə-dăp′tər) device used to join one part of equipment to another.

adduction (ə-dŭk′shən) drawing toward the midline.

adjacent (ə-jā′sənt) adjoining; next to.

administer (ăd-mĭn′ĭst-tər) to give.

aerosol (âr′ə-sôl) mist; fine spray.

air conditioning (âr′kən-dĭsh′ən-ing) treatment of air that controls its temperature, movement, moisture, and dust content.

airtight (âr′tīt′) impermeable to air.

airway (âr′wā′) passageway for ventilation; may be natural or artificial.

alcohol (ăl′kə-hôl′) colorless, flammable, volatile liquid; used as an antiseptic and as a vehicle for medicine; an intoxicating beverage.

alignment (ə-līn′mənt) bringing into line for correct arrangement or position.

allergen (ăl′ər-jən) anything that induces a state of allergy.

allergic (ə-lûr′jĭk) hypersensitive.

allergy (ăl′ər-jē) abnormal sensitivity to a substance.

alveoli (ăl-vē′ə-lī′) air cells formed by the terminal dilatation of air passages in lungs.

ambulation (ăm′byə-lā-shən) act of walking.

ampule (ăm′pyo͞ol) sealed glass container of sterile drug; usually intended for injection.

anatomic (ăn′ə-tŏm′ĭk) pertaining to the anatomy.

anchor (ăng′kər) to fasten.

anesthetic (ăn′ĭs-thĕt′ĭk) drug that causes loss of sensation; general anesthetic produces loss of consciousness, also.

anomaly (ə-nŏm′ə-lē) deviation from normal anatomy.

anorexia (ăn′ə-rĕk′sē-ə) loss of appetite.

antacid (ănt-ăs′ĭd) counteracts acidity.

antecubital (ăn′tĭ-kyo͞o′bĭ-təl) in front of the forearm.

antihistamine (ăn′tĭ-hĭs′tə-mēn′) drug that acts against histamines.

antiseptic (ăn′tə-sĕp′tĭk) drug or agent that arrests or prevents growth of microorganisms.

appliance (ə-plī′əns) device designed for a particular use.

apply (ə-plī′) to put on; to lay on.

arrest (ə-rĕst′) to stop completely.

arterial (är-tîr′ē-əl) pertaining to the arteries; vessels through which the blood flows away from the heart.

aspiration (ăs′pə-rā′shən) drawing into or out of, that is, drawing secretions into the lungs; suctioning secretions; withdrawal of secretions.

astringent (ə-strĭn′jənt) medication that has the effect of limiting secretions by contracting and hardening tissues.

atelectasis (ă-tə-lĕk′tə-sŭs) obstruction that prevents air from reaching a portion of the lung.

auditory (ô′də-tôr′ē) pertaining to hearing.

autoclave (ô′tō-klāv′) machine for sterilization under pressure.

Aveeno (ə-vē′nō) finely powdered oatmeal used for medicated baths.

axilla (ăk-sĭl′ə) armpit.

B

baking soda (bā′kĭng sō′də) bicarbonate of soda.

balloon (bə-lo͞on′) inflatable bag made of material impermeable to air or solution.

Band-Aid (bănd′ād) trade name for small, commercially prepared, adhesive bandage with gauze dressing in the center.

benzalkonium chloride (bĕn-zăl′kōn′ē-ŭm klôr′īd′) disinfectant; inactivated by presence of soap.

bevel (bĕv′əl) slanted line but not at a right angle; may refer to slanted portion at the end of a needle used for injection.

bikini (bĭ-kē′nē) brief swimsuit; refers to a cloth used to cover loin.

bile (bīl) secretion of the liver; emulsifies fats during digestion.

biologic death (bī′ə-lŏj′ĭk dĕth) characterized by cellular anoxia; occurs 3 to 8 minutes after clinical death.

blister (blĭs'tər) saclike elevation of skin containing fluid.

blot (blŏt) to touch gently; to dry with absorbent material by pressing gently.

body mechanics (bŏd'ē mĭ-kăn'ĭks) concerned with the movements of the whole or parts of the body.

bronchi (brŏng'kī) major branches leading from the trachea to the lungs.

bronchitis (brŏng-kī'tĭs) inflammation of the trachea and bronchi.

bronchogram (brŏng'kō-grăm) used for visualization and study of bronchi and bronchioli not accessible by bronchoscope; contrast medium injected and radiographs taken.

bronchographic (brŏng'ka-grăf'ĭk) pertains to examination of bronchi with radiography and contrast medium.

bubble suction (bŭb'əl sŭk'shən) *see* Suction.

buccal (bŭk'əl) cheek; buccal cavity refers to area between the teeth and the cheek.

burette (byo͝o-rĕt') graduated device designed to measure fluid accurately.

buttocks (bŭt'əks) gluteal prominences.

C

calibration (kăl'ə-brā'shən) marking that indicates a specific measurement of volume.

canthus (kăn'thəs) corner of the eye; inner canthus refers to angle proximal to the nose; outer canthus refers to angle formed by eyelids at outside edge of the face.

capillary (kăp'ə-lĕr'ē) tiny blood vessel connecting artery and vein.

cardiac massage (kär'dē-ăk mə-säzh') rhythmic compression and release of the heart.

cardiopulmonary (kär'dē-ō-po͝ol'mə-nĕr'ē) pertaining to the heart and lungs.

cardiotonic (kär'dē-ō-tŏn'ĭk) stimulating to the heart.

cardiovascular (kär'dē-ō-văs'kyə-lər) pertaining to the heart and blood vessels.

carminative (kär-mĭn'ə-tĭv) agent used to remove gases from the gastrointestinal tract.

cast (kăst) moisturized materials that mold to body part and harden as drying occurs; used to immobilize parts in orthopedics.

catheter (kăth'ə-tər) tube used to remove or instill fluids.

catheterization (kăth'ə-tər-ī-zā'shən) insertion of a catheter.

catheterize (kăth'ə-tə-rīz') to insert a tube for removal or instillation of fluids; often used in reference to the urinary bladder.

cellular response (sĕl'yə-lər rĭ-spŏns') reaction of cells.

cervix (sûr'vĭks) portion of uterus also known as the neck of the uterus.

chemical (kĕm'ĭ-kəl) pertaining to the composition of substances.

chest physical therapy (chĕst fĭz'ĭ-kəl thĕr'ə-pē) specialty that deals with medical prevention and treatment of diseases of the lungs.

chill (chĭl) sensation of being cold, accompanied by shivering.

cilia (sĭl′ē-ə) tiny hairlike processes arising from the epithelial cells and possessing a waving or sweeping action.

circular (sûr′kyə-lər) round; like a circle.

circulation (sûr′kyə-lā′shən) movement in a recurrent fashion.

clamp (klămp) to shut off; device used to press down and compress.

clavicle (klăv′ĭ-kəl) collarbone.

clean (klēn) free of soil.

cleanse (klĕnz)to make clean.

clinical death (klĭn′ĭ kəl dĕth) occurs at time of respiratory and/or cardiac arrest.

clinical response (klĭn′ĭ-kəl rĭ-spŏns′) reaction of the body to treatment.

clitoris (klĭt′ə-rĭs) small organ of erectile tissue located behind the juncture of the labia minora.

coagulation (kō-ăg′yə-lā′shən) change to a clot.

colloid (kŏl′oid′) gelatinous; suspension of large particles in a solvent.

colon (kō′lən) large intestine, specifically the portion from the cecum to the rectum.

colostomy (kə-lŏs′tə-mē) surgically created artificial opening into the colon through the abdominal wall.

compress (kəm-prĕs′) to press together; (kăm′prĕs) a dressing formed by several layers of material.

compression (kəm-prĕsh′ən) act of pressing together.

computation (kŏm′pyōō-tā′shən) method of determining an amount; mathematical.

concentration (kŏn′sən-trā′shən) strength of a solution.

conjunctiva (kŏn′jŭngt-tī′və) mucous membrane that lines eyelids and covers eyeball.

conscious (kŏn′shəs) state of awareness.

constrict (kən-strĭkt′) to squeeze, bind, tighten; to narrow the lumen as of vessels.

contact (kŏn′tăkt′) to touch; exposure to an infectious disease.

contaminant (kən-tăm′ə-nənt) anything that contaminates.

contaminate (kən-tam′ə-nāt′) to make impure or unsterile; to touch a sterile object with anything unsterile.

contamination (kən-tăm′ə-nā′shən) impure state; may refer to act of rendering a sterile object unsterile.

contiguous (kən-tĭg′yōō-əs) touching; neighboring.

contour (kŏn′tōŏr) outline or boundary.

contraindicated (kŏn′trə-ĭn′də-kāt′ĕd) treatment that is inappropriate due to adverse circumstances.

costal (kŏs′təl) pertaining to the ribs.

crepitation (krĕp′ə-tā′shən) crackling sound in tissues; grating sound of broken bones rubbing together.

crevice (krĕv′ĭs) cleft, fissure, crack.

crust (krŭst) hard covering, scab, eschar.

cyanosis, cyanotic (sī′ə-nō′sĭs, sī′ə-nŏt′ĭk) bluish or grayish discoloration of skin due to insufficient oxygen.

cycle (sī′kəl) a sequence that recurs at regular time intervals.

D

Dakin's (dā′kənz) a weak solution of sodium hypochlorite; used to cleanse wounds; a disinfectant.

decompression (dē′kəm-prĕsh′ən) removal of pressure.

decubiti (dĭ-kyŏŏ′bĭ-tī) pressure sores.

defecate (dĕf′ə-kāt′) evacuate the bowels.

defibrillation (dĕ-fī′brə-lā′shən or dĕ-fĭb′rə-lā′shən) direct application of high voltage; direct shock to the heart; used to treat irregularities of cardiac rhythm.

deformity (dĭ-fôr′mĭ-tē) congenital or acquired disfigurement.

dehiscence (dĭ-hĭs′ĕnz) refers to a wound breaking or splitting open.

deltoid (dĕl′toid′) triangular muscle originating at the shoulder.

demarcation (dē′mär-kā′shən) boundary; point of reference.

denuded (dĭ-nōōd′ĕd) condition in which protective covering or layer such as the skin has been removed.

dependent (dĭ-pĕn′dənt) hanging down; needing support.

depilatory (dĭ-pĭl′ə-tôr′ē) agent used to remove hair.

depression (dĭ-prĕsh′ən) area that is lower than the surface.

dermatology (dûr′mə-tŏl′ə-jē) science of the skin and its diseases.

deviation (dē′vē-ā′shən) departure from normal.

diaphragm (dī′ə-frăm) anatomic structure that separates thorax from abdomen.

diarrhea (dī′ə-rē′ə) frequent, liquid bowel movements.

digital (dĭj′ə-təl) pertaining to the fingers.

dilute (dī-lōōt′) to weaken, as by adding water.

disposable (dĭs-pō′zə-bəl) intended to be discarded after use.

disruption (dĭs-rŭp′shən) separation or breaking apart.

dissipate (dĭs′ə-pāt′) to scatter; to exhaust.

distention (dĭs-tĕn′shən) to inflate; to stretch out.

distill (dĭs-tĭl′) process of purifying water by vaporizing it and then condensing it.

dorsal-recumbent (dôr′səl rĭ-kŭm′bənt) lying on one's back.

douche (dōōsh) stream of solution directed against a part; often refers to cleansing vagina and vulva with a stream of solution.

drain (drān) tube through which fluid escapes; to flow freely.

drainage (drā′nĭj) fluids flowing from or being withdrawn from the body.

dressing (drĕs′ĭng) protective covering for injured or diseased part.

duodenum, duodenal (dōō′ə-dē′nəm, dōō′ə-dē′nəl) the part of the small intestine leading from the stomach to the jejunum.

dysfunction (dĭs-fŭngk′shən) abnormal function or lack of function of an anatomic structure.

dyspnea (dĭsp-nē′ə) labored or difficult breathing.

E

electrolyte (ĭ-lĕk′trə-līt′) any substance that dissociates into ions when placed in solution; a solution that conducts electricity.

elimination (ĭ-lĭm'ə-nā'shən) act of expelling; destruction.

emollient (ĭ-mŏl'yənt) an agent that soothes and softens.

enema (ĕn'ə-mə) solution injected into the rectum usually for the purpose of cleansing the rectum or the lower bowel or both.

engorgement (ĕn-gôrj'mənt) distention or congestion.

epigastric (ĕp'ĭ-găs'trĭk) over the abdomen; over the pit of the stomach.

evaporation (ĭ-văp'ə-rā'shən) process of turning into vapor.

exhale (ĕks-hāl') to breathe out.

extension (ĕk-stĕn'shən) anything that lengthens or stretches out.

extremities (ĕk-strĕm'ə-tēs) the arms or legs.

F

fascia (făsh'ē-ə) connective tissue that supports and separates muscles.

fillers (fĭl'ərs) substances used to give bulk, absorbability, firmness, or other qualities to materials.

filter (fĭl'tər) device that removes impurities; removal of impurities.

flannel (flăn'əl) a soft fabric; often cotton but may be a blend of cotton and another fiber such as rayon.

flare (flâr) to intensify; to spread; to increase in redness.

flatus (flā'təs) an accumulation of gas in the digestive tract.

flexion (flĕk'shən) bending as a joint of the body bends.

fluctuation (flŭk'choo-ā'shən) changing back and forth.

fluoroscopic (floor'ə-skŏp'ĭc) type of examination using a screen to view shadows with the aid of x rays.

folliculitis (fə-lĭk'yə-līt'ĭs) inflammation of a follicle; hair follicle is an invagination of epidermis from which the hair develops.

footboard (foot'bôrd') upright device designed to support the feet.

forceps (fôr'səps) instrument used for grasping and holding.

Fowler's position (Fou'lər's pə-zĭsh'ən) semisitting position.

friable (frī'ə-bəl) easily broken or torn.

G

gag reflex (găg rē'flĕks') act of retching that results from irritation of the fauces; may produce vomiting.

gastrointestinal (găs'trō-ĭn-tĕs'tə-nəl) pertaining to the stomach and intestines.

gastrostomy (găs-trŏs'tə-mē) surgically created opening that leads from the stomach through the abdominal wall; may be used for removal of secretions or for introducing tube for feeding.

gauge (gāj) standard of measurement; used to indicate size of the diameter of a needle used for injection.

gauze (gôz) a thin, loosely woven fabric.

genitalia (jĕn'ə-tā'lē-ə) reproductive organs; usually refers to external sex organs.

genitourinary tract (jĕn′ə-tō-yoor′ə-nĕr′ē trăkt) reproductive and urinary systems.

germicidal (jûr′mə-sīd′əl) agent that kills microorganisms.

gloving (glŭv′ĭng) to put on gloves.

gluteal area (gloo′tē-əl âr′ē-ə) the buttocks; specifically a portion of the upper outer quadrant.

granulation (grăn′yə-lā′shən) small projections of tissue formed in healing process; usually observed when wound does not heal by first intention.

gravitation (grăv′ə-tā′shən) tendency to move toward a particular point.

gravity (grăv′ə-tē) possessing weight.

green soap (grēn sōp) solution of soft soap in alcohol.

groin (groin) depression or fold between the body and the thigh.

gynecology (gī′nə-kŏl′ə-jē) study of the diseases of women.

H

hammock (hăm′ək) specially designed cloth used to suspend the body in a lying position.

harness (här′nĭs) a combination of straps; may be used to support the patient in a particular position.

heat (hēt) degree of temperature; warmth.

hematoma (hē′mə-tō′mə) tumor filled with blood.

hemoptysis (hĭ-mŏp′tə-sĭs) expectoration of blood or bloody mucus from the level of the larynx or below.

hemorrhage (hĕm′ə-rĭj) abnormal discharge of blood from the body; loss of large amount of blood.

hepatitis (hĕp′ə-tī′tĭs) inflammation of the liver; may be caused by pathogens or toxins such as certain drugs to which the patient is sensitive.

hernia (hûr′nē-ə) protrusion of an organ or its part through the wall of the cavity that normally contains it.

humidifier (hyoo-mĭd′ə-fī′ər) device used to increase moisture content of inhaled gases.

hydraulic (hī-drô′lĭk) operated by fluid pressure.

hyperextend (hī′pər-ĭk′stənd) to stretch out as far as possible.

hypotension (hī′pō-tĕn′shən) decrease in blood pressure to a level below the normal range.

hypothermia (hī′pō-thûr′mĭ-ə) cooling; method of lowering the temperature of the body; may use a machine that circulates a coolant.

I

identification card (ī-dĕn′tə-fĭ-kā′shən kärd) small cardboard on which is printed specific information; used to identify single dose of drug and the patient for whom it is intended.

idiosyncrasy (ĭd′ē-ō-sĭng′krə-sē) characteristic or reaction peculiar to an individual.

iliac crest (ĭl′ē-ək′ krĕst) upper margin of the hipbone.

immerse (ĭ-mûrs′) to place under water or another solution.

immobilization (ĭm-mō′bə-lī-zā′shən) fixation in an immovable position.

impaction (ĭm-păk′shən) pressing together tightly; fecal impaction refers to a hard mass of stool packed tightly and wedged; manual removal may be necessary.

incision (ĭn-sīzh′ən) cut made with a knife for surgical purposes.

incontinent (ĭn-kŏn′tə-nənt) unable to retain urine or feces voluntarily.

indwelling (ĭn-dwĕl′ĭng) to remain in place for an extended period of time.

infection (ĭn-fĕk′shən) diseased state due to pathogenic organisms.

infiltration (ĭn′fĭl-trā′shən) passing of liquid or gas substance into or through tissue.

inflammation (ĭn′flə-mā′shən) a defensive reaction of the tissue to injury; characterized by redness, swelling, heat, and pain.

inflation (ĭn-flā′shən) distention with a liquid or gas.

inframammary (ĭn′frə-măm′ər-ē) below the breast.

infusion (ĭn-fyōō′zhən) injection of a sterile solution into a vein or tissue.

inguinal (ĭng′gwə-nəl) in the groin; pertaining to the groin.

inhale (ĭn-hāl′) to breathe in.

injection (ĭn-jĕk′shən) introduction of a liquid into a vessel, cavity, or tissue; sterile equipment and solution are usually used.

inline (ĭn′līn) incorporated into the main line of flow.

insomnia (ĭn-sŏm′nē-ə) inability to sleep.

inspire (ĭn-spīr′) to breathe in.

instillation (ĭn′stə-lā′shən) slow injection; putting in drop by drop.

insufficiency (ĭn′sə-fĭsh′ən-sē) a deficiency; not enough for its purpose.

interdigital (ĭn′tər-dĭj′ə-təl) between the fingers; sometimes used to pertain to the area between the toes.

intermittent (ĭn′tər-mĭt′ənt) stopping periodically.

intertriginous (ĭn′tər-trĭj′ə-nəs) affected with dermatitis in an area in which two surfaces of the skin touch each other.

intestinal (ĭn-tĕs′tən-əl) the part of the alimentary tract distal to the stomach.

intramuscular (ĭn′trə-mŭs′kyələr) into or within a muscle.

intravenous (ĭn′trə-vē′nəs) within a vein; often pertains to an injection or infusion into a vein.

intravesical (ĭn′trə-vĕs′ĭ-kəl) within the bladder.

intubate (ĭn′tōō-bāt′) to insert a tube into the larynx.

IPPB intermittent positive pressure breathing, inspiratory; often refers to machines that assist or control ventilation.

irreversible (ĭr′ĭ-vûr′sə-bəl) cannot be changed back to its former state.

irrigate (ĭr′ĭ-gāt′) to wash out with a flow of solution.

irritation (ĭr′ə-tā′shən) anything that stimulates an adverse reaction.

isolation (ī′sə-lā′shən) separation from others: used to prevent transmission of organisms from one person to another.

K

knee-chest (nē′chĕst′) position in which patient rests his weight on his knees and chest; head is supported by his forearms.

L

labia (lā'bē-ə) folds of tissue surrounding the orifice of the vulva.

larynx (lăr'ĭngks) voice box.

Lassar's paste (Lăs'ărz pāst) thick preparation of zinc oxide.

lateral (lăt'ər-əl) on the side; may refer to side-lying position.

leverage (lĕv'ər-ĭj) mechanical advantage.

Levin tube (Lĕv'ən tōōb) straight tube used to decompress the stomach or to introduce food into it.

lint (lĭnt) bits of thread.

liter (lē'tər) a unit of measure.

lithotomy (lĭ-thŏt'ə-mē) also called dorsosacral; position in which patient lies on back with thighs flexed toward abdomen and legs abducted but at a right angle to the thighs.

lotion (lō'shən) liquid preparation containing medicine patted onto the skin.

lozenge (lŏz'ĭnj) small, flat, discoid preparation containing medicine intended to be held in the mouth until it dissolves.

lubricate (lōō'brĭ-kāt') to make slippery.

lumbar (lŭm'bər) part of the body on either side of the spinal column; between the ribs and the hip.

M

maceration (măs'ər-ā'shən) process that softens tissue.

macroscopic (măk'rə-skŏp'ĭk) visible with the naked eye.

malignancy (mə-lĭg'nən-sē) tendency to spread and produce death.

manipulate (mə-nĭp'yə-lāt') to handle with a degree of skill.

mastication (măs'tə-kā'shən) act of chewing.

meatus (mē-ā'təs) opening.

mechanical (mĭ-kăn'ĭ-kəl) pertaining to machinery.

medication (mĕd'ə-kā'shən) drug used to prevent or treat illness; application of a drug.

medication card (mĕd'ə-kā'shən kärd) *see* Identification card.

meniscus (mə-nĭs'kəs) curvature on upper surface of fluid; caused by fluid clinging to the sides of the container.

microbe (mī'krōb') organism too small to be seen with the naked eye.

microorganism (mī'krō-ôr'gən-īz'əm) tiny plant or animal that cannot be seen without magnification.

micturition (mĭk'chə-rĭsh'ən) voiding of urine; urination.

midanterior (mĭd'ăn-tĭr'ē-ər) midpoint and front.

midstream (mĭd'strēm') middle of the flow; neither at the beginning nor at the end.

milk (mĭlk) pertains to milking a chest tube; to alternately apply and release pressure on the tube by squeezing it with the hand.

milliliter (mĭl'lə-lē'tər) unit of metric measure; equivalent to a cubic centimeter.

moisture (mois'chər) water.

mottled (mŏt'tləd) patterned with irregular discolorations or blotches.

mucosa (myōō-kō'sə) mucous membrane.

musculoskeletal (mŭs'kyə-lō-skĕl'ə-təl) pertaining to the muscles and skeleton.

myocardium (mī'ō-kär'dē-əm) muscle of the heart.

N

narcotic (när-kŏt'ĭk) drug with addicting properties that also depresses the central nervous system.

nasogastric (nā'zō-găs'trĭk) pertaining to the nose and stomach.

nebulization (nĕb'yə-lī-zā'shən) act of breaking a liquid into a fine spray; vaporization.

negative pressure (nĕg'ə-tĭv prĕsh'ər) mechanical withdrawal of force.

nephrectomy (nə-frĕk'tə-mē) removal of a kidney.

neurosurgery (nōōr'ō-sûr'jər-ē) surgery on the nervous system.

nostril (nŏs'trəl) external opening of the nose.

nutrition (nōō-trĭsh'ən) food; process of converting food into tissue.

O

obstruction (əb-strŭk'shən) blockage of a passageway; prevents normal functioning.

occlusive (ə-klōō'sĭv) tending to shut in moisture or heat, often applied to dressings used for this purpose.

ointment (oint'mənt) semisolid preparation of medicine in a fatty base; applied externally by stroking.

oral (ôr'əl) pertaining to the mouth.

orifice (ôr'ə-fĭs) opening; an entrance or outlet.

orogastric (ôr'ō-găs'trĭk) pertaining to the mouth and stomach.

orthopedic (ôr'thə-pē'dĭk) pertaining to locomotor structures of the body, their diseases and deformities.

overdosage (ō'vər-dōs'ĭj) excessive amount or dose of medicine.

oxygen (ŏk'sĭ-jən) colorless, odorless gas necessary for life; supports combustion but does not burn.

P

palate (păl'ĭt) roof of the mouth.

pallor (păl'ər) unnatural paleness.

paralyzed (păr'ə-līz'd) unable to move because of loss of motor and sensory function.

patency (pāt'n-sē) state of being open; not obstructed.

pathogen (păth'ə-jən) organism capable of producing disease.

pathophysiologic (păth'ə-fĭz'ē-ə-lŏj'ĭk) study of disease state as it is related to normal functioning of the body.

pelvic (pĕl′vĭk) pertaining to the area of the body formed by the innominate bones, the pubis, the sacrum, the coccyx, and the ligaments uniting them.

percussion (pər-kŭsh′ən) tapping or striking a part of the body to diagnose or treat.

perineum (pĕr′ə-nē′əm) area between the vulva or the scrotum and the anus; sometimes includes the vulva.

peripheral (pə-rĭf′ər-əl) near the outside.

pharynx (făr′ĭngks) anatomic area between the oronasal passages and the esophagus.

physical therapist (fĭz′ĭ-kəl thĕr′ə-pĭst) person trained to treat with physical and mechanical means.

physiologic (fĭz′ē-ə-lŏj′ĭk) related to normal body functioning.

pivot (pĭv′ət) to turn or rotate.

pledget (plĕj′ət) a small mass of cotton or rayon fibers.

pleural cavity (plo͞or′əl kăv′ə-tē) space between the two layers of membrane that enclose the lungs.

ply (plī) thickness.

pneumothorax (no͞o′mō-thôr′ăks′) air in the pleural cavity; causes collapse of the lung.

popliteal (pŏp′lĭ-tē′əl) behind the knee.

positioning (pə-zĭsh′ən-ĭng) manner of arranging the body.

posterior (pŏ-stîr′ē-ər) caudal end of the body, dorsal side or back.

postural drainage (pŏs′-chər-əl drā′nĭj) positioning of patient that promotes drainage of secretions from the lungs and bronchi.

precaution (prĭ-kô′shən) to guard against.

precipitation (prĭ-sĭp′ə-tā′shən) separation of solid from liquid by allowing or causing it to settle out.

pregnancy (prĕg′nən-sē) period of time during which a developing fetus is present within the uterus.

pressure, direct (prĕsh′ər, dĭ-rĕkt′) compression or force exerted on a part.

probe (prōb) instrument inserted into a body cavity.

profound (prə-found′) extreme or intense, as profound cooling.

prostatic fluid (prō-stăt′ĭk) secretion produced by the prostate gland.

prosthesis (prŏs-thē′sĭs) an artificial part used to replace a missing part or to correct a defect.

pruritus (pro͞o-rī′təs) itching.

psoriasis (sə-rī′ə-sĭs) a chronic skin disease identified by characteristic lesions.

pulmonary (po͞ol′mə-nĕr′ē) pertaining to the lungs.

pylorus (pī-lôr′əs) opening from the stomach into the duodenum.

R

radiopaque (rā′dē-ō-pāk′) property of not being penetrated by x rays; visible by use of x rays.

radius (rā′dē-əs) outer bone of the lower arm.

range of motion (rānj ŭv mō′shən) extent to which the body part can be moved.

rectal (rĕk′təl) pertaining to the lower part of the rectum; between the sigmoid flexure and the anus.

recumbent (rĭ-kŭm′bənt) lying down; *see also* Dorsal-recumbent.

reducing sock (rĭ-dōōs′ing sŏk) device made of stockinette and used to cover stump after amputation.

regurgitation (rē-gûr′jə-tā′shən) return of stomach contents to the mouth; may refer to backflow of blood.

resection (rĭ-sĕk′shən) excision of part of a body structure.

reservoir (rĕz′ər-vwär′) collecting or storage containers for fluids.

residual (rĭ-zĭj′ōō-əl) quantity remaining or left over.

respiration (rĕs′pə-rā′shən) act of breathing.

respirator (rĕs′pə-rā′tər) machine, such as the IPPB machine, used for artificial breathing or used to assist respiration.

restrain, restraint (rĭ-strān′, rĭ-strānt′) to hinder or restrict action; device or method used to prevent patient from injuring himself.

resuscitation (rĭ-sŭs′ə-tā′shən) bringing back to life.

resuscitator (rĭ-sŭs′ə-tā′ter) person who resuscitates or machine that resuscitates.

retract (rĭ-trăkt′) to draw back or curl away.

reverse isolation (rĭ-vûrs′ ī′sə-lā′shən) special precautions or methods used to protect patient whose resistance to microorganisms is low; *see also* Isolation.

rinsing (rĭns′ing) washing lightly with water or another liquid.

S

salivary (săl′ə-vĕr′ē) glands that discharge secretions into the mouth.

scale (skāl) thin, flat, hard, flakelike materials on the skin that resemble the scales on a fish.

scalp (skălp) integument of head containing hair.

scapula (skăp′yə-lə) shoulder blade.

scrub (skrŭb) to cleanse the hands as thoroughly as possible; surgical scrub includes the forearms.

sebaceous (sĭ-bā′shəs) pertaining to fat; pertains to glands in the skin that secrete oil.

secretion (sĭ-krē′shən) product produced by glands; a fluid.

sedative (sĕd′ə-tĭv) a drug that calms; the effect of lowering activity.

sediment (sĕd′ə-mənt) residual matter that settles out of a liquid.

sensitivity (sĕn′sə-tĭv′ə-tē) state of being affected readily by outside influences.

septum (sĕp′təm) partition between two body cavities.

shampoo (shăm-poo′) washing the hair; may include gentle massage of the scalp.

shivering (shĭv′ər-əng) to shake from cold; a physiologic reaction that tends to increase body temperature.

shock (shŏk) state of collapse resulting from circulatory failure; known to be precipitated by many causes; recognized by many signs and symptoms.

shoulder blade (shōl′dər blād) scapula.

sidearm (sīd'ärm) extension of, but to one side of, an apparatus.

sigh (sī) periodic deep inspiration.

silicone (sĭl'ĭ-kōn') chemical that provides lubrication; gel is a semisolid form.

Sims' position (Sĭms' pə-zĭsh'ən) patient lying on side with upper leg flexed forward and toward abdomen.

single dose (sĭng'gəl dōs) amount of medicine to be administered at one time; used to refer to units prepared and packaged by manufacturer or by a pharmacist.

siphon (sī'fən) to remove liquids with the aid of a tube and atmospheric pressure.

sitz bath (sĭts băth) bath that patient sits in for designated period of time; water usually covers the hips.

skate (skāt) device attached to foot for purpose of exercising leg.

sling (slĭng) device used to support an injured extremity; used on some mechanical lifts to aid in transferring patient.

solution (sə-lōō'shən) homogeneous mixture of gas, liquid, or solid in one of the former; parts cannot be separated by ordinary means.

Soyaloid (soi'ə-loyd') commercial product prepared from soybeans and used in the treatment of selected skin diseases.

spasm (spăz'əm) a muscular contraction that is sudden and involuntary.

specimen (spĕs'ə-mən) a part intended to be representative of the whole, such as a specimen of urine.

sphincter (sfĭngk'tər) band of muscle that encircles a body orifice; its relaxation and constriction are voluntary or involuntary depending on its function.

sphygmomanometer (sfĭg'mō-mə-nŏm'ə-tər) device used to measure arterial blood pressure.

splint (splĭnt) any of a number of devices used to immobilize a body part.

sponge (spŭnj) absorbent material used to remove fluids.

spontaneous (spŏn-tā'nē-əs) unaided.

sterile (stĕr'əl) free of living organisms; unfertile.

sterilization (stĕr'ə-lə-zā'shən) act of making sterile.

stertorous (stûr'tər-ŭs) breathing characterized by snoring sounds.

stethoscope (stĕth'ə-skōp') instrument used to hear sounds within the body.

stimulus (stĭm'yə-ləs) anything that causes part or all of organism to react with activity.

stockinet, stockinette (stŏk'ə-nĕt') machine-knitted fabric; used to line orthopedic casts.

stoma (stō'mə) opening, either artificial or a small natural opening.

stopcock (stŏp'kŏk') a special valve used to control flow of fluid from a reservoir

strip (strĭp) referring to chest tubes: to remove contents from the tube with a simultaneous stroking aod compressing motion.

stump (stŭmp) part of an extremity or organ remaining after amputation.

stylet (stī'lĭt) a slender piece of rigid material inserted through a catheter, needle, or cannula to make it rigid or to block its opening; may be solid or hollow.

subcutaneous (sŭb'kyōō-tā'nē-əs) lying directly under the skin.

sublingual (sŭb'lĭng'gwəl) beneath the tongue.

suction (sŭk'shən) removal of gases or liquids by reducing the atmospheric pressure

suffocation (sŭf'ə-kā'shən) asphyxiation; effective ventilation is decreased appreciably or stopped; results in death if untreated.

sump drain (sŭmp drān) tube used to remove accumulated secretions from deep body cavities; usually attached to suction machine for this purpose.

superficial (soo'pər-fĭsh'əl) near the top; without depth.

surgery (sûr'jə-rē) medical specialty that treats and diagnoses with operative procedures; area in which operative procedures are done.

swallow (swä'lō) to move food from mouth to stomach without the aid of tubes or other devices.

symphysis pubis (sĭm'fə-sĭs pyōō'bĭs) anterior point at which pubic bones join.

syringe (sə-rĭnj') instrument used to instill or inject solutions into cavities, vessels, or tissues; sometimes attached to a needle for injection.

systemic (sĭ-stĕm'ĭk) pertaining to the whole body or one of its organs.

T

temperature (tĕm'pər-ə-chŏŏr') degree of warmth or coldness.

temporary (tĕm'pə-rĕr'ē) for a limited period of time; not permanent.

tepid (tĕp'ĭd) lukewarm.

termination (tûr'mə-nā'shən) bringing to an end or close, as termination of an infusion.

therapeutic (thĕr'ə-pyōō'tĭk) possessing healing properties.

therapy (thĕr'ə-pē) treatment of an illness.

thermal (thûr'məl) pertaining to heat.

thermostatic (thûr'mə-stăt'ĭk) relating to the automatic regulation of temperature.

thigh (thī) part of leg between the knee and the hip joint.

thrombophlebitis (thrŏm'bō-flĭ-bī'tĭs) clot accompanied by inflammation of the affected vein.

thyroid (thī'roid) a ductless gland lying on either side of the upper part of the trachea and the lower part of the larynx.

tidal drainage (tīd'l drān'ĭj) automatic irrigation of the urinary bladder characterized by periodic rising and falling of the level of fluid in a tube.

tidal volume (tīd'l vŏl'yōōm) amount of air moved into and out of the respiratory system.

topical (tŏp'ĭ-kəl) the surface of the body; a definite area.

tourniquet (tŏŏr'nĭ-kĭt) any device used to decrease bleeding by compressing blood vessels; encircles extremity and applies pressure.

trachea (trā'kē-ə) the windpipe; a tube-shaped anatomic structure leading from the larynx to the bronchi.

tranquilizing (trăn'kwə-līz'ĭng) making calm; often refers to a group of drugs used to treat emotionally disturbed persons.

transfusion (trăns-fyōō′zhən) injection of another person's blood; used less commonly to mean infusion of liquids other than blood.

transmission (trăns-mĭsh′ən) act of transferring; applies to transfer of organisms from one person to another.

transurethral (trăns′yōō-rē′thrəl) through the urethra; as, a transurethral resection of the prostate gland.

trauma (trou′mə) injury to the body.

Trendelenburg (Trĕn-dĕl′ən-bûrg) dorsal-recumbent position with the head lower than the trunk of the body and the trunk lower than the legs; sometimes called the shock position.

trial (trī′əl) a test, such as trying a medication; an experiment.

trochanter roll (trō-kăn′tər rōl) roll of material placed against the hip to maintain its position and to prevent its outward rotation.

trough (trôf) long, narrow receptacle used to channel direction of flow of fluids.

trunk (trŭngk) torso of body, all of the body except the head, neck, and extremities.

T tube (tē′ tōōb) connector or drain shaped like a T.

tube (tōōb) long, hollow cylinder used to provide a passageway for liquids and gases.

Turkish towel (Tûr′kĭsh tou′əl) thick cotton towel made with loops of fiber; absorbent due to its long nap.

twist (twĭst) to rotate, wind together, intertwine.

U

ulcerated (ŭl′sə-rāt′əd) affected with an open lesion or lesions on the skin or on the mucous membrane; manifested by disintegration of tissues.

ulna (ŭl′nə) long bone on inner aspect of forearm.

ultraviolet (ŭl′trə-vī′ə-lĭt) invisible light rays; abbreviated U. V.

umbilicus (ŭm′bĭl′ĭ-kəs) navel; depression in midpoint of abdomen that indicates the place at which the umbilical cord was attached.

unconscious (ŭn′kŏn′shəs) state in which one is not aware of himself.

undine (ŭn-dēn′) small device used to irrigate the eye.

unilateral (yōō′nĭ-lăt′ər-əl) affecting one side only.

unsterile (ŭn′stĕr′əl) not known to be free of organisms or other contaminants.

urination (yōōr′ə-nā′shən) act of discharging urine.

urology (yōō-rŏl′ə-jē) science that deals with the urinary and genitourinary tracts.

V

vacuum (văk′yōō-əm) space devoid of gases and other matter.

vagina (və-jī′nə) musculomembranous, tubelike structure or passageway between the uterus and the vulva.

vaporizer (vā′pə-rī′zər) device that converts water to steam or a mist.

vastus lateralis (văs′təs lăt′ər-əl-ĭs) muscle in the thigh; extends the knee.

venipuncture (věn′ə-pŭngk′chər) piercing of a vein with a needle, usually for the purpose of injecting fluid or medicine or to obtain a sample of blood.

venous (vē′nəs) pertaining to the vein.

venous outflow (vē′nəs out′flō) flowing out of the veins, away from the heart through the veins.

venous pattern (vē′nəs păt′ərn) design or layout formed by the veins.

venous pressure (vē′nəs prěsh′ər) pressure within the veins.

venous return (vē′nəs rĭ-tûrn′) flowing back to the heart through the veins.

ventilate (věnt′l-āt) to transport air to and from the alveolar surfaces.

ventilation (věn′tə-lā′shən) act of ventilating.

ventilator (věnt′l-ā′tər) machine or person who ventilates.

ventrogluteal (věn′trō-glōō′tē-əl) anterior portion of the gluteal muscle.

vertebra (vûr′tə-brə) bony segment of the spinal column; pl., *-brae* or **bras.**

vial (vī′əl) sealed glass container for medicine.

vibration (vī-brā′shən) shaking movement; to oscillate.

viscosity (vĭs-kŏs′ə-tē) quality demonstrated by the resistance of a fluid to flow.

viscous (vĭs′kəs) tending to adhere to a surface; to flow slowly or with resistance.

vital signs (vī′təl sīns) usually refers to temperature, pulse, and respiration; commonly includes blood pressure also.

vulva (vŭl′və) external female genitalia.

vulvectomy (vŭl-věk′tă-mē) removal of external vulva surgically; radical vulvectomy includes removal of lymph nodes in groin.

W

water-seal drainage (wô′tər sēl′ drā′-nĭj) drainage system in which the tube leading from the body to the drainage receptacle is under water; water seals the drainage tube and prevents gases from ascending through it.

X

xiphoid process (zĭf′oid′ prŏs′ĕs′) distal end of the sternum.

Z

Zephiran chloride (zěf′ĭ-rən klôr′īd′) same as benzalkonium chloride.

Z *track* (zē′ trăk) method of applying tension that displaces the subcutaneous tissue during insertion of a needle; refers to Z formed in overlying tissue when tension is applied; used to inject irritating drugs, especially those containing heavy metals; useful when drugs are to be injected into the gluteal area.

Index

Removal
  of ointments, crusts, scales, dried secretions, 165-166
  of tube, 194-195
Rescue breathing, 343-349
Respiration; *see also* Emergency action; Ventilation
  assisted, 97-111
  controlled, 111-112
Respirator rate
  of exchange; *see* Ventilation
  and rhythm, 98
Respirators, 103-115
  resuscitation with, 111-114
  weaning from, 114-115
Restoring cardiac function, 350-353
Restoring respiration, 343-349
Restraints, 61-68
Resuscitation, 111-114, 339-353
Retec, 99-102
Retention catheter, 274-277
Retention enemas, 243
Reverse isolation, 16
Roll belt, 67, 68
Room vaporizers, 95
Rotation of positions, 27-28

S

Safety, 26-69; *see also* Administration of drugs
  dust-free environment, 22-23
  hand washing, 1-3
  isolation, 16-22
  roll belt, 67, 68
  skin preparation, 3-6
  straps; *see* Mechanical devices for transferring patients
  vest, 66, 67
Salem sump tube, 300
Saline enema, 244
Scales, removal of, 165, 166
Scalp medications, 182
Scrub; *see* Surgical scrub
Scultetus binder, 59
Second container of intravenous solution, 212-213, 224-225
Secretions, removal of, 165-166; *see also* Ventilation
Selection of needle for injection, 139-141
Selection of sites
  for intramuscular injection, 148-151
  for subcutaneous injection, 145-148
Self-protection; *see* Isolation
Shampoo, 182
Shave; *see* Skin preparation for surgery
Shock
  positioning for, 353

Shock—cont'd
  treatment of, 353, 355
  warmth in treatment of, 355
Shoulder rolls, 33
Side-lying position, 29, 32-33
Sighing, 112-114
Silicone grease, 88
Site care, venipuncture, 229
Sitting up, 49, 50
Skin; *see also* Abdominal stoma; Topical application of medications
  care, 250, 252
  cleansing for venipuncture, 202-205
  damage, 26
  preparation of, for surgery, 3-6
  prevention of irritation to, 27
Sling
  arm, 57-59
  use of, with hydraulic lift, 42, 43
Soapsuds enema, 244
Sock, reducing, 61
Sodium bicarbonate, 179; *see also* Emergency action; Odor control
Solutions for enemas, 244-245; *see also* Irrigations; Topical medications
Solvents for ointments; *see* Ointments
Soyaloid, 179
Specific units for assisted ventilation, 97-115
Specimens
  blood, 202-205
  tracheal, 117
  urine, 277-278
Sphygmomanometer, 202, 203
Spine, precautions for, in turning, 39
Splinting of incisions; *see* Breathing exercises
Splints, application of, 211
Sponge bath, alcohol, 316-318
Sprays, anal, 306-307
Starch enema, 245
Steel needle, venipuncture with, 204, 205, 206
Sterile aspiration of tracheal secretions, 117
Sterile compresses, 330-332
Sterile dressings, 336, 337
Sterile perineal care, 309-310
Sterile towel for drying hands, 11
Stoma, abdominal, 250-262
  colostomy dressings for, 251-252, 253
  control of odor with, 261-262
  drainage bags for, 257-261
  irrigations of, 253-256
  permanent appliances, 260-261
  skin care for, 250, 252-253
  rescue breathing through; *see* Resuscitation